Tributes
Volume 21

From Knowledge Representation to Argumentation in AI, Law and Policy Making

A Festschrift in Honour of Trevor Bench-Capon on the Occasion of his 60th Birthday

Tributes Series Editor
Dov Gabbay   dov.gabbay@kcl.ac.uk

From Knowledge Representation to Argumentation in AI, Law and Policy Making

Policy Making

A Festschrift in Honour of Trevor Bench-Capon on the Occasion of his 60th Birthday

edited by

Katie Atkinson,

Henry Prakken,

and

Adam Wyner

ISBN 978-1-84890-133-9

College Publications
Scientific Director: Dov Gabbay
Managing Director: Jane Spurr
Department of Computer Science
King's College London, Strand, London WC2R 2LS, UK

http://www.collegepublications.co.uk

Cover by Laraine Welch, based on an idea by Vania Castelfranchi
Printed by Lightning Source, Milton Keynes, UK

Table of Contents

Contents

Preface

KATIE ATKINSON* , HENRY PRAKKEN† , AND ADAM WYNER‡

This volume is a Festschrift in honour of Trevor Bench-Capon on the occasion of his 60th birthday. Trevor Bench-Capon is well recognised as an outstanding figure in Artificial Intelligence and Law, having published extensively over the long course of his career on legal knowledge representation, engineering methods for knowledge-based systems, theoretical and applied argumentation, case-based reasoning, policy-making, reasoning about evidence, and many other related topics.

The volume provides an excellent overview of Bench-Capon's work over more than 25 years of research on AI and Law and argumentation, starting with his earlier work on principled methods for legal knowledge representation and the engineering of knowledge-based systems, and continuing with his research on argumentation and legal case-based reasoning. Moreover, the chapters in this volume attest to his deep influence upon his colleagues in all these fields.

The book was presented to Bench-Capon at a workshop held in his honour on November 22, 2013 in the Department of Computer Science at the University of Liverpool, Liverpool, United Kingdom. In attendance were many of the authors of the articles, his departmental colleagues, his former students, and friends and family.

The editors of the volume gratefully acknowledge and thank the sponsors who provided financial support to cover expenses for the volume and the workshop - the Dutch Foundation for Legal Knowledge Based Systems (JURIX), the International Association of Artificial Intelligence and Law (IAAIL), and the University of Liverpool's Department of Computer Science.

*University of Liverpool, Department of Computer Science
†Utrecht University, Department of Information and Computing Sciences, and the University of Groningen, Faculty of Law
‡University of Aberdeen, Department of Computing Science

Overview of Trevor Bench-Capon's Research

KATIE ATKINSON* , HENRY PRAKKEN† , AND ADAM WYNER‡

Introduction

Trevor Bench-Capon is with no doubt one of the main figures in artificial intelligence and law and his work has been more widely influential across a number of topics in computer science. In this introduction we give a brief overview of his main contributions, with no hope to be complete. Looking at Trevor Bench-Capon's published work, one main development can be recognised: from knowledge representation to argumentation. In his earlier work, the main focus was on principled knowledge representation (often in logic programming) while the reasoning was secondary in that it followed the meaning of the representations. This focus is apparent from the title of a textbook on AI he wrote in 1990, titled *Knowledge Representation: An Approach to Artificial Intelligence* [6]. In his later work instead the focus was on forms of reasoning that go beyond the meaning of the representations. It is here that the notion of argumentation is central. In Bench-Capon's published work this shift becomes apparent roughly towards 2000. However, as Bench-Capon himself describes in [11], he has always had an interest in argument (meant to be persuasive) as opposed to proof (meant to be valid). This interest goes back to his years as a philosophy student in Oxford and as a trainee policy maker in the UK civil service. Some traces of this early part of his career can be found in his earlier publications, but that work is mainly on knowledge-based systems, with special emphasis on legal applications. Besides knowledge representation, this earlier work also concerned principled engineering methods for knowledge-based systems, with special emphasis on ontologies, which were a computing concept in their infancy at the time, and on validation and maintenance. This strand of work was very influential on more practically-oriented work in knowledge-based systems. His later work on argumentation is more

*University of Liverpool, Department of Computer Science
†Utrecht University, Department of Information and Computing Sciences, and the University of Groningen, Faculty of Law
‡University of Aberdeen, Department of Computing Science

foundational in nature since it laid the groundwork for a perspective on practical reasoning that is rooted in ideas from philosophy. Above all, Bench-Capon has put the persuasiveness of arguments and the importance in this respect of societal values on the research agenda of artificial intelligence.

As can be seen from inspecting his substantial personal bibliography, Bench-Capon has a vast collection of collaborators and rarely worked alone. His co-authors span various disciplines, both within and outside of computer science, and as such his collaborative work covers a rich variety of topics. Below we survey some of the more major milestones of his research record, though there remain many interesting individual papers beyond those that we cover below.

1   Early years

Bench-Capon's undergraduate degree was in Philosophy, Politics and Economics at St. John's College, Oxford. He studied for this from 1972-1975 and gained a BA(Hons) first class. He won the Henry Wilde Prize for the best Philosophy First across all faculties in 1975. He continued his studies at Oxford from 1975-1977, earning a B.Phil and winning the John Locke Prize for Mental Philosophy in 1976. In 1980 at Oxford, Bench-Capon defended his D.Phil thesis titled *Can God be an Object of Reference?*, supervised by Michael Dummett (later Sir Michael). His philosophical education would shine through all of his later work. Another important influence was his years in the UK civil service (1978–1984). He first became a trainee policy maker, having the task to draft the arguments from which the minister responsible for the policy area chose to be the ones used in Parliament. This experience with policy argumentation in practice was invaluable for his later academic work on modelling argumentation about policy- and decision-making. In his last years in the civil service (at the Department of Health and Social Security) Bench-Capon worked on a project that investigated the potential for using knowledge-based systems in large legislation-based organisations. This sparked his interest in legal knowledge-based systems and later, legal argument, but also in software engineering methods for knowledge-based systems and ontologies. His work at the DHSS resulted in an edited volume [7].

2   Knowledge-based systems and ontologies

During his work at the DHSS Bench-Capon met Marek Sergot and Bob Kowalski, and he moved to the Department of Computing of Imperial College London in 1984, as a research assistant in the then world-famous Logic Programming Group led by Bob Kowalski. At Imperial Bench-Capon worked on the representation of legislation in logic programs [16, 31], and he further developed his interest in software engineering methods for knowledge-based systems. In 1987 Bench-Capon moved to Merseyside to work as a lecturer in the Department of Computer Science of the University of Liverpool and progressed to become a professor in 2004, remaining in this institute until his retirement in 2012.

A classic paper from his early Liverpool years is [12], about software engineering for knowledge-based systems. Its explicit focus is on legislation-based applications but its relevance is much wider. Among other things, it is one of the first papers in the literature on knowledge-based systems in which the importance of ontologies is stressed. The focus on ontologies became prominent in the KRAFT project, a collaborative research project between the Universities of Aberdeen, Cardiff and Liverpool, and British Telecom. Four of Bench-Capon's ten most cited papers (according to Google Scholar, accessed 21 October 2013) are from this period and are on ontologies. This may counter any impressions that younger AI students might have of Bench-Capon being 'just' an argumentation researcher.

3 Shift towards argumentation

While 1995 Bench-Capon was mainly known as an expert on (legal) knowledge-based systems, he is nowadays primarily known as an argumentation researcher. It is hard to say when exactly this change occurred. As mentioned above, Bench-Capon had been interested in argumentation since his years as a philosophy student. One of his very first papers was [15] (presented at a conference in 1985), in which in fact the idea of rule-based argumentation systems was proposed (though not yet formalised). Although the paper was about legal reasoning, the ideas were of much wider relevance. It is fair to say that much of the work in the 1990s on argumentation-based inference was foreseen in this paper. However, Bench-Capon himself did not really do anything with these ideas until much later, in the new millennium.

A second route to argumentation came via Bench-Capon's interest in explanation facilities of legal knowledge-based systems. In [17] the authors had the brilliant idea to annotate logic programs in terms of Stephen Toulmin's famous argument scheme [32], indicating the different roles of various elements in the knowledge base by linking them to different elements of Toulmin's scheme. For example, uses of negation as failure were linked to Toulmin's rebuttals. This may have been Bench-Capon's first encounter with the notion of an argument scheme, which later became so prominent in his research since 2000. Nevertheless, the main focus here was not on argumentation but on explanation dialogues, a line of research that was continued until [18].

Bench-Capon's first paper that explicitly addressed legal argument as a central topic was his JURIX 1995 invited address, published in revised form as [8]. However, this paper mainly commented on work of others and Bench-Capon had not yet really found his own approach. There was, for instance, no reference in [8] to [22], while yet Dung's abstract argumentation frameworks would become a major element of Bench-Capon's work after 2000.

4 Argumentation as the central topic

Around 2000-2005 Bench-Capon found his approach through a combination of value considerations, abstract argumentation frameworks and (a bit later) argumentation schemes. It was in these years that Bench-Capon truly became an argumentation scholar. Since 2000 Bench-Capon consistently emphasised that arguments, as opposed to mathematical proofs, are not meant to be formally valid but to be persuasive, and he stressed that the persuasive force of an argument to a large extent depends on the legal or societal values held by the audience to which the argument is addressed. With "values" Bench-Capon did not mean numbers but values in the sense of [28, 27], that is, qualitative notions like health, economic competition, social equality, sanctity of property, avoidance of litigation, or legal certainty. The work of the legal philosopher and argumentation scholar Chaim Perelman served as inspiration for Bench-Capon's work on value-based argument. His work since 2000 has several main strands, which are all based on the same coherent approach in which abstract argumentation frameworks capture the context-dependent evaluation of arguments, argument schemes account for the structure and content of arguments, and values capture the persuasiveness of arguments. We now briefly review his main work during these years, again with no hope to be complete.

Legal case-based reasoning with factors, dimensions and values [9] applied his newly found approach to factor-based legal reasoning with precedents. In AI & Law a tradition had emerged since the HYPO system of [24] to represent legal precedents as collections of (boolean) factors pro and con a decision and to express the decision with a preference over the factors. Bench-Capon now proposed to base these preferences over factors on preferences over values, so that cases that are different on the factors could still be regarded as similar in terms of values. Later he extended this view to HYPO's so-called dimensions (essentially multi-valued factors) and, with Giovanni Sartor [14], he applied these ideas in a theory-construction approach, in which alternative theories that explain a given set of precedents are constructed. The approach was later implemented in software as part of work with Alison Chorley [21]. More recently, Bench-Capon has worked on re-casting these ideas in the form of argument schemes embedded in a formal framework for structured argumentation [35, 22]. Finally, the work on legal case-based reasoning was in [33] broadened to a multi-agent account of generating classification arguments from a database of examples.

Value-based abstract argumentation frameworks In [4], his most cited paper, Bench-Capon abstracted these ideas to the level of [22]'s abstract argumentation framework (AFs). Dung's AFs are just a set of arguments with all structure abstracted away, plus a binary relation of attack. Bench-Capon proposed to assign to each argument in an AF a legal or societal value and to allow for different orderings of these values, reflecting different audiences, or different ways to resolve the attacks. This results in so-called Value-based Argumentation Frameworks (VAFs). This paper gave rise to a series of follow-up papers of Bench-Capon and others in which VAFs were computationally studied; e.g. [19].

Argument schemes for practical reasoning and policy debates Having abstracted his initial ideas to the level of abstract argumentation frameworks to demonstrate how argument evaluation concerns defeasible matters of subjectivity, Bench-Capon together with Katie Atkinson and Peter McBurney then turned attention to studying the instantiation of VAFs through argument schemes for practical reasoning, e.g. in [3, 4, 2, 20] (a preliminary version of this scheme was already in [4]). This in effect resulted in an argumentation-based theory of decision making, which has been applied in various contexts, such as legal case-based reasoning [1], democratic policy deliberation [34] and multi-agent systems [5].

Formal and computational analysis of abstract argumentation Above and beyond issues of knowledge representation and reasoning, other computational aspects related to value-based argumentation frameworks have also interested Bench-Capon. With Paul Dunne he published in *AI Journal* papers on computational aspects of abstract argumentation ([24, 25]), and with Sanjay Modgil he developed the idea of meta-argumentation frameworks [26].

5 Final observations

Although Bench-Capon mainly used logic-based techniques, he has methodologically always been open-minded, having used such diverse techniques as neural networks, constraint satisfaction, data-mining and heuristic search in his models of argumentation. Bench-Capon liked logic but he has never been a logician (and has often mused about not considering himself to be a computer scientist), perhaps because he was too interested in real knowledge, real reasoning and real argumentation. One thing that makes Bench-Capon's work so valuable is that he has always tried to connect his ideas to the real world. In his earlier work on knowledge-based systems the examples were always from real knowledge-based systems with real legislation, and in his later work on argumentation the modelled arguments were always real or realistic, from law, politics or related domains. It seems fair to say that Bench-Capon is not primarily known and influential for formalisms and theorems but for methods, ideas and ways of thinking and for lucid analyses of actual examples of argumentation. Having said so, he was not afraid of technical work, and his most-cited paper [4] on value-based argumentation frameworks is a technical one, and has been so influential because of the formalism presented in it that captures his ideas. Moreover, as briefly indicated above, he has published other technical papers of very high quality, such as his recent joint papers with Paul Dunne and with Sanjay Modgil. And there is this mysterious AI Journal research note from 1997 [23] that has received his first citation in this Festschrift in the chapter of Paul Dunne . . .

Bench-Capon's legacy contains more than just his published work. With Paul Dunne, Bench-Capon founded the International COMMA conferences on Computational Models of Argument. Although the first COMMA conference in 2006 was technically a deliverable of the European ASPIC project led by John Fox, it was organised by Bench-Capon and Dunne at the University of Liverpool, while they also founded the COMMA Steering Committee and thus gave the conference a solid grounding to build on, the success of which can be seen through the continued popularity of this bi-annual event.

In 2007 Bench-Capon and Dunne jointly edited a special issue on argumentation of the AI Journal, the world's premier journal in Artificial Intelligence [13]. This issue has been extremely influential in making argumentation a mainstream research topic in AI.

In December 2012 Bench-Capon became the fourth honorary member of JURIX, the Dutch Foundation for Legal Knowledge and Information Systems, for his outstanding contributions over the years to the annual JURIX conference. This conference has, very much helped by the fact that Bench-Capon decided to attend the third edition of in 1991 and to return virtually every year, developed from a modest national event into the main European conference in the field.

In his capacity of an editor-in-chief of the journal *Artificial Intelligence and Law* Bench-Capon has recently edited an extremely interesting special issue on 25 years of the International ICAIL conferences on Artificial Intelligence and Law. In this issue, 50 papers from these conferences are reviewed by 24 prominent scholars in the field in light of today's state-of-the-art, resulting in an excellent overview of a field in which Trevor Bench-Capon has been very much at home since he entered the academic profession.

Finally, while Bench-Capon's work has been a major source of inspiration for many, the same can be said of his oral contributions. Everybody who has had a chance to meet with Bench-Capon in person must agree that there are very few people who are so engaging, stimulating, interesting, witty, insightful, original, and intelligent as Trevor Bench-Capon. Many of us have learned at least as much from talking to him as from reading his work. We hope that this volume provides a fitting tribute to Bench-Capon to recognise his contributions both through his work and his personal presence in the academic community.

Bibliography

[1] K. Atkinson and T. J. M. Bench-Capon. Legal case-based reasoning as practical reasoning. *Artificial Intelligence and Law*, 13(1):93–131, 2005.

[2] K. Atkinson and T.J.M. Bench-Capon. Practical reasoning as presumptive argumentation using action based alternating transition systems. *Artificial Intelligence*, 171:855–874, 2007.

[3] K. Atkinson, T.J.M. Bench-Capon, and P. McBurney. A dialogue game protocol for multi-agent argument over proposals for action. *Autonomous Agents and Multi-Agent Systems*, 11:153–171, 2005.

[4] K. Atkinson, T.J.M. Bench-Capon, and P. McBurney. Computational representation of persuasive argument. *Synthese*, 152:157–206, 2006.

[5] T. J. M. Bench-Capon, K. Atkinson, and P. McBurney. Using argumentation to model agent decision making in economic experiments. *Autonomous Agents and Multi-Agent Systems*, 25(1):183–208, 2012.

[6] T.J.M. Bench-Capon, editor. *Knowledge Representation: An Approach to Artificial Intelligence*. Academic Press, San Diego, CA, 1990.

[7] T.J.M. Bench-Capon, editor. *Knowledge-based Systems and Legal Applications*. Academic Press, San Diego, CA, 1991.

[8] T.J.M. Bench-Capon. Argument in artificial intelligence and law. *Artificial Intelligence and Law*, 5:249–261, 1997.

[9] T.J.M. Bench-Capon. The missing link revisited: the role of teleology in representing legal argument. *Artificial Intelligence and Law*, 10:79–94, 2002.

[4] T.J.M. Bench-Capon. Persuasion in practical argument using value-based argumentation frameworks. *Journal of Logic and Computation*, 13:429–448, 2003.

[11] T.J.M. Bench-Capon. The long and winding road: forty years of argumentation. In B. Verheij, S. Woltran, and S. Szeider, editors, *Computational Models of Argument. Proceedings of COMMA 2012*, pages 3–10. IOS Press, Amsterdam etc, 2012.

[12] T.J.M. Bench-Capon and F.P. Coenen. Isomorphism and legal knowledge based systems. *Artificial Intelligence and Law*, 1:65–86, 1992.

[13] T.J.M. Bench-Capon and P.E. Dunne (eds.). Special issue on Argumentation in Artificial Intelligence. *Artificial Intelligence*, 171, 2007.

[14] T.J.M. Bench-Capon and G. Sartor. A model of legal reasoning with cases incorporating theories and values. *Artificial Intelligence*, 150:97–143, 2003.

[15] T.J.M. Bench-Capon and M.J. Sergot. Towards a rule-based representation of open texture in law. In C. Walter, editor, *Computing Power and Legal Language*, pages 39–60. Greenwood/Quorum Press, Westport, 1988.

[16] T.J.M. Bench-Capon, G.O. Robinson, T.W. Routen, and M.J. Sergot. Logic programming for large scale applications in law: a formalisation of supplementary benefit legislation. In *Proceedings of the First International Conference on Artificial Intelligence and Law*, pages 190–198, New York, 1987. ACM Press.

[17] T.J.M. Bench-Capon, D. Lowes, and A.M. McEnery. Argument-based explanation of logic programs. *Knowledge-Based Systems*, 4:177–183, 1991.

[18] T.J.M. Bench-Capon, T. Geldard, and P.H. Leng. A method for the computational modelling of dialectical argument with dialogue games. *Artificial Intelligence and Law*, 8: 233–254, 2000.

[19] T.J.M. Bench-Capon, P.E. Dunne, and S. Doutre. Audiences in argumentation frameworks. *Artificial Intelligence*, 171:42–71, 2007.

[20] T.J.M. Bench-Capon, H. Prakken, and W. Visser. Argument schemes for two-phase democratic deliberation. In *Proceedings of the Thirteenth International Conference on Artificial Intelligence and Law*, pages 21–30, New York, 2011. ACM Press.

[21] A. Chorley and T.J.M. Bench-Capon. AGATHA: Using heuristic search to automate the construction of case law theories. *Artificial Intelligence and Law*, 13:9–51, 2005.

[22] P.M. Dung. On the acceptability of arguments and its fundamental role in nonmonotonic reasoning, logic programming, and n–person games. *Artificial Intelligence*, 77:321–357, 1995.

[23] P.E. Dunne and T.J. Bench-Capon. The maximum length of prime implicates for instances of 3-SAT. *Artificial Intelligence*, 92:317–319, 1997.

[24] P.E. Dunne and T.J.M. Bench-Capon. Coherence in finite argument systems. *Artificial Intelligence*, 141:187–203, 2002.

[25] P.E. Dunne and T.J.M. Bench-Capon. Two party immediate response disputes: Properties and efficiency. *Artificial Intelligence*, 149:221–250, 2003.

[26] S. Modgil and T.J.M. Bench-Capon. Metalevel argumentation. *Journal of Logic and Computation*, 21:959–1003, 2011.

[27] Ch. Perelman. *Justice, Law and Argument*. D. Reidel Publishing Company, Dordrecht, Holland, 1980.

[28] Ch. Perelman and L. Olbrechts-Tyteca. *The New Rhetoric. A Treatise on Argumentation*. University of Notre Dame Press, Notre Dame, Indiana, 1969.

[22] H. Prakken, A.Z. Wyner, T.J.M. Bench-Capon, and K.D. Atkinson. A formalisation of argumentation schemes for legal case-based reasoning in ASPIC+. *Journal of Logic and Computation*, 2013. In press.

[24] E.L. Rissland and K.D. Ashley. A case-based system for trade secrets law. In *Proceedings of the First International Conference on Artificial Intelligence and Law*, pages 60–66, New York, 1987. ACM Press.

[31] T. Routen and T.J.M. Bench-Capon. Hierarchical formalisations. *International Journal of Man-Machine Studies*, 35:69–93, 1991.

[32] S.E. Toulmin. *The Uses of Argument*. Cambridge University Press, Cambridge, 1958.

[33] M. Wardeh, F. Coenen, and T. J. M. Bench-Capon. Multi-agent based classification using argumentation from experience. *Autonomous Agents and Multi-Agent Systems*, 25(3): 447–474, 2012.

[34] A. Z. Wyner, K. Atkinson, and T. J. M. Bench-Capon. Model based critique of policy proposals. In *Proceedings of the Fourth International Conference on eParticipation*, pages 120–131, 2012.

[35] A.Z. Wyner and T.J.M. Bench-Capon. Argument schemes for legal case-based reasoning. In A.R. Lodder and L. Mommers, editors, *Legal Knowledge and Information Systems. JURIX 2007: The Twentieth Annual Conference*, pages 139–149. IOS Press, Amsterdam etc., 2007.

Evaluating the Uses of Values in a Model of Legal Reasoning

KEVIN ASHLEY *

Abstract

Trevor Bench-Capon's study with Giovanni Sartor, "A Model of Legal Reasoning with Cases Incorporating Theories and Values", is a classic contribution to the field of Artificial Intelligence and Law. It exemplifies a model of argument with cases and values as theory construction. While the particular kind of theory the model constructs has predictive utility in a machine learning sense, however, it does not correspond to a reasonable legal argument scheme. Instead of reasoning with rules concerning preferences among factors or values, a model of legal argument with values should reason about the meanings of intermediate legal concepts.

Introduction

As an instructor who regularly teaches a law school seminar in Artificial Intelligence and Law (AI and Law) to a mixed group of law students and graduate students in intelligent systems, I grapple regularly with Trevor Bench-Capon's classic study with Giovanni Sartor, "A Model of Legal Reasoning with Cases Incorporating Theories and Values" (the "B-CS Paper") [8].

One reason for teaching an AI and Law Seminar in law school is to use the AI and Law models to teach law students lessons about legal rules, reasoning with legal cases, and legal argument. For instance, one can teach how legal rules are subject to semantic and logical ambiguities and unstated conditions by illustrating how AI and Law researchers have addressed or finessed such issues in their computational models [3].

In this respect, the B-CS Paper is an excellent vehicle for teaching law students a lesson that reasoning with cases is "a process of constructing, evaluating and applying a theory." After all, that is exactly how Bench-Capon and

---

*University of Pittsburgh, School of Law

Sartor have modeled reasoning with cases, as constructing theories with cases and values and applying them to decide new cases.

Their theory construction and application approach relates to an insight of Thorne McCarty in another classic AI and Law paper [21]. I also assign this paper in the AI and Law seminar to emphasize to law students the importance of reasoning with cases as theory construction. McCarty also developed a computational model of legal argument as theory construction. In particular, he modeled the legal arguments in a U.S. Supreme Court case, *Eisner v. Macomber*, where the majority and dissent offered different theories of the case based on different selections of and alignments among past precedents and made-up hypotheticals. Each competing theory proposed a different invariant property of the targeted legal concept. The invariant property aligned the precedents and hypothetical examples differently and offered a different explanation of what they and the problem shared or did not share. The goal of McCarty's program was to model the process of constructing these competing theory-based arguments. The program would examine the precedents and hypotheticals favorable to an arguer's desired result, and use what the program knew about the underlying transactions to make explicit the invariant property that would explain the result in the cases and justify the same result in the problem.

Both papers are challenging for law students. In reading [21], it is hard for law students to grasp the lesson because of the fairly abstract and unfamiliar nature of the (tax law) theory constructed and the fairly complex description of how the program constructs the theory. Bench-Capon's and Sartor's description of the theories and methods employs a logical formalism for automating construction of a theory based on precedents that would explain similar cases and justify the same result in a new problem. Logical formalisms challenge American law students, as well, but the authors provide an extended example of the theory construction in a domain of cases that is fairly intuitive and may even be familiar. (Some first year law school casebooks in property law discuss the *Pierson v. Post* case).

The theories generated in the Bench-Capon and Sartor (B-CS) model, moreover, are based on values underlying the regulatory domain. This in itself was an advance as compared to McCarty's model, which did not explicitly take values into account (although, presumably, values pertinent to the constitutionality of income taxation did inform the Justices' arguments.) The B-CS account makes reasoning with values explicit; the law is assumed to exist

> to serve certain social ends [and the] rules derived from cases draw
> their justification from the fact that following them promotes some

desirable end. Thus when rules conflict, we resolve this conflict through a consideration of the purposes served and their relative desirability. Precedent decisions record the ways in which conflicts have been resolved in the past and can be seen as revealing preferences amongst different purposes. Once revealed, these preferences can be used to resolve further disputes. [8, p. 98].

Finally, in the B-CS model, the theories constructed can be compared in terms of their coherence, a process that the authors implement computationally in terms of explanatory power, consistency, and simplicity. This is a second advance. McCarty acknowledged the importance of coherent theories but his model did not seem to operationalize assessing coherence.

There is just one problem with teaching Bench-Capon's and Sartor's model to law students. While it sounds plausible enough, does it really correspond to reasonable legal argumentation? Does it construct the right kinds of theories regarding values and are the assumed uses of values correct from a legal viewpoint? I do not believe that the model or the constructed theories are legally reasonable, or at least, I have not believed that they are. Consequently, I decided to take the advantage of the opportunity presented by the invitation to write something for this festschrift in honor of Trevor Bench-Capon to more closely examine those questions.

In this paper, I will briefly recapitulate the B-CS model and the nature of the legal theories it constructs and applies, focusing on the ways in which values are used in the theories, theory construction and theory application. I will compare that with: (1) McCarty's conception of a legal theory based on cases in [21], (2) discuss the interplay of past cases, values, and legal rules in legal reasoning, (3) briefly present the model of reasoning with cases and values of Melvin Eisenberg, a University of California at Berkeley law professor and jurisprudential scholar who has written extensively on the role of social values in common law reasoning and argumentation, (4) take a closer look at McCarty's sense of legal theory construction and (5) compare it with an example of argument from a theory constructed by the B-CS model and (6) with an approach my student, Matthias Grabmair, has been developing in the value judgment formalism. Finally, (7) I will discuss some criteria for an adequate model of legal theory construction with values and cases and draw appropriate conclusions.

My aim is not to be contentious, especially on the occasion of this celebration of Trevor Bench-Capon's profound contributions to AI and Law. I believe that his and Sartor's paper with its model is a milestone, and I continue to teach it. For law students, [8] teaches an important lesson. The question of how legal practitioners reason with values is somewhat vexed. Law students continually express confusion about that and they have good reason. Indeed, Bench-Capon and Sartor recommend that "a principled way of comparing sets of values ... has not so far been much studied, but is something that needs to be investigated" and that "given that the role of values has only recently been identified, ... some investigation [should be conducted] into the way in which they are used in actual legal practice." [8, pp. 136-7]. As discussed below, in their subsequent contributions they have engaged in doing exactly that. This paper is my attempt to be clear about how I think lawyers use values in legal argument.

1   Theories and values in the B-CS Model

In the B-CS model, past cases are represented in terms of factors representing reasons that explain their outcomes. Factors are abstractions from the facts of the cases in the regulatory domain. The factors provide not only a way of describing cases, but the presence of a factor in a case is "taken to strengthen the case for one or other of the parties to the dispute." [8, p. 102]. The factors also connect the case facts to the often-competing values underlying the regulatory domain. Each factor is associated with a value that it promotes [8, p. 103]. (The authors acknowledge that a factor might be associated with multiple values. This simplifying assumption does not play a role in my critique.)

Their multi-tiered representation enables a kind of theory construction, where the constructed theory can be used to explain the outcomes in the past cases and to determine the outcome of a new case. According to Figure 1: Construction and Use of Theories [8, p. 101] the "outcomes and factor descriptions in decided cases" "reveal" "preferences between sets of factors" which explain the case outcomes but also "reveal" "preferences between sets of values." These value preferences "explain/determine" the factor preferences, which "determine" the "outcomes in new cases." I should make clear, that I interpret the authors' use of "determine" in Figure 1 and elsewhere in their paper in the sense of providing a defeasible rule in favor of an outcome. As they repeatedly state, "case law can never give us such [necessary] conditions, but only defeasible rules," [8, p. 117], a position with which I agree.

Thus, in the B-CS model, a program can infer from decided cases a theory of preferences between competing factors and between competing values. A legal argument based on cases predicts or proposes resolving a new case's competing factors and values consistently with a theory of how such conflicting factors and values have been resolved in past cases; the argument explains and justifies the proposed outcome in terms of this theory. I will characterize this model, in which preferences between sets of values revealed in past cases, defeasibly "determine" outcomes in new cases, as a "precedential" model of values. Based on their repeated statements in the following quotations and elsewhere, I believe that is what Bench-Capon and Sartor intended:

> Preferences between factors are expressed in past decisions, which thus indicate priorities between these rules. From these priorities we can abduce certain preferences between values. Thus the body of case law as a whole can be seen as revealing an ordering on values. Figure 1 gives a diagrammatic representation of the process.... Figure 1 depicts the three levels we need in our theory. Starting from decided cases (precedents), we construct the next levels by identifying the rule-preferences revealed in these cases, and the value preferences which these rule-preferences show. When the theory is constructed it can be used to explain the precedents and to yield a predicted outcome in new cases. [8, p. 101].

> This assumption [of preference among rules based on a past case] is not arbitrary, but rather grounded on the evidence provided by precedent c (similar to the way in which scientific theories are grounded in the evidence provided by empirical observations). Accepting this preference between two rules also commits us to a preference for the values promoted by the preferred rule over those promoted by the defeated rule. We therefore introduce a theory constructor to include such abductions based on the evidence of previous decisions in our theories. [8, p. 108].

> These arbitrary [value] preferences are often required to enable a theory to justify a position when no position is determined by previous cases. What they do is make quite explicit the preferences that are being used to justify that position. In so doing they can pinpoint points of disagreement between the disputants, which will be resolved when the case is decided. [8, p. 109].

> Remember that one's [sic] preference is arbitrary when it does not explain any precedent, but only supports the decision one wishes to have in current case. [8, p. 112].

It is this "precedential" use of values, however, to which I object as a law professor. I do not believe that past cases "determine" preferences among values or an ordering of values that may be properly addressed in a reasonable legal argument to a judge deciding a new case. I believe it is conceptually misleading to characterize a teleological argument in this manner and that it overly simplifies legal argument from values. In short, it simply is not how legal advocates and judges argue with values.

To be clear, I do not deny that the B-CS model generates theories that may have predictive utility. From numerous instances, they could conceivably (and do, as noted below) abstract information that can improve predictive accuracy. The theories are more in the nature of machine learning theories or statistical models; they lack a semantic content adequate to support the kind of reasoning that human advocates perform with the cases and values. They do not correspond to reasonable legal arguments. My objection is similar to the objection to presenting an argument to a judge that the reasons in favor of a position quantitatively outweigh the reasons against the position based on a statistical analysis of past cases. That might well be useful information from a strategic viewpoint, but it does not constitute a reasonable legal argument.

As a law student in my AI and Law seminar once summed it up in her critique of [8], "It is not so easy to compare sets of values." I once asked Paul Brest, a law professor and former Dean of the Stanford Law School and an outside member of my Ph.D. Committee, about the idea of using precedents to resolve conflicting values (i.e., to determine that certain values outweigh other values). With an indulgent smile, he responded quickly, "But that is not how we do it."

2   Interplay of past cases, values, and legal rules

Then how *do* we do it? In the process of legal reasoning with values, an advocate or judge invokes underlying values in order to critique a rule or test that has been proposed for deciding the case. The effects on relevant values are the means for determining if the rule leads to the right result in the case at hand, in past cases, and in future cases, some of which are anticipated explicitly in the form of hypothetical cases. The values have a semantic content and a significance of their own; they are independent of past cases.

The proposed rule is not a rule about values or preferences among values, and the question in focus is how well does the rule accommodate underlying values. I defend this conception of a process of legal reasoning with values below, but first, I will underline the contrasts with the B-CS model, in which preferences among competing values are inferred from the decisions of precedents and treated as determining, in some sense, the decision of new cases. (As noted below, Bench-Capon's more current work does focus on reasoning about effects on values. See e.g., [6].)

In the B-CS model, a theory "contains descriptions of all the cases considered relevant by the proponent of the theory, descriptions of all factors chosen to represent those cases, all rules available to be used in explaining the cases, and all preferences between rules and values available to be used in resolving conflicts between rules [8, p. 106]. The rules referred to in the model are rules "based on factors: the antecedent of a rule is formed from factors favouring the outcome which forms the consequent."

Conspicuously absent from the B-CS model are rules that a law professor or jurisprudential scholar would recognize as the kinds of rules a legal advocate would propose for deciding a case. In proposing a legal rule, advocates and judges commonly employ an intermediate legal concept (ILC) "in order to characterize abstractly the value-laden factual patterns they deem legally significant." [17, p. 164]. The proposed rule or the intermediate legal concepts may be taken or adapted from a legal rule found in a precedent case, or an advocate may propose a new rule or invent a new concept, perhaps by analogy to some other area of law.

The ILCs have content. The intermediate legal concepts embody legal values and principles, as Lindahl explained in his response to Alf Ross's skeptical view of legal concepts [20, pp. 183-4]. Legal rules fashioned in terms of intermediate legal concepts that embody underlying principles, generate transparent, normatively coherent explanations of decisions that provide guidelines for handling new and problematic cases. "A judge finding it necessary to make law for this case must nevertheless decide how wide a range of future cases to control." [23, p. 458]. The choice of intermediate legal concepts with which a legislature or judge formulates a legal rule is one way in which they attempt prospectively to accommodate the conflicting underlying social values that are anticipated in the scenarios that will arise.

In addition, in case comparison, the ILCs play a crucial role in expressing the analogy between cases. In speaking of legal concepts and case comparison, Levi explained,

> It is true that similarity is seen in terms of a word....The movement of concepts into and out of the law makes the point. If the society has begun to see certain significant similarities or differences, the comparison emerges with a word. When the word is finally accepted, it becomes a legal concept. Its meaning continues to change. But the comparison is not only between the instances which have been included under it and the actual case at hand, but also in terms of hypothetical instances which the word by itself suggests. [19, p. 8].

The ILCs also have predictive utility. In an experiment involving predicting new case outcomes based on a database of trade secret law cases represented in terms of factors and intermediate legal concepts, it was demonstrated empirically that taking account of the intermediate legal concepts improved the accuracy of the case-based (factor-based) predictions [4].

Thus, ILCs are a locus of interaction between the values associated with legal principles and case facts in a regulatory domain in a way that factors are not, or have not been so far, even when factors are associated with particular values as in the B-CS model. Although the B-CS model incorporates rules based on factors, the model does not involve arguing about the meaning of those factors as intermediate legal concepts. In realistic legal arguments about cases and values, the meanings and scope of the intermediate legal concepts are at issue.

3   Eisenberg's Model of Reasoning with Cases and Values

With respect to the question of how legal advocates and judges reason with values, Melvin Eisenberg, Jesse H. Choper Professor of Law at the University of California, Berkeley, is a major authority. In his book, *The Nature of the Common Law*, Eisenberg devotes a great deal of attention to legal reasoning with values in addressing the question of the binding-ness of precedents.

3.1   Reasoning with Precedent Cases and Values

According to his account, a precedent imposes a substantive constraint on future decision making for courts subject to the precedent:

> [T]he announced rule of a precedent should be applied and extended to new cases if the rule substantially satisfies the standard of social congruence and a failure to apply or extend the rule to a new case would not be justified by applicable social propositions, given the social propositions that support the rule. [15, p. 55].

The applicable social propositions referred to are the values underlying the legal rules, "those moral norms, policies, and experiential propositions that it is proper for a court to employ," including "usages (experiential propositions about how the world works in a relevant subgroup)" [15, p. 43]. "[S]ocial propositions always figure in determining the rules the courts establish and the way in which those rules are extended, restricted, and applied. [15, pp. 2–3]. I assume that social propositions in Eisenberg's sense roughly correspond to values in the sense of the B-CS model. This seems consistent with Fred Schauer's reading of Eisenberg's text, as well. He says, "the values that guide a common law court in modifying or discarding what had previously been thought to be a rule of law are moral, economic, social, and political. [23, p. 456]. Then, he states,

> This account proceeds from what is probably Eisenberg's most illuminating distinction, the distinction between doctrinal propositions and social propositions. Doctrinal propositions include all those 'propositions that purport to state legal rules and are found in or easily derived from textual sources that are generally taken to express legal doctrine' (p. 1). Social propositions encompass essentially everything else, including moral propositions like 'it is wrong to abandon one's [sic] ill parents,' policy propositions like 'hindering the progress of the automobile industry will decrease the gross national product of the United States,' and experiential propositions such as 'Williamsburg is prettier than Newark' (pp. 14-42). [23, p. 460].

In Eisenberg's view, reasoning about whether a precedent is binding involves reasoning about an announced rule in the precedent. One can take it for granted that such an announced rule will not be expressed in terms of values but, rather, in terms of intermediate legal concepts. He describes the process as follows:

> [I]f the rule announced in a precedent substantially satisfies the standards of social congruence and systemic consistency, it should be consistently applied and extended even though another rule would be marginally better. [15, p. 75].

The standard of social congruence represents an ideal:

> that the body of rules that make up the law should correspond to the body of legal rules that one would arrive at by giving appropriate weight to all applicable social propositions and making the best choices where such propositions collide. [15, p. 44].

If the court determines in light of underlying values (i.e., applicable social propositions) that there is no good reason, or an insufficient reason, to treat the case at hand differently, it should follow the precedent and apply its announced rule to the new case. If, however, the balance of values (i.e., applicable social propositions) favors not applying the rule announced in the precedent, the court may distinguish it, formulating an exception.

> In distinguishing, a court normally begins with a rule, announced
> in a prior case, that is in terms applicable to the case at hand, and
> then determines that there is good reason to treat the case at hand
> differently. The court therefore reformulates the announced rule
> (or, what is the same thing, formulates an exception) in a way that
> requires the two cases to be treated differently. [15, p. 87].

If the court finds applying the rule of the precedent is seriously inconsistent
with underlying values, the court may even radically reconstruct or overrule
the rule of the precedent. "Whether a deciding court applies, extends, refor-
mulates, radically reconstructs, or overrules an announced rule will always
depend in part on whether the rule is socially congruent or incongruent." [15,
p. 75].

The process of reasoning with values described by Eisenberg, which Schauer
confirms subject to some qualifications, is very different from that in the B-
CS model. Eisenberg emphasizes the role of the rules of decision announced
in a precedent. Significantly, the values that, on Eisenberg's account, judges
should apply in reasoning about precedent, are not inferred from or determined
by past cases. According to Schauer's account, "Eisenberg's first tack is an attempt to pedigree his social propositions. Not all social propositions, it turns
out, can push aside doctrinal propositions: only those with a requisite degree
of a particular kind of social support." [23, p. 465]. The pedigree comes in part
from the judges' engaging in professional discourse with other judges, advocates, and via treatises and law review articles, which identifies, and mediates
judges' reception of social propositions. "[T]he social propositions used are
screened and translated by the perceptions of those acculturated into the legal
system." [23, pp. 486–9].

In short, Eisenberg's highly elaborated account of where judges find social
propositions belies any attempt to assert that they are determined by precedents
and there certainly is no reference to any role of past cases in determining preferences among sets of values. In all of Eisenberg's many examples of reasoning with cases and values, one does not observe the kind of theory building
and application of the B-CS model. Nor does Eisenberg refer to any fixed or
induced ordering, partial ordering, or hierarchy among values or social propositions. To the extent that he mentions preferences (specifically "a preference
for not suffering a particularized harm resulting from the violation of a moral
norm" versus "a colliding preference for producing a general benefit through
effectuation of a policy"), he says, in effect, it depends: "Of course, the former preference does not always trump the latter.... [T]here will be some cases
where the weighting of colliding policies and moral norms must lie within the

court's judgment.... The process of rendering judgment cannot be rendered judgment-free." [15, p. 35].

3.2 Values and Eisenberg's Model of Reasoning by Analogy and with Hypotheticals

Eisenberg's accounts of analogical reasoning and reasoning with hypothetical cases are similarly focused on testing announced or proposed rules (i.e., the kind of rules that employ intermediate legal concepts) against values in the form of social propositions.

> In reasoning by analogy, a court normally begins with a rule, announced in a prior case, that is not in terms applicable to the case at hand, and then determines that there is no good reason to treat the case at hand differently. The court therefore reformulates the announced rule (or, what is the same thing, formulates a new rule) in a way that requires the two cases to be treated alike. [15, p. 87].

In reasoning by analogy, a court can extend a rule from a case that the rule covers by its terms to one it does not where "neither applicable social propositions nor a deep doctrinal distinction justifies different treatment of the new cases." Or reasoning by analogy can help a court consolidate rules in a consistent manner, "determining that one rule... should be adopted in preference to a competing rule... because neither applicable social propositions nor any deep doctrinal distinction justifies adopting [the latter rule] while adhering to some other previously announced rule." [15, p. 93].

Arguing from hypothetical cases is another kind of arguing from legal analogy that involves proposed rules and values. Indeed, it seems especially designed for that purpose. "A hypothetical is an imagined situation that involves a hypothesis." In arguing from a hypothetical, an "arguer designs and poses the hypothetical in order to help demonstrate and test [the] consequences [of the arguer's] proposed test or standard for deciding an issue in the case before a court" (i.e., of the arguer's hypothesis). [2, p. 323].

For Eisenberg reasoning from hypotheticals is comparable to reasoning by analogy, "since it turns on the question whether two cases can be distinguished." He maintains, however, that it is substantively different, since it "depends on an interplay between applicable social propositions and conceivable doctrinal propositions and cases." [15, p. 102]. Scott Brewer regards arguments from hypotheticals more simply as a kind of analogical argument in which the items compared are hypothetical cases rather than authoritative precedents. [13, pp. 964–5].

According to Eisenberg, a court may argue from hypotheticals in deciding which legal rule to apply to a case at hand or whether to apply the rule. If the hypothetical case is (a) factually different from the problem but (b) seems easier to decide than the problem, and is (c) indistinguishable "under applicable social propositions," the court can decide to apply the rule from the hypothetical or an extension of that rule. If, however, (d) it "seems clearly improper" to apply the proposed rule to the hypothetical, the court is justified in not applying the rule to the problem because the rule cannot be generalized to cover the hypothetical. [15, pp. 99–101] see [2, p. 324].

Eisenberg provides an example based on a first year torts case, Vincent, plaintiff v. Lake Erie Transportation Co., defendant, 109 Minn. 456, 560 (1910). The defendant had moored a vessel to Vincent's dock to unload cargo when a fierce storm struck. Since the vessel rode out the storm in the relative safety of the dock, the vessel escaped injury, but the wave-tossed vessel damaged Vincent's dock. Vincent sued the plaintiff for the cost of the damage to the dock.

Based on an analogous case, the court satisfied itself that the defendant had a right to keep his vessel moored at Vincent's dock during the storm.

> The situation was one in which the ordinary rules regulating property rights were suspended by forces beyond human control, and if, without the direct intervention of some act by the one sought to be held liable, the property of another was injured, such injury must be attributed to the act of God, and not to the wrongful act of the person sought to be charged.... In *Ploof v. Putnam*, 71 Atl. 188, 20 L. R. A. (N. S.) 152, the Supreme Court of Vermont held that where, under stress of weather, a vessel was without permission moored to a private dock at an island in Lake Champlain owned by the defendant, the plaintiff was not guilty of trespass, and that the defendant was responsible in damages because his representative upon the island unmoored the vessel, permitting it to drift upon the shore, with resultant injuries to it. 109 Minn. 459.

But the court considered whether or not to extend that rule to prevent the plaintiff's recovery for the damages caused. Specifically, the court considered the question whether, although the defendant had a right to keep the vessel moored at the plaintiff's dock, the defendant was nevertheless liable to pay for the damage.

After considering a hypothetical, the court settled on the following rule for deciding: "where the defendant prudently and advisedly availed itself of the plaintiffs' property for the purpose of preserving its own more valuable property, the plaintiffs are entitled to compensation for the injury done".

> [I]magine that for the better mooring of the vessel those in charge of her had appropriated a valuable cable lying upon the dock. No matter how justifiable such appropriation might have been, it would not be claimed that, because of the overwhelming necessity of the situation, the owner of the cable could not recover its value. [15, p. 100].

The hypothetical differed from the case's facts; it did not involve the damage caused by the vessel but the intentional appropriation of the plaintiff's cable. It was, however, easier for the court to decide. The court believed that the hypothetical could not rationally be distinguished from the case at hand. As Eisenberg put it, "Surely one who appropriates another's goods, even for the best of reasons, should make compensation." [15, p. 100]. Thus, the court decided that the defendant was liable for the damage to plaintiff's dock. In Eisenberg's terminology, the court considered "applicable social propositions", which include moral principles and policies, and found they do not support treating the case differently from the hypothetical [15, p. 100]. In terms of the proposed test, both are instances of a defendant's availing itself of plaintiff's property.

Another jurisprudential account of analogical reasoning confirms the crucial role of proposed rules or tests for deciding a case. For Scott Brewer, an analogy-warranting rule (AWR) provides a legal analogy its rational force. The AWR is a rule under which the source case is relevantly similar to the target case with respect to the shared characteristics of each and the inferred conclusion the rule warrants [13, pp. 971, 975, 1015–6]. Underlying values elaborated in the analogy-warranting rationale (AWRa) make the analogy compelling. The rationale explains why, in the "eyes of the law", "the logical relation among the characteristics articulated by the analogy-warranting rule either does obtain or should obtain." [13, pp. 965, 1025].

While the B-CS model provides a computational account and concrete examples of theories involving cases and values, these jurisprudential accounts of reasoning with cases and values illustrate that a more complex kind of theory is required. While neither Eisenberg nor Brewer characterizes legal argument with cases explicitly as theory construction, one can, at least, try to imagine what such a constructed theory might look like in their accounts. It would be a theory relating the facts of a case or hypothetical to the announced or proposed rule for decision in light of the values (i.e., applicable social propositions or analogy-warranting rationale) underlying the legal rule and associated with the intermediate legal concepts.

4   McCarty's Sense of Legal Theory Construction

I agree with Bench-Capon and Sartor when they assert that "A better way of seeing reasoning with cases is to see it as a process of constructing and using a theory." [8, p. 98]. They quote McCarty for this central insight:

> The task for a lawyer or a judge in a 'hard case' is to construct a theory of the disputed rules that produces the desired legal result, and then to persuade the relevant audience that this theory is preferable to any theories offered by an opponent. [21, p. 285].

When McCarty speaks of theory construction, however, he, of course, means constructing a legal theory, a theory that relates the problem and past cases to values via a proposed rule for deciding the case. This is apparent in McCarty's phrase, "*to construct a theory of the disputed rules*" (emphasis added), as well as from his next sentence:

> Empirically, *legal theories* seem to have a prototype-plus-deformation structure, as in *Eisner v. Macomber*, and one important component of a persuasive argument is an appeal to the coherence of the theory thus constructed. (emphasis added) [21, p. 285].

The whole point of McCarty's approach was to model argument about intermediate legal concepts offered by advocates in proposed rules or tests for deciding the case, tests that judges evaluate in terms of how coherently they account for precedent cases and hypotheticals in light of the underlying values. The prototype-plus-deformation structure refers to McCarty's model of legal concepts, the kinds of concepts employed as intermediate legal concepts in proposed tests or rules for deciding a case. McCarty's discussion of Justice Pitney's argument for the majority and Justice Brandeis's response in dissent makes clear that the arguments were about proposed tests for deciding the case.

> Although ... this analysis of stock ownership in terms of the underlying deontic modalities is Justice Pitney's strongest argument, it does not by itself provide a workable test for taxability.... But this test, a measure of 'constant value' before and after the transaction, applies also to the cash distribution in *Lynch v. Hornby* and the stock distributions in *Peabody v. Eisner*, a fact that the commentators were quick to point out. A better suggestion is that the stock dividend 'does not alter the pre-existing proportionate interest of any stockholder,' 252 U.S. 189, 211 (1920), a verbal test that survives and appears frequently in subsequent decisions....

> Let us call this the 'no-transfers-out-of-assets' test, and see how it is constructed and attacked in our computational simulation. (emphasis added) [21, p. 283].

It would be surprising if McCarty agreed that the kind of theories in the B-CS model, theories about preferences among factors and values induced from past cases, counted as legal theories. Not only do they fail to refer to proposed rules or tests for deciding a case, but they do not correspond to the ways in which precedents and hypotheticals are used in legal argument.

> For instance, Justice Brandeis attacks the tests proposed by Justice Pitney: The overall strategy in this passage is to show: (i) that the tests proposed in Justice Pitney's opinion fail to make the distinction he really wants; and, a much stronger claim: (ii) that the distinction itself is incoherent. [21, p. 284].

The tools Justice Brandies employs for the attack are hypothetical cases that illustrate the failure of the test and its lack of coherence. As McCarty summarizes it:

> In this way, we have obtained the full sequence of hypothetical cases that appears in the passage quoted above from Justice Brandeis' opinion. The second stage of the computation compares these hypothetical cases with the cases from which they were derived to see if there would be any difference in tax treatment under Justice Pitney's analysis. Since each case was derived by replacing the distribution of a security with the distribution of cash, this becomes the main difference to analyze. [21, p. 284].

Thus, McCarty's legal theory construction mandate requires, at the least, a model that employs proposed rules or tests that incorporate intermediate legal concepts and that can adequately represent fact situations in sufficient detail to assess effects of the proposed rule on underlying values and to compare those effects across factual contexts.

And, it will take one thing more: argument schemes that legal practitioners recognize as reasonable. Although at the time he was writing the terminology was not yet in vogue, the fact is that McCarty identified a number of argument schemes, arguments from a counterexample or from a hypothetical, that any second or third year law student would recognize, and he described their implementation in a manner that should seem authentic if only law students could understand the descriptions.

5   Example of Argument from Constructed Theory

Bench-Capon and Sartor provide examples of theories in connection with *Young v. Kitchens*, 6 QB 606 (1844), a case involving the question of property rights in wild game, which has been studied in Artificial Intelligence and Law at least since Berman and Hafner discussed it in [12] and which is discussed in some first year law school casebooks in connection with the *Pierson v. Post* case. Plaintiff Young, a fisherman, had partially surrounded a large number of fish with his net, which was not yet closed. Defendant Hitchens rushed the gap in Young's net and caught the nearly corralled fish with his own net. The court decided in favor of defendant Hitchens.

The example is presented here very briefly to give the reader a flavor of the kind of theories the B-CS model constructs and of the kind of information the theories omit.

The B-CS model can generate theories justifying a decision for the defendant Hitchens based on two cases, *Pierson v. Post* and *Keeble v. Hickeringill*; the first held for defendant and the second for plaintiff in similar circumstances. Each theory represents the *Young* problem and one or both of *Pierson*, and *Keeble*, in terms of the factors that apply and their outcomes in the two decided cases as well as various rules and preferences between rules. Each rule is of a form in which a set of factors F is its antecedent and its consequent is an outcome for the case. The resulting theories are compared in terms of their coherence, which takes into account their explanatory power (i.e., the number of cases it explains) their consistency, and their simplicity.

The preferences among rules indicate that one rule is preferred over another. The preferences are derived either from cases or from values. A decided case to which a pair of conflicting rules applies has an outcome from which one may conclude that the rule with that outcome is preferred over the other. In addition, a decided case to which conflicting values apply (based on the values linked to the factors that apply in the case) is evidence that one set of values is preferred over another, and this preference can also be used to justify a preference among factor-based rules.

Based on the model, the authors construct seven theories that explain how the *Young* case should be decided in terms of the outcomes of the other two, the values of promoting productivity, enjoyment of property rights, and decreasing litigation, and the four factors: (1) *pLiv* = Plaintiff was pursuing his livelihood (*Keeble, Young*), favoring *P*, (2) *pLand* = Plaintiff was on his own land (*Keeble*), favoring *P*, (3) *pNposs* = Plaintiff was not in possession of the animal (*Pierson, Keeble* and *Young*), favoring defendant, and (4) *dLiv* = Defendant was pursuing his livelihood (*Young*), favoring *D*.

Since the *Pierson* case favored the defendant and the *Keeble* case favored the plaintiff, the defendant's theory should rely on one and distinguish the other as, indeed it can, but I will focus on the latter (as in theories T_{3b} and T_{3c} [8, p. 111-112]).

> In this way the theory distinguishes *Keeble* from *Young*: it explains why *Keeble* was decided for P without implying the same decision for *Young*. The plaintiff had a remedy (P) in *Keeble* since he was both pursuing his livelihood (*pLiv*) and on his own land (*pLand*), and the combination of these two factors supports P more strongly than not having possession of the animal (*pNposs*) supports D (according to the [previously derived] preference *rpref*($\langle\{pLiv, pLand\}, P\}\rangle$, $langle\{pNposs\}, D\rangle$)). Note that ... *Keeble* is explained by giving priority to the rule $\langle\{pLiv, pLand\}, P\rangle$ .... Therefore, the reasoning of *Keeble* cannot now be applied to *Young*, where there is only *pLiv* (and not *pLand*) to support decision P. [8, p. 111-112].

Thus far, the authors continue, the theory explains the negative case but does not make an affirmative argument that the defendant should win in the *Young* case. That is provided for in T_{3c}:

> Unfortunately T_{3c} does not explain why *Young* should be decided for D. For this purpose, one would need the rule preference *rpref*($\langle\{pNposs\}, D\rangle, \langle\{pLiv\}, P\rangle$), which would have to be either added arbitrarily or derived from the arbitrarily added value preference *vpref*(*Llit,Mprod*). (Remember that one's preference is arbitrary when it does not explain any precedent, but only supports the decision one wishes to have in current case.) [8, pp. 111–112].

The arbitrary preference is not desirable, of course, but that is, in part, simply an artifact of the rather impoverished set of cases the example provides, including only one pro-defendant case. This, however, is rather realistic. Advocates frequently need to make the best arguments possible given poor facts and few precedents. The arbitrary value preference should be seen as a placeholder, and indication of the kind of case ammunition the advocate needs to find.

In the B-CS model, it is a placeholder for a case supporting the desired rule preference or the desired value preference. And, it is the latter that causes the jurisprudential problem introduced above. The case that satisfies the desired value preference may not necessarily be properly used to make a legal argument to present to a judge. That is an instance of the precedential use of values, but from the point of view of legal theories or legal arguments with values, that is "not how we do it." Another way to think about this objection is that, although the B-CS model refers to some component argument moves that attorneys would recognize (e.g., an argument from distinguishing), the theory construction moves do not correspond to actual legal arguments, and the manner in which the moves are elaborated using value and rule preferences is foreign. In addition, some expected argument moves (and the associated argument schemes) associated with case comparison in terms of intermediate legal concepts are missing.

In other words, I do not believe that there is a valid scheme for legal-argument-from-theory, into which one can plug a value preference from the value-preference-determining case and that uses the values in a constructed theory in the way that Bench-Capon and Sartor describe. Their model does not do justice to the way we reason with values. I do believe that there are valid schema for legal argument-from-theory, but these schema involve additional components, namely a proposed test or rule for deciding the case, a rule that employs intermediate legal concepts, the kind of rule that McCarty had in mind when he recommended modeling argument with cases as construction of a *legal* theory.

In addition, to implement a scheme for legal argument-from-theory successfully, I suspect, a program will need a richer representation for facts than factors provide. One can use past cases as a guide to resolving conflicting values in a current case, but it is a matter of mapping arguments about the values at stake in the past case to the context of the current facts. One needs to compare the current case facts and those of a past case in sufficient detail to make sure how well the mapped arguments apply in the new circumstances. SIROCCO, for instance, employed an enriched representation of the facts of engineering ethics cases and of the ethics code principles, which embodied professional and social values. The expert board's opinions were annotated to flag the case facts that the board emphasized in discussing, for example, how conflicting principles were resolved in a specific case. The utility of these techniques was demonstrated empirically in improved information retrieval performance [22].

In practice, when one needs to resolve conflicting values, one can always use well-crafted hypotheticals. Even if there is no on-point precedent, one can pose a hypothetical scenario that seems, for teleological reasons, "easier to decide than the problem," to use Eisenberg's phrase, and employ it to evaluate and modify a proposed test. The B-CS model makes no provision for posing hypotheticals. As explained below, our approach does, with its value judgment formalism and representations of event progressions and relevant common sense knowledge.

I imagine that Thorne McCarty would agree with the assertion that modeling legal theory construction requires an enriched fact representation. After all, his knowledge representation for the *Macomber* argument, as described in Section 3 of [21, pp. 278-281], employed his Language for Legal Discourse (LLD), with its representation of states, events, actions and deontic modalities such as permission and obligation to represent the facts of the corporate distributions not only in the case itself, but in the precedents and hypotheticals. This included representing such things as permitted distributions to common stockholders and their resulting states of affairs in sufficient detail that the program could discover invariants shared by subsets of the various taxable or non-taxable events in the cases and hypotheticals (e.g., distribution of a corporation's cash, of its preferred stock or of its common stock, distribution of the stock of another corporation, or mere appreciation in the corporation's stock value.)

The latter point, representing the resulting states of affairs of various actions, is particularly important. It is only from examining the before-and-after states of affairs of an action, including legal actions such as deciding a case according to a particular legal rule, that a reasoner can assess the effects of the action on the underlying values. While I do not necessarily advocate applying LLD to model arguments from legal theories constructed from cases and values, I do take McCarty's point that a richer factual representation is required, one that is more detailed than a factor representation and one that explicitly represents the states of affairs resulting from various actions.

6 The Value Judgment Formalism

Matthias Grabmair, my advisee in the University of Pittsburgh Intelligent Systems Program, has been developing a computational model of legal argument with legal rules, values, cases, and hypotheticals. The value judgment formalism [16, 17, 18] see also [2] defines and implements a set of schemes for arguing about the consequences that certain decisions have on underlying values, namely decisions to apply (or not to apply) legal rules in specific scenarios. The rules, proposed tests for deciding a case, are expressed in terms of intermediate legal concepts. The consequences are characterized in terms of whether the positive effect of a decision on the applicable legal values outweighs the negative effect. The argument schemes explicitly refer to these effects.

In order to represent the situations entailing these effects in more concrete terms that a program can reason about, Grabmair has developed a new knowl-

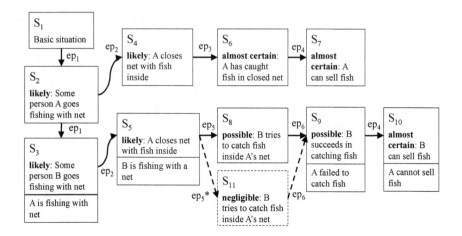

Figure 1. Example event progression space for the domain underlying *Young v. Hitchens*.

edge representation formalism called "event progressions" and is implementing it computationally. Event progressions are transition operators that modify a given scenario into a new scenario in a particular way under certain circumstances and with a known likelihood.

For example, Figure 1 depicts a sample event progression space for the scenarios in the *Young v. Hitchens* case. Each node represents a situation. The arcs represent transitions from one situation to the next. The facts added in a transition are indicated along with their likelihood represented in boldface. Other facts of interest are shown under the line in a node. [18].

In this example, a proposed test is under consideration: If a person (P1) has visibly commenced to acquire possession of one or more movable things (T), then any subsequent intervening acquisition (A) of possession by another person is wrongful. It is formalized as:

Acquisition protection [AP] rule:

commAcqPoss(P1, T) ∧ intrvAcqPoss(P2, T) ⇒
wrongful(intervene, P2, P1)

In this legal rule "Commenced to acquire possession" (commAcqPoss) is an intermediate legal concept.

In Figure 1, the dashed arc indicates that S11 is only available when the AP legal rule is adopted. States S8 and S11 are mutually exclusive. If the AP rule is adopted, then the "threat" of wrongfully acquiring possession by taking them from the other fisherman's net makes it less likely that the second fisherman would actually do it. In the diagram, this is represented by the change in likelihood from S8 (possible) to S11 (negligible), thereby providing greater protection of the first fisherman's efforts to earn his livelihood but demoting competition. This change in the progression space hence informs policy arguments about whether the AP rule should be adopted or not. (See argument *a1* below) [18].

The program uses basic argument schemes including *argument from common sense rule*, *argument from norm*, and *argument from value effect*. It also employs more complex schemes such as *argument from desirable consequence*, *from more likely desirable consequence*, *from less likely desirable consequence*, and corresponding arguments *from undesirable consequences*. Examples of the kinds of arguments we believe the implementation will be able to generate for the *Young* case include:

> *a1 (for Plaintiff Young)*: The AP rule should be adopted as it provides better protection of peoples' efforts to earn their livelihood. Mr. Young made an effort to maintain his livelihood by pursuing the fish with his net. It would be unjust not to grant him the reward and render his efforts futile. Without adopting the AP rule in this case, it is possible that a fisherman's efforts are rendered futile by others. Adopting the rule would virtually eliminate this risk.

> *a2 (for Defendant Hitchens)*: The AP rule should not apply because it would entail Mr. Hitchens losing his earnings from catching the fish, an endeavor he also spent effort for in order to maintain his livelihood.

> *a3 (for Plaintiff Young)*: The AP rule should be adopted because it promotes the protection of property, where such private property extends to movable things that an individual is visibly making efforts to gain possession over. Young was visibly closing his nets, and it was only a matter of time until Mr. Young's net would have almost certainly been closed.

> *a4 (for Defendant Hitchens)*: The AP rule is too broad. While property deserves protection, someone has a protectable property interest in a thing only when he or she has already acquired full possession over the thing.

> *a5 (for Plaintiff Young)*: If the AP rule is not adopted, it would allow unfair hunting practices. Mr. Hitchens could not have caught

the fish so easily without the prior efforts of Mr. Young to corral
the fish into his net. [18].

In addition, the formalism models, and we plan to implement, argument
schemes for drawing analogical inferences from cases with values. The analogies are drawn in terms of intermediate legal concepts. And, the knowledge
representation will be sufficiently detailed to enable the program to generate
arguments about whether the analogy holds.

For starters, the program, arguing on behalf of say, the plaintiff, would use
a scheme for an *argument from sufficient similarity* to draw an analogy to a favorable precedent, in effect, proposing a test for deciding the case and using an
intermediate legal concept to characterize the analogy. Following the scheme,
the plaintiff's advocate cites a precedent with a pro-plaintiff outcome whose
facts include a pattern of facts characterizable in terms of an intermediate legal concept like "commenced to acquire possession". By citing the precedent,
the advocate implicitly affirms that the positive effects on relevant values of
assigning that outcome in the precedent outweighed the negative effects [17].

To justify the imposition of the same outcome in the current case, the advocate establishes that the positive effects on relevant values of assigning that
outcome in the current case outweigh the negative effects. To do that, the advocate points out a pattern of facts in the current case associated with the same
intermediate legal concept (i.e., commenced to acquire possession) and hence
shared with the precedent. She submits this similarity as justifying the inference that the positive effects on relevant values of assigning that outcome in
the current case also outweigh the negative effects [17].

For the defendant's advocate, the program can challenge this analogy with
an *argument from a distinction due to a missing feature*. First, the advocate
points out a fact pattern associated with an intermediate legal concept present
in the precedent but absent from the case, say, "with no possibility of escape
or interference by competitors" and argues that the positive balance of value
effects in the precedent was due to its presence. Second, the advocate asserts
an undesirable consequence on relevant values if this additional intermediate
legal concept is omitted from the analogy and a desirable consequence if it is
included, for instance, "a more exacting standard reduces litigation". Third, if
possible, the advocate points to the actual opinion in the precedent, where the
additional intermediate legal concept was explicitly considered to have been
relevant for the decision. Fourth, the advocate can present an argument from
an undesirable consequence in the precedent, hypothesizing that one of the
purposes of the rule in the precedent was to prevent that consequence. Then,
the advocate shows that the case at bar does not entail that consequence and

hence the precedent's rule should not apply in any case because the purpose it serves is inapplicable. [17].

Using other argument schemes, the defendant's advocate may cite her own precedent in an *argument from counterexample*, ideally one that shares intermediate legal concepts with the case at hand and the plaintiff's precedent but has the opposite outcome, suggesting that the effects on relevant values of not assigning an outcome for plaintiff were greater. [17].

The plaintiff's advocate can mount a surrebuttal to a distinction. She can downplay the distinction by pointing out an undesirable consequence if the distinguishing intermediate legal concept is required for the analogy to the precedent and a desirable consequence if it is not required. The distinction's undesirability argument can also be countered with another intermediate legal concept which is present in the case at hand but absent from the precedent and which compensates for the absence of the distinguishing intermediate legal concept, an *argument from feature substitution*. [17].

In sum, the value judgment formalism, with its representation of event progressions and related common sense knowledge, supports computationally modeling schemes for arguing about the effects on values of proposed rules that employ ILCs. This will enable us to model kinds of argument that are closely related to legal theory construction, including arguments using hypotheticals to assess the effects of proposed rules on values and analogical arguments with even very small numbers of precedents.

7 Discussion

While much work remains to implement and evaluate the value judgment formalism, I believe that the resulting arguments by analogy as applied in a microworld of cases such as the property cases and hypotheticals in the *Pierson v. Post* arena [1] will more closely resemble constructing a legal theory in McCarty's sense than the B-CS model. This is because:

1. The value judgment approach models argument schemes that are recognizable to legal practitioners and in a way that is familiar to them.

2. The argument schemes concern proposed tests for deciding cases where the tests employ intermediate legal concepts, whose function it is to "characterize abstractly the value-laden factual patterns they deem legally significant." The consequents of the proposed tests include the fulfillment of an intermediate legal concept as well as the outcome of a case.

3. The case analogies are framed as facts subsumed under shared intermediate legal concepts.

4. The knowledge representation is detailed enough to model the effects of decisions on the balance of values so that a program can argue about the aptness of the analogy.

5. The value judgment formalism includes argument schemes for reasoning with hypotheticals [16]. While we intend to implement them, we are still working through the ramifications of the event progression representations for posing meaningful hypothetical variations.

Of course, the focus of this piece, on [8] as a vehicle for teaching law students about arguing with cases and values as legal theory construction, should not obscure the fact that Trevor Bench-Capon has made significant progress: his more recent models display a number of the hallmarks above. Bench-Capon and Atkinson present an approach to using argumentation schemes and critical questions to conduct defeasible reasoning, using social values to represent individual motivations, representing knowledge of actions, their pre- and post-conditions, and the values promoted by actions, and handling time. See [6] and the work cited therein. This work supports reasoning about effects on values and has important ramifications for modeling legal arguments with cases and values as theory construction.

Bench-Capon and Prakken have developed a model of legal reasoning with hypotheticals that deals with proposed tests employing intermediate legal concepts and that uses information about the values advanced and demoted by a rule to derive priorities between rules. [7]. I believe that the use of the event progressions representation [18] provides a finer-grained representation of factual effects on values. It seems to us to be better grounded legally than their introduction of abstract and somewhat arbitrary thresholds to talk about degrees of values in cases. Although Bench-Capon provides support for the use of thresholds in his analysis of certain Supreme Court oral arguments [10], there does not seem to be an argument scheme focused explicitly on thresholds; rather, thresholds are a method for computationally implementing contextual value balancing in order to model arguments where the Court directs, in effect, for example, that one should "consider first if exigency is sufficient and if not whether privacy is sufficiently low" in deciding cases involving the legality of a warrantless search of an automobile.

Thus, in respect to computational implementation, thresholds might be useful (but see a technical problem with cascading thresholds identified in [16]). Indeed, even though the theories generated by the B-CS model do not correspond to legal theories in the sense explained above, they, too, may be practically useful. They may help a computer program to select cases for fulfilling a scheme for an argument-from-legal-theory, guide a program's search in deciding which of many possible argument moves to pursue, or help it to assess an argument's *apriori* likelihood of success.

This would be especially true if a large number of cases were available (instead of just three as in [8].) For example, Chorley and Bench-Capon used the Agatha and related models to explore generating predictive theories with much larger sets of cases and taking values into account using the precedential approach. Although the theories do not appear to be legal theories in the sense explained above (e.g., they do not involve intermediate legal concepts) but are more in the nature of machine learning theories, they have explanatory power based on many cases and they make accurate predictions [14]. In addition, they are a novel kind of theorizing made possible by the value- and factor-based case representational and intelligent search techniques developed by Bench-Capon and his student. The development of new technologies for recording and retrieving cases has made the development of new legal argument schemes possible before (e.g., the development of English law reports in the 1200s) and they will surely do so again.

8 Conclusion

Trevor Bench-Capon's and Giovanni Sartor's "A Model of Legal Reasoning with Cases Incorporating Theories and Values" is a classic contribution to the field of Artificial Intelligence and Law. It exemplifies a model of argument with cases and values as theory construction. McCarty was right: in a hard case an advocate or judge needs to construct a theory with the rules and cases at hand. Bench-Capon and Sartor are right: that theory needs to take values into account and the resulting theories have to satisfy criteria of coherence. In addition, they deserve much credit for actually creating a computational data structure for a theory. By making theories involving cases and values computational, they reawakened the field to the importance of modeling this aspect of legal argumentation, and they provided concrete examples of such theories to ponder. Bench-Capon's implementations of these aspects of theory construction, in [8]and his follow-on work, are major contributions, and the theories constructed have explanatory power and potential practical significance.

The particular kind of theory their model constructs, I maintain, however, does not correspond to a recognizably reasonable legal argument scheme. That would require a proposed test or rule for deciding a case, involving intermediate legal concepts, to play a central role. In addition, a more detailed representation of case facts will, I predict, be necessary for computationally modeling a contextually-sensitive comparison of cases to determine if an analogy drawn in terms of the concept applies or not. Of course, theory construction is only one of Trevor Bench-Capon's classic contributions to Artificial Intelligence and Law that any serious attempt at teaching the subject in an AI and Law Seminar like mine must cover, including his foundational work on isomorphic representations of statutes [9], legal ontologies [11], and argumentation schemes and critical questions to conduct defeasible reasoning [5]. And, no doubt, there will be many more such contributions. Trevor Bench-Capon may have retired from his university position, but, I predict, he will become the most prolific "Honorary Visiting Professor" in history.

9 Acknowledgements

I am very grateful to my graduate student advisee in the University of Pittsburgh Intelligent Systems Program, Matthias Grabmair, for his careful reading of and incisive comments and suggestions on a draft of this manuscript.

Bibliography

[1] K. D. Ashley. Ontological requirements for analogical, teleological, and hypothetical legal reasoning. In *Proceedings of the 12th International Conference on Artificial Intelligence and Law*, ICAIL '09, pages 1–10, New York, NY, USA, 2009. ACM.

[2] K. D. Ashley. Teaching a process model of legal argument with hypotheticals. *Artificial Intelligence and Law*, 17(4):321–370, Dec. 2009.

[3] K. D. Ashley. Teaching law and digital age legal practice with an ai and law seminar. *Chicago Kent Law Review*, 88, 2013.

[4] K. D. Ashley and S. Brüninghaus. A predictive role for intermediate legal concepts. In D. Bourcier, editor, *Legal Knowledge and Information Systems: Jurix 2003 the Sixteenth Annual Conference, Frontiers in Artificial Intelligence and Applications*, pages 153–162. IOS Press, Inc., 2003.

[5] K. Atkinson and T. Bench-Capon. Argumentation and standards of proof. In *Proceedings of the 11th International Conference on Artificial intelligence and Law*, ICAIL '07, pages 107–116, New York, NY, USA, 2007. ACM.

[6] T. Bench-Capon and K. Atkinson. Action-state semantics for practical reasoning. In *AAAI Fall Symposium - Technical Report*, pages 8–13, 2009.

[7] T. Bench-Capon and H. Prakken. Using argument schemes for hypothetical reasoning in law. *Artificial Intelligence and Law*, 18(2):153–174, June 2010.

[8] T. Bench-Capon and G. Sartor. A model of legal reasoning with cases incorporating theories and values. *Artificial Intelligence*, 150(1–2):97 – 143, 2003.

[9] T. J. M. Bench-Capon. Exploiting isomorphism: Development of a KBS to support British coal insurance claims. In *Proceedings of the 3d International Conference on Artificial Intelligence and Law*, ICAIL '91, pages 62–68, New York, NY, USA, 1991. ACM.

[10] T. J. M. Bench-Capon. Relating values in a series of supreme court decisions. In K. Atkinson, editor, *Legal Knowledge and Information Systems - JURIX 2011: The Twenty-Fourth*

Annual Conference, University of Vienna, Austria, 14th-16th December 2011, volume 235 of *Frontiers in Artificial Intelligence and Applications*, pages 13–22. IOS Press, 2011.

[11] T. J. M. Bench-Capon and P. R. S. Visser. Ontologies in legal information systems; the need for explicit specifications of domain conceptualisations. In *Proceedings of the 6th International Conference on Artificial Intelligence and Law*, ICAIL '97, pages 132–141, New York, NY, USA, 1997. ACM.

[12] D. H. Berman and C. D. Hafner. Representing teleological structure in case-based legal reasoning: the missing link. In *Proceedings of the 4th International Conference on Artificial Intelligence and Law*, ICAIL '93, pages 50–59, New York, NY, USA, 1993. ACM.

[13] S. Brewer. Exemplary reasoning: Semantics, pragmatics, and the rational force of legal argument by analogy. *Harvard Law Review*, 109(5):pp. 923–1028, 1996.

[14] A. Chorley and T. Bench-capon. Agatha: Using heuristic search to automate the construction of case law theories. *Artificial Intelligence and Law*, 13:9–51, 2006.

[15] M. Eisenberg. *The Nature of the Common Law*. Thomas M. Cooley lectures. Harvard University Press, 1988.

[16] M. Grabmair and K. D. Ashley. Argumentation with value judgments - an example of hypothetical reasoning. In R. Winkels, editor, *Legal Knowledge and Information Systems - JURIX 2010: The Twenty-Third Annual Conference on Legal Knowledge and Information Systems, Liverpool, UK, 16-17 December 2010*, volume 223 of *Frontiers in Artificial Intelligence and Applications*, pages 67–76. IOS Press, 2010.

[17] M. Grabmair and K. D. Ashley. Facilitating case comparison using value judgments and intermediate legal concepts. In K. D. Ashley and T. M. van Engers, editors, *Proceedings of the 13th International Conference on Artificial Intelligence and Law*, ICAIL '11, pages 161–170. ACM, 2011.

[18] M. Grabmair and K. D. Ashley. Using event progression to enhance purposive argumentation in the value judgment formalism. In *The 14th International Conference on Artificial Intelligence and Law, Proceedings of the Conference, June 10-14, 2013, Rome*. ACM, 2013.

[19] E. H. Levi. *An Introduction to Legal Reasoning*. University of Chicago Press (Phoenix), Chicago, 1949.

[20] L. Lindahl. Deduction and justification in the law. the role of legal terms and concepts. *Ratio Juris*, 17(2):182–202, 2004.

[21] L. T. McCarty. An implementation of Eisner v. Macomber. In *The 5th International Conference on Artificial Intelligence and Law, Proceedings of the Conference, May 21-24, 1995, College Park, MD*, pages 276–286, New York, NY, USA, 1995. ACM.

[22] B. M. McLaren. Extensionally defining principles and cases in ethics: an ai model. *Artificial Intelligence Journal*, 150:145–181, 2003.

[23] F. Schauer. Is the common law law? *California Law Review*, 77:455–471, 1989.

The Value of Values in Computational Argumentation

KATIE ATKINSON * AND ADAM WYNER[†]

Abstract

Value-based argumentation has had a big impact in the computational argumentation literature and work in AI and Law. This paper presents a survey of this line of work that covers the seminal contributions on the topic by Trevor Bench-Capon and the subsequent lines of research that have been followed by others to make use of and extend Bench-Capon's ideas.

Introduction

A fundamental concern of work in artificial intelligence is how to enable automated practical reasoning, which is reasoning about what to do. Over the past decade some researchers in the AI community have been addressing this issue using the notion of argument. In order to account for differing points of view in debates about what to do, it has been recognised that the parties within a debate will have different perspectives on what is important to pursue, according to their subjective aspirations and preferences. Trevor Bench-Capon has been central in developing analyses for representing and reasoning about *value-based arguments* in general and *value-based practical reasoning* in particular, whereby the social interests of debate participants are accounted for. Bench-Capon's work in these areas touches on many different aspects, covering abstract argument systems to concrete representations. His work has been applied in a number of different domains, with a particular focus falling on work in AI and Law.

This paper provides a survey of the work of Bench-Capon and his colleagues on value-based arguments, and also reviews other authors' work that has built on the main ideas. The paper is structured as follows. Section 1 discusses

---

*University of Liverpool, Department of Computer Science
†University of Aberdeen, Department of Computing Science

some of the work that has motivated Bench-Capon's ideas on value-based argument, with a particular focus on philosophical background material. Section 2 recounts the use of values in abstract frameworks for representing and reasoning about argument, which is the first major contribution that Bench-Capon made on the topic of value-based argument. Section 3 surveys past and current work on structured arguments that capture value-based reasoning. Section 4 discusses how value-based argument has been applied in a variety of domains, with a particular focus on work in AI and Law. Section 6 considers some open issues related to value-based argument and points to future work related to the topic.

1 Arguments and Values

Artificial Intelligence has made use of a wide range of concepts from philosophy and psychology about human reasoning processes. For example, one well-known model for constructing autonomous agents is the Belief-Desire-Intention model [39], which is intended to capture essential elements of reasoning [10]. Over the past decade it has been recognised that computational models of argument may provide a useful mechanism for automating reasoning in artificially intelligent systems [14]. As part of rational argument in practical reasoning, Bench-Capon has advocated the central role that social values play. Thus, we should briefly survey some of the motivations and sources from a diverse range of literature in philosophy, psychology, and law that have influenced Bench-Capon's work on value-based argument.

What exactly is a value? Briefly, values are social interests that a person/agent wishes to promote. Values are often referred to in everyday reading material, such as newspapers, political party manifestos, religious material, and so on. Perhaps one of the best examples to cite of values is the French national motto "Liberté, égalité, fraternité" (Liberty, equality, fraternity). People widely recognise and understand such concepts. Tom van der Weide in his PhD thesis [43] discusses the characterisation of values given in [40] and [41] whereby abstract values are deemed to have the following five features: 1) *Values are beliefs*; they are a conception of the desirable and are tied to emotions but are not objective beliefs. It is possible to discuss what a value means and what importance is given to values. 2) *Values are a motivational construct*; they describe desirable goals that people want to achieve. 3) *Values are what is called 'trans-situational'*; they transcend specific actions and situations and are therefore 'abstract goals'. The abstract nature of values distinguishes values from concepts like norms and attitudes, which usually refer to specific actions, objects, or situations. 4) *Values guide selection and evalua-*

tion of behaviour and events; they serve as standards or criteria. 5) *Values are relatively ordered according to importance*; the values people pursue are structured in a value system in which each value is given a relative importance to other values. This hierarchical feature of values also distinguishes them from norms and attitudes.

For the important role of values in argument, we consider Chaim Perelman and Lucie Olbrechts-Tyteca's work [36], which influenced Floriana Grasso's research in AI on dialectical argumentation for the domain of health promotion and in turn motivated some of Bench-Capon's work on value-based argument. In [29] Grasso et al. discuss that, following Perelman and Olbrechts-Tyteca's observations, that "people do not rely on what they know when they argue with an opponent, but rather they try to justify their views by appealing to the values and opinions of the people to whom they are addressing." The two important points to take from this are the *appeal to values* and the notion of an *audience* to whom the views are being addressed. These concepts are key to successful *persuasion*, which is a central aspect addressed by value-based argumentation. Values provide us with an explanation as to why it is not always possible to persuade others to accept an opinion simply by demonstrating facts and proofs. It may well be that a particular individual will accept the facts of a particular decision but she may reject the conclusion to act because it does not support the values she holds.

In addition to Perelman and colleagues' writing on the topic, the philosopher John Searle [42] recognises the instrumental role that values play in practical reasoning. In particular, Searle points out that disagreement between rational agents can occur precisely because different agents subscribe to different values; he argues that practical reasoning does, and should, typically involve the adjudication of conflicting desires, needs, commitments. However, classical models of rationality do not have any mechanism by which we can decide what constitutes the 'best' way to do something and how we can reconcile inconsistent conclusions of valid derivations.

While value-based argumentation has found application in a number of different domains, it is particularly important in the legal domain. The landmark paper [15] drew attention to the need to account for values in AI and Law research. The authors, Donald Berman and Carole Hafner, argue that, following the practice of legal professionals, computational accounts that are intended to model legal case-based reasoning need to take into account the *purposes* behind legal rules. They term such purposes the 'teleological component' that explains why one particular rule is preferable to another. Since the law is constructed to serve social ends, conflicts that arise about the application of rules in legal cases can be resolved by considering the purposes of the rules and their relative applicability to the case in question. This enables preferences amongst purposes to be revealed, and then the argument can be presented appropriately to the audience through an appeal to the social values that the argument promotes or defends. Some examples of such purposes, taken from the well-documented 'wild animals' cases that are discussed in [15], are: protection of right of property owners; protection of free enterprise and competition; and respect of the judiciary for the powers of the legislature.

Having introduced some of the key background literature and concepts related to values, some of which have influenced Bench-Capon's work, in the following sections we discuss particular aspects in greater depth.

2   Value-Based Arguments in Abstract Frameworks

In this section, we look at the representation of, and reasoning with, values in computational argumentation through abstract argumentation frameworks. In the following section, we consider structured instantiations of arguments.

One of the landmark pieces of research in computational argumentation is Dung's abstract argumentation frameworks (AFs) [26]. The underlying idea of AFs is to model and evaluate arguments by considering how well they can be defended against other arguments that can attack and defeat them. The relationships between arguments can be modelled as directed graphs showing which arguments attack one another. No concern is given to the internal structure of the arguments; the status of an argument is evaluated by considering whether or not it is able to be defended from attack from other arguments with respect to a set of arguments. Essentially, an argument can be justified with respect to a set of arguments if it is not attacked by a member of that set, and all its attackers are attacked by a member of that set [26].

A number of extensions and variations to Dung's model have been proposed to handle preferences [2], probabilities [32], and a variety of other notions. Here we focus on Value-based Argumentation Frameworks (VAFs) [9], which are one of the seminal contributions that Bench-Capon has made to the computational argumentation literature. VAFs are essentially an extension to Dung's argumentation frameworks to allow arguments to be evaluated not only in respect of the attack relation existing between arguments, but also in consideration of the values the arguments promote. The inclusion of values in such frameworks enables distinctions to be made between different audiences' preferences, in Perelman's sense as discussed in the previous section. Whereas in AFs an argument is always defeated by an attacker, unless that attacker can itself be defeated, in VAFs, attack is distinguished from *defeat for an audi-*

ence. This allows a particular audience to choose to reject an attack, even if the attacking argument cannot itself be defeated, provided that audience ranks the value associated with the attacked argument as more important than that associated with the attacker. Within a VAF, therefore, which arguments are accepted depends on the ranking that the audience (characterised by a particular preference ordering on the values) gives to the values. Other extensions to Dung's AFs to capture preferences have been set out, such as Amgoud et al.'s Preference-based Argumentation Frameworks [2], but in these frameworks the preference relation is entirely abstract; VAFs give more content to the notion of preferences by relating the strength of arguments to the values promoted by accepting them.

VAFs are clearly applicable for modelling scenarios where deciding how to act is the key concern since it is in practical reasoning that values play their important role. Bench-Capon and his colleagues have shown in a variety of work how VAFs can be used to model scenarios involving practical reasoning, such as legal decisions [5, 54], moral problems [2], and political debates [4].

Since they were first introduced in 2002, VAFs have been used in other work that extends Dung's framework to give richer accounts of argumentation. In [33] Sanjay Modgil proposes Extended Argumentation Frameworks in which attacks between arguments can themselves be attacked. The idea is to provide a natural way to represent and reason about preferences (enabled through the representation of values) between arguments. Modgil and Bench-Capon build on this work in [34], where they formalise reasoning *about* argumentation within the Dung argumentation paradigm itself. As such, they distinguish between an object-level and a meta-level whereby a meta-level Dung argumentation framework is itself instantiated by arguments that make statements about arguments, their interactions, and their evaluation in an object-level argumentation framework. They show how Dung's theory, and object-level extensions of Dung's theory such as VAFs, can then be uniformly characterised by meta-level argumentation in a Dung framework.

There is also work that has investigated complexity issues related to VAFs, see e.g. [27], and many other authors have made use of VAFs in their work on computational argumentation; space precludes us giving the full list, so we leave here our discussion of abstract accounts of value-based argumentation. In the next section we turn our attention to instantiated value-based arguments.

3 Instantiating Value-Based Arguments

Abstract argumentation frameworks represent arguments as atomic entities, so they are not useful when we are concerned with the *internal structure and con-*

tent of the arguments, the relationships between the arguments in virtue of their content, and the application of argumentation. In this section, we discuss the theory of *instantiated argumentation*, where the internal structure and content of arguments is elaborated, while applications and some examples of instantiated argumentation are presented in section 4. The main focus of our discussion is how to use *semantic models* to *instantiate argumentation schemes* in order to *generate* value-based arguments; in particular, we discuss arguments using the *practical reasoning argumentation scheme with values* [5], which is key to the applications discussed in section 4 [53]. The section starts with a general overview about instantiated argumentation, moves to value-based practical reasoning, touches on how auxiliary schemes are represented, then concludes with a recent approach to structuring arguments in terms of the use of ASPIC+ [37]. It represents a synopsis of work by Bench-Capon and his colleagues on instantiated argumentation [5, 4, 38, 48].

3.1   Instantiated Argumentation and Argumentation Schemes

Abstract argumentation treats arguments as atomic elements and attacks as relations between the elements. Instantiated argumentation considers the internal structure and content of the arguments. In the following, we take a neutral stance on terminological issues [37, 48] and particular theory of instantiated argument (see [37, 16, 28] among several others).

In classical propositional logic, an argument is an application of the classical syllogistic reasoning pattern of *Modus Ponens*: supposing propositional variables $\mathcal{P}$ and $\mathcal{Q}$, a rule $\mathcal{P} \to \mathcal{Q}$, where $\to$ is *material implication*, $\mathcal{P}$ is the *antecedent*, $\mathcal{Q}$ is the *conclusion*, and the assertion that $\mathcal{P}$ holds, we infer $\mathcal{Q}$, where is the *claim*. Given a *knowledge base* (KB), e.g. $KB_1 = \{P, P \to Q\}$, we can generate an argument a_1 as an instance of *Modus Ponens* by substituting the variables in the syllogism with propositions from KB_1.

Argumentation frameworks were introduced and have been developed to reason *non-monotonically* and *defeasibly*. This is achieved by allowing arguments to be generated with respect to KBs that allow inconsistency, relating the arguments by attack, then reasoning with them at the abstract level. Broadly speaking, we can reason with inconsistency rather than ruling it out. In the following, we provide several semi-formal examples of KBs with $\to$ and $\Rightarrow$ in order to sketch the main ideas. For example, given $KB_2 = \{P, P \to Q, P \to \neg Q\}$, we generate arguments a_1 and a_2 (along with others given *contraposition* and *closure under entailment*), which contradict with respect to their claims Q and $\neg$Q. In virtue of this, we say that a_1 and a_2 attack one another, and can use this information to reason in an abstract argumentation framework. One argument can attack another by having a claim that contradicts the claim of the other argument (rebutting), or a premise (undermining), or provides a reason to believe that the rule is inapplicable (undercutting). Such an example represents a simple, small illustration of *instantiated arguments* as found in the various approaches to instantiated argumentation.

In addition the KBs can have *strict rules*, indicated with →, as well as *defeasible rules*, ⇒: for strict implication, whenever the antecedents hold, the conclusion always holds, e.g. *Emus are birds*; in contrast, defeasible implications can be defeated by contrary examples, rules, or circumstances, e.g. *Birds typically fly*. Given KBs with strict and defeasible rules, we generate strict and defeasible arguments. In many approaches (e.g. [37, 35]), there is a *preference* relation between defeasible rules to resolve which argument "wins" where they otherwise equally attack one another. Given our focus in this section on instantiated arguments for value-based practical reasoning, we do not consider preferences or strict rules further.

We have, to this point, considered KBs based on propositions. As our objective is value-based argumentation related to practical reasoning, we turn to KBs expressed with predicate logic (without quantifiers). For instance, suppose a domain of disourse {a,b}, one-place predicates {P(x),Q(y)}, where P and Q each denote the set {a,b}, and KB_3 = {P(x), P(x) ⇒ Q(y), P(x) ⇒ ¬Q(y)}. The KB along with the domain of discourse and denotations of predicates constitute a *semantic model*. With respect to the semantic model, we can generate four arguments, for example: a_3, *P(a), P(a) ⇒ Q(b), therefore Q(b)*; and a_4, *P(a), P(a) ⇒ ¬Q(b), therefore ¬Q(b)*. The arguments a_3 and a_4 are contradictory on their claims, so attack one another.

Argumentation schemes (ASs) [45, 46] are instantiated arguments of particular interest as they are the mechanism that has been used widely by Bench-Capon and his colleagues in a variety of work to ground the arguments that appear in practical reasoning debates. An AS is a *stereotypical pattern of reasoning* in which the premises give a presumptive reason, indicated with ⇒, to accept the conclusion. ASs can be used in a dialogical context as justifications for a conclusion and are subject to critiques that address points characteristic of the particular scheme. An interlocutor might offer a critique that elicits a response that either contradicts, reaffirms, or otherwise weakens the rhetorical force of the AS. Consider, for example, the well-known *Argument From Position to Know*, where *E* is a variable over individuals, *P* is a variable over propositions, and the predicates are *is in a position to know* and *asserts*.

- If *E is in a position to know P*; and
- *E asserts P*.
- Therefore *P*.

While this is *not a logically sound* argument, it is nonetheless widely used and often accepted. It can be rebutted, undermined, or undercut. For example, supposing we ground the variables for the first premise as *Prof. Hayes is in a position to know that eggs are rich in cholesterol.*; we can undermine the argument with the claim that *Prof. Hayes is not in a position to know that eggs are rich in cholesterol*, justifying it by pointing out that Prof. Hayes is not a nutritionist.

3.2 Practical Reasoning with Values

With the context set, we can consider a particularly well-developed and applied instantiated argumentation scheme that has featured in a focussed line of work of Bench-Capon and his colleagues for over a decade; this is the *practical reasoning argumentation scheme with values* (PRAS), developed in a series of papers [3, 5, 5, 1, 4]. The scheme is used to systematically and transparently argue about actions; given a range of actions that might be carried out by an agent, which one should be selected and how is the selection justified? As there can be several agents with conflicting action selections and justifications, arguments can arise. *Values* play a key role in practical reasoning since agents can debate what values are promoted by a given action. In this section, we outline the PRAS and how it is instantiated with respect to a semantic model. We also relate the PRAS to auxiliary schemes that can be used to justify particular components of the PRAS. As discussed in section 4, the scheme and associated semantic model are very useful in representing and reasoning about public policy-making. Our presentation here is a summary of [4].

The PRAS proposes an argument for an action that should be done, based on an understanding of the current situation, the consequences of actions, a goal, and the desire to promote particular social values. For our purposes, the relevant part of the scheme is:

> PRAS
>
> In the current circumstances R, we should perform action A, which will result in new circumstances S, realise goal G, and promote value V.

In this scheme, an action that realises a goal is proposed that *promotes* a social value; a similar scheme can be given that recommends *not* to perform action A since this would *demote* a social value. A variety of critiques can be made of this scheme, some transparent (e.g. *The current circumstances are not as stated*) and some implicit (e.g. *There are unintended consequences of the action*).

To use instantiations of the schemes in computational systems, the PRAS has been represented formally in a computational model based on the Action-Based Alternating Transition System with Values (AATS+V); AATSs were introduced in [47] and extended in [1, 4] to AATS+V in order to represent social values. The PRAS is recast in terms of the AATS+V. The AATS+V is then given a model, i.e. denotations of the components of the system, which is in turn used to instantiate the PRAS, generating arguments for or against a proposed action. The arguments that can be generated are, in principle, all and only those that represent instantiations of the PRAS relative to a given semantic model, though in a given exercise, one might only use a selection of the arguments. In section 4, we use the PRAS and a semantic model to generate arguments.

In this section, we have reviewed some of the key elements of work by Bench-Capon and his colleagues on instantiated value-based and related argumentation schemes, semantic models, and how the schemes are used together with the models to generate instances of the schemes. In the next section, we outline how such instances of schemes are applied.

4 Application Areas for Value-Based Argumentation

In 3, we introduced key elements of instantiated value-based argumentation. In this section, we focus on how such argumentation has been applied to legal case-based reasoning and policy-making, focussing primarily on recent developments.

4.1 Legal Case-based Reasoning and Values

In Artificial Intelligence and Law, reasoning with cases has been one of the main lines of investigation, where the issue is to decide a current undecided case with respect to prior cases, e.g. precedents. In a series of papers culminating in [11] and followed by implementations and experiments [22], legal case-based reasoning (LCBR) is presented as *theory construction*. As disputation is an essential aspect of LCBR, subsequent approaches turned to implemented argumentation, particularly *LCBR using argumentation schemes with values* [5, 50, 51, 52, 38, 10]. In this section, we give an overview of each of these approaches.

LCBR and Theory Construction Reasoning with cases is seen as the process of *constructing and using a theory of the rules* that are derived from the cases and that bear on a legal decision. Where conflicts amongst the rules arise, the purposes of the law are invoked, which are the *social values* that the rule promotes or defends; such values may be ordered with respect to preferences. Precedent cases represent, in effect, prior application of a rule, implying (or explicitly giving) the social value that is promoted or defended. The precedent cases themselves present *abstract fact patterns*, factors, that are compared and contrasted and that contribute to the decision for one party or the other: given a constellation of factors and a legal rule that bears on the factors, a legal decision for a party is given. The significance of the factors can be *emphasised* or *downplayed* in relation to other factors in the case. As the rules are themselves subject to dispute, they are *defeasible*. Following the legal principle of *stare decisis*, a current undecided case with the same factors as a precedent case is decided in the same way. However, should the current case vary in certain ways, then other, relevant precedents are invoked and used to argue about the relative importance of the different factors, legal rule, and case decision. As the factors and decision reflect social values, the argument thus is an argument about those values.

To construct a theory, a knowledge background is given of: cases, factors, outcomes, values, factor descriptions, and case factor-based descriptions. Cases are described in terms of the factors that are present in the case, where the factors are associated with the party that they strengthen in the decision. The analysis of cases in terms of factors is taken as a given. The outcomes are those for the plaintiff Π or for the defendant Δ, and values are linked to factors. Factor descriptions are constructed from factors, outcomes and values. Case factor-based descriptions are the set of cases that are described by the factors that hold of a case and the outcomes; a case base that is used to reason about the cases can be given by such descriptions. Legal rules associate a set of factors with a decision for a party, where the factors themselves are associated with a decision and the social value that is promoted. Legal rules can attack one another should the outcomes be complementary, and there can be asymmetrical preferences of one rule over another such that one rule is said to defeat the other. A theory is an explicit selection of material from the background, containing: descriptions of all the cases considered relevant by the proponent of the theory; descriptions of all factors chosen to represent those cases; all rules available to be used in explaining the cases; and all preferences between rules and values available to be used in resolving conflicts between rules. A variety of means are described to construct theories from an initial (perhaps empty) theory by including cases, factors, rules, and preferences.

The objective is to construct a theory for a current case, using the resources provided by the case background, to explain the desired outcome of the case. Informally, a case is explained if: (a) given some of the factors of the case, f_1, and a rule, r_1, with f_1 as antecedent gives the outcome of the case, o_1; and (b) there is set of factors of the case, f_2, and a rule, r_2, with the outcome of the case, o_2, such that r_2 defeats r_1.

One example of a theory is from the analysis of *wild animal* cases, e.g. *Pierson v Post*, *Keeble v Hickeringill*, and *Young v Hitchens*, which are used in [15]. In the following, we use prefix π for plaintiff and δ for defendant; Π and Δ are for respective outcomes. In *Pierson v Post*, π was fox hunting on open land when δ killed and carried off the fox; π was held to have no right to the fox because he had not possessed it; δ won. In *Keeble v Hickeringill*, π owned a pond and made a living by attracting ducks to the pond with decoys, shooting them, and selling them for food. δ scared the ducks away from the pond. In this case π won. In *Young v Hitchens*, both parties were fisherman. Just as π was closing his nets on the fish, δ sped into the gap, spread his net, and caught the fish. In this case δ won. We represent some aspects of these cases with the following factors and values:

Factors:

πLiv = π was pursuing his livelihood, favouring π;

πLand = π was on his own land, favouring π;

δNposs = δ was not in possession of the animal, favouring δ;

δLiv = δ was pursuing his livelihood, favouring δ.

Values:

Llit = Less Litigation;

Prop = Enjoyment of property rights;

Mprod = More productivity

From this information, we can construct a theory **T2** (where T1 is a precursor), which is a structure that has the following constituents:

cases: $\{<$Young, $\{\pi$Liv, πNposs, δLiv$\}$, $\Pi >$, $<$Pierson, $\{\pi$Nposs$\}$, $\Delta >$, $<$Keeble, $\{\pi$Liv, πNposs, πLand$\}$, $\Pi >\}$

factor descriptions: $\{< \pi$Nposs, Δ, Llit$>$, $< \pi$Liv, Π, Mprod$>\}$

rules: $\{<\{\pi$Nposs$\}$, $\Delta >$,$<\{\pi$Liv$\}$, $\Pi >\}$

rule preferences: $\{$rpref($<\{\pi$Liv$\}$, $\pi >$,$<\{\pi$Nposs$\}$, $\Delta >)\}$

value preferences: $\{$vpref(Mprod,Llit)$\}$

We suppose that *Young* is an as yet undecided case, but want to construct a theory that can successfully explain that it should be decided for the plaintiff Π. Amongst the cases, we have *Pierson*, which was decided in favour of the defendant, and *Keeble*, which was decided in favour of the plaintiff. The cases have different arrangements of overlapping factors. How can we decide *Young*? In *factor descriptions*, we see the relationship between factors, outcomes, and values; in *rules*, we are given the inference from factors to outcomes. If we just followed the rules, we might expect there to be a conflict in *Keeble*, deciding both for Δ and for Π, since each of the rules applies to the factors, but this is not so, as *Keeble* is decided for Π. This follows from the rule preferences, where π *was pursuing his livelihood, favouring* π trumps δ *was not in possession of the animal, favouring* δ. Applying this same reasoning to *Young*, the decision is for Π. Thus, precedents are used to reason for a decision in an undecided case. Other theories can be constructed to argue for different outcomes, until the background of cases is fully exploited.

In [11], there are several ways to evaluate alternative theories as well as various argument moves. The approach was subsequently developed, implemented, and experimented with in [22].

LCBR with Argumentation Schemes and Values Recent work in AI and Law by Bench-Capon and his colleagues has examined how argumentation schemes with values can be represented precisely and formally in ASPIC+ [37] as part of a well-developed framework for LCBR [50, 52, 38]. A formalisation in ASPIC+ means that the analysis is precise and unambiguous and that formal properties can be demonstrated.

For [38], ASPIC+ contains a first-order logical language with equality, classical negation, and strict and defeasible rules. The knowledge base contains axioms and ordinary premises. Arguments are built from the knowledge base; attacks are determined as outlined previously. LCBR is represented in terms of the logical language, a knowledge base, and argumentation schemes for reasoning about the decisions of the cases. Cases are represented in terms of sets of factors; various partitions of factors are used to support or undermine a plaintiff's argument that a current case should be decided in favour of the plaintiff. In addition, a *factor hierarchy* [1] enables reasoning about relationships *between* factors such that one factor may, for example, be substituted for another. Preferences between sets of factors are also expressed. Instantiated argumentation schemes are used, with respect to sets of factors, the factor hierarchy, preferences, to reason about combinations of and counter-balancing between factors in the cases. While this is a well-developed analysis of LCBR in terms of argumentation frameworks, values are not represented or reasoned with.

LCBR with values and instantiated argumentations schemes appears in [30, 51, 10]. The case *Popov v. Hayashi*, which concerns disputed possession of a baseball, is modelled using the PRAS discussed in section 3.2 (though not with respect to a semantic model) [51]. For example, parts of the judge's reasoning in the case can be represented informally using PRAS: If the interruption of Popov completing the catch of the baseball was illegal (due to an assault on him), the case should be decided for Popov, which would prevent assault being rewarded and promote the value of public order. Other patterns of reasoning in the case can be modelled, giving rise to an argumentation framework of arguments in attack relations. However, such reasoning patterns are informal.

To systematically argue about values in LCBR, several argumentation schemes are formalised in ASPIC+ [10] such as: one to establish a value preference from a precedent case, one to apply a value preference to a new case, and one to establish that a value is promoted by deciding a case for a particular party when a given factor is present. These schemes are linked, such that premises of the main scheme *VAS1* are justified by subsidiary schemes. We present the first two schemes informally to illustrate the approach:

VAS1: Decision Based on Value Scheme

Promotion Premise 1: Decision for party 1 in current case promotes value1

Promotion Premise 2: Decision for party 2 in current case promotes value2

Preference Premise: Value1 is preferred to value 2

Conclusion: Decide current case for party 1

Another scheme is used to establish the promotion premises of *VAS1* (either 1 or 2 depending on how it is instantiated):

VAS2: Promotion Scheme

Factor Premise: Factor is present in case

Value Premise: Decision for party when factor is present promotes value

Conclusion: Decision for party in case promotes value

Additional schemes establish the preference order, critique the applicability of the preference order, and introduce ways of comparing sets of values. The analysis is used to illustrate various examples of reasoning about cases.

4.2 Policy-making Using Instantiated Argumentation Schemes with Values

Bench-Capon and his colleagues have fruitfully applied their work on practical reasoning with values to a domain that has risen to prominence over the past decade or so, namely e-Democracy and e-Participation [3, 21, 20, 4, 53, 6]. In this section, we discuss some of the key points and outline recent tools for *Structured Consultation* and *Critique* that show how some of the formal theories developed in value-based argumentation can be applied.

The theory and tools address the question *What should be the process of formation of political will?* A current view is that the political will, where the government serves as the agent of the citizenry, is achieved by *deliberative democracy*, where citizens are not only *recipients* of government policies made by well-informed officials who work in the interests of society, but are also *producers* of political information and policies by participating in political processes and debate. A citizen identifies and publicizes issues of personal or social concern as well as argues with other citizens for and against various policy options; thus, in *deliberative democracy*, citizens pool their judgements about what should be done, passing these judgements to government officials for further action.

However, deliberative democracy requires communication between the government and the people. To meet the communication needs, governments leverage technologies, e.g. the Internet, to give the public greater access to government information, to offer virtual venues for public discussion and feedback, and to respond to public enquires. A variety of systems are available such as e-voting, web-based questionnaires, discussion boards, crowd-sourced legislative proposals, and e-petitions [21]. While useful, the information from these systems is often not sufficiently structured to facilitate fine-grained analysis of just what participants agree to or desire as alternatives. For example, in an e-petition, a citizen may be asked to agree or disagree with a particular policy-making proposal, e.g. *smoking should be banned from all public buildings*, whereas the signatory has a range of concerns about just what the facts are, how the ban will be implemented, what counts as a public building, and so on. In order for a government's policy to be effective, the specific concerns of the effected parties must be understood and addressed. More generally, given the volume and complexity of the information received from the public, issues arise about how to analyse, evaluate and respond to the volume of data gathered. In addition, tools for facilitating such interactions have to be easy to use.

Tools for Deliberation To facilitate fine-grained, well-structured consultations about policy-making proposals, easy to use prototype web-based tools have been developed. The first tool developed by Bench-Capon and his colleagues was *Parmenides*, which implemented argumentation schemes such as the PRAS and aspects of Argumentation Frameworks [20]. Parmenides was re-engineered into the *Structured Consultation Tool* (SCT) and *Critique Tool* (CT), making use of a wider variety of argumentation schemes along with semantic models and giving the tools greater underlying structure, precision and flexibility [4, 53, 6, 49].

The SCT and CT address complementary issues. The government may provide a policy proposal and wish to understand what specific components citizens agree with or object to; for this, the SCT provides the means to serve a survey type list of well-structured questions. Alternatively, a citizen may wish to make her own proposal, then understand how it compares to the government's own policy proposal; for this, the CT facilitates input of a citizen's proposal, which is then systematically critiqued. At the end of a session using the CT, a citizen has aired her proposals, understood their implications, and received a critique in relation to the government's position.

The SCT and CT use and present argumentation schemes such as Practical Reasoning, Credible Source, and Value Recognition that have been formalised and grounded in semantic models [1, 4], providing a systematic way to structure, investigate, and critique the policy proposal. Given the argumentation schemes, the various associated critiques either guide the structure of presentation (for the SCT) or provide feedback to the user (for the CT). Among the critiques from [1], we have:

1. Is the action possible?
2. Does the action promote the value?
3. Are there negative side effects?
4. Do the other agents do what they are supposed to do?

The PRAS is taken as the main scheme, while subsidiary schemes relate to particular challenges; the *Credible Source* scheme (CS) examines the justification for circumstances or consequences of the action, while the *Value Credible Source* (VCS) and *Value Recognition* (VR) schemes justify the values in different ways. The tools are web-based applications written in PhP; they access the same MySQL database, though with different queries.

Structured Consultation Tool The SCT is designed for a consultation where the policy-maker presents a policy to citizens as a survey and solicits their opinion on the particulars of the policy. The consultation has a *main* line and *digressions*. The main line is structured by the components of the Practical Reasoning scheme, which are presented with default responses (e.g. *agree* or *demote*) that represent the position of the policy-making body. Should the user select something other than the default, a digression opens, wherein the user can investigate further the justification for the defaults, then return to the main line. Digressions are structured around the constituents of the relevant subsidiary argumentation schemes justifying the statement disagreed with. Each

proposition in the circumstances and consequences has a digression with respect to the CS; each of the values has a digression with respect to either the
VCS or the VR. For each of the digressions, the user indicates what she accepts
or rejects the default (thereby justifying why she did not accept the main line
statement). In this way, the user gives a fine-grained, structured opinion about
the circumstances, consequences, and values along with her justifications for
these opinions.

Critique Tool For the CT, the citizen *interactively creates* her own policy
proposal by selecting from a menu of choices, which is then critiqued from the
standpoint of the government's policy proposal.

The program generates the logical space of justifications of actions from the
database representation of the semantic model. Menus are formed to solicit
the user's beliefs as to the current state, a proposed action, the state the user
believes will be reached as a consequence of the action, and the value the
action will promote. For each part of the user's proposal, the program applies
some of the critiques in [1], and where appropriate, offers the corresponding
criticism or *caveat* to the user. The user then freely chooses from a menu
of alternatives, which are checked against the policy-maker's proposal. The
policy-maker's proposal is only incrementally revealed to the user over the
course of the interview. In this way, the user gets the opportunity to represent
what she believes to be the case, what can be done, what the consequences are,
and whether values are promoted (demoted, unaffected), receiving in the end a
thorough analysis of implications of her proposal.

4.3   Application in General AI and Multi-Agent Systems

We now turn to the field of multi-agent systems, which is a natural application
area for formal frameworks for representing and reasoning about value-based
arguments. The AATS+V model mentioned above has been applied in a variety of different work. In [13] Bench-Capon and colleagues showed how it can
be used to model scenarios from experimental economic studies, the Dictator
Game and the Ultimatum Game, in which it must be decided how a sum of
money will be divided between the players in the games. Studies have been
conducted into how humans act in such games, and the results are not explained by a decision-model that assumes that the participants are purely self-
interested utility-maximisers. The AATS+V representation has been shown to
effectively model behaviour in the scenarios, precisely because of the use of
value-based argument in the representation and reasoning.

Black and Atkinson have used value-based argumentation to investigate dialogical interactions in agent systems where agreement needs to be reached on
how to act [17]. In [18] they present a dialogue system that lets agents agree to

an action that each finds acceptable, but does not necessarily demand that they resolve differing preferences that might occur. As part of their system they develop a mechanism with which an agent can develop a model of another's preferences, which is a concern in persuasion scenarios. Further in the agents literature, Tom van der Weide's work [44] provides automated support for decision making in complex scenarios, using argumentation, decision theory, and values as part of a formal dialogue framework. Dechesne at al. investigate the relationship between norms, values and culture to study norm acceptance and norm compliance [24]. They report on agent-based simulations that account for all these concepts in order to explain the differences in uptake of policies in different cultures. They apply their model to the introduction of the anti-smoking legislation. It has also been shown how value-based argumentation can be used to address the issue of ontology alignment between autonomous agents [31]. Since agents differ in the choice of vocabulary used to represent concepts, as represented in their domain ontologies, they need to be support with mechanisms to enable them to align their ontologies. This is achieved through a process of argumentation using VAFs in which candidate correspondences are accepted or rejected, based on the ontological knowledge and the agents' preferences. Similar issues have been investigated in [25]. Finally, we note that research has been conducted into showing how VAFs can be translated into neural networks [23]. An algorithm to perform this translation is presented with the aim of facilitating learning capabilities in VAFs, since arguments may evolve over time with respect to their strength, and also to enable the parallel computation of argumentation frameworks by making use of the machinery of neural networks.

Our survey of the use of value-based argumentation in the variety of domains discussed above is not exhaustive, but gives a flavour of the rich and diverse types of problem that Bench-Capon's work has been used to address.

5 Concluding Discussion

Over the course of this paper, we have discussed what values are, how they appear in abstract and instantiated argumentation, and how they have been applied to support reasoning in legal and political domains. Bench-Capon's work took up, initiated, and developed ideas about values and argumentation, influencing many others to develop related or distinct lines of research. There is clearly scope for continued research. In the legal and political domains, one might reason about values using quantitative, statistical approaches, e.g. data mining or neural net systems, rather than the sorts of symbolic, heuristic approaches that have been discussed above. There are advantages and disadvantages of each: quantitative approaches gain applications over large, extensible volumes of data, but lose transparency and explanatory force; the symbolic approaches are crafted for small, constrained domains, gaining transparency and explanatory force. Perhaps some integration would be of use. Another general consideration is the relationship between the factors and the values in legal cases as factors vary widely in form and meaning while the values may be implicit in a decision. In current work on values in legal reasoning, values may be ranked in preference orderings, but there may be richer ways of reasoning about values such as giving them weights and reasoning by accrual. Finally, for many applications, it will be important to find the means to scale up information extraction from legal case decisions or policy consultations to identify arguments, factors, and values.

6   Some Personal Remarks

Katie Atkinson I have known Trevor since 2001 when I was a second year student on my undergraduate degree in Computer Information Systems in the Department of Computer Science at the University of Liverpool. Trevor was then lecturing on that year's group project module and he went on to co-supervise my final year individual project. It was at this early juncture in my interactions with Trevor that I first encountered his skills of persuasion. Having committed to implementing my project software in a Java-based language, at Trevor's suggestion, I learnt Prolog and ended up producing a second implementation that changed the expected conclusions of my project (which, of course, were all the better for this change). In my final year Trevor suggested to me that I consider continuing my studies on a PhD programme. This career route had not even registered on my list of options until Trevor proposed it, but having someone place faith in my abilities was a significant factor in my decision to follow this path. I approached Peter McBurney to ask him if he would be willing to supervise my PhD on a topic that was of mutual interest to us, agent-based negotiation. Peter accepted and Trevor expressed a willingness to be involved as co-supervisor (- Peter elucidates on this arrangement in his own personal note in his joint contribution to this volume). I have very fond memories of the meetings that the three of us had; the learning curve about my research topic seemed steep at the time but I benefitted from having Peter's and Trevor's combined knowledge imparted to me, and I got to witness argument in action, though this was always for the higher purpose of getting the ideas right. Through our joint research Trevor has (perhaps not always intentionally) helped me to sharpen my skills in argumentation, and not just when applied to discussion about our work on argumentation. Outside of our shared research interests, Trevor has taught me much about philosophy, AI, law, religion and academia, and also, importantly, how to have a good time at a conference. I never expected that conference trips with Trevor would result in such memorable events as meeting a legendary blues singer, beating Trevor at poker in an airport lounge (though this was one minor victory since he is currently ahead in the overall stakes), discovering the 'best bar in the world' and witnessing Trevor show appreciation on a dance floor for Fatboy Slim's music.

Trevor once told me that he thought I would make a good Computer Science PhD student because of my 'flaky background' (by which he meant, in some kind of complementary way, that my pre-university studies were not in science subjects). I am glad I followed his advice since it contributed to me following a career path into academia, which I never expected, but find thoroughly enjoyable and stimulating. When I was appointed Lecturer at Liverpool after completing my PhD in 2005, I was most pleased to have the opportunity to continue my research on argumentation with Trevor and Peter, both of whom welcomed me wholeheartedly now as a colleague, as well as have the opportunity to establish new collaborations (such as that with my co-author of this contribution). I am very grateful for the support Trevor has given me in developing my own career in academia, as well as the friendship that has come hand-in-hand with this. I look forward to us tackling new (and old remaining) lines of research in argumentation, and with the aspiration of trying to promote one of Trevor's highly-ranked values, I will try my best to get a paper on our work accepted at a US conference during the World Series.

Adam Wyner I first met Trevor in April 2006 when I interviewed for a job as Research Associate on the ESTRELLA Project at the University of Liverpool. Trevor was PI on the project and Katie Atkinson was the CI. Over the following two years and several months, I worked on the project under Trevor's direction. Work on the ESTRELLA Project lasted until September 2008. In September 2010, I had the opportunity to rejoin working with Trevor on the IMPACT Project with Katie as PI and Trevor as CI till December 2012. Thus, over the last seven years (except for some 16 months between jobs), Trevor and I have been in regular contact, whether meeting in person or by email. Though I currently work in Aberdeen, Scotland, we continue to correspond about ongoing projects and research.

While I had a background in Linguistics (formal syntax and semantics of natural language) and in Computer Science (deontic concepts and contracts), many of the topics that Trevor and I worked on over these years were new to me such as using XML-based standards of the Semantic Web to define a legal knowledge exchange framework, legal case-based reasoning, ontologies, policy making, and argumentation. Initially, there was quite a lot to take on board. Trevor was a very patient, engaged, and thoughtful supervisor, bringing me into and upwards in the work. He takes his pastoral role with his students and junior colleagues very seriously. Throughout my time working with Trevor, he encouraged me in my career by suggesting activities (e.g. workshops, journal editing), pointing out what to avoid, targeting conference venues, setting research agendas, and structuring our publication schedule. Indeed, his prolific, high standard publication effort provided a very motivating (and charmingly competitive) context for my own efforts, leading me to be very productive during my time at Liverpool. For me, Trevor has been an exceptional supervisor, project leader, and colleague. As a consequence of what I have learned from Trevor along with our collaborative publications and joint efforts, I have landed a permanent academic position and completed a career transition. For that, I am hugely and gratefully in Trevor's debt.

Perhaps because he started out academically as a philosopher, Trevor takes inquiry and debate very seriously. He is full of ideas, eager to explore and interrogate them. In discussions, he asserts and raises counterpoints. As I came with my own *back story*, we initially had different ways of looking at matters, leading to passionate and vigorous discussions that usually developed into a common view. Such intense discussions extended to our disciplined hobby on spelling, grammar, and word choice with the highly advantageous result that we often got reviews back complimenting us on our style and clarity. Such a style of close, intense intellectual discussions Trevor recalled and highly valued from his Oxford days. As I understood more about the substance of the various work we did, I gained confidence to return some of his fire. Discussions became louder (as Katie would attest), more complex, and also imbued with humour and warmth. Trevor enjoys engaging in an argument, especially if he wins, but he's a good sport if he does not. Based on my experience with Trevor as supervisor, colleague, and discussant, I am proud to call him my *don*.

There were some dark days when Trevor was gravely ill, and we all were worried. Yet, he was graced not only with pulling through, but also regaining his capacity to work and talk. For me, it has been a great privilege and honour to work for and with Trevor, and I am very pleased that I can be amongst others in appreciation of his long, productive, and continuing life's work.

Bibliography

[1] V. Aleven. *Teaching case-based argumentation through a model and examples.* PhD thesis, University of Pittsburgh, 1997.

[2] L. Amgoud and C. Cayrol. On the acceptability of arguments in preference-based argumentation. In G. F. Cooper and S. Moral, editors, *Proceedings of the Fourteenth Confer-*

ence on Uncertainty in Artificial Intelligence (UAI 1998), pages 1–7. Morgan-Kaufmann, 1998.

[3] K. Atkinson. *What Should We Do?: Computational Representation of Persuasive Argument in Practical Reasoning*. PhD thesis, Department of Computer Science, University of Liverpool, Liverpool, UK, 2005.

[4] K. Atkinson, T. Bench-Capon, D. Cartwright, and A. Wyner. Semantic models for policy deliberation. In *Proceedings of the Thirteenth International Conference on Artificial Intelligence and Law (ICAIL 2011)*, pages 81–90, Pittsburgh, PA, USA, 2011. ACM Press.

[5] K. Atkinson, T. Bench-Capon, and P. McBurney. Arguing about cases as practical reasoning. In *Proceedings of the Tenth International Conference on Artificial Intelligence and Law (ICAIL 2005)*, pages 35–44, New York, NY, USA, 2005. ACM Press.

[6] K. Atkinson, T. Bench-Capon, and A. Wyner. Opinion gathering using a multi-agent systems approach to policy selection. In V. Conitzer, M. Winikoff, W. van der Hoek, and L. Padgham, editors, *AAMAS 2012*, pages 1171–1172. IFAAMAS, 2012.

[7] K. Atkinson and T. Bench-Capon. Practical reasoning as presumptive argumentation using action based alternating transition systems. *Artificial Intelligence*, 171(10–15):855–874, 2007.

[8] K. Atkinson and T. Bench-Capon. Addressing moral problems through practical reasoning. *Journal of Applied Logic*, 6(2):135–151, 2008.

[9] K. Atkinson, T. Bench-Capon, and P. McBurney. Computational representation of practical argument. *Synthese*, 152(2):157–206, 2006.

[10] T. Bench-Capon, H. Prakken, A. Wyner, and K. Atkinson. Argument schemes for reasoning with legal cases using values. In *Proceedings of 26th International Conference on Legal Knowledge and Information Systems (JURIX 2013)*, pages xx–xx, Amsterdam, 2013. IOS Press. To appear.

[11] T. Bench-Capon and G. Sartor. A model of legal reasoning with cases incorporating theories and values. *Artificial Intelligence*, 150 1-2:97–143, 2003.

[12] T. J. M. Bench-Capon. Persuasion in practical argument using value-based argumentation frameworks. *Journal of Logic and Computation*, 13(3):429–448, 2003.

[13] T. J. M. Bench-Capon, K. Atkinson, and P. McBurney. Using argumentation to model agent decision making in economic experiments. *Autonomous Agents and Multi-Agent Systems*, 25(1):183–208, 2012.

[14] T. J. M. Bench-Capon and P. E. Dunne. Argumentation in artificial intelligence. *Artificial Intelligence*, 171(10-15):619–641, 2007.

[15] D. H. Berman and C. D. Hafner. Representing teleological structure in case-based legal reasoning: the missing link. In *Proceedings of the Fourth International Conference on AI and Law (ICAIL 1993)*, pages 50–59, New York, NY, USA, 1993. ACM Press.

[16] P. Besnard and A. Hunter. Argumentation based on classical logic. In Iyad Rahwan and Guillermo Simari, editors, *Argumentation in Artificial Intelligence*, pages 133–152. Springer, 2009.

[17] E. Black and K. Atkinson. Dialogues that account for different perspectives in collaborative argumentation. In C. Sierra, C. Castelfranchi, K. S. Decker, and J. Simão Sichman, editors, *AAMAS (2)*, pages 867–874. IFAAMAS, 2009.

[18] E. Black and K. Atkinson. Choosing persuasive arguments for action. In L. Sonenberg, P. Stone, K. Tumer, and P. Yolum, editors, *AAMAS*, pages 905–912. IFAAMAS, 2011.

[19] M. E. Bratman. *Intention, Plans, and Practical Reason*. Harvard University Press, Cambridge, MA, 1987.

[20] D. Cartwright. *Digital Decision-Making: Using Computational Argumentation to Support Democratic Processes*. PhD thesis, University of Liverpool, 2011.

[21] D. Cartwright and K. Atkinson. Using computational argumentation to support e-participation. *IEEE Intelligent Systems*, 24(5):42–52, 2009.

[22] A. Chorley. *Reasoning with Legal Cases seen as Theory Construction*. PhD thesis, University of Liverpool, Department of Computer Science, Liverpool, UK, 2007.

[23] A. S. d'Avila Garcez, D. M. Gabbay, and L. C. Lamb. Value-based argumentation frameworks as neural-symbolic learning systems. *Journal of Logic and Computation*, 15(6):1041–1058, 2005.

[24] F. Dechesne, G. di Tosto, V. Dignum, and F. Dignum. No smoking here: values, norms and culture in multi-agent systems. *Artificial Intelligence and Law*, 21(1):79–107, 2013.

[25] C. Trojahn dos Santos, P. Quaresma, and R. Vieira. An argumentation framework based on confidence degrees to combine ontology mapping approaches. *IJMSO*, 3(2):142–150, 2008.

[26] P. M. Dung. On the acceptability of arguments and its fundamental role in nonmonotonic reasoning, logic programming and n-person games. *Artificial Intelligence*, 77:321–357, 1995.

[27] P. E. Dunne and T. J. M. Bench-Capon. Complexity in value-based argument systems. In J. J. Alferes and J. A. Leite, editors, *JELIA*, volume 3229 of *LNCS*, pages 360–371. Springer, 2004.

[28] T. Gordon, H. Prakken, and D. Walton. The Carneades model of argument and burden of proof. *Artificial Intelligence*, 171:875–896, 2007.

[29] F. Grasso, A. Cawsey, and R. B. Jones. Dialectical argumentation to solve conflicts in advice giving: a case study in the promotion of healthy nutrition. *Int. J. Hum.-Comput. Stud.*, 53(6):1077–1115, 2000.

[30] K. Greenwood, T. Bench-Capon, and P. McBurney. Towards an account of persuasion in law. In *Proceedings of the Ninth International Conference on AI and Law (ICAIL 2003)*, pages 22–31, New York, NY, USA, 2003. ACM Press.

[31] L. Laera, I. Blacoe, V. A. M. Tamma, T. R. Payne, J. Euzenat, and T. J. M. Bench-Capon. Argumentation over ontology correspondences in mas. In E. H. Durfee, M. Yokoo, M. N. Huhns, and O. Shehory, editors, *AAMAS*, page 228. IFAAMAS, 2007.

[32] H. Li, N. Oren, and T. J. Norman. Probabilistic argumentation frameworks. In S. Modgil, N. Oren, and F. Toni, editors, *TAFA*, volume 7132 of *LNCS*, pages 1–16. Springer, 2011.

[33] S. Modgil. Reasoning about preferences in argumentation frameworks. *Artificial Intelligence*, 173(9-10):901–934, 2009.

[34] S. Modgil and T. Bench-Capon. Metalevel argumentation. *Journal of Logic and Computation*, 21(6):959–1003, 2011.

[35] D. Nute. Defeasible logic. In Dov Gabbay, Christopher J. Hogger, and J. A. Robinson, editors, *Handbook of Logic in Artificial Intelligence and Logic Programming, Volume 3: Nonmonotonic Reasoning and Uncertain Reasoning*, pages 353–395, Oxford, 1994. Oxford University Press.

[36] C. Perelman and L. Olbrechts-Tyteca. *The New Rhetoric: A Treatise on Argumentation*. University of Notre Dame Press, Notre Dame, IN, USA, 1969.

[37] H. Prakken. An abstract framework for argumentation with structured arguments. *Argument and Computation*, 1(2):93–124, 2010.

[38] H. Prakken, A. Wyner, T. Bench-Capon, and K. Atkinson. A formalisation of argumentation schemes for case-based reasoning in ASPIC+. *Journal of Logic and Computation*, 0(0):0–0, 2013. To appear.

[39] A. S. Rao and M. P. Georgeff. BDI agents: From theory to practice. In Victor R. Lesser and Les Gasser, editors, *ICMAS*, pages 312–319. The MIT Press, 1995.

[40] M. Rohan. A rose by any name? the values construct. *Personality and Social Psychology Review*, 4(3):255–277, 2000.

[41] S. Schwartz and W. Bilsky. Toward a universal psychological structure of human values. *Journal of Personality and Social Psychology*, 53(3):550–562, 1987.

[42] J. R. Searle. *Rationality in Action*. MIT Press, Cambridge, MA, USA, 2001.

[43] T. L. van der Weide. *Arguing to Motivate Decisions*. PhD thesis, Universiteit Utrecht, The Netherlands, 2011.

[44] T. L. van der Weide and F. Dignum. Reasoning about and discussing preferences between arguments. In P. McBurney, S. Parsons, and I. Rahwan, editors, *ArgMAS*, pages 117–135. Springer, 2011.

[45] D. Walton. *Argumentation Schemes for Presumptive Reasoning*. Erlbaum, Mahwah, N.J., 1996.

[46] D. Walton, C. Reed, and F. Macagno. *Argumentation Schemes*. Cambridge University Press, 2008.

[47] M. Wooldridge and W. van der Hoek. On obligations and normative ability: Towards a logical analysis of the social contract. *Journal of Applied Logic*, 3(3-4):396–420, 2005.

[48] A. Wyner, K. Atkinson, and T. Bench-Capon. A functional perspective on argumentation schemes. In P. McBurney, S. Parsons, and I. Rahwan, editors, *ArgMAS*, pages 203–222. Springer, 2012.

[49] A. Wyner, K. Atkinson, and T. Bench-Capon. Model based critique of policy proposals. In *Proceedings of the 4th International Conference on eParticipation (ePart 2012)*, pages 120–131, 2012.

[50] A. Wyner and T. Bench-Capon. Argument schemes for legal case-based reasoning. In A. R. Lodder and L. Mommers, editors, *Legal Knowledge and Information Systems. JURIX 2007*, pages 139–149, Amsterdam, 2007. IOS Press.

[51] A. Wyner, T. Bench-Capon, and K. Atkinson. Arguments, values and baseballs: Representation of Popov v. Hayashi. In A. R. Lodder and L. Mommers, editors, *Legal Knowledge and Information Systems. JURIX 2007*, pages 151–160, Amsterdam, 2007. IOS Press.

[52] A. Wyner, T. Bench-Capon, and K. Atkinson. Towards formalising argumentation about legal cases. In *Proceedings of the Thirteenth International Conference on Artificial Intelligence and Law (ICAIL 2011)*, pages 1–10, Pittsburgh, PA, USA, 2011.

[53] A. Wyner, K. Atkinson, and T. Bench-Capon. Towards a structured online consultation tool. In E. Tambouris, A. Macintosh, and H. de Bruijn, editors, *ePart*, volume 6847 of *LNCS*, pages 286–297. Springer, 2011.

[54] A. Z. Wyner, T. J. M. Bench-Capon, and K. Atkinson. Arguments, values and baseballs: Representation of popov v. hayashi. In A. R. Lodder and L. Mommers, editors, *JURIX*, volume 165 of *Frontiers in Artificial Intelligence and Applications*, pages 151–160. IOS Press, 2007.

Values as the Point of a Story

FLORIS BEX *

Abstract

Stories can be powerful vehicles of persuasion, because they convince not by imparting facts and rules, but rather by encouraging the right choices through a change in values. In this article I intend to lay the conceptual foundations for a mature theory of stories for value-based argumentation. The article discusses how stories can be used in argumentation, and how values can be seen as the point, or the conclusion, of stories.

Introduction

Stories can be powerful argumentative vehicles: we often persuade not by imparting facts and rules, but rather by providing an interesting and convincing narrative. This is particularly important when we are trying to convince others to adopt particular values by which their actions are guided. For instance, it is much more convincing to tell a child the story of *The Boy Who Cried Wolf* instead of simply saying that they should not lie because then even if they tell the truth, no one will believe them. Here, the story is meant to encourage right choices through a change in values rather than through a rule to be followed and thus a value is adopted by the person rather than imposed.

The combination of stories and values in argumentation has been central to the research Trevor and I have performed together since my visit to Liverpool in 2008. With Katie Atkinson [11] we discuss abductive argumentation schemes for arguing about past actions, where values serve as motives for these actions. More recently with Bart Verheij [12] we have looked at how case-based reasoning (CBR) techniques from AI and Law [1] can be applied to arguing with factual stories; thus we implicitly show how factual stories would fit in Bench-Capon and Sartor's [7] CBR model of reasoning with values. However, for various reasons joint work on a full theory of persuasive stories for value-based argumentation has never progressed beyond an exchange

---

*University of Groningen, Artificial Intelligence Department

of notes and a short paper [9]. In this article I intend to lay the conceptual
foundations for such a theory.[1]

In [9], we pose three important questions regarding the role of stories in
(value-based) persuasion: (i) What is the relation between arguments and stories? (ii) What are the elements of a typical story? and (iii) When is a story
persuasive for a particular person? I will propose tentative answers to these
questions, paving the way for future collaborations. The perspective of this article is clearly that of computational arguments, computational narratives and
multi-agent approaches to communication. However, formal definitions will
be kept to a minimum but possible formalisations will be indicated where appropriate.

1   Stories in Argumentation

Structurally, stories and arguments are different things: a story is a coherent
sequence of events, whereas an argument is a reason for some conclusion .
However, a story can be used for a variety of different goals: to explain, to
entertain, to persuade and so on. Whether a story should be considered as an
explanation, as a source of entertainment or as an argument depends not on its
structure but rather on the intention of the author or speaker. This idea stems
from speech act theory [23]: it is the intention of uttering some locution - the
illocutionary force of the speech act - that determines how the contents of the
speech act should be treated. So if a story is told with the intention of persuading or arguing, we can consider it to be an argument, a reason for a conclusion,
whereas if it is told with the intention of explaining we can consider it to be
an explanation [15]. This is vital, as the criteria by which we judge arguments,
explanations or entertainment are wholly different.

In Bex and colleagues' *hybrid theory* [13] arguments are used to reason
about stories. The hybrid theory is one of Inference to the Best Explanation
(IBE), in which observations are first explained by hypothetical stories and
arguments based on evidence are subsequently used to support or attack these
stories. For example, a hypothetical story about a shooting can be supported
by witnesses stating that it was the suspect who shot the victim. However, the
suspect's own denial of the shooting counts as evidence that attacks this story.
Ultimately, the objective of IBE is to find the best explanation, that is, the one
that is supported by the greatest number of evidential arguments and attacked
by the least number of evidential arguments. Figure 1 shows a stylised picture

---

[1]Interestingly, my work on the first version of this article for Trevor's Festschrift has given
impetus to new work with Trevor on stories and argumentation [10, 6].

of arguments supporting (closed arrow) and attacking (open arrow) elements in a story.

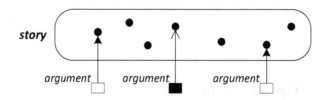

Figure 1. Arguments supporting and attacking a story

Another example in which arguments and stories are closely intertwined is in Case-based Reasoning (CBR). The field of CBR in Artificial Intelligence [17] essentially stems from the early work on story understanding [21]. Ideas from this early work were later on used in formal approaches to legal CBR in AI and Law [2, 1]. In this work, cases are collections of factors, stereotypical fact situations with legal relevance, such as *plaintiff was pursuing his livelihood* or *plaintiff was not in possession of the animal* in cases relating to the chase and ownership of game. Recently, the work on CBR has come full circle. Bex and colleagues [12] focus on factual stories, which are very similar to legal cases in that both stories and cases present a coherent set of facts; the main difference is that in legal cases the elements of the case (factors) are somehow legally relevant, whilst this is not a requirement for stories. Thus, the argumentative moves of legal CBR [1] can be used to explore similarities between stories in an argumentative way. For example, it can be argued that *Hamlet* is similar to *Cavelleria Rusticana*, as in both stories one man (Hamlet / Turrido) defends himself because he is attacked by another man (Laertes / Alfio). However, this similarity can be countered by arguing that in Hamlet the attacker, Laertes, was acting to avenge the death of his sister Ophelia, whilst Alfio did not have a similar reason to attack Turrido. Figure 2 shows a stylised representation of two such arguments.

The work on the hybrid theory and the work on arguments and stories in CBR focus on arguments about stories: in the hybrid theory arguments are used to reason about the truth of a single story, and the CBR approach uses arguments to reason about the similarity of multiple stories. However, as was discussed above, it is also possible to use a story as an argument, that is, propose a story as a reason for some conclusion. In the case of IBE, once the best explanation is inferred, we can infer further conclusions from this explanatory story. For instance, from a factual story containing the elements *S shot V* and

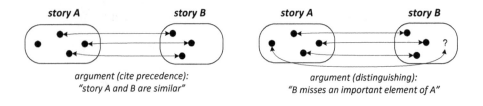

Figure 2. Arguments about the similarity of stories

S shooting V caused V to die we can infer both that *S intended to kill V* - otherwise S would not have shot V - and that *S killed V*, which together leads to the conclusion that S murdered V. Here the elements of the story serve as the conditions of legal rules [14] and thus as premises to an argument (Figure 3). So in addition to reasoning about stories we can also construct arguments with stories.

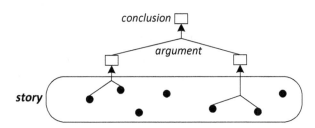

Figure 3. Drawing conclusions from elements in a story

CBR also involves both reasoning about and with stories: first we infer that story B is similar to story A' from which previously conclusion C was inferred (reasoning *about* stories, left side of Figure 4). This then allows us to infer C from B (reasoning *with* stories, right side of Figure 4). In legal CBR, the conclusion C that we want to argue for is typically a legal conclusion. For example, in *Pierson v. Post*, plaintiff was chasing a fox and defendant interrupted the chase, killing the fox and claiming it. It was concluded that plaintiff had no right to the fox since he had not gained possession of it. A similar case was *Young v. Hitchens*: in this case plaintiff, a fisherman, was closing his nets when defendant sped into the gap and caught the fish in his own nets. The two cases are similar because in both cases, plaintiff was not in possession of the animals. Hence, by citing Pierson v. Post as a precedent we can draw the same conclusion in Young v. Hitchens, namely that the case should be decided in favour of defendant.

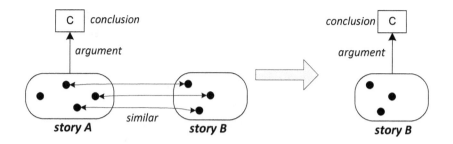

Figure 4. Drawing the same conclusion from a similar story

1.1 Value-based argumentation

Values have been incorporated into formal argumentation frameworks by Trevor [5]. The basic idea is that accepting a particular conclusion promotes or demotes some abstract social or cultural value such as *liberty* or *equality*. In a sense, people's world views can be said to represent an ordering of such values; for example, a Democrat will generally prefer equality over liberty, whilst for a Republican this will be the other way around. Whenever a person has to choose between competing arguments, they choose the argument that best matches their value ordering, that is, the argument that promotes their favoured value.

Atkinson and Bench-Capon [5, 4] show how discussions about moral issues can be represented as practical reasoning with values. Such arguments are of the following form[2]:

I have goal G.
Performing action A in situation S will realise goal G, which will promote some value V.
Therefore I should perform action A.

The idea is that by performing an action and reaching a goal, a value is promoted. For example, if you find a wallet with a large sum of money you can bring it back to its rightful owner (promoting *honesty*) or take out the money (promoting *wealth*). The choice whether or not to perform an action is ultimately governed by one's value ordering (i.e. whether honesty or wealth is preferred).

Atkinson and colleagues' model does not capture reasoning with stories or cases: the premises of arguments are simple propositions. Value-based rea-

---

[2]The exact argumentation scheme used by Atkinson and Bench-Capon is slightly different; here I have adapted it into a slightly abbreviated standard form.

soning with cases has been tackled, however, by [7], who present a model of legal CBR in which combinations of individual factors and decisions promote values. So, for example, if based on the factor plaintiff was pursuing his livelihood we would decide for plaintiff, the value productivity would be promoted. Thus, a case promotes all the values that are promoted by its individual factors. Note that we can essentially consider CBR to be a model of practical reasoning [3], where the action is making a legal decision (e.g. "decide for plaintiff"). In this way, the reasoning in Bench-Capon and Sartor's model can be interpreted as practical reasoning with more complex situations and multiple values: given situation $x_1, \ldots, x_n$, where x_i is a factor, performing action A (deciding for plaintiff or defendant) promotes values $v_1, \ldots, v_n$, where v_i is the value promoted by the combination of factor x_i and decision A.

1.2   Issues for Stories in Value-based Argumentation

The objective of this article is to lay the foundations for a model in which stories can be used to influence the actions of others. The current work on stories and argumentation discussed above shows that stories can form the basis of arguments by providing the conditions for the application of one or more rules, and that these arguments can promote values in the usual way. However, there are a number of open issues.

First, note that the existing approaches mainly use stories to infer legal conclusions such as "the defendant is guilty" or "the case should be decided for plaintiff". The legal rules used to infer these conclusions can be derived from previous decisions (in the case of CBR, 4) or found in legislation (for models that adhere to a more continental legal approach, 3). An important aim is to figure out which non-legal conclusions we want to derive from stories and which inference rules allow us to do so. The work on practical reasoning provides some important basics here: if stories are told to influence the behaviour of others, they can be considered as premises to arguments for practical reasoning. In other words, we might use stories to infer the standard conclusion in models for practical reasoning, namely *action A should be performed*.

One issue with treating value-based reasoning with stories as standard practical reasoning is that current conceptions of practical argument are mostly concerned with specific, goal directed actions (e.g. "stop eating cake", "install speed cameras", "decide for plaintiff"). However, when one tells a story such as a parable or a fable, the objective is often not to influence a single future action but rather the way in which someone lives their life in general. Basically, what one is trying to accomplish by telling a story is a shift in values, a change in someone else's worldview, so the conclusions of arguments based on stories should be the values or value orderings themselves, or at least a more abstract rendition of actions which is not directly aimed at building a plan but rather at providing the basic tenets for how one should live one's life.

Another open question is exactly how stories serve as the premises of arguments for practical reasoning. As discussed earlier, Bench-Capon and Sartor's model (implicitly) uses cases as premises of practical arguments. So, given the similarities between stories and cases [12, 14], it should be possible to model value-based reasoning with stories in a similar way; instead of one case setting a precedent for which legal decision needs to be made in a similar case, a story sets a precedent for how one should behave in a similar situation. What needs to be determined now is which elements of a story cause it to be an argument for or against a particular value. For this, we turn to research on narratives and story points.

2   The Structure and Point of a Story

Since Aristotle's *Poetics*, there have been numerous theories about the elements and the structure of narratives, mainly in literature theory. The first formalisation of the structure of stories came from Vladimir Propp [18], who identified standard event types and structures for folk tales. Following Propp's work, researchers from the field of cognitive psychology and artificial intelligence became interested in story structure, mainly with the aim of defining and automating story understanding. Influenced by the work on generative grammars, researchers such as [20] developed so-called story grammars, which express the structure of stories as a Context Free Grammar. For example, most story grammars divide a story into a series of episodes ($story \longrightarrow episode*$), each of which has a basic goal-driven structure ($episode \longrightarrow setting + goal + action + consequence$). Others, most notably [21], argued that whilst stories consist of goal-driven action sequences, story understanding is more content-driven, in that more specific information in the form of scripts is used when understanding stories. Scripts model the way things tend to happen in the world; for instance, the restaurant script lists the roles (customer, waiter) and sequence of events (ordering, eating, paying) for a typical restaurant visit.

Wilensky [27] argued against story grammars and scripts, saying that a piece of text can only be a proper story if it has a point. Wilensky distinguishes between external points, goals a storyteller might have when telling a story such as persuading someone or communicating information, and internal points, parts of the story text that generate interest. Wilensky's theory mainly focuses on internal points. As an example of an internal point, consider the following sequence of events: "John loved Mary. He asked her to marry him. She agreed, and soon after they were wed. Then one day John met Sue, a new employee in his office, and fell in love with her". This text has an internal point, that is, there is a dramatic situation that involves goals and the interaction between them. In the example, a new goal (the love for Sue) interferes with an old goal (the marriage with and love for Mary). So, according to Wilensky, the point of a story is a summary of the events that comprise interesting ("dramatic") goal relationships in the story ("John loves someone but is already married to someone else").

Wilensky thus argues that the dramatic content in a story can be found by looking at the relationships between the goals of the various characters. Wilensky's idea of dramatic content, however, can be further generalised by taking into account Schank and Abelson's scripts: often, it is a deviation of the standard script that counts as "dramatic content". In the example, people might expect John and Mary to live happily ever after, as the (original) idea behind marriage is that it lasts "until death do you part". This script-based approach to dramatic content allows for a broader definition of the term. For example, in Searle's Chinese room story [24], the Chinese Room satisfies the Turing test (i.e. it answers questions in a seemingly intelligent way). Our standard script is that if something satisfies the Turing test, it can be said to be intelligent. Searle's dramatic twist is then that there actually no intelligence being engaged even with a human inside [10].

Wilensky thus argues that the dramatic content in a story can be found by looking at the relationships between the goals of the various characters. Wilensky's idea of dramatic content, however, can be further generalised by taking into account Schank and Abelson's scripts: often, it is a deviation of the standard script that counts as dramatic content. In the example, people might expect John and Mary to live happily ever after, as the (original) idea behind marriage is that it lasts "until death do you part"[3]. This script-based approach to dramatic content allows for a broader definition of the term. For example, in Searle's Chinese room story [24], the Chinese Room satisfies the Turing test (i.e. it answers questions in a seemingly intelligent way). Our standard script is that if something satisfies the Turing test, it can be said to be intelligent. Searle's dramatic twist is then that there actually no intelligence being engaged even with a human inside [10].

Schank and colleagues [22] also discussed points in the context of story understanding. They perceive points to be interplay between the speaker's intentions on how the listener should process the story and the listener's ability

---

[3]However, considering the high number of divorces, the standard script might nowadays be marriage to A - divorce - marriage to B - divorce. In this case the story would be contain a dramatic twist if John and Mary actually lived happily ever after!

to correctly process and categorise a story. For example, affective points are meant to change the listener's goals, explanatory points are meant to explain situations, prescriptive points are meant to present the listener with rules, argumentative points are meant to persuade the listener, and so on. These point categories are very similar to the differences in illocutionary force discussed earlier: a story may be told with the intention of explaining, arguing and so forth[4]. Very often, this illocutionary force depends on the dialogical context in which a story is told [19]. For example [6, 25], in the bible Jesus is often asked a question to which he responds with a story, a parable: the story of the Good Samaritan is told to answer the question "Who is my neighbour?", and the story of the Prodigal Son is told in response to the Pharisees negative comments on Jesus' consorting with sinners. Jesus tell these stories with the intention of explaining who can be considered a neighbour, or why he consorts with sinners, and at the same time these stories argue for a particular value or value ordering.

Dorfman and Brewer [16] provide a model in which the point of a story is not a structural characteristic of the story (as in Wilensky's work) or specifically tied to the intention of the speaker (as in Schank et al.'s work). Rather, Dorfman and Brewer argue that the point is a higher level concept, a moral or an "abstract truth". The point of many stories, such as fables, is about whether we should or should not exhibit certain behaviour, for example, "don't be overconfident", "be honest" and so on. The point of the story can be explicitly mentioned in the text, as is often the case for the various renditions of Aesop's fables where the moral of the story is explicitly included. Take, for example, the tale of The Boy Who Cried Wolf, which concerns a shepherd boy who repeatedly tricks nearby villagers into thinking a wolf is attacking his sheep. After a while, a wolf actually does appear, the villagers do not believe the boy's cries for help, and the flock is destroyed. Caxton's medieval version this tale of ends with the explicit point *"For men bileue not lyghtly hym / whiche is knowen for a lyer"*.

In many cases, however, the point of a text is not explicit: mentioning the point of a story is often considered to be quite a thought-terminating clicher. The question is then how the contents and structure of a story influence its point. Dorfman and Brewer try to answer this question by proposing and testing a model of point comprehension. In this model, readers infer the point or moral of a story based mainly on the positive or negative valence of the story's central action combined with the positive or negative valence of the story's outcome. The central action of a story is the morally significant action of the

---

[4]In fact, Schank and colleagues explicitly connect their work to Searle's work.

story; for example, lying in the case of *The Boy Who Cried Wolf* or being lazy and overconfident in *The Tortoise and The Hare*. The outcome describes how the central action was resolved. Actions and outcomes can be perceived as positive or negative (according to Western standards): lying is a negative action, losing one's sheep is a negative outcome, being diligent is a positive action, winning a race is a positive outcome. In their experiments, Dorfman and Brewer presented subjects with a variety of short fables. Base fables are the original versions, where positive actions are paired with positive outcomes and negative actions are paired with negative outcomes. Reversed outcome fables were the base fables with reversed outcome valences (e.g. the Hare wins the race), so a positive action is tied to a negative outcome and vice versa. Neutral and no-outcome fables had a non-morally significant central action or no outcome, respectively.

The experiments showed that in the case of base fables, subjects nearly always (95%) correctly understood the moral point of the story correctly, that is, the fable's moral was understood as originally intended. For neutral and no-outcome fables, most subjects (93% and 85% respectively) could not find a point to the story. In the case of reversed-outcome fables, about 60% of the subjects argued that there was no point to the fable. Of the remaining 40%, most subjects (40%) assigned a new, reversed moral point to the story that coincided with the new outcome. For example, in the reversed-outcome The Goose and the Golden Eggs, the farmer kills the Goose, as in the original fable, but instead of losing his source of income is rewarded with a huge sum of gold. The new point assigned by subjects was then something like "greed and impatience are good". However, quite a lot of subjects (30%) replied that the reversed-outcome fable had the original point (e.g. "greed is bad"). This is attributed to the "just-world" hypothesis: people will always believe that good behaviour will or should be rewarded and bad behaviour will or should be punished, even if a story tells them otherwise.

It seems that there are various ideas about what constitutes the point of a story: dramatic story content ("John loves someone but is already married to someone else"), the intention of the author (to argue for fidelity in marriage), morals in the form of a lesson about one should or shouldn't do ("you should not look at other women once you're married"), or perhaps more abstract values one should follow (fidelity).

The dramatic story content and the intention of the author are, in my view, not the point of the story but they play an important part in *establishing* the point of a story. So-called neutral stories, in which there is no dramatic resolution to some central event, are usually regarded as pointless. The intention of the narrator, which can sometimes by gathered from the context, is also important as the above discussion shows. Finally, the knowledge and beliefs of the reader also guide the inference of a point from a story: deeply entrenched beliefs influence the point that people read in a story (cf. the just world hypothesis), and a reader will identify more with a character who is in a similar situation or who has a similar world view. The point of the story is thus the interaction between the structure and contents of the story and the knowledge and beliefs of the reader. The story teller intends the story to have such an interaction and thus change the knowledge and beliefs of the reader in a particular way.

Which knowledge and which beliefs are usual targets of storytelling? This of course depends on the type of story and the context in which it is used in [24], the point of the story is that "Syntax by itself is neither constitutive of nor sufficient for semantics" or, in other words, being able to manipulate strings of symbols does not mean that one understands the meaning of these symbols. In this article I mainly discuss stories with an explicit moral, that is, stories that are meant to teach us values and influence our behaviour. As indicated earlier, here the interest is not in stories that are intended to influence a rather simple, single action but rather in stories that are aimed at influencing the (order of) the values people believe in and live their lives by.

3 Stories in Value-based Argumentation

In section 1, it was discussed how stories can be used as arguments: if the intention of the speaker is to persuade someone using a story, they can argue for some conclusion by telling a story. As the discussion in section 2 demonstrates, this conclusion will be what is normally called the point of the story: a lesson on how we should live our lives, which values we should strive for. Clearly, these types of conclusions are very close to the conclusion of a value-based practical argument: action A should be performed to promote value V. Note that, as discussed in the previous section, this conclusion is often left implicit, as stories are as much intended to provoke thought as to lay down explicit rules.

The premise of the argument, the reason for performing the action, is in this case the story itself. This story tells us what will happen if and when the action is performed. The following provisional argument scheme for practical reasoning based on stories can now be constructed:

Character x performs action A, which promotes (demotes) value V, and gets
  positive (negative) results
Therefore I should (not) perform action A, promoting (demoting) value V.

The premise is the story, in which a character performs an action and gets a certain positive or negative result, promoting or demoting a value. For example, the boy lies about the wolf, demoting honesty, and gets negative results, namely none of the villagers help him when the wolf does turn up. From this story, we can conclude that we should not lie.

The above scheme presents a generic situation, in which a story is told and we expect people to accept the conclusion. Whilst we can expect that, given a story, people can infer the conclusion that they should exhibit certain behaviour, it is certainly not clear that people can be persuaded just by giving them a story. Persuasion requires a person to somehow identify with the character in a story. As an example, consider the parable of the Prodigal Son (Luke 15:11-32). In this story, a father gives the younger of his two sons his inheritance before he dies. The son goes off and wastes his money, but after a while goes hungry during a famine. The son repents and returns home, where the father holds a feast to celebrate his return. The older son is angry that the father holds a big feast for his wasteful sibling, stating that he never got such a feast even though he always obeyed his father and worked hard. The father reminds the older son that everything the father has is the older son's, but that they should still celebrate the return of the younger son as he has come back to them. As a young student, identifying with the younger son, one might take from this story that it is not forbidden to make mistakes, as long as you can later see the error of your ways. As a father, one might see this story mainly as a tale of forgiveness: no matter what your children do you should always forgive them.

So a story sets an example by having the listener or reader identify with one of the characters. More precisely, the story acts as a precedent for the current situation and thus, arguing with stories takes the form of Case-based Reasoning, as described in section 2.2:

> Character x performs action A, which promotes (demotes) value V, and gets positive (negative) results
> I am in a similar situation as character x
> *Therefore* I should (not) perform action A, promoting (demoting) value V.

This scheme effectively combines practical reasoning and argument from analogy. A similar scheme is Walton and colleagues' [26] scheme for practical reasoning from analogy, which says that if in situation S, action A is the right (wrong) thing to do and S' is similar to S, then in S' one should (not) do A. The scheme proposed here is a more detailed version of this scheme, focusing on how people are persuaded by stories. Furthermore, the idea of story similarity has recently been explored in [12]. This work builds on the idea of story schemes [8] - generalised patterns of events akin to scripts [21] - for comparing stories: two stories are relevantly similar if both are an instance of the same story scheme.

The conclusion of the above scheme, however, still points to a specific action, whereas we want stories to influence the (orderings of) values others use to live their life by. This more general effect of arguments based on the above scheme also influences the relation of these argument to the kind of value orderings proposed by [5]. Where in standard practical arguments value orderings are meant to allow us to choose between competing arguments, arguments following the above scheme are meant to influence precisely these value orderings: values attached to actions that lead to positive results should be preferred to values attached to actions that lead to negative results. So we could further rewrite the scheme as follows, focusing on the values instead of the actions.

Character x performs action A, which promotes (demotes) value V, and gets positive (negative) results

I am in a similar situation as character x

Therefore I should (not) prefer actions that promote (demote) value V.

4   Conclusions and future work

In this article, I have discussed the role of stories in argumentation and how the content of stories and their structure influence the arguments based on them. I have shown that by combining ideas from practical and case-based reasoning, a simple argumentation scheme can be constructed that captures, in my opinion, the essence of story-based persuasion. Because the work clearly builds on existing formal approaches to CBR and practical reasoning, further formalising and integrating it with these approach should be fairly straightforward.

There are, however, still a number of issues that are somewhat harder to solve. Simple stories such as Aesop's fables usually have one protagonist and a clear action-outcome structure. However, when we start looking at, for example, parables things start getting more complex: the Prodigal Son has three important actors, each with his own behaviour and set of values. Furthermore, the positive or negative outcome is only one way to determine the point of a story. In the fables, the outcomes are quite clearly positive or negative. In Biblical parables, they are less so: is the party really a positive outcome for the older son? In such cases, the actual point of the story (i.e. the value promoted) is often more dependent on context, intention of the narrator and expectations of the hearer. In addition, more complex stories do not necessarily convince because the hearer is in a similar situation, but rather they convince by evoking an emotion. For example, the parable of the Good Samaritan is not just meant to persuade people to help persons who have been robbed and beaten, but rather to show mercy and compassion in all relevant situations.

In sum, two important questions for future research are: (i) how do we find the point of a story, the conclusion for which it argues?; and (ii) why exactly are some stories convincing and others not? I have tentatively answered these questions for simple fables in this article, but for parables things start getting more complex, and full-length novels seem almost impossible to analyse thus. This is not a problem that is exclusive to the formalisation of stories and story-based reasoning, however; much of the work in computational argumentation, whilst mathematically and formally sound, does sadly not transcend the basic examples of flying penguins and Quaker presidents. When looked at from this perspective, stories add a great deal to a more knowledge intensive and realistic theory of argumentation.

A related question, one that is often presented with respect to stories in argumentation, is: why exactly should we use stories in formal argumentation? Are they not simply a different and sometimes confusing way of representing knowledge that can also be summarised as a simple sentence? Why should we tell the whole story when we can just use the argumentation scheme from section 4? Admittedly, stories are more interesting to read and more thought-provoking than fairly dry, rule-based if ... then ... arguments. However, of what use is this in situations aimed at automated reasoning? A software agent will not be more easily persuaded by a beautiful story than by a simple rule. And what about the dangers of stories? We are all familiar with the idea that, for example in court, a well-told story can trump a solid and strong argument. Summarising: are stories not just a rhetorical device, interesting to study when looking at informal argument, rhetoric and human communication but of no direct use in artificial intelligence models?

In this regard, it is (again) instructive to consider the similarities between reasoning with stories and reasoning with legal cases. Legal cases often have a so-called *ratio decidendi*, which consists of the rules of law or the reasons given to justify a decision in a case. In a sense, the ratio decidenci can be viewed as the point of a legal case: what does it mean to choose one decision over another? As [7, 25] mention, there are essentially two camps in the debate as to whether the ratio should be seen as being explicitly given (i.e. by an explicit argumentation underlying the decision) or whether the ratio decidendi is implicit and can be considered as flowing naturally from the facts of the decision and its outcome. We can also adhere to the second viewpoint when considering the points of stories: the point follows quite naturally from a coherent story and the hearer's interpretation of it. A computational theory of human argumentation (or, more broadly, of human intelligence) needs a concept of stories and story-based reasoning because storytelling and understanding are central [28]. As an intelligent person with an almost unmatchable capacity for absorbing and using a wide variety of stories, I suspect that Trevor will agree with this and I look forward to continuing our work for years to come.

Bibliography

[1] V. Aleven. *Teaching Case Based Argumentation Through an Example and Models*. PhD thesis, University of Pittsburgh, 1997.

[2] K. Ashley. *Modeling Legal Argument*. MIT Press, 1990.

[3] K. Atkinson and T. Bench-Capon. Legal case-based reasoning as practical reasoning. *Artificial Intelligence and Law*, 13:93–131, 2005.

[4] K. Atkinson and T. Bench-Capon. Addressing moral problems through practical reasoning. *Journal of Applied Logic*, 6:135ñ151, 2007.

[5] T. Bench-Capon. Persuasion in practical argument using value-based argumentation frameworks. *Journal of Logic and Computation*, 3:429–448, 2003.

[6] T. Bench-capon. The parable of the good samaritan. Personal communication, 2013.

[7] T. Bench-Capon and G. Sartor. A model of legal reasoning with cases incorporating theories and values. *Artificial Intelligence*, 150:97–143, 2003.

[8] F. Bex. Analyzing stories using schemes. In H. Kaptein, H. Prakken, and B. Verheij, editors, *Legal Evidence and Proof: Statistics, Stories, Logic*, Applied Legal Philosophy Series. Ashgate, Aldershot, 2009.

[9] F. Bex and T. Bench-Capon. Persuasive stories for multi-agent argumentation. In *Proceedings of the 2010 AAAI Fall Symposium on Computational Narratives. AAAI Technical Report FS-10-04*, Menlo Park, CA, 2010. AAAI press.

[10] F. Bex and T. Bench-Capon. Arguing with stories. Workshop on Computational Models of Natural Argument (CMNA), 2013.

[11] F. Bex, T. Bench-Capon, and K. Atkinson. Did he jump or was he pushed? abductive practical reasoning. *Artificial Intelligence and Law*, 17:79–99, 2009.

[12] F. Bex, T. Bench-Capon, and B.Verheij. What makes a story plausible? the need for precedents. In K. Atkinson, editor, *Legal Knowledge and Information Systems. JURIX 2011: The Twenty-Fourth Annual Conference*, pages 23–32, 2011.

[13] F. Bex, P. van Koppen, H. Prakken, and B. Verheij. A hybrid formal theory of arguments, stories and criminal evidence. *Artificial Intelligence and Law*, 2:123–152, 2010.

[14] F. Bex and B. Verheij. Legal stories and the process of proof. *Artificial Intelligence and Law*, 2012. to appear.

[15] F. Bex and D. Walton. Combining explanation and argumentation in dialogue. In *Computational Models of Natural Argument - Proceedings of CMNA12*. Springer, 2012. to appear.

[16] M. Dorfman and W. Brewer. Understanding the points of fables. *Discourse Processes*, 17:105–129, 1994.

[17] D. Gentner and K. Forbus. Computational models of analogy. *Wiley Interdisciplinary Reviews: Cognitive Science*, 2:266–276, 2011.

[18] V. Propp. *The Morphology of the Folktale*. University of Texas Press, Austin, TX, 1968.

[19] C. Reed. Implicit speech acts are ubiquitous. why? they join the dots. In *Proceedings of the Conference on Argumentation: Cognition and Community (OSSA-2011)*, 2011.

[20] D. Rumelhart. *Notes on a schema for stories*. Academic Press, NY, 2013.

[21] R. Schank and R. Abelson. *Scripts, Plans, Goals and Understanding: an Inquiry into Human Knowledge Structures*. Lawrence Erlbaum, Hillsdale, NJ, 1977.

[22] R. Schank, G. Collins, E. Davis, P. Johnson, S. Lytinen, and B. Reiser. What's the point? *Cognitive Science*, 6:255–275, 1982.

[23] J. Searle. *Speech Acts: An Essay in the Philosophy of Language*. Cambridge University Press, 1969.

[24] J. Searle. Minds, brains and programs. *Behavioral and brain sciences*, 3:417–457, 1980.

[25] W. Twining. The ratio decidendi of the parable of the prodigal son. In *Rethinking Evidence - Exploratory Essays*, chapter 13. Cambridge University Press, 2nd edition, 2006.

[26] D. Walton, C. Reed, and F. Macagno. *Argumentation Schemes*. Cambridge University Press, Cambridge, 2008.

[27] R. Wilensky. *Points: A Theory of the Structure of Stories in Memory*. Erlbaum, Hillsdale, NJ, 1982.

[28] P. Winston. The strong story hypothesis and the directed perception hypothesis. In *Proceedings of the 2010 AAAI Fall Symposium on Computational Narratives. AAAI Technical Report FS-10-04*, Menlo Park, CA, 2010. AAAI Press.

A Data Mining Approach to Extracting Debate Graphs

ZAHER SALAH* , FRANS COENEN† , AND DAVIDE GROSSI‡

Abstract

A mechanisms for extracting debate graphs from debate transcriptions is described. The idea is to represent the structure of a debate as a graph with speakers as nodes. Nodes are labelled according to the "attitude" of the speaker, whether they "agree" or "disagree" with the motion, using a classifier constructed from a training set of labelled speeches. Links between nodes are established according to the semantic similarity between speeches. The graph links are labelled as being either "supporting" or "opposing". If both speakers have the same attitude (both negative or both positive) the link is labelled as being supporting; otherwise the link is labelled as being opposing. To act as a focus for the work, and for the evaluation reported in this paper, transcriptions of UK "House of Commons" debates were used.

Introduction

In his early career Bench-Capon worked for the civil service and during this time wrote parliamentary speeches for cabinet ministers. Bench-Capon is also internationally recognised as a leading expert within the domain of argumentation. In this paper we introduce a graph based mechanism for modelling debates (a form of argument) in terms of the speakers and the relationships between speakers. More specifically we illustrate the process using UK parliamentary debates focussing on the individual speeches of ministers and other members of parliament. The objective is to provide a mechanism whereby debates can be summarised and consequently analysed. As such debate graphs may considered to be structurally similar to argument graphs *à la*

*University of Liverpool, Department of Computer Science
†University of Liverpool, Department of Computer Science
‡University of Liverpool, Department of Computer Science

Dung [Dung 1995], except for two key differences: nodes represent speeches instead of arguments; edges are symmetric and of two types (supporting or opposing). By constructing graphs from debate transcriptions we can obtain an overview of the debate which can then be analysed with respect to how the individual participants interact and with respect to patterns that might allow us to predict debate outcomes. In this paper we consider a debate graph to comprise nodes representing "speakers" (participants) and links representing connections between speakers. Nodes also have the concatenated speeches of individual speakers associated with them. To allow for analysis we propose a mechanism whereby nodes are labelled according to the attitude of each speaker, either "agree" or "disagree" indicating whether they agree with the motion or not. Links are established according to the semantic similarity between speeches and labelled as being either "supporting" or "opposing" according to the attitude of the speeches that represented by the end nodes; "supporting" if both nodes have the same attitude and "opposing" if both nodes have a different attitude. The attitude is determined by applying text classification [Jiang *et al.* 2010, Wang *et al.* 2009] to the concatenated speeches. To do this we first generate a classifier using labelled training data which can then be applied to "unseen" data. We can gain confidence in our classifier by applying it to labeled test data.

The research contribution presented in this paper is directed at extracting debate graphs, describing political debates, from political textual data using data mining techniques. More specifically a mechanism is described whereby political debates can be represented as graphs generated from debate transcripts. To act as a focus for the work the graph generation process was applied to a parliamentary proceedings corpus consisting of verbatim transcripts of debates held within the UK House of Commons. To the best knowledge of the authors, no one has performed such experiments on this kind of data before.

The rest of this paper is structured as follows. Section 1 overviews some previous works relevant to the research topic, while Section 2 discusses the application domain. Section 3 presents the proposed debate graph extraction process. An illustrative example is then given in Section 4 and an evaluation of the proposed framework in Section 5. Section 6 then provides some conclusions and considers some future extensions of the proposed work.

1 Related work

There is little work on the generation of debate graphs as formulated in this paper. However, in [Kaptein *et al.* 2009] annotations of meeting notes and knowledge of "interruptions" are used to capture debate structure which are then visualised using a graph format. In this case the process relies on the annotations associated with the debate transcripts and does not employ the concept of text mining (specifically text classification) as advocated in this paper.

Although there has been very little reported work on debate graphs there has been significant work on the visualisation of arguments which has some overlap with the work described in this paper. A number of mechanisms have been proposed each founded on some specific theory of argumentation such as Dung's argument framework [Dung 1995]. The distinction between debate graphs, as conceived in this paper, and argument graphs is that in the latter case each node is usually taken to represent one argument (of some inferential kind) and links, which are directed, are taken to represent that the source node undermines (in some way) the target node. Besides the abstract theory of argumentation frameworks, research in argumentation has developed a number of more concrete, and application-oriented systems. Two frequently cited systems are Araucaria [Reed *et al.* 2004] and Carneades [Gordon 2007]. These systems, however, do not build on corpora of existing debates and aim at the internal representation of the logical structure of arguments. Finally, in the context of debate analysis, as opposed to visualisation, there is also existing work directed at identifying and displaying keywords in, for example, a tabular format, with time along the x-axis and selected words along the y-axis.

Text mining is concerned with the application of data mining techniques to document collections. A typical task is to classify news paper articles according to a set of categories [Jiang *et al.* 2010, Wang *et al.* 2009]. The key challenge of text mining is not the data mining techniques themselves, these tend to be well understood, but the data preprocessing that must first be undertaken. This preprocessing requires that the input data be translated into some format that: (i) minimises information loss and (ii) allows for the application of data mining techniques. A common representation is the bag of words model where documents are encoded in terms of feature vectors whose elements represent keywords (a similar approach can be adopted using key phrases). The procedure for generating debate graphs as described in this paper utilises ideas and mechanisms from the domain of text mining.

2 Application

To act as a focus for the work described in this paper UK House of Commons debates were used. Both houses in the UK parliament, the House of Commons and the House of Lords, reach their decisions by debating and then voting with either an "Aye" or a "Nay" at the end of each debate. Proceedings

Iain Stewart (Milton Keynes South, Conservative)

I reassure the hon. Gentleman that many of us who passionately believe that we have to address the West Lothian question also believe in the equality of the work loads of Members. I do not believe that that is an intractable problem. Although some of my colleagues might believe that for Members from devolved areas there is a lighter load from postbags or parliamentary work, not all of us hold that view.

Ian Paisley Jnr (North Antrim, DUP)

I do not think that the view is necessary commonly held, but we should caution ourselves. When we speak in **this place** on behalf of the Union and such points are made-not in jest, but seriously-that seriously undermines the standing of the House and its Members. That is not what we should be about. We should bear that in mind.

Chris Bryant (Rhondda, Labour)

Has the hon. Gentleman had the following experience, as I have had in the past couple of weeks? As a Welsh **Member of Parliament**, I have had a lot of e-mails and correspondence from my constituents on the issue of selling off forests. That does not apply in Wales, but the issue is deeply felt by many in my **constituency**.

Ian Paisley Jnr (North Antrim, DUP)

I appreciate that **intervention**. I got at least three forest trees of letters through my door from people passionately asking me to oppose or support the plan, depending on where the correspondence came from, even though it does not directly affect Northern Ireland. I exercised some caution. I recognised that although it did not directly affect Northern Ireland, I could attend the debate and listen to the arguments. However, I did not vote; I deliberately made a choice not to do so, because I believed that it was a matter for Members who were directly affected and whose **constituency** issues rested on it. The issues were addressed in the devolved Assembly. I had the right to vote, but I also had the choice of whether to exercise it.

If Members feel that they are missing out, they should look at the devolved Assemblies. What exactly are they doing? Last week, our Assembly in Northern Ireland, of which I am no longer a Member, was dealing with legislation for safety helmets for bicycle riders. A dog fouling Bill was also introduced. We are not missing a lot. We should not think that there is stuff going on in those regions that we should really be getting our teeth into and ask why Members there are getting it while we are not. We are not missing that much, and we should bear that in mind.

I turn to the substantial point that I have in mind. I am a Unionist, and a proud one, but my Unionism is as strong only as each component part of the Union. My Unionism is deleted if Scottish or Welsh Unionism is deleted or English Unionism is not strong. As a Member for Northern Ireland, I have a responsibility to encourage the Union and see that it is strengthened. The Union is as strong only as each of its component parts. If Northern Ireland or Scotland are made weaker by legislation such as this, Unionism is made weaker. We should tread very carefully.

Harriett Baldwin (West Worcestershire, Conservative)

I thank the hon. Gentleman for coming along to participate in the debate, because his perspective is valuable. Will anything in the Bill prevent him from voting on anything? The Bill could allow our unwritten constitution to evolve so that Members might indeed choose to abstain in the way that he describes.

Figure 1. Fragment of a UKHCD2 Debate as published on the TheyWork-ForYou.com www site.

of the Commons Chamber are published on-line in XML format (at They-WorkForYou.com) three hours after they take place. Figure 1 shows an extract from a debate transcript taken from the "Legislation (Territorial Extent) Bill, Friday 11 February 2011"[1] debate (Debate number 20 in our dataset). The highlighted text indicates MPs who voted Aye at the end of the debate while the unhighlighted text indicates MPs who voted Nay. The advantage offered by this collection is that the outcome of the debates are known and thus we can (at least in part) evaluate the veracity of our debate graphs so that some confidence can be gained in the technique when it is applied to debates where the result is not known (or not yet known).

The authors extracted the speeches associated with 100 debates from the TheyWorkForYou.com www site. QDAMiner4[2] was used to extract the desired textual information from the debate records. For each debate the speeches associated with the same MP were concatenated together. Concatenated speeches with fewer than 50 words were ignored as it was conjectured that little meaning could be associated with these speeches. The remaining concatenated speeches were collected together to form a single dataset. We refer to this dataset as the UK House of Commons Debate version 2 (UKHCD2) dataset[3]. The dataset comprised 9473 concatenated speeches (4581 speeches made by speakers who voted Aye and 4892 speeches made by speakers who voted Nay) associated with 617 distinct Members of Parliament (MPs). The speeches comprised a total of 5,617,126 words or unigrams (34,097 unique words after stemming and stop-word removal). A statistical overview of the UKHCD2 dataset is provided in Table 2. Some specific statistics concerning a selected sample of individual speeches are presented in Table 2. Note that the number of concatenated speeches featured in a debate also equates to the number of MPs taking part. The average number of words in a concatenated speech was 592.96. The significance of the speaker's vote (Aye or Nay) is that this was used for evaluation purposes (as reported in Section 5). As noted above, the proposed debate graph extraction mechanism utilises various techniques taken from the domains of text mining, hence we also refer to individual concatenated speeches as documents.

---

[1]Hansard source citation: from HC Deb, 11 February 2011, c599 to HC Deb, 11 February 2011, c645

[2]http://provalisresearch.com/products/qualitative-data-analysis-software/

[3]Version 2 to distinguish it from an earlier version of this dataset used by the authors with respect to some initial proof-of-concept work (unpublished at present) that only featured 21 debates, UKHCD1 ⊂ UKHCD2.

Speakers			Concatenated Speeches		
9473 (617 distinct MPs)			9473 (5,617,126 words)		
Min # speakers	Max # speakers	Avg # speakers	Min # words	Max # words	Avg # words
13	156	94.73	50	5814	592.96
Voted Aye			Voted Nay		
4581			4892		
Min # votes	Max # votes	Avg # votes	Min # votes	Max # votes	Avg # votes
0	115	45.81	4	90	48.92

Table 1. UKHCD2 statistical overview

3 Debate Graph Extraction

An overview of the proposed debate graph extraction system is presented in Figure 2. The input is the concatenated speeches associated with a single debate, the output is a graph representing the structure of the debate. More formally the input is a set of n concatenated speeches $S = \{s_1, s_2, \ldots, s_n\}$, and the output is a graph of the form $G(V, E, L_v, L_E, f_{map})$ where: (i) V is a set of n vertices (one per concatenated speech) such that $V = \{v_1, v_2, \ldots, v_n\}$, (ii) E is a set of m edges such that $E = \{e_1, e_2, \ldots, e_m\}$, (iii) L_V is a set of two vertex labels (positive or negative), (iv) L_E is a set of two edge labels (supporting or opposing) and (v) f_{map} is some mapping function that maps the vertex and edge labels on to vertices and edges. The process encompasses four stages: (i) document/data preprocessing, (ii) attitude detection and node labelling, (iii) edge identification and labelling and (iv) debate graph generation. Each of these stages is described in more detail in the following four sub-sections.

3.1 Preprocessing

The input to the proposed process, as already noted above, is a set of speeches. In terms of text processing each speech is conceptualised as a document which in turn is said to represent a speaker. Each "document" is thus comprised of all the speeches associated with a particular speaker concatenated together. The pre-processing phase commenced with the conversion of all uppercase alphabetic characters to lower case, and punctuation mark and numeric digit removal.

The next stage is stop word removal [Chin & Deng 2008] (for further examples see [Hariharan & Srinivasan 2008] and [Poomagal & Hamsapriya 2011]).

debate	speeches	voted aye	voted nay	Min words	Max words	Avg words	SD words	Total words
D1	97	52	45	50	5456	606.19	1105.02	58800
D2	81	50	31	52	5615	731.04	1187.80	59214
D3	91	39	52	51	5612	561.05	1086.07	51056
D4	116	42	74	50	4603	583.73	772.93	67713
D5	75	40	35	50	5740	770.40	1234.36	57780
D6	134	80	54	50	5779	552.91	879.96	74090
D7	13	0	13	115	5772	1850.15	2046.59	24052
D8	82	36	46	50	5617	798.88	1299.86	65508
D9	68	29	39	51	5684	798.53	1254.60	54300
D10	67	12	55	50	5615	590.49	1292.76	39563
...	...	...	...	...	...	...	...	...
D20	20	12	8	68	4483	1612.90	1263.37	32258
...	...	...	...	...	...	...	...	...
D46	19	4	15	63	5661	1515.00	1791.49	28785
D47	120	66	54	50	5510	443.42	924.47	53210
D48	97	51	46	50	5326	594.10	1052.71	57628
D49	116	57	59	51	4515	574.49	880.54	66641
D50	75	51	24	50	2792	664.93	618.46	49870
D51	148	74	74	50	4306	368.68	594.33	54564
D52	112	34	78	51	5448	605.32	976.03	67796
D53	99	46	53	52	5573	685.90	1043.71	67904
D54	83	43	40	53	5630	628.22	1149.16	52142
D55	103	41	62	51	5694	438.84	844.35	45201
...	...	...	...	...	...	...	...	...
D91	107	55	52	51	5175	564.44	887.08	60395
D92	107	48	59	50	5637	491.69	993.55	52611
D93	125	66	59	51	3684	538.58	773.24	67323
D94	88	41	47	50	5626	569.33	1251.18	50101
D95	124	62	62	50	5273	499.10	841.93	61888
D96	70	32	38	50	5515	746.37	1219.12	52246
D97	142	61	81	52	5603	463.07	945.48	65756
D98	93	45	48	50	5571	648.33	1018.46	60295
D99	99	50	49	50	5505	662.78	971.50	65615
D100	151	68	83	52	5597	397.05	882.95	59954
min	13	0	4	50	2161	368.42	520.17	24052
max	156	115	90	515	5814	2436.57	2046.59	90297
avg	94.73	45.81	48.92	56.32	5199.84	674.04	1025.52	56171.26
stdev	33.17	21.15	20.45	46.84	723.54	309.70	264.42	13532.38
total	9473	4581	4892	5632	519984	67403.96	102552.26	5617126

Table 2. UKCHD2 statistics for selected debates

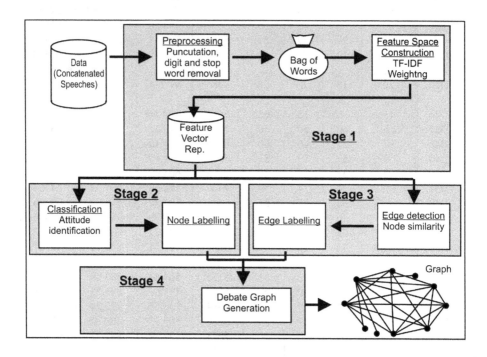

Figure 2. Schematic of the debate graph generation process

Stop words are words that carry little meaning (such as "and" or "the") and can therefore not be expected to make a significant contribution to the debate graph generation process. Stop words are thus removed from the document set. Given a specific domain there will also be additional words, other than stop words, that occur frequently. In the case of our UKHCD2 dataset words like: "hon.", "house", "minister", "government", "gentleman", "friend" and "member" are all very frequent words. For similar reasons as for stop and rare word removal these domain specific words are also removed. This was done by appending them to the stop-words list. The names of all the members of parliament, political parties and constituencies were also added to our bespoke stop-word list.

The following stage is to produce a Bag-Of-Words (BOW) representation containing all the remaining words in the document collection (speeches), $BOW = \{t_1, t_2, \ldots, t_{|BOW|}\}$. Each document will then be represented by some subset of the BOW. To reduce the number of individual words to be considered in the BOW stemming was applied. Stemming is concerned with the process of deriving the stem of a given word by removing the added affixes so that "inflated" words that belong to the same stem (root) will be "counted together" [Hariharan & Srinivasan 2008]. For example "compute", "computes", "computer", "computation" and "computing" will be counted together because they share the common stem "compute". Many mechanisms have been proposed to perform stemming, in the context of the work described in this paper Snowball stemming was used.

The bag of words is then used to define feature spaces from which sets of feature vectors can be generated. The feature vector elements hold term weightings. The most widely used mechanism for generating term weightings, and that adopted with respect to the DAP framework, is the TF-IDF weighting scheme which aims to "balance out the effect of very rare and very frequent" terms in a vocabulary [Kuhn *et al.* 2007]. TF-IDF also tends to reflect the significance of each term by combining local and global term frequency [Li *et al.* 2009]. TF-IDF can be defined as follows:

$$W_{ij} = TFIDF(i,j) = tf(i,j) \cdot \left(log \frac{N}{df(j)} \right) \qquad (1.1)$$

where: (i) $tf(i,j)$ is the frequency of term j in document d_i (local weight for the term), (ii) N is the total number of documents in the corpus (concatenated speeches in the debate), and (iii) $df(j)$ is the number of documents (speeches) containing term j (global weight for the term). Alternative schemes to TF-IDF include: Term Frequency (TF), Document Frequency (DF), Term Strength (TS) and Term Contribution (TC). Table 3.1 shows the DF counts for a number of example terms taken from the UKHCD2 collection. The table also shows the document count with respect to documents (speeches) where the MP in question voted Aye and where the MP voted Nay. The final column gives the document frequency difference between the number of Aye and Nay counts. Inspection of this final column clearly indicates that some terms can be associated with an Aye vote, while other terms can be associated with a Nay vote.

Term	DF (Aye)	DF (Nay)	DF (Total)	Diffe-rence	Term	DF (Aye)	DF (Nay)	DF (Total)	Diffe-rence
people	406	338	744	68	timetable	23	23	46	0
cuts	87	38	125	49	taxpayer	11	29	40	-18
change	154	111	265	43	generous	10	28	38	-18
worse	52	17	69	35	fully	34	53	87	-19
simply	101	70	171	31	sustainable	11	33	44	-22
care	69	39	108	30	funding	41	64	105	-23
confidence	60	31	91	29	improve	40	63	103	-23
recession	42	13	55	29	assure	34	59	93	-25
women	64	36	100	28	inherited	9	38	47	-29
military	42	16	58	26	previous	101	131	232	-30
hope	136	120	256	16	raises	8	38	46	-30
existence	15	0	15	15	reduce	38	73	111	-35
wonderful	24	10	34	14	encourage	30	72	102	-42
deep	21	7	28	14	european	59	105	164	-46

Table 3. Document Frequency (DF) values associated with selected terms occurring in the UKHCD2 dataset with respect to MPs who voted Aye and Nay.

On completion of the pre-processing phase the input collection of speeches are represented using the vector space model such that each speech can be described by a feature vector. More formaly a speech i is represented as a vector $S_i = \{w_{i1}, w_{i2}, \ldots, w_{iz}\}$ where w_{ij} is the TF-IDF value for term j in speech i. It should also be noted that each element in S_i corresponds to a term in the BOW. We will indicate the list of terms associated with feature vector S_i using the notation $T_i = \{t_{i1}, t_{i2}, \ldots, t_{iz}\}$. Thus we have a set if feature vectors $S = \{S_1, S_2, \ldots, S_z\}$ and a set of term lists $T = \{T_1, T_2, \ldots, T_z\}$ with a one-to-one correspondence between the two.

3.2   Attitude Detection and Node Labelling

Once the input data has been translated into the desired BOW format, whereby each speaker (node in the debate graph) is defined by a subset of words contained in the BOW, text classification can be applied to determine each speakers "attitude" (positive or negative). The idea is founded on the natural assumption that speeches of Members of Parliament (MPs) can be used as cues to how they are going to vote [Thomas *et al.* 2006].

With respect to this paper the classifier was generated using the entire dataset, in practice we would continue to use this classifier to generate debate graphs describing "new" debates. Classifier generation is a supervised learning mechanism that requires labelled training data (something which we would only have with respect to historical data). In our case we can use the known vote associated with each speaker in the UKHCD2 dataset as the label. Using this training set we first applied a feature selection (dimension reduction) mechanism to identify those features (words) which served as good discriminators. More specifically we used the χ^2 feature selection mechanism to identify the top k words that served as the best discriminators. Once the classifier had been generated it could be applied. Note that the training data used to generate the classifier, the data used to test it and the data to which it is to be applied all has to be preprocessed in the same way as described above.

3.3 Link Identification and Labelling

Links between node pairs, as noted above, are established when the speeches associated with two nodes (speakers) are deemed to be similar. There are a number of measures that can be used to determine the similarity between two feature vectors, such as: the Euclidean or Manhatten distance, or the Jaccard measure [Madylova & Oguducu 2009]. For the work described in this paper the cosine similarity measure was adopted because of its wide usage and acceptance. Cosine similarity is computed as follows:

$$CosSim(d_i, d_j) = \frac{d_i \times d_j}{|d_i| \times |d_j|} = \frac{\sum_{k=1}^{k=z} w_{ik} \times w_{jk}}{\sqrt{\sum_{k=1}^{k=z} w_{ik}^2 \times \sum_{k=1}^{k=z} w_{jk}^2}} \qquad (1.2)$$

Cosine similarity is the normalised dot product between two document vectors. Cosine similarity values range between 0 and 1. A value of 1 indicates that the two documents under consideration are identical, and a value 0 means that the two documents are entirely unrelated. With respect to the proposed framework similarities between all document (node) pairs are determined by constructing an affinity matrix. This matrix is then used to determine where links exist between nodes. A link is deemed to exist if the similarity value is greater than the average of all pair-wise similarities. Links are labelled using the terms "support" and "oppose". The label support is applicable if both of the linked nodes have the same attitude, and the label oppose is used if they have different attitudes.

3.4 Argument Graph Genration

The final phase, Phase four, of the proposed framework comprises debate graph generation. Graph generation is conducted using the outputs from Phases 2 and 3 (see Figure 2), and is fairly straightforward. Although any suitable graph drawing package can be used to visualise the generated result the authors used NetDraw[4], a Windows program for visualising social network data [Borgatti 2002].

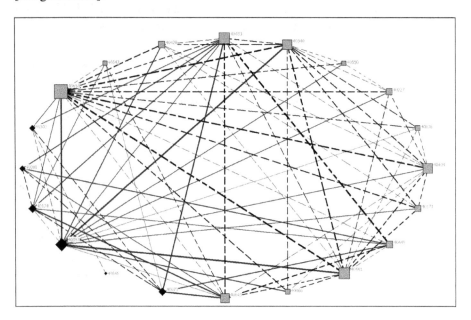

Figure 3. Debate graph generated from UKHCD2 debate number 20 using semantic similarity between speeches to indicate links.

4 Illustrative Example

In this section the proposed process is illustrated using one of the smaller debates contained in the UKHCD2 dataset, the "Legislation (Territorial Extent) Bill, Friday 11 February 2011" (Debate number 20), a fragment of which was presented in Figure 1 for illustrative purpose. Applying the proposed process to this debate the graph presented in Figure 3 was generated. With reference to the figure each speaker is represented by a node labelled with a speaker-ID (the official MP ID numbers used in Hansard). A square node indicates a positive

---

[4]https://sites.google.com/site/netdrawsoftware/home

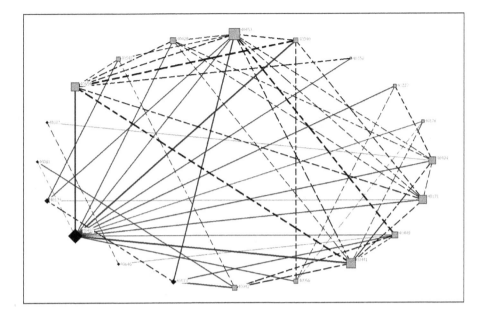

Figure 4. Debate graph generated from UKHCD2 debate number 20 using interruption data to indicate links.

attitude and a diamond node a negative attitude. The size of a node reflects the number of links connected to it. The "thickness" of a link reflects the semantic similarity between the two connected speakers; supporting links are indicated by dashed links while negative links are indicated by solid links.

An alternative option to using the semantic similarity between speakers' concatenated speeches to represent the exchanges (links) between debaters is to use interruptions made by MPs during the debate (who interrupted whom), as for example considered in [Kaptein *et al.* 2009] (see Section 1 above). Figure 4 shows the same debate used to generate Figure 3 but using the interruptions made by individual speakers to establish links.

From Figure 4 it can be seen that using interrupting information, instead of semantic similarity, is not sufficient to disclose the complexity of the debates. In fact MPs take turns to speak according to a pre-agreed list or when the "chief officer" (chair) calls each MP to speak, thus interruptions are not necessarily a good means of generating a debate graph.

Classifier	Precision (P)			Recall (R)			F-Measure (F)			Accuracy (A)		
	Aye	Nay	Avg.	Aye	Nay	Avg.	Aye	Nay	Avg.	Aye	Nay	Avg.
J48	0.934	0.938	0.936	0.938	0.938	0.936	0.934	0.938	0.936	0.934	0.938	0.936
JRip	0.731	0.938	0.838	0.953	0.672	0.808	0.827	0.783	0.805	0.953	0.672	0.808
SMO	0.600	0.627	0.614	0.602	0.624	0.614	0.601	0.626	0.614	0.602	0.624	0.614
NB	0.511	0.554	0.533	0.607	0.456	0.529	0.555	0.500	0.527	0.607	0.456	0.529
IBk	0.487	0.580	0.535	0.955	0.059	0.492	0.645	0.107	0.367	0.955	0.059	0.492
Min	0.487	0.554	0.533	0.602	0.059	0.492	0.555	0.107	0.367	0.602	0.059	0.492
Max	0.934	0.938	0.936	0.955	0.938	0.936	0.934	0.938	0.936	0.955	0.938	0.936
Average	0.653	0.727	0.691	0.811	0.550	0.676	0.712	0.591	0.650	0.810	0.550	0.676
SD	0.184	0.194	0.185	0.189	0.324	0.190	0.161	0.317	0.225	0.188	0.324	0.190

Table 4. Comparison of classification performance (using all features) with respect to a number of classifier generators

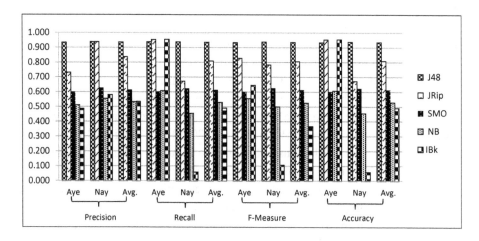

Figure 5. Data presented in Table 4 in presented in the form of a bar chart.

5 Evaluation

One of the challenges of work on debate graph generation is the lack of "ground truth" data. In some cases it is possible to construct such graphs by hand, however this still entails subjectivity and requires a considerable resource (to the extent that it is not possible to derive significant bench mark data). However, it was possible to test the operation of the classifier by training it on a proportion of the data and testing it on the remainder. More precisely Ten-fold Cross Validation (TCV) was adopted. Two sets of experiments were conducted. The first tested the operation of the proposed approach in the context of classifier generation without feature selection. The second tested the effect of feature selection. To this end a number of different classification techniques were considered from those available in the Weka-3.6 workbench[5]: (i) Naive Bayes, (ii) Support Vector Machine SMO, (iii) J48 decision tree learner, (iv) JRip rules-based classier and (v) IBk nearest neighbour classier.

The classification results (without feature selection) are presented in Table 4. Note that for each classifier the overall precision, recall, accuracy and F-measure (with respect to both the Aye and the Nay classes) were recorded. The F-measure (the harmonic mean of precision and recall) combines the precision and recall values and is a good overall measure. The same results as presented in Table 4 are presented in Figure 5 using a bar-chart format. From the table (and the figure) it can be observed that excellent results were obtained using the J48 classifier generator which outperformed all the other classifiers including the SMO classifier, this was a surprising result as SVMs are usually considered to be well suited to text classification [Joachims 1998]. Good results were also obtained using the JRip classifier. The worst recorded average recall and F-measure (0.492, and 0.367 respectively) were obtained using the IBk classifier, while the worst recorded average precision (0.533) was obtained using the Naive Bayes classifier. Inspection of Table 4 also indicates that there is no discernible difference with respect to the operation of the classifiers with respect to either the Aye or the Nay class.

The results with respect to the experiments directed at determining the effect that feature selection had on the process is presented in Figure 6 which presents a plot of recorded F-measures against different values of k for χ^2 feature selection using the different classifier mechanisms considered. From the figure it can be seen that best results were obtained when $k = 1000$ in conjunction with J48. It is also interesting to note that feature selection makes very little difference to JRip, while higher values of k have an adverse effect on SMO, NB and IBk.

---

[5]http://www.cs.waikato.ac.nz/ml/weka/downloading.html/

6 Conclusions

In this paper we have described a data mining approach to the generation of debate graphs from transcripts of debates. The objective of the research described was to assess the use of text mining techniques for extracting debate graphs from debate transcriptions in order to use the generated graphs to predict debate outcomes in future work. The operation of the framework was illustrated and evaluated using 100 debates taken from the proceedings of the Commons Chamber which are published on-line at TheyWorkForYou.com (in XML form). The promising results obtained so far indicate that: (i) it is possible to capture debate structure using text mining techniques to accurately label nodes in the graph according to speaker attitude and links in the graph according to whether pairs of speakers support or oppose each other, and (iii) the graphs can be effectively used to visualise political debates. Future work will initially be directed at consideration of lexicon based techniques, more specifically the utilisation of a "sentiment lexicon" to identify the attitude of speakers from their speeches. It is also deemed desirable to obtain a larger collection of debates (UKHCD3) with which to conduct further experiments. In the longer term the authors wish to be able to predict debate outcomes using the structure of the debate graph so far.

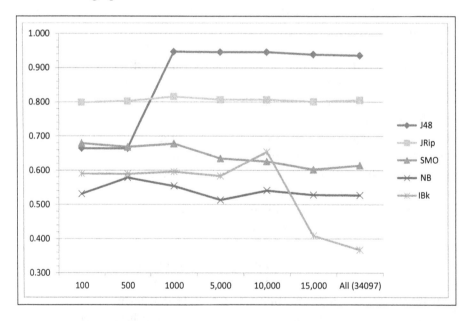

Figure 6. Plot of recorded F-Measure values against different k values for χ^2 feature selection in the context of a number of different classifiers.

Bibliography

[Borgatti 2002] Borgatti, S.P. (2002). NetDraw Software for Network Visualization. Analytic Technologies: Lexington, KY, USA.

[Braak *et al.* 2006] van den Braak, S.W., van Oostendorp, H., Prakken, H. and Vreeswijk, G.A.W. (2006). A critical review of argument visualization tools: do users become better reasoners? Workshop Notes of the ECAI-2006 Workshop on Computational Models of Natural Argument (CMNA VI), pp67-75.

[Chin & Deng 2008] Chim, H. and Deng, X. (2008). Efficient Phrase-Based Document Similarity for Clustering. IEEE Transactions on Knowledge and Data Engineering, 20(9), pp1217-1229.

[Dung 1995] Dung, P.M. (1995). On the acceptability of arguments and its fundamental role in non monotonic reasoning, logic programming and n-person games. Artificial Intelligence, Vol 77, pp321-357.

[Gordon 2007] Gordon, T. (2007) Visualizing Carneades Argument Graphs. Law, Probability and Risk, Vol. 6. Issue 1-4, pp109-117.

[Hariharan & Srinivasan 2008] Hariharan, S. and Srinivasan, R. (2008). A Comparison of Similarity Measures for Text Documents. Journal of Information Knowledge Management, 7(1), pp1-8.

[Jiang *et al.* 2010] Jiang, C., Coenen, F., Sanderson, R. and Zito, M. (2010). Text Classification using Graph Mining-Based Feature Extraction. Knowledge Based Systems, Vol 23(4), Oct. 2010, pp302-308.

[Joachims 1998] Joachims, T. (1998). Text Categorization with Support Vector Machines: Learning with Many Relevant Features Proc. 10th European Conference on Machine Learning (ECML'98), pp137-142.

[Kaptein *et al.* 2009] Kaptein, K., Marx, M. and Kamps, J. (2009). Who said what to whom? capturing the structure of debates. Proc. 32nd international ACM SIGIR conference on Research and development in information retrieval (SIGIR'09), pp831-832.

[Kuhn *et al.* 2007] Kuhn, A., Ducasse, S. and Gírba, T. (2007). Semantic clustering: Identifying topics in source code. Information and Software Technology, 49(3), pp230-243.

[Li *et al.* 2009] Li, H.-M., Sun, C.-X. and Wan, K.-J. (2009). Clustering web search results using conceptual grouping. Proc. 8th International Conference on Machine Learning and Cybernetics, pp12-15.

[Madylova & Oguducu 2009] Madylova, A. and Oguducu, S.G. (2009). Comparison of similarity measures for clustering Turkish documents. Intelligent Data Analysis, 13, pp815-832.

[Poomagal & Hamsapriya 2011] Poomagal, S. and Hamsapriya, T. (2011). K-Means for Search Results Clustering Using URL and Tag Contents. Proc. International Conference on Process Automation, Control and Computing (PACC), pp1-7.

[Reed *et al.* 2004] Reed, C.A. and Rowe, G.W.A. Rowe, G. and Reed, C. (2004). Argument Diagramming: The Araucaria Project. International Journal of AI Tools, 13 (4), pp961-980.

[Thomas *et al.* 2006] Thomas, M., Pang, P. and Lee, L. (2006). Get out the vote: Determining support or opposition from Congressional floor-debate transcripts. Proc. EMNLP, pp327-335.

[Wang *et al.* 2009] Wang, Y.J., Coenen, F. and Sanderson, R. (2009). A Hybrid Statistical Data Pre-processing Approach for Language-independent Text Classification. Proc. 5th Int. Conf. on Advanced Data Mining and Applications (ADMA 2009), Springer Springer LNCS 5678, pp338-349.

Propositional Encodings of Value-based Argumentation Questions

PAUL E. DUNNE*

Abstract

A common approach used to deal with computationally hard problems, i.e. NP-hard or higher levels of complexity, is that of expressing instances, x, of a problem as a propositional formula, φ_x so that models of φ_x can be mapped to solutions of the problem itself. In this way, it becomes possible to exploit the considerable technology available in the form of highly-tuned satisfiability solvers. In this paper we examine encodings of the standard subjective acceptance *problem in value-based argumentation as propositional formulae.*

Introduction

Argumentation is established as a central sub-discipline within AI – an overview of its importance in this regard may be found in the survey of [13]. The abstract model of argumentation frameworks (AFs) put forward by [21] nearly twenty years ago, has been the focus of extensive study as a paradigm for computationally effective treatment of argument analysis. Such studies have embraced issues including semantics, see e.g. the survey of [4]; algorithms and complexity, e.g. [20], [22], [23], [27], [30], [36, 38, 39], [51]; proof-theoretic matters, e.g. [28], [50, 54, 55, 56]; game-theoretic approaches, e.g. [48], [52]; dynamic and update approaches, e.g. [9, 17, 18], [45], *et cetera*.

One of the richest sources of recent work stemming from Dung's proposal is the consideration of formalisms which extend the basic graph-theoretic abstraction underpinning the model from [21]. Amongst such methods one finds divers approaches to *weighted* argumentation frameworks such as [8, 34], formulations and treatments of "attack strength" [47, 31]; and several proposals through which attacks may be "disregarded" under certain conditions. This last group includes both methods operating purely within Dung's model itself, e.g.

---

*University of Liverpool, Department of Computer Science

the resolution-based semantics from [7] and techniques based on configuring some additional structural element, e.g. [1, 6, 5], [16, 15, 19, 35, 49].

Of these developments it is Bench-Capon's proposal of *value-based argumentation frameworks* in [5] (henceforward referred to as VAFs) that has, arguably, attracted the most intensive subsequent study. In the VAF model, Bench-Capon offers a rationale (built on ideas originating from [53]) by which the plurality of "conflicting acceptable" arguments[1] in classical AFs can be formally explained. This stems from Searle's insight that the mutual acceptability of superficially conflicting positions can be explained in terms of differing (qualitative) value judgements. That is to say, an individual, X say, may accept an argument x attacked by another argument y, by reason of viewing the social or ethical *value* promoted by x as having greater import than that endorsed by y. In total, VAFs retain much of the elegant abstract flavour of Dung's approach wherein arguments are treated as atomic entities interacting through an "attack relation". They add to this, however, the awareness that attacks may *rationally* be ignored: i.e. by agents (*audiences* in the terminology of [5]) for whom the value of an attacked argument outweighs the value(s) of its attackers.

The semantics of Dung's model and those proposed in its wake from VAFs onwards offer a rich panoply of representation and reasoning capabilities. In at least one *computational* aspect, however, all of these approaches must contend with one issue: the underlying computational complexity of fundamental decision questions, e.g. determining whether an argument is justified with respect to a particular semantics in a given model.

Starting from the pioneering analysis of [20] and continuing through contributions of [27], [38], [22, 23], [7] and [37] has led to a near complete appreciation of the complexity landscape in Dung's AFs. As a result, *pace* some rare exceptions such as Dung's grounded semantics, the standard acceptability questions are known to range in hardness from NP and coNP-complete ([20]) up to Σ_2^p and Π_2^p-complete ([27, 38]). Such phenomena continue (and are, arguably, exacerbated) within the enhancements of AFs outlined earlier: for example, weighted systems [34], strength of attack models, [31], and extended AFs [35].

Unsurprisingly, VAF semantics have proved to be no exception: the standard acceptance problems being classified as NP and coNP-complete in [29], (see also [11]). Within VAFs a further obstacle arises: while classical AFs have a number of so-called *tractable fragments*[2] such cases do not, however, retain

---

[1]The reader should note that the terms "conflicting" and "acceptable" are used informally rather than with the technical meaning presented in Section 1.

[2]That is, special instances for which decision questions can be dealt with efficiently.

their tractable status when treated as VAFS. Thus even severely limited topologies, such as binary trees in which no value is common to more than three arguments, fail to yield tractable domains [22]. In fact until quite recently with the work of [24, 43] no non-trivial tractable fragments, insensitive to the number of values involved, had been identified.

Our aim in this article is to examine one mechanism to developing feasible methods for decision problems in VAFS. The underlying motivation for our approach comes from the extensive body of research into efficient propositional satisfiability solvers. Not only has this produced an effective battery of highly-tuned heuristic solvers, e.g. as presented in the survey of Gu *et al.* [42], it has also provided a supporting base with which the usefulness of general paradigms for tackling notionally intractable problems can be explored, e.g. fixed-parameter tractability, [41], randomised methods building on average-case behaviour such as [57] or so-called phase-transition phenomena, see, e.g [26, 32, 33].

The existence of such systems is one of the key reasons for considering the following approach to constructing algorithms: given an instance, I, of some problem, build a propositional formula, φ_I from I, for which models of φ_I can be mapped to solutions for I (and *vice-versa*). The concept of finding propositional encodings for argumentation settings has already been adopted in earlier work. For example [40] construct quantified formula representations capturing various decision properties within the assumption-based frameworks of [14]. Within Dung's formalism itself, encodings of some standard problems as propositional formulae have been given in [27].

In the remainder of this article we present background from [21] and [5] in Section 1. In Section 2 we present our encodings for the two principal decision questions in VAFS and discuss some consequences of these. Conclusions and further directions for research are offered in Section 3.

1 Background

We begin by recalling the concept of abstract argumentation framework and terminology from [21] and outline the main computational problems that have been of interest within it.

1.1 Dung's abstract model of argument

Definition 1. An *argumentation framework* (AF) is a pair $\mathcal{H} = \langle \mathcal{X}, \mathcal{A} \rangle$, in which $\mathcal{X}$ is a finite[3] set of *arguments* and $\mathcal{A} \subseteq \mathcal{X} \times \mathcal{X}$ is the *attack relationship* for $\mathcal{H}$. A pair $\langle x, y \rangle \in \mathcal{A}$ is referred to as '*y is attacked by x*' or '*x attacks y*'.

---

[3]In Dung's original article, this restriction to finite sets of arguments is not used.

Table 1. Decision Problems in AFs

Problem Name	Question
Verification (VER$_\sigma$)	Is $S \in \mathcal{E}_\sigma(\mathcal{H})$?
Credulous Acceptance (CA$_\sigma$)	$\exists S \in \mathcal{E}_\sigma(\mathcal{H})$ for which $x \in S$?
Sceptical Acceptance (SA$_\sigma$)	$\forall T \in \mathcal{E}_\sigma(\mathcal{H})$ is $x \in T$?
Existence (EXISTS$_\sigma$)	Is $\mathcal{E}_\sigma(\mathcal{H}) \neq \emptyset$?
Emptiness (VER$_\sigma^\emptyset$)	Is $\mathcal{E}_s(\mathcal{H}) = \{\emptyset\}$?

For $S \subseteq \mathcal{X}$,

$$S^- =_{\text{def}} \{ p : \exists q \in S \text{ such that } \langle p, q \rangle \in \mathcal{A} \}$$
$$S^+ =_{\text{def}} \{ p : \exists q \in S \text{ such that } \langle q, p \rangle \in \mathcal{A} \}$$

An argument $x \in \mathcal{X}$ is *acceptable with respect to* S if for every $y \in \mathcal{X}$ that attacks x there is some $z \in S$ that attacks y. A subset, S, is *conflict-free* if no argument in S is attacked by any other argument in S. A conflict-free set S is *admissible* if every $y \in S$ is acceptable w.r.t S and S is a *preferred extension* if it is a maximal (with respect to $\subseteq$) admissible set. A subset, S, is a *stable extension* if S is conflict free and every $y \notin S$ is attacked by S. The *grounded extension* of $\langle \mathcal{X}, \mathcal{A} \rangle$ is the subset $\mathcal{X}$ obtained by iterating the following process: given $S \subseteq \mathcal{X}$, let $\mathcal{F}(S)$ be the set of arguments *acceptable* to S. Letting $\mathcal{F}^0(S)$ denote S and $\mathcal{F}^{i+1}(S) = \mathcal{F}(\mathcal{F}^i(S))$ ($i \geq 0$), the *grounded extension* of $\langle \mathcal{X}, \mathcal{A} \rangle$ is the least fixed point of $\mathcal{F}(\emptyset)$, i.e. the set of arguments $\mathcal{F}^k(\emptyset)$ where k is the smallest value satisfying $\mathcal{F}^k(\emptyset) = \mathcal{F}^{k+1}(\emptyset)$. It is shown in [21] that the grounded extension is well-defined and unique.

For a given semantics σ and AF, $\mathcal{H}(\mathcal{X}, \mathcal{A})$ we use $\mathcal{E}_\sigma$ to denote the set of all subsets of $\mathcal{X}$ that satisfy the conditions specified by σ.

Informally, the canonical decision problems are *Verification* (VER), *Credulous Acceptance* (CA) and *Sceptical Acceptance* (SA): VER$_\sigma$, refers to the decision problem of verifying that a given set of arguments satisfies the conditions of the semantics σ, i.e. that the set is in the collection $\mathcal{E}_\sigma$; CA$_\sigma$ that of deciding if a given argument, x, is a member of some set, S, in $\mathcal{E}_\sigma$; while $\mathcal{S}_\sigma$ asks whether an argument belongs to *every* set in $\mathcal{E}_\sigma$. The formal definitions of these problems for AFs is presented in Table 1. In the case of preferred extensions we note that $\mathcal{S}_{pr}(\mathcal{H}, x)$ is captured by the quantified formula:

$$\forall S \subseteq \mathcal{X} \exists T \subseteq \mathcal{X}(x \in S) \vee (S \notin \mathcal{E}_{adm}(\mathcal{H})) \vee ((S \subset T) \wedge (T \in \mathcal{E}_{adm}(\mathcal{H}))$$

whose satisfiability can be decided in Π_2^p: i.e. x is sceptically accepted w.r.t. preferred extensions if and only if every admissible subset S of $\mathcal{X}$, either contains x or fails to be a *maximal* admissible set.

1.2 Bench-Capon's value-based argumentation frameworks

In [5], *value-based* argumentation frameworks (VAFs) are introduced. These provide a mechanism for describing the phenomenon that the acceptability status of an argument may be coloured by the fact that its endorsers view the value (in the sense of ethical, legal or other qualitative assessment) as having greater importance than the values promoted by the argument's attackers.

Definition 2. A *value-based argumentation framework* (VAF) is defined by a tuple $\mathcal{H} = \langle \mathcal{X}, \mathcal{A}, \mathcal{V}, \eta \rangle$ in which the pair $\langle \mathcal{X}, \mathcal{A} \rangle$ forms a standard AF (in the sense of Defn. 1), $\mathcal{V} = \{v_1, v_2, \ldots, v_k\}$ is a set of *values* and $\eta : \mathcal{X} \to \mathcal{V}$ a mapping which associates a value in $\mathcal{V}$ with each $x \in \mathcal{X}$. A *specific audience* over $\mathcal{V}$ is a total ordering, $\succ$, of $\mathcal{V}$. For such an audience, α, an attack $\langle x, y \rangle \in \mathcal{A}$ is said to be *successful* if it is *not* the case that $\eta(y) \succ_\alpha \eta(x)$, i.e. when x and y have the same value then $\langle x, y \rangle$ is always successful otherwise $\langle x, y \rangle$ succeeds with respect to α only if $\eta(x) \succ_\alpha \eta(y)$: the value promoted by x is considered more important (to the audience α) than that supported by y.

For a specific audience α and VAF $\mathcal{H}(\langle \mathcal{X}, \mathcal{A}, \mathcal{V}, \eta \rangle)$ the standard AF *induced by* α, $\mathcal{H}^{(\alpha)}$, has arguments $\mathcal{X}$ and attack set $\mathcal{A}_\alpha$ given by

$$\mathcal{A}_\alpha = \mathcal{A} \setminus \{\langle x, y \rangle : \eta(y) \succ_\alpha \eta(x)\}$$

so that $\mathcal{A}_\alpha$ contains only those attacks in $\mathcal{A}$ which are successful w.r.t. α.

The concept of induced framework now allows the set of subsets, $\mathcal{E}_{pr}^{vaf}$ to be described through,

$$\mathcal{E}_{pr}^{vaf}(\mathcal{H}) = \bigcup_\alpha \mathcal{E}_{pr}(\mathcal{H}^{(\alpha)})$$

In Bench-Capon's original presentation the restriction that VAFs do not contain *directed* cycles of arguments with identical values is imposed: this suffices to ensure that $\mathcal{E}_{pr}(\mathcal{H}^{(\alpha)})$ contains exactly one set since the induced AF is acyclic.

The decision problems *subjective* (SBA) and *objective* (OBA) acceptance whose instances are a VAF, $\mathcal{H}$, and argument x, are given by,

$$\text{SBA}(\langle \mathcal{H}, x \rangle) \quad \Leftrightarrow \quad \exists \alpha \ s.t. \ \text{CA}_{pr}(\langle \mathcal{H}^{(\alpha)}, x \rangle)$$
$$\text{OBA}(\langle \mathcal{H}, x \rangle) \quad \Leftrightarrow \quad \forall \alpha \ \text{CA}_{pr}(\langle \mathcal{H}^{(\alpha)}, x \rangle)$$

2 Propositional Encodings of SBA and OBA

We now turn to the main technical material of this article: given a VAF, $\mathcal{H}$, we construct a propositional formula $\varphi_\mathcal{H}(Z)$ for which subjectively and objectively accepted arguments are determined via suitable (i.e. satisfying) assignments to Z.

We recall that a propositional formula, ψ over variables $X = \langle x_1, \ldots, x_n \rangle$ is in *conjunctive normal form* (CNF) if ψ has the form

$$C_1 \quad \& \quad C_2 \quad \& \quad \cdots \quad \& \quad C_m$$

where each C_j (*clause*) is of the form

$$y_{j,1} \quad \vee \quad y_{j,2} \quad \vee \quad \cdots \quad \vee \quad y_{j,t_j}$$

and each $y_{j,k}$ is a *literal* – $\neg x$ or x – over some variable from X. An assignment $\alpha = \langle a_1, \ldots, a_n \rangle$ of Boolean values to X *satisfies* a CNF $\psi(X)$ if every clause of ψ contains at least one literal that evaluates to $\top$ under α, i.e. some $\neg x_i$ with $a_i = \bot$ or x_i with $a_i = \top$.

Given a VAF, $\mathcal{H} = \langle \mathcal{X}, \mathcal{A}, \mathcal{V}, \eta \rangle$ in which $\mathcal{X} = \langle x_1, \ldots, x_n \rangle$ and $\mathcal{V} = \{v_1, \ldots, v_m\}$ the propositional formula $\varphi_{\mathcal{H}}$ uses variables

$$\begin{aligned} X &= \{ x_i \,:\, 1 \leq i \leq n \} \\ V &= \{ v_{i,j} \,:\, 1 \leq i, j \leq m \} \end{aligned}$$

The formula, $\varphi_{\mathcal{H}}(X, V)$ is built as

$$\varphi_{\mathcal{H}}(X, V) \;=\; Audience(V) \quad \& \quad cf(X, V) \quad \& \quad defensive(X, V)$$

For the construction presented we will show,

Theorem 1. *Given $\mathcal{H} = \langle \mathcal{X}, \mathcal{A}, \mathcal{V}, \eta \rangle$ and $x \in \mathcal{X}$ it holds that*

$$\text{SBA}(\mathcal{H}, x) \quad \Leftrightarrow \quad (x) \quad \& \quad \varphi_{\mathcal{H}}(X, V) \text{ is satisfiable.} \tag{SBA}$$

Now let $\mathcal{H}' = \langle \mathcal{X}', \mathcal{A}', \mathcal{V}, \eta' \rangle$ be the VAF obtained from $\mathcal{H}$ by adding arguments $\{x' \,:\, x \in \mathcal{X}\}$ with $\eta'(x') = \eta(x)$ and attacks $\{\langle x, x' \rangle \,:\, x \in \mathcal{X}\}$. For each $x \in \mathcal{X}$ it holds that

$$\text{OBA}(\mathcal{H}, x) \quad \Leftrightarrow \quad \neg \, \text{SBA}(\mathcal{H}', x') \tag{OBA}$$

The proof of Theorem 1 is given following the detailed construction of $\varphi_{\mathcal{H}}$.

We now turn to the role of the variable sets V and X and the specification of the sub-formulae *Audience*, *cf*, and *defensive*.

2.1   The variable set V and the sub-formula $Audience(V)$

The propositional variables V are used in $\varphi_{\mathcal{H}}$ as follows: $v_{i,j}$ taking the value $\top$ in a satisfying assignment of $\varphi_{\mathcal{H}}$ corresponds to the value preference $v_i \succ v_j$.

In describing value-based acceptability (subjective or objective) we are only interested in valuations of $v_{i,j}$ which map to specific audiences. This requirement imposes three conditions on the propositional values that $v_{i,j}$ may assume:

V1. For $i \neq j$, *exactly* one of $v_{i,j}$, $v_{j,i}$ is assigned $\top$, i.e. in a specific audi-ence exactly one of $v_i \succ v_j$ or $v_j \succ v_i$ holds.

V2. For all i, $v_{i,i}$ cannot be assigned $\top$, i.e. the ordering relation is *irreflex-ive*.

V3. For each triple $\langle i, j, k \rangle \in [1, \ldots, m]^3$ if both $v_{i,j}$ and $v_{j,k}$ are assigned $\top$ then $v_{i,k}$ must be assigned $\top$, i.e. a specific audience is a (total) *ordering* of $\mathcal{V}$ and, therefore, *transitive*.

The first of these is captured through the CNF formula,

$$ExactlyOne(V) \;=\; \bigwedge_{i=1}^{m-1} \bigwedge_{j=i+1}^{m} (v_{i,j} \lor v_{j,i}) \land (\neg v_{i,j} \lor \neg v_{j,i})$$

It is easily seen that that (V2) is described through

$$Irreflexive(V) \;=\; \bigwedge_{i=1}^{m} \neg\, v_{i,i}$$

Finally for the transitivity condition (V3) we have

$$Trans(V) \;=\; \bigwedge_{i=1}^{m} \bigwedge_{j=1}^{m} \bigwedge_{k=1}^{m} (v_{i,j} \;\&\; v_{j,k} \to v_{i,k})$$

which translates to CNF through the equivalence

$$(v_{i,j} \;\&\; v_{j,k} \to v_{i,k}) \;\equiv\; (\neg v_{i,j} \lor \neg v_{j,k} \lor v_{i,k})$$

In total the sub-formula $Audience(V)$ is the CNF corresponding to

$$ExactlyOne(V) \;\;\&\;\; Irreflexive(V) \;\;\&\;\; Trans(V)$$

2.2 The variable set X and sub-formulae $cf(X, V)$, $defensive(X, V)$

The variable set X is used to encode membership in admissible sets, i.e. should x_i be assigned $\top$ then the formula $\varphi_{\mathcal{H}}(X, V)$ will be satisfiable in such an assignment if and only x_i belongs to the resulting preferred extension of the (acyclic) AF induced through some specific audience.

In such a preferred extension its set of arguments must be conflict-free within the framework induced through the relevant specific audience, i.e. should $\langle x_i, x_j \rangle \in \mathcal{A}$ and we have a satisfying assignment of $\varphi_{\mathcal{H}}(X, V)$ with $x_i =$

$x_j = \top$ then the audience must be configured so that $\eta(x_j) \succ \eta(x_i)$. This yields,

$$cf(X,V) \;=\; \bigwedge_{\langle x_i, x_j \rangle \in \mathcal{A}} \left(\neg x_i \vee \neg x_j \vee v_{\eta(x_j),\eta(x_i)} \right)$$

For defensiveness we need to ensure that whenever $x_i = \top \; x_j = \bot$, and $\langle x_j, x_i \rangle \in \mathcal{A}$ that any potential satisfying assignment of $\varphi_{\mathcal{H}}$ is such that either $\eta(x_i) \succ \eta(x_j)$ or x_i will have a defence (counter-attacker) available to x_j *and* that the value ordering does not rank the value of x_j as having greater importance than the value of this defender. We thus obtain the sub-formula for *defensive*(X,V):

$$\bigwedge_{\langle x_i, x_j \rangle \in \mathcal{A}} \left(\neg x_j \vee v_{\eta(x_j),\eta(x_i)} \vee \bigvee_{x_k \in \{x_i\}^-} x_k \; \& \; \left(\neg v_{\eta(x_i),\eta(x_k)} \right) \right)$$

Of course, this encoding of the conditions *defensive*(X,V) is not in CNF. Before dealing with this minor complication we return to the

Proof: (of Thm 1) For the first part (subjective acceptance) consider $\mathcal{H}$, x_i and $\varphi_{\mathcal{H}}(X,V)$. Suppose that x_i is subjectively accepted in $\mathcal{H}$ via the specific audience α and the subset S of $\mathcal{X}$. Consider the assignment, $(\underline{x}, \underline{v})$ to (X,V) in which

$$x := \top \quad \text{if} \quad x \in S \quad ; \quad x := \bot \quad \text{if} \quad x \notin S$$
$$v_{i,j} := \top \quad \text{if} \quad v_i \succ_\alpha v_j \quad ; \quad v_{i,j} := \bot \quad \text{if} \quad (i = j) \text{ or } (v_j \succ_\alpha v_i)$$

It is not hard to see that $\underline{v}$ satisfies the formula $Audience(V)$: α is a specific audience so for distinct values v_i and v_j exactly one of $v_i \succ_\alpha v_j$, $v_j \succ_\alpha v_i$ holds. Similarly such audiences define irreflexive and transitive orderings of V ensuring that the corresponding sub-formulae of $Audience(V)$ are satisfied by the assignment constructed. Similarly, since S must be conflict-free (and defensive) with respect to the specific audience α it follows that $(\underline{x}, \underline{v})$ will satisfy the formula $(x_i) \; \& \; cf(X,V) \; \& \; defensive(X,V)$. Hence from SBA$(\mathcal{H}, x_i)$ we have formed a satisfying assignment of $(x_i) \; \& \; \varphi_{\mathcal{H}}(X,V)$ as required. That $(\underline{x}, \underline{v})$ also satisfies $cf(X,V) \; \& \; defensive(X,V)$ is immediate from the construction of these formulae and the fact that S with respect to the specific audience α is conflict-free and defends itself against attacks.

For the converse implication, suppose that $(\underline{x}, \underline{v})$ satisfies $x_i \; \& \; \varphi_{\mathcal{H}}(X,V)$. Consider the subset S of $\mathcal{X}$ for which $x_j \in S$ if and only if $x_j = \top$ in

$\underline{x}$ together with the specific audience, α, in which $v_i \succ_\alpha v_j$ if and only if $v_{i,j} = \top$ in $\underline{v}$. That α is well-defined follows from the fact that $\underline{v}$ satisfies *Audience*(V). In addition $x_i \in S$ and S is conflict-free w.r.t. α: $(\underline{x}, \underline{v})$ satisfies the associated sub-formulae, (x_i), $cf(X, V)$ and $defensive(X, V)$.

We deduce that SBA$(\mathcal{H}, x_i)$ if and only if (x_i) & $\varphi_\mathcal{H}(X, V)$ is satisfiable.

For the second part (objective acceptance) it suffices to observe that were some x' to be subjectively acceptable in $\mathcal{H}'$ then x could not be objectively accepted in $\mathcal{H}$ (or $\mathcal{H}'$): since $\eta'(x') = \eta'(x)$ we cannot have both present in a preferred extension induced by any α. Similarly, if x' is *not* subjectively acceptable, from the fact that the preferred extension induced by a specific audience is, in fact, a *stable* extension, it must be the case that any such extension not containing x' thereby contains x. Since no specific audience induces an AF in which x' is accepted (by the premise) it follows that for every specific audience x is in the corresponding extension. That is, x is objectively accepted. □

We now deal with the fact that our formula encoding $defensive(X, V)$ is not in CNF, i.e. the formula

$$\bigwedge_{\langle x_i, x_j \rangle \in \mathcal{A}} \left(\neg x_j \vee v_{\eta(x_j), \eta(x_i)} \vee \bigvee_{x_k \in \{x_i\}^-} x_k \ \& \ (\neg v_{\eta(x_i), \eta(x_k)}) \right)$$

There are a number of alternative ways of dealing with this. We could modify $\mathcal{H}$ so that $\max\{|\{x\}^+|, |\{x\}^-|\} \le 2$ (following the construction outlined in [22])[4] so that we could directly apply equivalences translating

$$(p \vee q_1 \ \& \ r_1 \vee q_2 \ \& \ r_2)$$

without incurring significant increase (i.e. exponentially larger) in the formula size. While such translations to bound the number of attacks on a given argument result in only a linear increase in the overall size of $\mathcal{X}$, rather than amend the structure of $\mathcal{H}$ we adopt a solution that modifies the form of $\varphi_\mathcal{H}$. This will incur the cost of having to introduce an additional set of variables, denoted

$$Y = \{ y_{i,j} : \langle x_i, x_j \rangle \in \mathcal{A}\}$$

We then replace the formula above by,

$$\bigwedge_{\langle x_i, x_j \rangle \in \mathcal{A}} \left(\neg x_j \vee v_{\eta(x_j), \eta(x_i)} \vee \bigvee_{x_k \in \{x_i\}^-} y_{i,k} \right)$$

---

[4]This construction preserves the acceptability status of arguments in $\mathcal{X}$ in the sense that $x \in \mathcal{X}$ is subjectively (objectively) accepted in the original VAF if and only if x is subjectively (objectively) accepted in the modified VAF.

Of course in order to preserve the properties proven in Thm. 1 it is necessary to ensure that $y_{i,k}$ cannot be arbitrarily assigned Boolean values in satisfying assignments, i.e. we need to ensure that for each $y_{i,k}$,

$$y_{i,k} \equiv (x_k) \; \& \; (\neg v_{\eta(x_i),\eta(x_k)}) \tag{EQ}$$

thereby introducing (at most) $|\mathcal{A}|$ further terms in the specification of $\varphi_{\mathcal{H}}$. We now can use three clauses to replace each (EQ) term, i.e.

$$(\neg y_{i,k} \vee x_k) \; \& \; (\neg y_{i,k} \vee v_{\eta(x_i),\eta(x_k)}) \; \& \; (y_{i,k} \vee \neg x_k \vee v_{\eta(x_i),\eta(x_k)})$$

To summarise, the encodings presented above yield two translations of a VAF $\mathcal{H} = \langle \mathcal{X}, \mathcal{A}, \mathcal{V}, \eta \rangle$ to propositional formulae.

T1. The (non-CNF) formula $\varphi_{\mathcal{H}}(X, V)$ for which $x \in \mathcal{X}$ is subjectively acceptable in $\mathcal{H}$ if and only if $(x) \; \& \; \varphi_{\mathcal{H}}(X, V)$ is satisfiable.

T2. The CNF $\varphi_{\mathcal{H}}(X, V, Y)$ (with $|Y| = |\mathcal{A}|$) in which, again, $x \in \mathcal{X}$, is subjectively acceptable in $\mathcal{H}$ if and only if $(x) \; \& \; \varphi_{\mathcal{H}}(X, V, Y)$ is satisfiable.

3   Conclusion

In the preceding section we have presented a number of encodings of acceptability questions in the VAF model of [5] in terms of satisfiability problems on propositional formulae: the initial encoding for subjective acceptance being presented in a non-CNF style and subsequent representations into equivalent CNF forms given. For the CNF translation one may either choose a "direct" translation with the cost of of introducing additional arguments into the source VAF or (if the source VAF is unaltered) accomplish this by the use of auxiliary propositional variables. In this concluding section we, briefly, discuss some aspects of these translations together with possible directions for future exploitation.

3.1   Directing search strategies

Many satisfiability solvers seek solutions through identifying (either dynamically or by fixing a static ordering) variables which are "best suited" to pruning the potential search space. Thus one has mechanisms such as first dealing with "unit" clauses in CNF instances such cases forcing exactly one setting of the variable involved that could be consistent with a satisfying setting. The literal phrasing of SBA (in terms of "there exists an audience") suggests exploring heuristics which reduce the number of potential value orderings to examine.[5] Inspecting the structure of $\varphi_{\mathcal{H}}(X, V)$ suggests that there may be cases where progress towards a satisfying assignment may be more rapidly attained by concentrating on the sub-formulae represented by $cf(X, V)$ and $defensive(X, V)$ and subsequently identifying an audience consistent with a putative satisfying assignment of these. Overall it would be of interest to consider variable selection strategies and their interpretation within VAFs in order to gain further insight into the nature and obstacles to efficient decision processes.

3.2 Propositional Proof Theories and Value-based Reasoning

A considerable body of literature has been dedicated to the development of sound and complete proof stategies for determining the validity of propositional tautologies. Similarly in Dung's abstract AFs a significant line of research has focused on sound and complete "dialogue" games for determining argument status under various semantics, e.g. [28, 50, 54, 55, 56]. Explicit links between the TPI game of [56] and the CUT-free sequent (Gentzen) calculus for propositional validity were demonstrated in [28]. In [11] similar methods are developed directed at value-based argumentation. A detailed analysis and exploration of mappings between propositional proof calculi and reasoning games within value-based frameworks *á la* [28] has, however, yet to be undertaken. It would be of interest to examine the extent to which translations such as those on which this article has focused might facilitate such study.

3.3 Reducing Number of Variables

An immediate (possible) concern regarding the encodings above is, of course, the fact that VAFs involving n arguments, m values and t attacks translate to propositional formulae with $n+m^2$ variables (an additional t being used for the CNF form) and that the number of clauses involved is $\max\{O(m^3), O(n^2)\}$. The quadratic increase in variable together with the cubic blow up in the actual formula size (as measured by the total number of occurrences of literals) presents a possible obstacle to gauging how effective the translation may prove to be. Preliminary empirical studies indicate that the space overheads, incurred in translating even moderate size (several hundred arguments and values) to CNF, are problematic. Finding improved translations (in the sense of reducing numbers of clauses used) of hard decision problems into CNF satisfiability has become increasingly important in recent years. It would, therefore, be of some interest to examine to what extent our translation is sub-optimal. Here the ob-

---

[5]It is worth noting that [24] adopts a similar approach in its identification of topologies for which the number of "relevant audiences" (in the paper's terminology) is polynomially bounded.

vious barrier is in representing the conditions that are encoded in the formula $Audience(V)$.

Afterword – Trevor Bench-Capon (a personal appreciation)

Given the occasion marked by this volume, it is only appropriate to add to the technical content some element of personal introspection.

I have worked at Liverpool University since 1985 and so Trevor's involvement in the department (from 1987) overlaps almost my entire professional career. Looking back over nearly a quarter of a century, I am struck not only by the extensive range of our collaboration but also by the manner in which much of this originated. We first worked together on [12][6] a paper whose genesis (if not subject matter!) was symptomatic of many future articles. Following the growth of interest in hypertext and computer supported cooperative writing in the later 1980s – an interest which turned out to be just one of those occasional obsessions in which Computer Science periodically becomes embroiled – the department at Liverpool had established a research group in this area. As often happens in such cases, technical reports and recent publications dedicated to the new specialism were readily available, with the result that I found myself perusing one of these – [44] – and managed to put together a short rather involved technical report building on this work. Just after this had appeared, Trevor came to my office, announcing "You should be doing another paper!" and proceeded to describe how this could be structured. The resulting article follurd the pattern of most of our subsequent joint work: with me concentrating on theoretical analysis, particularly involving computational complexity (what I referred to as "the easy stuff") while Trevor would elaborate motivation, significance and applicability (that is, "the difficult stuff"). While I could easily fill many more pages recalling the background and work on our subsequent collaborations, with regret on account of space limitations, I will focus on just four.

The first of these is [25][7]: a paper which was the first Liverpool article to be published in *Artificial Intelligence* and which owes its origins to Trevor's drawing my attention to the wealth of theoretical work appearing in this journal. My interest in formal computational properties of argumentation – in particular Dung's model – came about following Henry Prakken visiting Trevor and presenting a seminar based on [56]. Ultimately this led not only to [27] but also the article which (eventually) appeared as [28].[8] Finally, there is our in-

---

[6]This, in fact, was the first paper I had co-authored with anyone.

[7]The first – and very possibly last – citation this article receives.

[8]As Trevor will confirm, this paper had an unusual odyssey before eventually landing in the competent editorial harbour of AIJ.

troduction to the special issue of *Artificial Intelligence* on Argumentation [13] – an issue which Trevor and I co-edited – and which, it is fair to say, resulted in an increased awareness of argumentation as a computational paradigm. In his critique of film-making [46], the writer David Mamet has commented that an actor ought to feel satisfied if only a handful of memorable performances are achieved over their whole career. In this light, where Computer Science in common with so many scientific disciplines, all too often seems to produce only road signs confirming the destination of Gray's paths of glory, these papers are, I feel, noteworthy.

Most of the preceding commentary has concentrated on the significant benefits I feel have resulted from working with Trevor. It would be a huge oversight, however, to write about nothing outside this arena. Trevor, as is well-known, is a great aficionado of quiz competitions. Having some slight knowledge of those few areas where Trevor does not feel completely confident (obscure arthouse cinema, opera and classical music), I frequently accompanied him visiting local hostelries that had installed quiz machines offering cash payouts. In Liverpool in the late 1980s through to the mid 1990s, it was possible to obtain a moderate supplement to one's salary through careful investment of time in these. It was inevitably the case, however, that individuals who demonstrated some prowess with these machines, were liable to attract a modicum of attention. Of several such incidents, one particularly memorable, is that of Trevor, who disliked carrying large amounts of small change, filling at least half a dozen ash-trays (this being a time when bars still stocked such items as standard fittings) with assorted coins just won from the pub's machine, and asking the bar staff to exchange the contents for notes: an action which attracted the attention of the landlord sufficiently strongly as to result in him "requesting" we leave his establishment when we next visited about a week a later.

Another occurred in the now defunct *Black Horse and Rainbow* pub on Liverpool's Berry Street. For reasons which even now I find difficult to fathom, in addition to the presence of their quiz machine, Trevor felt this had some attractions as a place to have a beer. Being, myself, rather more cautious by nature, I tend to shy away from bars whose window display is reminiscent of the vitriol distillery from *L'assommoir* and whose habitués appeared to enjoy rousing games of heaving pint mugs at each other. Soon after entering and starting the machine, Trevor and I were approached by someone whom I recall as looking identical to the lead singer of the band *Hot Chocolate*. Apparently concerned that I was standing, he asked if I wanted a seat and then, ignoring my indication that this was unnecessary, proceeded by dragging a bar stool away from its current occupant and over to the machine. At this point I was informed that I had been brought a chair. I again indicated that this wasn't required, however, having gone to the effort of obtaining it, its donor was quite insistent that it be used. In order to minimise further debate, I perched on the bar stool, only for this action to be met with the following: "Good. and if you move I'm gonna kill you". Trevor, still standing next to the machine, later told me that while he hadn't felt significant trepidation at this information, became more concerned when the subsequent intended action was stated: "and then I'm gonna kill your mate". At this point, fortunately, a member of the bar staff decided to intervene.

While Trevor has now retired from the more tedious aspects of academic activity, it is good that he continues to participate in, engage with and contribute to research. It is particularly satisfying to be able to produce something for this volume in his honour. Trevor has often expressed mild bemusement at my interest in opera (much as I am puzzled by his enjoyment of five-day test matches). One finds, therefore, something of a fitting irony that this celebration of Trevor's achievement should take place in the year marking the bicentennial birth anniversaries of the two giants of 19th century opera – Richard Wagner and Giuseppe Verdi. In the *Preislied* scene of *Die Meistersinger*, the acceptability of radical new directions at variance with tradition is justified through the argument "One may judge the quality of the rules by the fact they can bear exceptions".[9] When one considers the increasingly irksome emphases on bureaucratic paper-chasing, form-filling exercises, and largely counter-productive academic audit regimes that have slowly infected almost all aspects of UK university procedure over the last 30 years, to be able to continue presenting significant new ideas, suggests that Wagner's sentiment is now, more accurately expressed as "One can judge the quality of exceptions by the fact that they can bear the rules": in this sense it would not be overstating things to see Trevor as exceptional and I wish him all the best in the future.

---

[9]"*Der Regel güte daraus man erwägt, dass sie auch 'mal 'ne Ausnahm verträgt*".

Bibliography

[1] L. Amgoud and C. Cayrol. A reasoning model based on the production of acceptable arguments, *Annals of Math. and Artificial Intelligence*, **34**, 197–215, (2002)

[2] K. Atkinson. *What Should We Do?: Computational Representation of Persuasive Argument in Practical Reasoning.* Ph. D. thesis, Dept. of Comp. Sci., Univ. of Liverpool, 2005

[3] K. Atkinson and T. J. M. Bench-Capon. Practical reasoning as presumptive argumentation using action based alternating transition systems. *Artificial Intelligence*, 171:855–874, 2007

[4] P. Baroni, M. Caminada, M. Giacomin, An introduction to argumentation semantics, The Knowledge Engineering Review 26 (4) (2011) 365–410.

[5] P. Baroni, F. Cerutti, P.E. Dunne, and M. Giacomin. Computing with infinite argumentation frameworks: the case of AFRAs. In *Proc. 1st Intnl. Workshop on Theory and Appl. of Formal Argumentation (TAFA)*, Springer LNCS 7132, 2012, pages 197–213

[6] P. Baroni, F. Cerutti, M. Giacomin, and G. Guida. AFRA: argumentation framework with recursive attacks. *Int. J. Approx. Reason.*, 51(1):19–37, 2011.

[7] P. Baroni, P. E. Dunne and M. Giacomin. On the resolution-based family of abstract argumentation semantics and its grounded instance. *Artificial Intelligence*, 175(3–4):791–813, 2011

[8] H. Barringer, D. M. Gabbay, and J. Woods. Temporal dynamics of support and attack networks: From argumentation to zoology. In *Mechanizing Mathematical Reasoning (LNCS Volume 2605)*, pages 59–98. Springer-Verlag: Berlin, Germany, 2005.

[9] R. Baumann, G. Brewka, and R. Wong. Splitting argumentation frameworks: An empirical evaluation. In *TAFA*, pages 17–31, 2011.

[5] T. J. M. Bench-Capon. Persuasion in practical argument using value-based argumentation frameworks, *Jnl. of Logic and Computation*, **13**(3):429–48, 2003.

[11] T. J. M. Bench-Capon, S. Doutre, and P. E. Dunne. Audiences in argumentation frameworks. *Artificial Intelligence*, 171:42–71, 2007.

[12] T. J. M. Bench-Capon and P. E. S Dunne. Some computational properties of a model for electronic documents. *Electronic Publishing - Origination, Dissemination and Design*, 2:231–256, 1989.

[13] T. J. M. Bench-Capon and P. E. Dunne. Argumentation in artificial intelligence. *Artificial Intelligence*, 171:619–641, 2007.

[14] A. Bondarenko, P. M. Dung, R. A. Kowalski and F. Toni. An abstract, argumentation-theoretic approach to default reasoning, *Artificial Intelligence*, **93**(1–2):63–101, 1997

[15] G. Brewka, P. E. Dunne, and S. Woltran. Relating the semantics of abstract dialectical frameworks and standard AFs. In *Proc. 22nd IJCAI*, Barcelona, July 2011, pages 780–785

[16] G. Brewka and S. Woltran. Abstract dialectical frameworks. In *Proc. Principles of Knowledge Representation and Reasoning*, pages 102–111, 2010.

[17] C. Cayrol, F. Dupin de Saint-Cyr and M.-C. Lagasquie-Schiex. Change in abstract argumentation frameworks: adding an argument. *J. Artif. Intell. Res. (JAIR)*, 38:49–84, 2010.

[18] S. Coste-Marquis, C. Devred, S. Konieczny, M.-C. Lagasquie-Schiex, and P. Marquis. On the merging of Dung's argumentation systems. *Artificial Intelligence*, 171:730–753, 2007.

[19] S. Coste-Marquis, C. Devred, and P. Marquis. Constrained argumentation frameworks. In *Proc. Principles of Knowledge Representation and Reasoning*, pages 112–122, 2006.

[20] Y. Dimopoulos and A. Torres. Graph theoretical structures in logic programs and default theories. *Theor. Comput. Sci.*, 170(1-2):209–244, 1996.

[21] P. M. Dung. On the acceptability of arguments and its fundamental role in nonmonotonic reasoning, logic programming, and N-person games. *Artificial Intelligence*, **77**:321–357, 1995.

[22] P. E. Dunne. Computational properties of argument systems satisfying graph-theoretic constraints. *Artificial Intelligence*, 171(10-15):701–729, 2007.

[23] P. E. Dunne. The computational complexity of ideal semantics. *Artificial Intelligence*, 173:1559–1591, 2009.

[24] P. E. Dunne. Tractability in value-based argumentation. In *Proc. 3rd COMMA*, volume 216 of *FAIA*, pages 195–206. IOS Press, 2010.

[25] P. E. Dunne and T .J. M. Bench-Capon. The maximum length of prime implicates for instances of 3-SAT. *Artificial Intelligence*, 92:317–329, 1997.

[26] P.E. Dunne and T.J.M. Bench-Capon. A sharp threshold for the phase transition of a restricted satisfiability problem for horn clauses. *Journal of Logic and Algebraic Programming*, 47(1):1–14, 2001.

[27] P. E. Dunne and T. J. M. Bench-Capon. Coherence in finite argument systems. *Artificial Intelligence*, 141(1/2):187–203, 2002.

[28] P. E. Dunne and T. J. M. Bench-Capon. Two party immediate response disputes: Properties and efficiency. *AI*, 149(2):221–250, 2003.

[29] P. E. Dunne and T. J. M. Bench-Capon. Complexity in value-based argument systems. In *Proc. 9th JELIA*, volume 3229 of *LNAI*, pages 360–371. Springer-Verlag, 2004.

[30] P. E. Dunne and M. Caminada. Computational complexity of semi-stable semantics in abstract argumentation frameworks. In *Proc. JELIA'08*, volume 5293 of *LNCS*, pages 153–165. Springer, 2008.

[31] P. E. Dunne, A. J. García, D. C. Martínez and G. R. Simari. Computation with varied-strength attacks in abstract argumentation frameworks. *Proc. 3rd COMMA*, FAIA 216, IOS Press, 2010, pages 207–218

[32] P.E. Dunne, A. Gibbons and M.Zito. Algorithmic and complexity issues concerning phase-transition phenomena in combinatorial problems, Proc. AWOCA'99, Perth WA, pages 76–90, August 1999.

[33] P. E. Dunne, A. Gibbons, and M. Zito. Complexity-theoretic models of phase-transitions in search problems. *Theoretical Computer Science*, 294(2):243–263, October 2000,

[34] P. E. Dunne, A. Hunter, P. McBurney, S. Parsons and M. Wooldridge. Weighted argument systems: basic definitions, algorithms, and complexity results. *Artificial Intelligence*, 175(2):457–486, 2011

[35] P. E. Dunne, S. Modgil and T. J. M. Bench-Capon. Computation in Extended Argumentation Frameworks. *Proc. 19th ECAI*, FAIA 215, IOS Press, Lisbon 2010, pages 119–124

[36] P. E. Dunne and M. Wooldridge. Complexity of abstract argumentation. In I. Rahwan and G. Simari, editors, *Argumentation in AI*, chapter 5, pages 85–104. Springer-Verlag, 2009.

[37] W. Dvořák. *Computational aspects of abstract argumentation*, Ph. D. Dissertation, Tech. Univ. Vienna, 2012

[38] W. Dvořák and S. Woltran. Complexity of semi-stable and stage semantics in argumentation frameworks. *Inf. Process. Lett.*, 110(11):425–430, 2010.

[39] W. Dvořák, R. Pichler, and S. Woltran. Towards fixed-parameter tractable algorithms for argumentation. In *KR*, 2010.

[40] U. Egly and S. Woltran. Reasoning in argumentation frameworks using quantified Boolean formulas. *Computational Models of Argument (Proc. COMMA 2006)*, volume 144 of *Frontiers in Artificial Intelligence and Applications*, pages 133–144, IOS Press, 2006

[41] J. Flum and M. Grohe. *Parameterized Complexity Theory* EATCS Monographs on Theoretical Computer Science, Springer-Verlag, 2006.

[42] J. Gu, P. W. Purdom, J. Franco, and B. W. Wah. Algorithms for the Satisfiability (SAT) Problem: A Survey. In: *Satisfiability Problem: Theory and Applications*, DIMACS Series in Discrete Mathematics and Theoretical Computer Science, American Mathematical Society, 1997, pages 19–152.

[43] E. J. Kim, S. Ordyniak, and S. Szeider. Algorithms and complexity results for persuasive argumentation. *Artificial Intelligence*, 175:1722 – 1736, 2011.

[44] R. Koo. A model for electronic documents. *SIGOIS Bull.* 10(1):23–33, 1989.

[45] B. S. Liao, L. Jin, and R. C. Koons. Dynamics of argumentation systems: A division-based method. *Artif. Intell.*, 175(11):1790–1814, 2011.

[46] D. Mamet. *Bambi vs. Godzilla: On the nature, purpose, and practice of the movie business.* Vintage, 2008.

[47] D. Martinez, A. Garcia, and G. Simari. An abstract argumentation framework with varied-strength attacks. In *Proceedings of the 11th International Conference on Principles of Knowledge Representation and Reasoning (KR'08)*, 2008.

[48] P. Matt and F. Toni. A game-theoretic measure of argument strength for abstract argumentation. In *Proceedings of 11th European Conference on Logics in Artificial Intelligence (JELIA'08)*, volume 5293 of *LNAI*, pages 285–297. Springer, 2008.

[49] S. Modgil. Reasoning about preferences in argumentation frameworks. *Artificial Intelligence*, 173(9–10):901–934, 2009.

[50] S. Modgil and M. Caminada. Proof theories and algorithms for abstract argumentation frameworks. In I. Rahwan and G. R. Simari, editors, *Argumentation in AI*, pages 105–129. Springer, 2009.

[51] S. Ordyniak and S. Szeider. Augmenting tractable fragments of abstract argumentation. In *IJCAI*, pages 1033–1038, 2011.

[52] I. Rahwan and K. Larson. Pareto optimality in abstract argumentation. In *Proceedings of 23rd Conference on Artificial Intelligence (AAAI'08)*. AAAI Press, 2008.

[53] J. R. Searle. *Rationality in Action*. MIT Press, Cambridge Mass., 2001

[54] P.M. Thang, P.M Dung, and N.D. Hung. Towards a common framework for dialectical proof procedures in abstract argumentation. *Logic and Computation*, pages 1071–1109, 2009.

[55] B. Verheij. A labeling approach to the computation of credulous acceptance in argumentation. In *IJCAI*, pages 623–628, 2007.

[56] G. Vreeswijk and H. Prakken. Credulous and sceptical argument games for preferred semantics. In *JELIA*, pages 239–253, 2000.

[57] L. C. Wu and C. Y. Tang. Solving the satisfiability problem by using randomized approach. *Inf. Proc. Lett.*, 41:187–190, 1992.

Structured Consultation with Argument Graphs

THOMAS F. GORDON *

Abstract

This article presents the Carneades opinion formation and polling tool, which was inspired by work by Katie Atkinson, Trevor Bench-Capon and Adam Wyner at the University of Liverpool on the Structured Consultation Tool (SCT) they developed in the European IMPACT project. The Carneades polling tool generalises and extends their results by using argument graphs to support consultations about any argument, independent of the argumentation schemes used to reconstruct the arguments, by collecting feedback on the arguments put forward on all sides of a debate, rather than only the arguments of a single position of one party, such as the government agency proposing some policy, and by providing a convenient way for respondents to rank stakeholders by the extent to which they share opinions. Argument graphs abstract away details of the argumentation schemes used to construct or reconstruct the arguments but not needed for the purposes of conducting the poll. Moreover, Carneades provides a high-level declarative language for argumentation schemes, enabling humanities scholars, such as lawyers or argumentation experts, to define and configure the set of argumentation schemes to be used to construct the argumentation graphs, without requiring technical computer-science skills or modifications to the implementation of the polling tool.

Introduction

It is a great personal pleasure for me to be able to contribute to this Festschrift in honor of Trevor Bench-Capon. We have known each other for many years in the field of Artificial Intelligence and Law, having both participated in many, perhaps most, ICAIL and Jurix conferences, and have worked together rather intensively since 2006, in a couple of European research projects, ESTRELLA

---

*Fraunhofer FOKUS, Berlin

and IMPACT. I believe we first met 26 years ago at the first ICAIL conference, which took place in Boston in 1987. Trevor and his colleagues presented *two* papers on modeling legislation using logic programming [6, 7], an approach I had been constructively criticizing for its insufficient support for isomorphic modeling of exceptions [14, 16] and made an early attempt to rectify with the Oblog system [15] I presented at the same conference. Trevor's work on modeling dialogue games [8, 9] directly influenced my research on the procedural aspects of legal argumentation in dialogues, for my doctoral thesis on the Pleadings Game, first presented at the 1993 ICAIL in Amsterdam [17]. I have always enjoyed Trevor's company and good humor and consider him a good friend. And I don't want to neglect to take this opportunity to thank Trevor for his generous support over the years, in particular for his positive and helpful review of my habilitation thesis [18], for which I am extremely grateful and will always be in his debt.

My contribution here, however, was inspired by more recent work by Trevor and his colleagues Katie Atkinson and Adam Wyner on the Structured Consultation Tool (SCT) they developed in the European IMPACT project [1, 26]. I present a fully implemented polling tool, based on the Carneades argumentation system, which generalizes and extends their results by using argument graphs to support consultations about any argument, independent of the argumentation schemes used to reconstruct the arguments, by collecting feedback on the arguments put forward on all sides of a debate, rather than only the arguments of a single position of one party, such as the government agency proposing some policy, and by providing a convenient way for respondents to rank stakeholders by the extent to which they share opinions. The polling tool advances the state-of-the-art by using argument graphs to abstract away details of the argumentation schemes used to construct or reconstruct the arguments but not needed for the purposes of conducting the poll. This enables the tool to be used to conduct polls about all arguments in an argument graph, no matter which argumentation schemes have been applied to construct the graph. The process of applying argumentation schemes to construct the argument graph is cleanly separated from the process of using the argument graph to generate poll questions. Moreover, Carneades provides a high-level declarative language for argumentation schemes, enabling humanities scholars, such as lawyers or argumentation experts, to define and configure the set of argumentation schemes to be used to construct the argumentation graphs, without requiring technical computer-science skills or modifications to the implementation of the polling tool.

The Carneades argumentation system provides web-based, collaborative software tools for:

- reconstructing the arguments of a debate in an argument graph
- visualizing, browsing and navigating argument graphs
- critically evaluating arguments
- forming opinions, participating in polls and ranking stakeholders by the degree to which they share your views
- obtaining clear explanations, using argument graphs, of the different effects of alternative policies in particular cases

Carneades is open source software, available for downloading from `http://carneades.github.com`.

The focus of this paper is the polling tool of the Carneades system, which serves two main purposes:

1. It guides users step by step through the arguments on all sides of a complex policy debate, in a kind of simulated debate, providing an overview of the issues, positions and arguments in a systematic way. The tool can help users to form an opinion, if they do not yet have one, or to critically evaluate and reconsider their current opinion, if they do. The tool also enables users to compare their opinions with the published opinions of stakeholders, such as political parties, which can be useful for finding persons and organizations which best represent or share their views and interests.

2. At the same time the tool conducts a poll to collect and aggregate views and opinions on the issues of a debate, taking care to protect privacy. The anonymous and aggregated results of the poll can provide valuable feedback, to the respondents and policy makers, going beyond the information provided by typical surveys and polls. It enables users to discover not only how much support policies enjoy, but also to learn precisely why particular aspects of the policies, or their underlying assumptions, are supported or not.

The rest of this paper presents an analysis of requirements for the polling tool, the algebraic model of argument graphs underlying all tools of the Carneades system, an overview of the design and implementation of the polling tool, a tour of its user interface, and a discussion comparing the results with prior, related work, in particular work in the European IMPACT project by Trevor, Katie and Adam at the University of Liverpool on the Structured Consultation Tool.

1   Requirements Analysis

Following an *agile* methodology [21], the functional requirements of the polling tool are defined here via *user stories*. User stories are brief, high-level statements describing users in particular roles (who) that would like to be able to use the system to perform some task (what) in order to achieve some benefit or value (why). They are typically specified by filling in templates, such as "As a *role*, I want to *action*, in order to *value*." There are various versions of these templates, but their differences are minor and not significant for our purposes.

Let us focus on the application scenario of the IMPACT project: supporting public policy deliberations. In this scenario, first a government agency publishes a green or white paper on the Web regarding some policy topic, such as "copyright in the knowledge economy".[1] Whereas green papers ask questions about some policy topic, without proposing a specific policy, white papers do propose a specific policy.[2] For both types of papers, at the time of publication, the agency invites interested parties to submit comments, proposals and arguments, by uploading documents in PDF format to the agency website. At the end of the commenting period, the agency analyses the comments and produces a report summarizing the arguments contained in the comments, along with any decisions taken by the agency as a result of the consultation process, which is then published on its website.

The question which interests us is how to use argumentation technology to support and improve this consultation process. Here we will focus mainly on the requirements for the polling tool, which would provide interested persons with an opportunity to learn about and evaluate claims and arguments put forward during the consultation process, both by the government agency and by the parties who submitted comments. One goal is to systematically generate polling questions from an argument graph containing reconstructions of arguments in the paper and comments, taking care to assure that all relevant critical questions are asked. The polls are conducted only after some arguments have been reconstructed in an argument graph, using argumentation schemes to guide the reconstruction process. If the initial paper contains arguments, for example arguments in a white paper used to justify the proposed policy, a poll could be conducted soon after publication of the paper, before any comments have been submitted. Another alternative would be to wait until the commenting period has expired to conduct the poll, to also collect feedback about the

---

[1]See http://ec.europa.eu/internal_market/copyright/docs/copyright-infso/greenpaper_en.pdf.

[2]For a description of the distinction between green and white papers, see http://en.wikipedia.org/wiki/Green_paper.

arguments put forward in the comments. A further alternative would be to conduct several polls during the consultation process, using the arguments which have been put forward thus far in the process at each stage.

Several roles can be identified in this scenario:

Agency. The government agency which published the green or white paper and manages the consultation process.

Analyst. The persons who have the job of using argumentation schemes to reconstruct the arguments in the paper and comments, to build the argument graph. Analysts are presumed to have had some training in how to reconstruct arguments, over a period of weeks, including how to use argumentation software tools designed to support this tasks.

Commentator. A person or organization who submits a comment, putting forward arguments in response to the green or white paper. Commentators are presumed to have some knowledge about the policy issue being debated, but no specialist knowledge about argumentation theory or information technology.

Respondent. Persons who take part in the polls, to express their opinions about the claims and arguments exchanged by the agency and the commentators. It is presumed that these persons have no specialist knowledge in argumentation, information technology, the policy domain being discussed, or any other field, and are unwilling to invest any time in learning how to use the polling software.

Humanities Scholar. Philosophers and others with the specialist knowledge required to formalize argumentation schemes.

Given this consultation scenario, with these roles, functional requirements for the polling tool can be formulated in the following user stories:

1. As an agency, I want to obtain feedback from the public with their opinions on the claims and arguments put forward in a green or white paper, as well as in the comments submitted during the consultation, in order to understand which policy proposals are acceptable or not by the public, along with the reasons for their opinions.
2. As an analyst, I want to be able to easily and quickly reconstruct the arguments in the paper and comments, in order to produce a report summarizing the arguments for the agency and the public.

3. As a poll respondent, I want to be able to participate in the poll in order to learn more about the policy issues, influence the policy-making process to protect my interests and discover which stakeholder organizations, such as political parties, share my views and represent my interests.

4. As a humanities scholar, I want to be able represent and model argumentation schemes using a high-level declarative language, in order to be able to customize or extend the schemes used by analysts to reconstruct arguments, without the help of IT experts or the need to modify the implementation of the argument reconstruction tool.

2   Argument Graphs

All tools of the Carneades system, including the polling tool which is the focus of this paper, are interoperable and tightly integrated due to their all being based on the same underlying model of argument graphs. Currently, the following tools are provided:

- A tool for creating and editing argument graphs using argumentation schemes to reconstruct arguments in source text;

- An argument visualization tool for interactively viewing maps of argument graphs containing links to source documents;

- The polling tool, for guiding users through argument graphs and collecting and aggregating opinions about the claims and arguments represented in the graphs;

- And a tool for analyzing the effects of rule-based models of policies in particular cases, via dialogues with a kind of legal expert system, which uses argument graphs to visualize and explain the results of the analysis.

Argument graphs play the role in argumentation of proof trees in classical logic. They are structures representing chains of reasoning and more general, nonlinear, relationships among inference steps. Whereas in proof trees the inference steps are applications of the strict inference rules of some calculus for classical logic, in argument graphs the steps are applications of more general argumentation schemes, which may be defeasible as well as strict.

An individual inference step in an argument graph is called an *argument node*. They are often also called "arguments", but this terminology is less precise, since the term "argument" has other uses. In particular, argument nodes are not arguments in the sense of Dung argumentation frameworks [12]. Another term for argument nodes, suggested by Trevor in a personal correspondence, would be "single-step argument". With this caveat, in contexts where there is little risk of confusion, we will use the term "argument node" and "argument" interchangeably.

A single argument graph can be used to represent all the arguments put forward in a debate, from all participants.

Argument graphs are abstract structures, which can be represented in various concrete ways in software systems. The Carneades system currently represents argument graphs in three different, but isomorphic ways:

1. In XML, using an XML schema called the Carneades Argument Format (CAF).

2. In relational databases, using a database schema defined in SQL.

3. Using data structures defined in the Clojure language, the Lisp dialect used to implement Carneades.

The rest of this section provides a formal, algebraic specification of argument graphs.

Definition (Argument Graph) An argument graph is a bipartite, directed, labelled graph, consisting of statement nodes and argument nodes connected by premise and conclusion edges. Formally, an argument graph is a structure $\langle S, A, P, C \rangle$, where:

- S is a set of *statement nodes*,
- A is a set of *argument nodes*,
- P is a set of *premises*, and
- C is a set of *conclusions*.

Argument graphs are bipartite, because they consist of two kinds of nodes, argument nodes and statement nodes, and all edges (premises and conclusions) link argument nodes to statement nodes, i.e. to nodes of different kinds.

Let L be a predicate logic *language*, containing a unary predicate symbol applicable. Each statement node in S is labelled with a well-formed formula of the language L.

Each argument node in A is a structure $\langle i, s, d \rangle$, where

- i is a term in L identifying the argument node (no two argument nodes in an argument graph have the same identifier),
- s is a Boolean value which is true if the argument node is *strict* and false if it is *defeasible*.

- *d* is a Boolean value, representing the *direction* of the argument, which is true if the argument is *pro* its conclusion and false if it is *con* its conclusion.

An atomic formula in *L* of the form `applicable(X)` is intended to denote that the argument node identified by the term X is applicable. This enables the applicability of argument nodes to be an issue in argument graphs. An argument node `a1` is undercut by an argument node `a2` if `a2` is an argument node con the conclusion `applicable(a1)`.

The premises and conclusions of an argument graph represent the edges of the graph, connecting the statement and argument nodes.

Each premise in *P* is a structure $\langle s, a, p \rangle$, where

1. $s \in S$,
2. $a \in A$,
3. *p* is a Boolean value denoting the *polarity* of the premise, i.e. positive or negative. If *p* is true, then the premise is positive, otherwise it is negative.

Each conclusion in *C* is a structure $\langle a, s \rangle$, where

1. $a \in A$, and
2. $s \in S$

Every argument node has exactly one conclusion. That is, for every argument $a \in A$ there exists exactly one $\langle a, \_ \rangle \in C$.

An argument node may have zero or more premises. That is, it need not be the case that for every $a \in A$ there exists a premise $\langle \_, a, \_ \rangle \in P$.

Figure 1 shows a visualization of an example argument graph, instantiating an argumentation scheme for value-based practical reasoning [5]. Argument nodes and statements nodes are represented by circles and boxes, respectively. Statements nodes are labeled, for readability, with a natural language representation of their formula. Argument nodes are labeled with their id and a plus or minus sign, indicating whether the argument is pro or con, respectively. The conclusion of the con argument, `a2`, is shown in the visualization with a link to the other argument node, `a2`. Thus it may appear that the argument graph is not actually bipartite. However, this is just a more readable visualization of an undercutting argument node. In the underlying argument graph, the conclusion of `a2` is actually a statement node containing the formula `applicable(a1)`, where by convention `applicable` is a standard predicate in every language

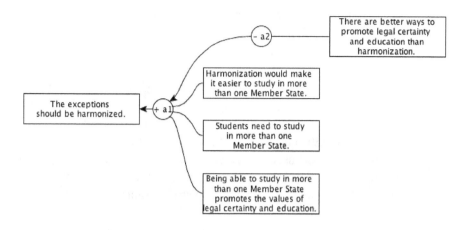

Figure 1. Visualization of a Simple Argument Graph

L of argument graphs. All the argument nodes in the example are defeasible. The example does not illustrate negative premises.

Prior conceptualizations of argument graphs, such as Beardsley/Freeman argument diagrams [4, 13] and the Argument Interchange Format (AIF) [11], do not distinguish pro and con argument nodes or positive and negative premises. Rather, in these prior approaches all argument nodes are pro and all premises are positive. An argument con a statement node P is represented in these prior approaches by an argument node having the conclusion $\neg P$. Similarly, if one argument node has a premise P and another has a premise $\neg P$, then two statement nodes are needed in the argument graph, using these prior approaches, one for P and one for $\neg P$. Explicit "refutation" or "conflict" links are used to express the information that P and $\neg P$ are complementary statements. Our approach has the advantage of reducing the number of statement nodes required by up to 50%. There is no room here for a deep or scholarly comparison of models of argument graphs, but a thorough comparison of Carneades argument graphs and the Argument Interchange Format has been published [10]. For the purpose of comparing the Carneades polling tool with the work of Trevor and his colleagues on the Structured Consultation Tool, it should be sufficient to note that the Structured Consultation Tool makes no use of any kind of argument graph for modeling structured arguments.

The above formalization of argument graphs defines the basic, abstract data model. In the implementation of the data model in the Carneades software, argument graphs have additional properties, omitted here, for associating weights with the argument and statement nodes, recording the results of formally evaluating the argument graph and for annotating the elements of the graph with metadata, quotations of and links to source documents, among other information.

The weights associated with the statement and argument nodes of an argument graph represent the aggregated opinion of an *audience* [22] about the truth or significance of the statement or argument, respectively. These weights can be computed from the data collected using the polling tool.

The weights can then be used to formally evaluate the argument graph using a computational model, based on an instantiation of the ASPIC+ framework [23] that maps the argument graph to an abstract argumentation framework [12]. As in earlier versions of Carneades [19, 20] proof standards are used to resolve conflicts between rebuttals, but by mapping argument graphs to Dung abstract argumentation frameworks, cyclic argument graphs can now be handled. Proof standards enable the risks of errors to be balanced against the costs of further argumentation, such as the costs of collecting evidence. This is important for practical reasoning in most domains, not just for legal reasoning.

3 Design and Implementation

The Carneades argumentation system, including its polling tool, is a three-tiered Web application, with a relational database backend, an application logic layer, and a Web client user interface.[3]

The relational database schema is a very simple and direct implementation of the algebraic model of argument graphs presented in Section 3. It consists of tables for statement nodes, arguments nodes, premises, and metadata. There are additional tables for storing poll responses and managing translations of text, to support multilingual application scenarios.

The database schema is independent of the argumentation schemes used to reconstruct arguments. A high-level declarative language for representing argumentation schemes is provided. A selection of about 20 of Doug Walton's schemes [25] have been modeled using the language, in collaboration with him. We have also used the language to represent versions of the schemes for value-based practical reasoning and arguments from a credible source developed by Trevor, Katie and Adam during the course of the IMPACT project [3]. The Carneades system is preconfigured to use these schemes, but they can be modified, extended or replaced with others. Restarting the web application is sufficient to reconfigure the system to use the new schemes. Existing argument

---

[3]Carneades is open source software, freely available for downloading from http://carneades.github.com.

graphs are not invalidated when the schemes are modified. Carneades includes a web application for editing argument graphs, which uses the argumentation schemes to generate forms for entering and modifying arguments. The editor can be used to update existing arguments to correctly instantiate modified schemes. A tool is planned, but not yet implemented, for checking arguments against the schemes and reporting errors.

The premises and conclusions of argumentation schemes are represented at a fine-level of granularity, at the level of a higher-order predicate logic. Premises are labelled by their roles in the scheme, e.g. "major" or "minor". All of this detail, including the identifiers of the schemes applied, is preserved in the relational database representation. Statements are represented in the database both in natural language and formally, in predicate logic. A logic-based query language is provided for retrieving statement nodes from the database which unify with (match) the query.

The application layer is implemented in a functional programming language, Clojure, which is compiled to byte codes for the Java Virtual Machine. A purely functional, declarative style has been used, with no mutable state and side effects only for input/output. The application layer is packaged as a Web service which can be accessed via HTTP. An inference engine is provided. It can be used to automatically generate argument graphs by applying argumentation schemes to sets of predicate logic formulas ("semantic models"). We have demonstrated this feature by reconstructing Liverpool's traffic law example [1]. Finally, the application layer also includes an argument graph evaluator, which uses a mapping to Dung abstract argument frameworks to label (in, out or undecided) the statement and argument nodes. Grounded semantics is currently used, but the system has been designed in a modular way to allow future implementations of other semantics to be selected at run-time.

The user interface, illustrated in the next section, is a Rich Internet Application (RIA), implemented in JavaScript and, more recently, ClojureScript. The client communicates with the Carneaedes Web service via HTTP and exchanges data using JSON. The style of the user interface was designed and implemented by the company User Interface Design (UID), a partner in the IMPACT project.

The entire code of the server-side of the system, including a relational database engine (H2) and a web server (Jetty), is packaged as a single, double-clickable JAR file. The system is very simple to install, requires no configuration or administration, and can be used stand-alone, on a personal computer, without an Internet connection.

4   User Interface

This section presents the user interface of the polling tool and illustrates how it is used.

The first page of the polling tool provides an overview of the features of the tool and explains the following procedure for using the tool:

1. Log in using a pseudonym to protect the respondent's privacy.

2. Read an introduction to the topic of the debate and select an issue of interest.

3. Answer a series of survey multiple-choice questions about the selected issue, asking whether the respondent agrees or disagrees with claims made in arguments.

4. View a summary of the questions and responses. The respondent is provided with an opportunity to change his or her answers.

5. Compare the respondent's opinions with those of the authors of the source documents reconstructed by analysts in the argument graph.

The procedure is flexible and the respondent is in control. The procedure can be stopped at any time, and continued later if desired. Moreover, the respondent can jump backwards or forwards to any step in the procedure.

4.1   Question Types

Three types of questions are asked during the poll. The questions are generated automatically by traversing, depth-first, the nodes of the argument graph. Figure 2 shows the form displayed the first time the respondent is asked for his opinion about some statement.

If the respondent first wants to see the arguments before answering, and thus chooses the third alternative, then the question will be put aside and he will be shown questions about the arguments pro and con this statement. As illustrated in Figure 3, this second type of question shows the argument, quoting the formulations of the argument in the source texts, and asks for each premise whether the respondent agrees or disagrees with the premise, or, if there are arguments in the graph about the premise, whether he would like to first see the arguments (not shown in this example, since there are no arguments in the graph for these premises). Note also that the default answer, "Skip this question", has not been changed in this example.

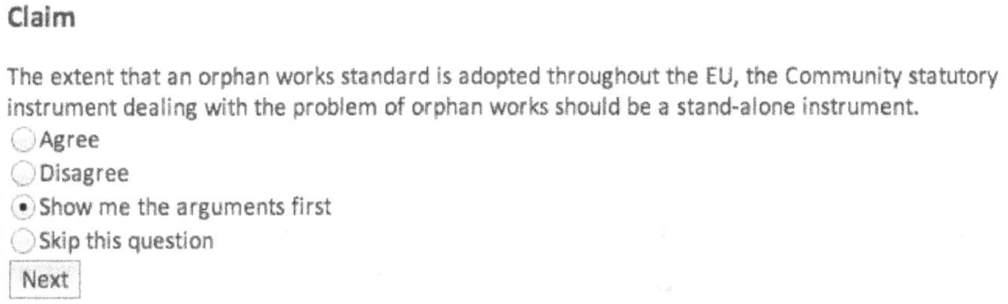

Claim

The extent that an orphan works standard is adopted throughout the EU, the Community statutory instrument dealing with the problem of orphan works should be a stand-alone instrument.

○ Agree
○ Disagree
● Show me the arguments first
○ Skip this question

Next

Figure 2. First Time Question About a Claim

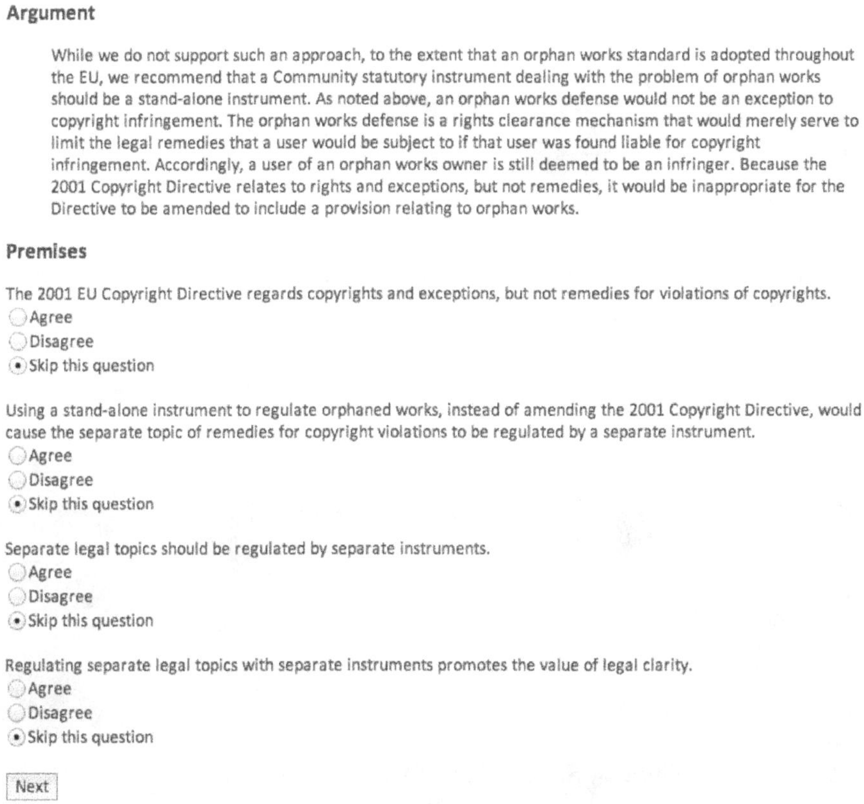

Argument

While we do not support such an approach, to the extent that an orphan works standard is adopted throughout the EU, we recommend that a Community statutory instrument dealing with the problem of orphan works should be a stand-alone instrument. As noted above, an orphan works defense would not be an exception to copyright infringement. The orphan works defense is a rights clearance mechanism that would merely serve to limit the legal remedies that a user would be subject to if that user was found liable for copyright infringement. Accordingly, a user of an orphan works owner is still deemed to be an infringer. Because the 2001 Copyright Directive relates to rights and exceptions, but not remedies, it would be inappropriate for the Directive to be amended to include a provision relating to orphan works.

Premises

The 2001 EU Copyright Directive regards copyrights and exceptions, but not remedies for violations of copyrights.
○ Agree
○ Disagree
● Skip this question

Using a stand-alone instrument to regulate orphaned works, instead of amending the 2001 Copyright Directive, would cause the separate topic of remedies for copyright violations to be regulated by a separate instrument.
○ Agree
○ Disagree
● Skip this question

Separate legal topics should be regulated by separate instruments.
○ Agree
○ Disagree
● Skip this question

Regulating separate legal topics with separate instruments promotes the value of legal clarity.
○ Agree
○ Disagree
● Skip this question

Next

Figure 3. Questions About the Premises of an Argument

After the respondent has seen the arguments, to the depth and level of detail chosen by his answers to the questions, he will be asked again for his opinion of the statement. (Recall that users can control the depth of the survey by skipping questions or asking to see the arguments before answering questions.) This second time, however, the question is formulated somewhat differently. He will first be asked to weigh arguments pro and con the statement. The respondent can easily adjust the relative weights of these arguments, using sliders, as shown in the figure. The user is asked to weigh an argument only if he has agreed with all of its premises, since we expect that it would be too confusing for most users to ask them to weigh arguments as if they accepted them, when they do not. In the example there is only one argument. Weighing the argument can be useful nonetheless, since the weights entered by all respondents are averaged to resolve conflicts among rebuttals when evaluating the argument graph, using weights and proof standards [19, 20].

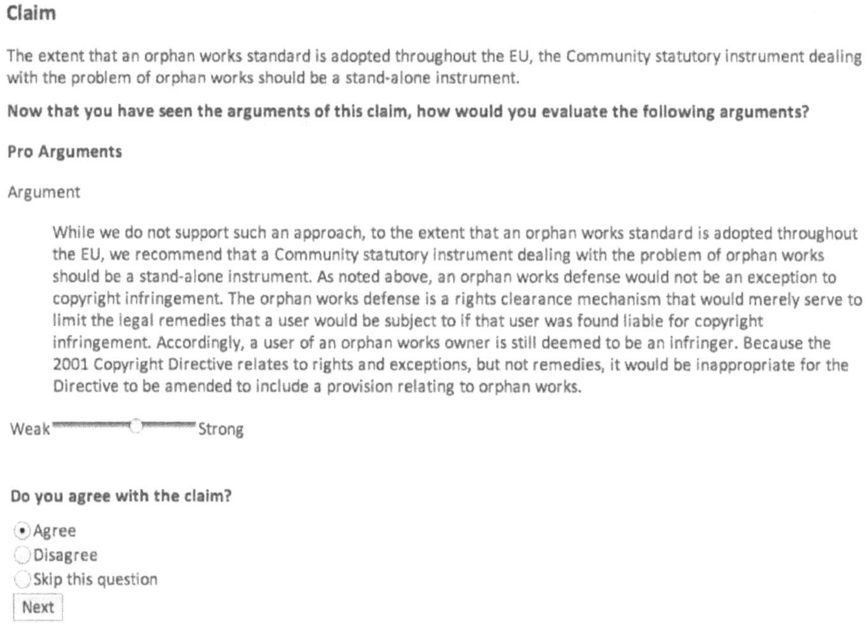

Claim

The extent that an orphan works standard is adopted throughout the EU, the Community statutory instrument dealing with the problem of orphan works should be a stand-alone instrument.

Now that you have seen the arguments of this claim, how would you evaluate the following arguments?

Pro Arguments

Argument

> While we do not support such an approach, to the extent that an orphan works standard is adopted throughout the EU, we recommend that a Community statutory instrument dealing with the problem of orphan works should be a stand-alone instrument. As noted above, an orphan works defense would not be an exception to copyright infringement. The orphan works defense is a rights clearance mechanism that would merely serve to limit the legal remedies that a user would be subject to if that user was found liable for copyright infringement. Accordingly, a user of an orphan works owner is still deemed to be an infringer. Because the 2001 Copyright Directive relates to rights and exceptions, but not remedies, it would be inappropriate for the Directive to be amended to include a provision relating to orphan works.

Weak ▭▭▭◯▭▭▭ Strong

Do you agree with the claim?

⦿ Agree
◯ Disagree
◯ Skip this question
[Next]

Figure 4. Second Time Question About a Claim

After the arguments have been weighed, the respondent is asked, at the bottom of the same page, whether he now agrees or disagrees with the claim.

4.2   Checking and Changing Answers

To check or change answers the respondent can go to the "summary" page, shown in Figure 5, listing all the claims with which the respondent has agreed or disagreed, showing the opinion entered and providing an opportunity to make changes. The sixth item in the list shows the user's position on the main claim, that a stand-alone statutory instrument should be used for standardizing the handling orphaned works. The user has agreed with this claim.

Summary

Thank you for having participated in this consultation process! Here's a list of your responses to the survey questions. Click on any item in the list to change your answer. Or compare your answers with the positions of other stakeholders by clicking the button below.

[Compare]

Your responses

* The cross-border aspects of the orphaned works issue are already provided for by the proposal of High Level Expert group, which recommends mutual recognition by Member States of each other's copryight exceptions. **Agree.** Change

* Regulating separate legal topics with separate instruments promotes the value of legal clarity. **Agree.** Change

* The policy proposed by the German Action Alliance should be adopted to address the cross-border aspects of orphaned works. **Agree.** Change

* The 2001 EU Copyright Directive regards copyrights and exceptions, but not remedies for violations of copyrights. **Agree.** Change

* Separate legal topics should be regulated by separate instruments. **Agree.** Change

* The extent that an orphan works standard is adopted throughout the EU, the Community statutory instrument dealing with the problem of orphan works should be a stand-alone instrument. **Agree.** Change

* The cross-border aspects of the orphaned works should be handled through an amendment to Directive 2011/29/EC. **Agree.** Change

* Using a stand-alone instrument to regulate orphaned works, instead of amending the 2001 Copyright Directive, would cause the separate topic of remedies for copyright violations to be regulated by a separate instrument. **Agree.** Change

Figure 5. A Summary Page

4.3   Comparing Opinions

Finally, the respondent can compare his opinions with those reconstructed from the source documents. The comparison page (Figure 6) shows the source documents grouped into several categories, ordered by how much the opinions expressed in the documents have in common with the opinions expressed by the respondent in his answers to the poll questions. In each category, full references to the documents are provided (author, title, etc). The title includes a hyperlink to the source of the document on the Web.

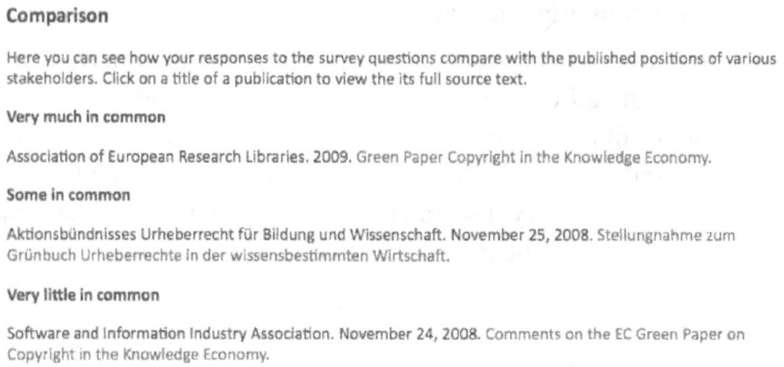

Comparison

Here you can see how your responses to the survey questions compare with the published positions of various stakeholders. Click on a title of a publication to view the its full source text.

Very much in common

Association of European Research Libraries. 2009. Green Paper Copyright in the Knowledge Economy.

Some in common

Aktionsbündnisses Urheberrecht für Bildung und Wissenschaft. November 25, 2008. Stellungnahme zum Grünbuch Urheberrechte in der wissensbestimmten Wirtschaft.

Very little in common

Software and Information Industry Association. November 24, 2008. Comments on the EC Green Paper on Copyright in the Knowledge Economy.

Figure 6. Opinion Comparison Page

Here is brief explanation of how the comparison is computed. All of the arguments modeled in the argument graph are tagged with the keys of source documents in which the argument has been made, from the corpus of source documents used by the analysts to construct the graph. These documents do not merely cite or quote the argument but rather express agreement with the argument, by claiming that the premises and the conclusion of the argument are true. Since the arguments are linked to their conclusion and premises in the argument graph, it is easy to compute from the source metadata of arguments the set of claims, i.e. statements claimed to be true or false, in each source document. These claims are then compared to the respondent's opinions. The similarity of opinions is currently measured by the percentage of claims in the document with which the respondent has expressed agreement, but other metrics are possible, such as "Euclidean distance" [24, pp. 9–15]. For every claim, the opinion of the user matches the position of a comment only if they both agree, disagree or have expressed no opinion about the claim. For example, if an argument graph contains 100 claims (statements) and the opinion of the user matches 20 of the opinions of the comment, then the comment is assigned a score of 20%. The comments are grouped into five qualitative categories: very little in common (< 20%), little in common (20-39%), some in common (40-59%), much in common (60-79%), and very much in common (80-100%).

5 Discussion

The Carneades polling tool presented here, which is fully implemented, has been inspired by the Structured Consultation Tool Trevor Bench-Capon and his Liverpool colleagues Katie Atkinson and Adam Wyner developed in the European IMPACT project [1, 26]. The SCT, in turn, builds on prior work at Liverpool by Katie, Trevor and Peter McBurney on the Parmenides system [2]. Our aim in developing and implementing the Carneades polling tool was not specifically for the purpose of this Festscrift, to allow comparison with Trevor's work, but rather with the aim to develop a practical tool meeting identified user requirements. This work was mostly completed before receiving the invitation to make a contribution to this Festschrift.

We have aimed to preserve all of the features of Parmenides and the SCT, but with a more flexible design supporting further use cases and enabling a tighter integration with tools for argument reconstruction, visualization and evaluation. These additional use cases include the provision of support for consultations about any argument, independent of the argumentation schemes used to reconstruct the arguments, the collection of feedback on the arguments put forward on all sides of a debate, rather than only the arguments of a single position of one party, and the ranking of stakeholders by the extent to which they share opinions. We believe these goals have been achieved with the polling tool presented here.

Argument graphs provided the key for this increased flexibility, by enabling the code for generating and conducting polls to be decoupled from the code for using argumentation schemes to (re)construct arguments. The SCT represents every argumentation scheme with a separate table in a relational database. Modifying the schemes, or extending the system to support further schemes, requires modifications to the database schema, the middleware (application layer) and the user interfaces, invalidating existing databases using prior versions of the schemes. All of these modifications are labor intensive and require specialist computer programming skills. Our approach, on the other hand, provides a high-level declarative programming language for specifying argumentation schemes, facilitating experimentation with various formulations of argumentation schemes, by humanities scholars as well as computer scientists, without requiring technical computer-science skills or modifications to the implementation of the polling tool. We find this feature especially useful, because we consider argumentation schemes to be an active field of research, with many schemes not yet well understood and waiting to be adequately formalized.

6 Acknowledgments

This work was partially funded by the European IMPACT project (FP7-IST-247228), 2010-2012. Carneades was conceived and designed by the author, with contributions by Douglas Walton and Henry Prakken. The current version of Carneades was programmed by Pierre Allix, Stefan Ballnat and the author.

Bibliography

[1] K. Atkinson, T. Bench-Capon, D. Cartwright, and A. Wyner. Semantic Models for Policy Deliberation. In *Proceedings of the Thirteenth International Conference on Artificial Intelligence and Law (ICAIL 2011)*, pages 81–90, New York, NY, USA, 2011. ACM Press.

[2] K. Atkinson, T. Bench-Capon, and P. McBurney. PARMENIDES: facilitating deliberation in democracies. *Artificial Intelligence and Law*, 14(4):261–275, 2006.

[3] K. Atkinson, A. Wyner, and T. Bench-Capon. Report on the structured consultation tool (sct). IMPACT Deliverable D5.2, University of Liverpool, 2012.

[4] M. C. Beardsley. *Practical Logic*. Prentice Hall, New York, 1950.

[5] T. Bench-Capon. Persuasion in Practical Argument Using Value-Based Argumentation Frameworks. *Journal of Logic and Computation*, 13(3):429–448, 2003.

[6] T. J. Bench-Capon. Support for Policy Makers: Formulating Legislation with the Aid of Logical Models. In *Proceedings of the First International Conference on Artificial Intelligence and Law*, pages 181–189, Boston, 1987.

[7] T. J. Bench-Capon, G. O. Robinson, T. Routen, and M. Sergot. Logic Programming for Large Scale Applications in Law: A Formalisation of Supplementary Benefit Legislation. In *Proceedings of the First International Conference on Artificial Intelligence and Law*, pages 190–198, Boston, 1987.

[8] T. J. M. Bench-Capon, P. E. S. Dunne, and P. H. Leng. Interacting with Knowledge Systems Through Dialogue Games. In *Proceedings of the 11th Annual Conference on Expert Systems and their Applications (vol. 1)*, pages 123–130, Avignon, 1991.

[9] T. J. M. Bench-Capon, P. E. S. Dunne, and P. H. Leng. A Dialogue Game for Dialectical Interaction with Expert Systems. In J. C. Rault, editor, *Proceedings of AVIGNON-92 (vol. 1)*, Nanterre, 1992.

[10] F. Bex, T. Gordon, J. Lawrence, and C. Reed. Interchanging arguments between Carneades and AIF. In B. Verheij, S. Szeider, and S. Woltran, editors, *Computational Models of Argument – Proceedings of COMMA 2012*, pages 390–397, Amsterdam, 2012. IOS Press.

[11] C. Chesnevar, J. McGinnis, S. Modgil, I. Rahwan, C. Reed, G. Simari, M. South, G. Vreeswijk, and S. Willmott. Towards an argument interchange format. *Knowledge Engineering Review*, 21(4):293–316, 2006.

[12] P. M. Dung. On The Acceptability Of Arguments And Its Fundamental Role In Nonmonotonic Reasoning , Logic Programming And N-Persons Games. *Artificial Intelligence*, 77:321–357, 1995.

[13] J. B. Freeman. *Dialectics and the Macrostructure of Arguments: A Theory of Argument Structure.* Walter de Gruyter, Berlin / New York, 1991.

[14] T. F. Gordon. The Role of Exceptions in Models of the Law. In H. Fiedler and R. Traunmüller, editors, *Formalisierung im Recht und Ans[ä]tze juristischer Expertensysteme*, pages 52–59. J. Schweitzer Verlag, Munich, 1986.

[15] T. F. Gordon. Oblog-2: A Hybrid Knowledge Representation System for Defeasible Reasoning. In *Proceedings of the First International Conference on Artificial Intelligence and Law*, pages 231–239, Boston, 1987.

[16] T. F. Gordon. Some Problems with Prolog as a Knowledge Representation Language for Legal Expert Systems. In C. Arnold, editor, *Yearbook of Law, Computers and Technology*, pages 52–67. Leicester Polytechnic Press, Leicester, England, 1987.

[17] T. F. Gordon. The Pleadings Game; Formalizing Procedural Justice. In *Proceedings of the Fourth International Conference on Artificial Intelligence and Law*, pages 10–19. ACM Press, New York, 1993.

[18] T. F. Gordon. *Foundations of Argumentation Technology – Summary of Habilitation Thesis.* PhD thesis, Technical University of Berlin, 2009.

[19] T. F. Gordon, H. Prakken, and D. Walton. The Carneades Model of Argument and Burden of Proof. *Artificial Intelligence*, 171(10-11):875–896, 2007.

[20] T. F. Gordon and D. Walton. Proof Burdens and Standards. In I. Rahwan and G. Simari, editors, *Argumentation in Artificial Intelligence*, pages 239–260. Springer-Verlag, Berlin, Germany, 2009.

[21] D. Leffingwell. *Agile Software Requirements: Lean Requirements Practices for Teams, Programs and the Enterprise.* Addison-Wesley, 2010.

[22] C. Perelman and L. Olbrechts-Tyteca. *The New Rhetoric.* University of Notre Dame Press, Notre Dame, 1969.

[23] H. Prakken. An abstract framework for argumentation with structured arguments. *Argument & Computation*, 1:93–124, 2010.

[24] T. Segaran. *Programming Collective Intelligence.* O'Reilly, 2007.

[25] D. Walton, C. Reed, and F. Macagno. *Argumentation Schemes.* Cambridge University Press, 2008.

[26] A. Wyner, K. Atkinson, and T. Bench-Capon. Towards a Structured Online Consultation Tool. In *Electronic Participation: Proceedings of Third IFIP WG 8.5 International Conference (ePart 2011)*, Lecture Notes in Computer Science (LNCS), pages 286–297, Berlin, 2011. Springer.

Revisiting Metalevel Argumentation

SANJAY MODGIL[*]

Abstract

This paper revisits a program of research work on metalevel argumentation conducted jointly with Trevor Bench-Capon. After a brief review of this research, I then discuss some potential uses of the metalavel approach. Specifically, I argue that one of the key benefits of the abstract argumentation paradigm is its potential for bridging between computational models of argumentation and human models of reasoning and debate, and that metalevel argumentation can play a key role in facilitating this bridging.

Introduction

I've known Trevor Bench-Capon since the first day I met him, and ever since have been glad to count him amongst my friends and academic collaborators. My early interest in argumentation owes much to his guidance and friendship. In 2003 John Fox offered me a postdoctoral position on the ASPIC project, and I enthusiastically accepted the opportunity of returning to the themes of my PhD – logic, reasoning and conflict – after a four year hiatus in medical informatics. It was at the project kick-off meeting, in Albi France, when I first met Trevor. My first impression, on the opening day of that meeting, was of a charmingly anarchic figure whose incisive contributions belied a look of indifference. As that first day drew to a close, I remember being somewhat underwhelmed by the prospect of the evening meal. After all, a Spanish philosopher once wrote that all human beings long for "the eternal persistence of consciousness", but my experience had been that this was not an easy state to maintain, especially when dining out with computer scientists. But conscious I remained, on that particular evening, for I discovered that many in the argumentation community constituted an altogether more entertaining breed of 'computer scientist', and chief amongst those who had me wide mouthed

[*]King's College London, Department of Informatics

with laughter and slack-jawed with alcohol (his appetite then was legendary, as well as infectious), was a certain Trevor Bench-Capon. From that night on, I relished project meetings and the chances they afforded to converse with this cultured and witty colleague; and I say "colleague", since it is a testament to his lack of pretension that he made a neophyte like me feel like a colleague. Since then our friendship has grown, and as I know to be the case with many other junior researchers, I have greatly benefitted from his advice, guidance and support (especially when at one point I felt that the chances of a permanent academic position were hopeless).

I have also enjoyed many fruitful academic collaborations with Trevor. In 2007, I asked him to comment on an early draft of what was to become my paper on Extended Argumentation Frameworks (*EAF*s) [15]. His comments were very helpful, and in particular, he suggested an idea that subsequently evolved into our work on metalevel argumentation [7], [16], [17], [18]. Essentially, the idea of metalevel argumentation is that given an object-level argumentation framework (such as a Dung framework (*AF*) [8] or an *EAF*), one can consider metalevel arguments that can be explicitly categorised according to the types of claim made about the arguments and their relations in the object level framework. These metalevel arguments can then themselves be related by an attack relation in a Dung framework, where this metalevel attack relation satisfies constraints imposed by the claim based categorisation. One can then show a correspondence between the object level framework and its metalevel formulation, such that the justified arguments of the object level framework can be computed directly from its metalevel formulation[1]. In this way, the full range of theoretical and practical results and techniques for *AF*s can now be inherited by their various extensions and developments, including *EAF*s, frameworks with support relations [2], recursive attacks [4], collective attacks [21], etc.

In this paper I will explore uses and applications of meta-argumentation that go beyond those described in our above mentioned papers on metalevel argumentation. Section 1 briefly reviews Dung's argumentation theory and metalevel argumentation as formalised in [18]. Section 2 then proposes the use of metalevel argumentation as a formalism for bridging between computational and human models of argument, whereby networks capturing interactions between human authored statements and arguments can be mapped to metalevel argumentation frameworks, so that evaluation of the latter under Dung's stan-

---

[1]The idea of metalevel argumentation first appeared in [16], and was subsequently adopted by Boella et.al [9]. In their work, formal correspondences with object level frameworks are not shown.

dard semantics can provide dialectical guidance to human users, and more sophisticated feedback prompting human users to submit dialogical moves that render explicit, information that is implicitly encoded in the relations holding between statements and arguments. The paper then concludes in Section 3.

1 Background: Abstract and Metalevel Argumentation Frameworks

1.1 Abstract Argumentation Frameworks

Many applications of argumentation build on Dung's seminal theory [8] and its various developments. A Dung *argumentation framework* (*AF*) consists of a binary conflict based *attack* relation R on a set A of arguments. Then, $x \in A$ is said to be *acceptable* w.r.t. $S \subseteq A$ iff $\forall y \in A$ such that yRx, implies $\exists z \in S$ such that zRy. This basic principle, whereby x is defended (or reinstated) against an attack by y, if some z attacks y, underpins evaluation of the winning/justified arguments of an *AF* in the following way:

Definition 1. Given an *AF* (A, R), Let $S \subseteq A$ be conflict free iff $\forall x, y \in S$, $(x, y) \notin R$, and let $S \subseteq A$ be an admissible extension iff S is conflict free and all arguments in S are acceptable w.r.t. S. The status of arguments is then evaluated w.r.t. extensions defined under different semantics:

Let S be an admissible extension of (A, R).

- S is *complete* iff S contains all arguments in A which are acceptable w.r.t S; *grounded* iff S is the minimal (w.r.t. set inclusion) *complete* extension; *preferred* iff S is a maximal *complete* extension, and *stable* iff $\forall y \notin S, \exists x \in S$ s.t. $(x, y) \in R$

- For $s \in \{\text{complete, preferred, grounded, stable}\}$:
If $x \in A$ is in at least one, respectively all, s extension(s) of (A, R), then x is said to be credulously, respectively sceptically, justified under the s semantics.

Dung's theory has been developed in a number of directions. Some works formalise collective attacks between *sets* of arguments [21]. In other works, the success of an attack from x to y, as a *defeat* by x on y, is contingent on y not being preferred to x according to some given preference relation on $\mathcal{A}$ [1], or the value promoted by y not being ranked higher than the value promoted by x, according to a given ordering on values [5]. [15]'s *Extended Argumentation Framework* (*EAF*) then extended Dung's framework to include arguments that attack attacks. *EAF*s thus accommodate argumentation based reasoning *about* possibly conflicting preference information, values, and value orderings, within the argumentation framework itself. [4] generalise the idea of attacks on attacks to recursive attacks on attacks, while a number of works also augment Dung's framework to include a *support* relation on arguments [2],[22], and weights on attacks [12].

1.2   Metalevel Argumentation Frameworks

Metalevel Argumentation Frameworks (*MAF*s) [18] categorise meta-arguments according to the claims they make *about* object level arguments and their properties and relations. These meta-arguments are organised into a Dung AF whose meta-attack relation obeys constraints imposed by the claim based characterisation.

Definition 2. A MAF is a tuple $\Delta_{\mathcal{M}} = (\mathcal{A}, \mathcal{R}, \mathcal{C}, \mathcal{L}, \mathcal{D})$, where $(\mathcal{A}, \mathcal{R})$ is a Dung AF, and:

- $\mathcal{L}$ is a language that includes a countable set of constant symbols and predicates. The set $wff(\mathcal{L})$ is defined by the following BNF (x, x_i range over constant symbols or variables)[2]:

  $\mathcal{L} : X ::= x, \{x_1, \dots, x_n\} \mid justified(X) \mid rejected(X) \mid$
  $attack(X, X') \mid defeat(X, X') \mid preferred(X, X') \mid support(X, X')$
  $\mid unsupported(X, X')$

- The claim function $\mathcal{C}$ is defined as $\mathcal{C} : \mathcal{A} \mapsto 2^{wff(\mathcal{L})}$

- $\mathcal{D}$ is a set of constraints on $\mathcal{R}$ of the form:

$$\text{if } l \in \mathcal{C}(\alpha) \text{ and } l' \in \mathcal{C}(\beta) \text{ then } (\alpha, \beta) \in \mathcal{R}$$

- $\mathcal{R}$ is said to be *defined by* $\mathcal{D}$ if whenever $(\alpha, \beta) \in \mathcal{R}$ then the claims of α and β satisfy the antecedent of some constraint in $\mathcal{D}$.

- The extensions and justified arguments of $\Delta_{\mathcal{M}}$ are the extensions and justified arguments of $(\mathcal{A}, \mathcal{R})$.

Henceforth, we may use abbreviations $j, r, d, p \dots$ for $justified, rejected, defeat, preferred$ etc., and may also denote an argument by the claim it makes. For example, $j(x)$ may denote the meta-argument claiming x is justified.

Consider now a given object level AF, (A, R). Then the existence of an argument $x \in A$, gives rise to a meta-argument $\alpha \in \mathcal{A}$ of the form 'there is an $x \in A$ that is an admissible extension of (A, R)', supporting the claim that 'x *is justified*'. The existence of an object level attack yRx, constitutes a meta-argument $\overrightarrow{\beta\alpha} = $ 'y attacks x' supporting the claim 'y *defeats* x'. Since the justified status of x in the object level framework is challenged by a defeat on x, then $\overrightarrow{\beta\alpha}$ attacks α at the metalevel, and so we have the following constraint

---

[2]In [18] $\mathcal{L}$ also includes val, val_pref, $audience$ and wff constructed from these predicates.

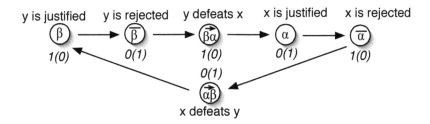

Figure 1. The MAF characterisation of a Dung AF $x \rightleftarrows y$

on the meta-level attack relation $\mathcal{R}$ (V, W, X, Y, Z will henceforth range over *wff* of $\mathcal{L}$):

D1 : if $d(Y, X) \in \mathcal{C}(\gamma)$ and $j(X) \in \mathcal{C}(\alpha)$ then $(\gamma, \alpha) \in \mathcal{R}$

y does not defeat x if y is rejected, and so $\overrightarrow{\beta\alpha}$ is attacked by a meta-argument $\overline{\beta}$ claiming 'y *is rejected*'. However, y does defeat x if y is justified, and so β claiming 'y *is justified*' attacks $\overline{\beta}$. We thus have the following metalevel constraints:

D2 : if $d(Y, X) \in \mathcal{C}(\gamma)$ and $r(Y) \in \mathcal{C}(\beta)$ then $(\beta, \gamma) \in \mathcal{R}$

D3 : if $j(X) \in \mathcal{C}(\alpha)$ and $r(X) \in \mathcal{C}(\beta)$ then $(\alpha, \beta) \in \mathcal{R}$

Fig 1 shows the MAF characterisation of a Dung AF $x \rightleftarrows y$ (together with the two labellings – the second in brackets – identifying the two preferred extensions). In [18] the following correspondence is shown:

> Let $\Delta = (A, R)$, Δ_M its MAF $(\mathcal{A}, \mathcal{R}, \mathcal{C}, \mathcal{L}, \mathcal{D})$, where $x \in A$ iff $j(x), r(y) \in \mathcal{A}$, $(y, x) \in R$ iff $d(y, x) \in \mathcal{A}$, and $\mathcal{R}$ is defined by $\{D1, D2, D3\}$. Then x is a justified argument of Δ iff $j(x)$ is a justified argument of Δ_M (under any semantics).

Note that in the spirit of Dung's AFs, MAFs adopt an abstract level approach in that they leave open the question of how meta-arguments might be formally constructed (in some meta-logic), and specify at the abstract level: 1) a function that maps meta-arguments to their claims, expressed in a language (that may be) distinct from that in which the arguments are formally constructed; 2) constraints on the attack relation defined in terms of these claims.

In [18], preference based *AF*s (*PAF*s) [1], value based *AF*s [5], hierarchical *EAF*s [15], and frameworks with collective attacks [21] are all characterised as metalevel Dung frameworks, and similar correspondences are shown. In addition, [17] shows how argument accrual can also by formalised in *MAF*s, so integrating accrual and dialectical modes of argumentation. An example of the correspondence shown in [18], involves characterising attacks on attacks in *hierarchical EAF*s, as metalevel attacks on arguments claiming object level defeats. Recall that in [15], it may be that in an *EAF*, x attacks y, but arguments may also attack attacks, so that z may attack the attack from x to y, indicating that z is an argument claiming that y is preferred to z. Hence, if z is a justified argument, then the attack from x to y fails to succeed as a defeat. Fig 2 shows the metalevel characterisation of the object level attack on an attack.

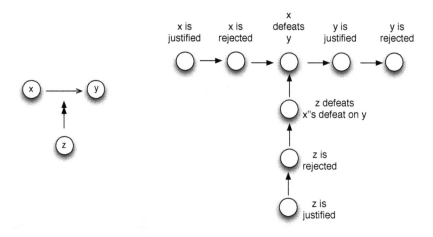

Figure 2. The EAF attack on an attack is shown on the left. The metalevel characterisation is shown on the right, with the claims of the metalevel arguments also shown.

2   Metalevel Argumentation: Bridging between Human and Formal Models of Argumentation

In our papers on metalevel argumentation we discuss various uses of metalevel argumentation frameworks. An obvious advantage of the approach is that *MAF* characterisations of object level formalisms allows for application of the full range of results and techniques developed for Dung *AF*s to be applied to the various object level developments of *AF*s (e.g.labelling algorithms and argument game proof theories [19] for Dung frameworks can now be applied to extensions of Dung's framework). Furthermore, MAFs provide a unifying formalism for integrating and further extending the various developments of Dung argumentation (e.g., integrating preference and value-based argumentation as shown in [18]). Specific uses of metalevel argumentation have been described in: [16], in which dialogue games for metalevel formulations of value-based argumentation were shown to have advantages over games defined for object level *VAF*s [6]; [7], in which argumentation about cases and their uses as precedents in legal reasoning can be modelled by dialogues defined over MAFs; and [3], in which MAFs are used for reasoning about firewall policies.

In what follows, I will discuss a further use of metalevel argumentation; in particular, as a bridging formalism between human and computational models of argument. To provide an appropriate context for the ensuing discussion it is worth reviewing what can be considered to be one of the key reasons for why argumentation has emerged as a prominent logic-based paradigm for reasoning under uncertainty and conflict [3].

2.1 Argumentation: The Added Value

The continuing impact of Dung's theory can be attributed to its level of abstraction and characterisation of non-monotonic inference relations in terms of general and intuitive principles. One is free to choose a logic and define what constitutes an argument and attack for that logic[4]. Then, given the arguments and attacks defined (instantiated) by a possibly inconsistent set of *wff* in that logic, one evaluates the justified arguments. The claims of these arguments then identify the non-monotonic inferences from the set of instantiating *wff*. Thus, abstract argumentation defines non-monotonic inference relations for instantiating monotonic logics. Furthermore, existing non-monotonic logics (e.g. logic programming, default, auto-epistemic and defeasible logic) can be given argumentation-based characterisations ([8],[13]), in the sense that the inferences defined though instantiation and evaluation of justified arguments correspond to the inference relations of the instantiating non-monotonic logic.

The fact that reasoning in existing non-monotonic logics can thus be characterised, testifies to the generality of the principle whereby one argument defends another from attack; a principle that is also both intuitive and familiar

---

[3]Five of the top ten most cited articles in the Journal of Artificial Intelligence, between 2007 and 2012, were on the topic of argumentation.

[4]Although as shown in [20], any given choice may be ill-conceived in that the resulting instantiated argumentation framework does not satisfy desirable properties (rationality postulates).

in human modes of reasoning, debate and dialogue. Indeed, recent ground breaking work in cognitive science argues that the human capacity for reasoning evolved primarily in order to assess and counter the claims and arguments of interlocutors in social settings [14]. Argumentation theory thus provides a *language independent* characterisation of both human and logic-based reasoning in the presence of uncertainty and conflict, through the abstract dialectical modelling of the process whereby arguments can be moved to attack and defend other arguments. The theory's value [5] can therefore in large part be attributed to its explanatory potential for making non-monotonic reasoning processes inspectable and readily understandable for human users, and its underpinning of dialogical and more general communicative interactions involving reasoning in the presence of uncertainty and conflict, where such interactions may be between heterogeneous agents (i.e., computational and/or human). Thus, computational reasoning processes can be informed by argumentation-based characterisations of human reasoning and interaction, and the reasoning processes of humans can be informed by argumentation-based characterisations of computational reasoning.

However, in order that argumentation can provide such a bridging role between computational and human reasoning, one requires development of models that account for human reasoning and argument as conducted in practice. Note that in this view, the oft heard critique aimed at abstract argumentation formalisms needs to be reformulated. This critique argues that in order to justify the addition of concepts and constructs extending AFs at the abstract level, one should relate these extensions to the underlying logical features that they abstract from; otherwise the abstraction counts for nothing, since it is an abstraction of nothing. However, the aforementioned requirement suggests that these various extensions can also be justified according to whether they accommodate modes of human reasoning and argument. Hence the critique might be better re-cast as a challenge for any such developed extension: *either* demonstrate that the extension provides a framework for instantiation by some underlying logical formalism, *or* demonstrate that the abstraction developed intuitively accommodates modes of human argumentation.

Given abstract extensions of AFs that do accommodate human modes of reasoning and argument, then in order to facilitate the bridging role of argumentation requires formally relating these extensions to the computational logic-based models of argument exemplified by Dung frameworks. This is where I believe metalevel argumentation can play an important role.

---

[5]Note that some of the material in this section draws from material presented in Section 21.1.2 of [24]

2.2 Dialectical Evaluation of Arguments Authored by Humans

To illustrate, a key anticipated use of computational argumentation is in informing human debate and argument so that interlocutors are guided by logical rational principles. The idea is that human dialogue and debate on online and offline tools (e.g., *Rationale* [8] and the tools developed at Dundee University that are reviewed in [24]) are mapped to Dung frameworks, and evaluated under Dung's various semantics. The provision of this evaluative functionality would: 1) ensure that the assessment of arguments is formally and rationally grounded; 2) enable humans to track the status of arguments so that they can be guided in which arguments to respond to; 3) enable 'mixed' argumentation integrating both computational and human authored arguments.

To achieve this functionality requires that tools accommodate interactive reasoning and debate as conducted in real life, where interlocutors sometime exchange complete arguments, incomplete arguments (enthymemes), individual statements (that may combine to form arguments), or indeed questions and challenges that prompt responses. They may also debate the relative strength of arguments, or whether one argument does indeed constitute a valid attack on another argument, or submit arguments supporting other arguments or accruing for a given claim, etc. The contributions of interlocutors then need to be organised into Dung frameworks and evaluated.

Let me illustrate with a simple example of a fictional exchange between myself and Trevor, an entirely appropriate advocate given his quickness to provoke and cajole one into a 'robust' argument, which is not to imply reproach; after all, mediocrity thrives on a diet of consent, and mediocrity is an anathema to Trevor as good football is an anathema to Portsmouth FC:

Sanjay : "The information about Tony Blair's affair should not have been published ($\neg pub$) because it was private information pr." (A)

Trevor : "So what ? Just because it is private, why should that mean it should not be published ?"

Sanjay : "Well, he's also no longer a public figure ($\neg p\_f$)." (B)

Trevor : "So what?"

Sanjay : "Well, also the information is not in the public interest ($\neg p\_int$)". (C)

Trevor : "But Blair has been appointed as UN envoy for the Middle East (un_env), and so the information is in the public interest". (D)

The exchange can be characterised in terms of an argument A, supported by arguments B and C, where C is then attacked by D. Of course, in this example the support relation essentially expresses a sub-argument relation, in that the support of B and C for A can be modelled as a single argument whose claim is $\neg pub$, inferred from the defeasible rule $pr \wedge \neg p\_f \wedge \neg p\_int \Rightarrow \neg pub$ and premises pr, $\neg p\_f$ and $\neg p\_int$. However, the point is to capture the arguments, statements, and their relations as interlocutors might present them.

While I acknowledge that the notion of support has been ascribed a variety of interpretations in the literature [6], it is often the case that illustrative examples suggest the sub-argument interpretation is the one implied (as in the above case), and this is confirmed by the fact that an attack on an argument X is extended to an attack on arguments supported by X [2]. Hence, the metalevel characterisation of this notion of support is that if X supports Y, and X is rejected, then Y is unsupported by X, and so rejected. Consider now the abstract framework shown in Figure 3 in which the arguments in the above dialogue are related by attack and support relations, and the associated metalevel interpretation. Then, one can apply standard techniques (such as labelling algorithms [19]) to evaluate the winning arguments; in this case providing me with feedback that my argument A is losing.

2.3 Prompting Dialogical Moves

In what follows I speculate on more sophisticated uses of metalevel argumentation in bridging between human and computational models of argument. Specifically, the previous section's use of metalevel frameworks, in providing dialectical feedback, did not rely on the internal structure of the metalevel arguments. Rather, the feedback relied on their organisation into a Dung graph, which in turn relied only on the claims these meta-arguments make about object level frameworks. As discussed in Section 1.2, we did not in [18] formally define instantiation of meta-arguments, but appealed to informal notions such as α is a meta-argument of the form 'there is an $x \in A$ that is an admissible extension of (A, R)', supporting the claim that x *is justified*, where this claim is associated with the argument at the abstract level (and so does not commit to the specifics of the language used for instantiating the meta-argument). I will now discuss how the following variation of the previous section's dialogue illustrates how future work on more formal instantiations of meta-arguments (e.g., of the type described in [25]) will enable more sophisticated user feedback.

---

[6]Another reasonable interpretation is that X supports Y if X's claim α is a premise or conclusion of a rule in Y so that X is an additional argument for α, i.e., we have an instance of arguments 'accruing' for α: X and the sub-argument Y' of Y that concludes α.

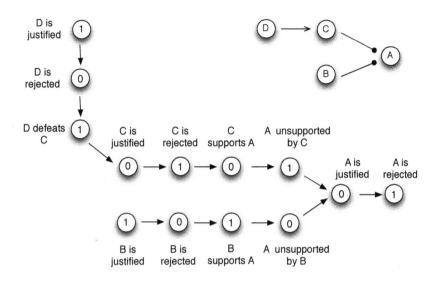

Figure 3. The framework above contains support relations (links with swollen ends). Its metalevel characterisation is shown below with the associated admissible/grounded labelling; 0 for losing (rejected) and 1 for winning (justified).

Suppose Sanjay argues that "Tony Blair is no longer a public figure, the information about his affair is not in the public interest, and the information is private, so the information should not be published" (X). Trevor counter-argues with "but Blair is UN envoy for the Middle East" (Y). Sanjay then counters by asking "why is this an argument against prohibiting publication ?" (Z). Trevor strokes his finely coiffeured goatee, and responds with "because his appointment as UN Middle East envoy implies that the information about his affair is in the public interest" (V).

This example raises a number of issues:

The distinct roles of attack in argumentation. Firstly note that I counter Trevor's attack on X, by Y, by questioning the validity of the attack. This question can then be represented as an attack on Y's attack on X, but *not* an EAF meta-attack [15], where an attack from Z to Y's attack on X invalidates the *dialectical* use of Y as a counter-argument to X, given that Z is an argument claiming that X is preferred to Y. Rather, I question the *declarative* basis for the attack.

To elaborate, object level attacks play two roles. Firstly, that Y attacks X is an abstract, declarative representation of the mutual incompatibility of the claim of the attacking argument and some element in the attacked argument. Secondly, the attack abstractly characterises the dialectical, procedural use of Y as a counter-argument to X. Definition 1's notion of a conflict free set accounts for the former declarative denotation, whereas the notion of acceptability of arguments accounts for the dialectical use of attacks. The question that then naturally arises is how can one question, in a formal *logical* context, the declarative basis of an attack from Y to X, since to do so would be to question the fundamental logical principle that a formula (i.e., the claim of Y) and its negation (i.e., a premise or conclusion of a rule in X) are in conflict ? Clearly one cannot do so in a logical context[7], but in informal human contexts in which enthymemes – arguments in which information is omitted – are commonplace, one can question the declarative rationale for an attack in those cases where the missing information is that which would provide such a rationale.

Attacking the declarative basis of attacks in enthymemes. In our example, Y is just such an enthymeme. The very fact that Y is moved as an attack on X (as indicated by the qualifying "but"), but the attack is not explicitly targeted, is indicative of an incomplete rule of the form 'if someone is a UN envoy for the Middle East then (s)he is ...', where the missing information is some proposition that negates an element in X. Note that if explicitly targeted, as for example in Trevor's argument D in the previous section's dialogue, it is clear that "the information is in the public interest" negates a premise in Y. In such a case it makes no sense to question the declarative basis of this attack; rather the rule $un\_env \Rightarrow p\_int$ in D would be targeted by an attack on D.

Metalevel prompting of dialogical moves. Suppose the locutions in this section's dialogue are represented together with the relations between them. Figure 4 shows the incremental construction of the framework[8], and the associated MAF.

1. My assertion of X, is associated with assertion of meta-arguments α claiming $justified(x)$ and $\overline{\alpha}$ claiming $rejected(x)$.

---

[7]Although this is not strictly true of approaches that make use of contrary relations (e.g., ABA [10] and ASPIC+ [20]) which generalise negation. But then in these approaches such relations cannot be subject to argument.

[8]I hesitate to call this an 'argument' framework; rather it is a dialogue framework given that the locutions represented by the nodes do not strictly equate with arguments construed as reasons in support of a claim; on the other hand the relations between the nodes are those we are familiar with in argument frameworks

2. Now, as suggested earlier, let us suppose construction of metalevel arguments using a metalogic of the type described in [25]. Trevor's assertion of the attacking Y yields meta-arguments β and $\overline{\beta}$ respectively claiming $justified(y)$ and $rejected(y)$. It also yields the premise $attack(y, x)$, which together with the defeasible rule '$attack(y, x) \Rightarrow defeat(y, x)$' yields the meta-argument $\overrightarrow{\beta\alpha}$ claiming $defeat(y, x)$. In other words, the launching of the attack allows one to defeasibly conclude that it succeeds, dialectically, as a defeat.

3. Now, a challenge on the premise of $\overrightarrow{\beta\alpha}$ is suggested, i.e.,
'why $attack(y, x)$?', shifting the burden of proof on Trevor to justify the attack. This is exactly the kind of dialogical move one sees in persuasion dialogues [23], where a *why* locution challenging a premise is effectively interpreted as an attack on the premise, in the sense that the burden of proof is then on the interlocutor submitting the premise to provide an argument for that premise. The metalevel arguments associated with this challenge are γ = 'there exists a challenge z' supporting the claim $justified(z)$ which attacks $\overline{\gamma}$ claiming $rejected(z)$, which in turn attacks $\overrightarrow{\gamma_{\beta\alpha}}$ claiming $defeat(z, attack(y, x))$, which in turn attacks $\overrightarrow{\beta\alpha}$ on its premise $attack(y, x)$. Notice the contrast with the meta-argument in Figure 2, representing the EAF attack on the dialectical success of the attack from x to y; it's claim thus being $defeat(z, defeat(x, y))$[9].

4. Finally, Trevor responds to the challenge by supplying the missing information, i.e., the rule $V = un\_env \Rightarrow p\_int$ that resolves the issue of which of X's premises is targeted by Y.

What the above suggests, is that the metalevel characterisation of the dialogue as a MAF, prompts submission of dialogical moves (Z) that then serve to render explicit, implicit information in enthymemes (V), so that this information is made available for debate. For example, I might then respond to Trevor by undercutting the rule $un\_env \Rightarrow p\_int$ (and thus the argument composed from Y and V). To reiterate, contrast this section's dialogue with that in the previous section, in which the targeted attack by D would yield a meta-argument composed from premise stating that 'D's claim negates the claim of C', which then strictly (rather than defeasibly) implies that 'D attacks

---

[9]Which, now that we take into account the logical structure of the meta-argument $\overrightarrow{\beta\alpha}$, could then be seen as either rebutting the claim $defeat(y, x)$ or undercutting of the rule $attack(y, x) \Rightarrow defeat(y, x)$

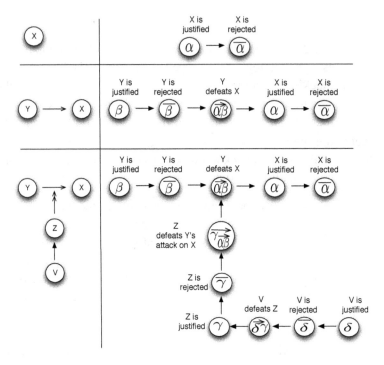

Figure 4. The frameworks on the left are those incremented during the dialogue, while the associated increments to the MAF are shown on the right.

C', which in turn defeasibly implies that 'D defeats C'.

From abstract argumentation to computational knowledge: Clearly, much of what is described above awaits a more formal analysis. However, I hope the intuitions are convincing enough to suggests a number of interesting research issues. Indeed, the above examples illustrate a more general research goal that I am currently pursuing; the exploitation of abstract relations between locutions/arguments, to, as it were, induce further information for updating computational knowledge. A simple example of this is suggested by the previous section's dialogue: the moving of B and C in response to Trevor's 'so whats' is indicative of B and C's (sub-argument) support for A, and so can be seen as inducing the rule $pr \land \neg p\_f \land \neg p\_int \Rightarrow \neg pub$. Also, in this section's dialogue, we showed how further dialogical moves can be prompted, serving both the overall dialectical goal of the dialogue, and in so doing eliciting the rule $un\_env \Rightarrow p\_int$.

3 Conclusions

In this paper I have briefly reviewed a program of research work on metalevel argumentation conducted jointly with Trevor Bench-Capon. I have also looked forward to what I believe are promising research directions that are complementary to commonly accepted views of the practical benefits that the argumentation paradigm has to offer. Essentially, I've suggested that metalevel argumentation can bridge between human modes of reasoning and debate, and computational models of argumentation. Human submitted arguments and statements can be captured in frameworks that can be represented as metalevel Dung frameworks. Further debate can then be informed by dialectical evaluation of these frameworks, and the prompting of further dialogical moves that seek to clarify and make available implicit information that can then be further interacted with.

Finally, I would like to emphasise the pleasure it gives me in being able to contribute to this Festschrift, especially in view of what I witnessed Trevor endure in these last few years. This paper is a testament not only to the importance of the metalevel paradigm that we developed, but also to my delight in seeing him triumph, against the odds.

Bibliography

[1] L. Amgoud and C. Cayrol. A reasoning model based on the production of acceptable arguments. *Annals of Mathematics and Artificial Intelligence*, 34(1-3):197–215, 2002.

[2] L. Amgoud, C. Cayrol, M. Lagasquie-Schiex, and P. Livet. On bipolarity in argumentation frameworks. *International Journal of Intelligent Systems*, 23(10):1062–1093, 2008.

[3] A. Applebaum, A.R. Syed, K. N. Levitt, S. Parsons, J. Rowe, and E. Skar. Firewall configuration: An application of multiagent metalevel argumentation. In *Proc. 9th International Workshop on Argumentation in Multiagent Systems (ArgMAS)*, 2012.

[4] P. Baroni, F. Cerutti, M. Giacomin, and G. Guida. AFRA: Argumentation framework with recursive attacks. *International Journal of Approximate Reasoning*, 52(1):19 – 37, 2011.

[5] T. J. M. Bench-Capon. Persuasion in practical argument using value-based argumentation frameworks. *Journal of Logic and Computation*, 13(3):429–448, 2003.

[6] T. J. M. Bench-Capon, S. Doutre, and P. E. Dunne. Audiences in argumentation frameworks. *Artificial Intelligence*, 171(1):42–71, 2007.

[7] T. J. M. Bench-Capon and S. Modgil. Case law in extended argumentation frameworks. In *Proceedings of the 12th International Conference on Artificial Intelligence and Law*, ICAIL '09, pages 118–127, 2009.

[8] T. Berg, T. van Gelder, F. Patterson, and S. Teppema. *Critical Thinking: Reasoning and Communicating with Rationale*. Amsterdam: Pearson Education Benelux, 2009.

[9] G. Boella, D.M. Gabbay, L. Van de Torre, and S. Villata. Meta-argumentation modelling 1: Methodology and techniques. *Studia Logica*, 93:297–355, 2009.

[10] A. Bondarenko, P.M. Dung, R.A. Kowalski, and F. Toni. An abstract, argumentation-theoretic approach to default reasoning. *Artificial Intelligence*, 93:63–101, 1997.

[11] P. M. Dung. On the acceptability of arguments and its fundamental role in nonmonotonic reasoning, logic programming and n-person games. *Artificial Intelligence*, 77(2):321–358, 1995.

[12] P. E. Dunne, A. Hunter, P. McBurney, S. Parsons, and M. Wooldridge. Weighted argument systems: Basic definitions, algorithms, and complexity results. *Artificial Intelligence*, 175(2):457 – 486, 2011.

[13] G. Governatori and M. J. Maher. An argumentation-theoretic characterization of defeasible logic. In *Proc. 14th European Conference on Artificial Intelligence*, pages 469–473, 2000.

[14] H. Mercier and D. Sperber. Why do humans reason? Arguments for an argumentative theory. *Behavioral and Brain Sciences*, 34(2):57–747, 2011.

[15] S. Modgil. Reasoning about preferences in argumentation frameworks. *Artificial Intelligence*, 173(9-10):901–934, 2009.

[16] S. Modgil and T. J. M. Bench-Capon. Integrating object and meta-level value based argumentation. In *Computational Models of Argument: Proceedings of COMMA 2008*, pages 240–251, 2008.

[17] S. Modgil and T. J. M. Bench-Capon. Integrating dialectical and accrual modes of argumentation. In *Computational Models of Argument: Proceedings of COMMA 2010*, pages 335–346, 2010.

[18] S. Modgil and T. J. M. Bench-Capon. Metalevel argumentation. *Journal of Logic and Computation*, 21(6):959–1003, 2011.

[19] S. Modgil and M. Caminada. Proof theories and algorithms for abstract argumentation frameworks. In I. Rahwan and G. Simari, editors, *Argumentation in AI*, pages 105–129. Springer-Verlag, 2009.

[20] S. Modgil and H. Prakken. A general account of argumentation with preferences. *Artificial Intelligence*, 195(0):361 – 397, 2013.

[21] S. H. Nielsen and S. Parsons. A generalization of Dung's abstract framework for argumentation: Arguing with sets of attacking arguments. In *Proc. 3rd Int. Workshop on Argumentation in Multi-agent Systems*, pages 54–73, 2006.

[22] N. Oren and T. J. Norman. Semantics for evidence-based argumentation. In *Computational Models of Argument: Proceedings of COMMA 2008*, pages 276–284, 2008.

[23] H. Prakken. Coherence and flexibility in dialogue games for argumentation. *Journal of Logic and Computation*, 15:1009–1040, 2005.

[24] S. Modgil and F. Toni et.al. Chapter 21: The added value of argumentation. In Sascha Ossowski, editor, *Agreement Technologies*, pages 357–403. Springer Netherlands, 2013.

[25] M. Wooldridge, P. McBurney, and S. Parsons. On the meta-logic of arguments. In *Proc. Fourth International Joint Conference on Autonomous Agents and Multiagent Systems*, pages 560–567, 2005.

Talking about Doing

PETER MCBURNEY * AND SIMON PARSONS †

Abstract

*Utterances regarding actions have several aspects that make them differ-
ent to utterances regarding beliefs or other mental states. First, they often
require uptake — agreement from another party — for a commitment to
be created on the part of the intended executor of the action. Second, the
power to revoke this commitment-to-action may lie with a different agent
than the one making the initial utterance or the one (possibly the same)
executing the action. In this paper we explore these different possible
combinations of executor, uptaker and revoker for utterances over action,
and present a game-theoretic semantics for such utterances.*

Introduction

Philosophers have studied propositions since Aristotle. They have devoted far
less attention to other types of utterance. Speech act theory, due primarily
to John Austin [4] and John Searle [37], has remedied that bias in modern
times, but there were at least two earlier precursors to this work. The Scottish
philosopher, Thomas Reid (1710–1796) [36], and the German philosopher,
Adolf Reinach (1883–1917) [35], both looked at the nature of promises and
similar utterances. Each observed that most utterances about action require
an audience: one cannot issue a command to oneself or meaningfully make
a request to oneself or pray to oneself. To that extent, such utterances about
action are *social acts*. Moreover, these utterances may only produce binding
commitments to undertake a particular action if someone *accepts* the utterance:
a promise by me to you to do some action only becomes a commitment on me
to do that action when you accept the promise; likewise, a request by me to you
to do some action only becomes a commitment on you to execute the action
if you accept the request. Reinach, whose explorations were motivated by an

*King's College London, Department of Informatics
†University of Liverpool, Department of Computer Science

attempt to understand the law of contractual obligations, called this acceptance event *uptake* [35].

Uptake is not a property of utterances about truth or knowledge, or utterances about the speaker's desires and preferences. In this respect, utterances about action are fundamentally different to those about beliefs. These two types of utterances differ in another important respect: for utterances over knowledge or beliefs, the original speaker may normally retract his or her prior statement of knowledge or belief and issue a new statement, asserting new knowledge or belief. Such retraction may revoke a commitment to defend a prior statement asserting knowledge or belief. In the case of utterances over actions, however, this power to revoke or retract the utterance or to annul any resulting commitment may not lie with the original speaker, but may be vested — through cultural tradition or linguistic practice — in someone else. For instance, it is not normal (at least in English-speaking cultures) for the maker of a promise that has already been accepted by the receiver of that promise to be able to un-make it: Only the receiver of the promise may — normally — annul it[1].

In previous work [27], we identified revocation as an aspect of utterances over action which had not been given any attention in the agent communications literature. In our earlier paper, we also proposed a syntax, where a speaker may indicate who is intended to execute the action, and who has power to revoke the action, and gave these utterances a denotational semantics in terms of manipulations of the contents of specified tuple spaces.

An example may make this clear. Suppose two agents, named Alice (A) and Bob (B), are engaged in conversation about the performances of some actions. Suppose that at different times in the interaction, A makes the following utterances to B:

Sentence 1: *I command you to wash the car.*

Sentence 2: *I promise you to wash the car.*

The syntactical form of these two statements is identical, despite the fact that almost everything else is different: the identity of the individual that the speaker intended to do the action (Bob for sentence 1, Alice for sentence 2); the illocutionary force of the two utterances (many people would view commands

---

[1]In contemporary society there is nothing to prevent the maker of the promise breaking it, but it is clear that a social norm has been violated. It was not so long ago, however, that if a man refused to marry a woman that he had agreed to marry, he could be sued for "breach of promise", and a woman who changed her mind about an offer of marriage that she had accepted was in danger of damaging her reputation, as discussed in [39].

creating stronger commitments than promises, for example); the nature of the commitment created in each case; the identity of the agent who would be obligated under any commitment to execute the action (Bob and Alice, respectively); the identity of the agent to whom the commitment would be due (Alice and Bob, respectively); and if a commitment was created, the identity of the agent with power to revoke it or accept that it had been fulfilled (Alice and Bob, respectively).

In this paper, we present in Section 1 a formal syntax for utterances over action which allows for different allocation of the responsibilities for doing, for uptaking and for revoking action commitments. We then provide a game theoretic semantics for such utterances, in terms of formal dialog games involving subsets of the participants; this is presented in Section 2. Section 3 discusses related work, and Section 4 concludes the paper with a brief discussion of potential future work.

1 Utterances over actions: Syntax

We begin by considering a dialog between two agents, identified as A and B respectively, who consider a single, atomic action, labeled α, to be undertaken at some time in the future. We assume that agent A makes an utterance about the potential action to agent B. The action α may be undertaken by agent A, or by agent B, or by a third agent (possibly not present in the interaction), agent C. It may help to think of the agents with first names: Alice (A) is the speaker of the utterance, Bob (B) is the hearer of the utterance, and Carol (C) is a possibly-non-present third-party. We ignore situations where the nature of the action needs two or more agents to execute it successfully.[2] Uptake (acceptance) of the action and thereby creating a commitment on the agent doing the action could be a power given to any one of the three agents. Likewise, once a commitment to execute α has been created, any one of the three agents could have the power to revoke or annul the commitment. Again ignoring cases where uptake or revocation requires joint or several participants, we therefore have $3^3 = 27$ possible cases, as shown in Table 1.

---

[2] Examples of such actions are: carrying a heavy object, operating a two-man saw (common in the lumber industry before the invention of the chain saw), and launching nuclear missiles [11].

Table 1. **Combinations of Actors, Uptakes and Revokers**. A speaks to B. C is not present.

No.	Who does action	Who up-takes	Who re-vokes	Type of Utterance
1.	A	A	A	Intention to act by A
2.	A	A	B	
3.	A	A	C	
4.	A	B	A	
5.	A	B	B	Promise by A to B
6.	A	B	C	
7.	A	C	A	
8.	A	C	B	
9.	A	C	C	
10.	B	A	A	Command by A to B (valid)
11.	B	A	B	
12.	B	A	C	
13.	B	B	A	Command by A to B (contested)
14.	B	B	B	Request by A to B
15.	B	B	C	
16.	B	C	A	
17.	B	C	B	
18.	B	C	C	
19.	C	A	A	Command by A to C (valid)
20.	C	A	B	
21.	C	A	C	
22.	C	B	A	
23.	C	B	B	
24.	C	B	C	
25.	C	C	A	Request or Prayer by A to C
26.	C	C	B	
27.	C	C	C	Request by A to C

Some of the cases in Table 1 correspond to the everyday usage of certain locutions in English; for instance, case 5 where the speaker, agent A intends to execute an action after acceptance by agent B, and with revocation power also vested in B describes the allocation of these roles in normal usage of *promise* locutions. However, most of the 27 cases do not have corresponding commonly-used English locutions. Even those cases which do have corresponding natural language locutions may be open to interpretation, or their meanings may differ in different cultures or language-groups.

An example is given by cases 10 and 12, *commands* from agent A to agent B. Legitimate commands are those where the commander has the legal or moral right to issue commands to the recipient of the command, the commandee. This right may well be contestable in specific cases, so it is reasonable to say that the recipient (say, agent B) may question or contest the command. Even if agent B accepts A's right to issue commands to B, the command may require clarification or explanation before it can be executed, as we have explored in [3]. Even organizations with strict hierarchies, such as military organizations, where members are empowered to issue commands to specified others, still permit recipients of commands to contest or refuse to obey unlawful commands.[3] Once uptaken, however, a command may only be revoked or annulled by the commander, not the commandee.

We now present a simple syntax for these utterances, which is:

$$actionloc(\alpha, S, \mathcal{H}, A, U, R)$$

where *actionloc* indicates that this is intended to be an utterance over action, α represents the proposed action, S is the identity of the speaker of the utterance, $\mathcal{H}$ is a finite set containing the identifiers of agents intended to be hearers of the utterance, A is the identifer of an agent intended to be the executor of the proposed action, U is the identifer of the agent empowered to accept (or uptake) the proposed action, thereby creating a commitment on agent A to execute the action, and R is the identifer of an agent empowered to revoke or annul the commitment on agent A to execute the action. We define $\mathcal{H}$ to be a set of agents, rather than only a single agent, to allow for multiple intended auditors to an utterance; the elements of $\mathcal{H}$ may or may not include agents

---

[3]The US television series, *Generation Kill*, for instance, based on the experiences of a US Marine Corp in the invasion of Iraq in 2003 provides many examples of military commands being contested or questioned in the course of the operation, and urban legend has it that in the POUM militia in the Spanish Civil War:

> You obeyed an order only after it had been explained in detail, you could refuse it if it didn't make sense [15, page 221].

A, U or R. The syntax of the utterance could also include terms to represent the intended starting time, completion time, or duration of the action α, as well as any necessary pre-conditions, concurrent conditions, or desired end-states of the action. For simplicity of presentation, we ignore such elements here.

This syntax is given in the two-layer structure now standard in agent communications, as defined, for example, in the Agent Communications Language ACL of FIPA [12]. The outer (or wrapper) layer is given by *actionloc*, with the elements $\alpha, S, \mathcal{H}, A, U$ and R all part of the inner layer. Note that in this syntax *actionloc* is a specific term, and does not stand in for, or represent, some other specific locution or locutions, such as *promise* or *command*. The use of *actionloc* as a specific term means that we can use this to embody any one of the 27 possible action locutions presented in Table 1, including those for there is no standard natural language term.

2   Game-theoretic semantics

The preceding discussion has shown how aspects of the meaning of a statement about actions may depend on the utterances of others, whether in creating a commitment via uptake, or in annulling a prior commitment via revocation. Insofar as these aspects of meaning do not relate to the truth-status of the utterance, some linguists would regard them as being part of the pragmatics rather than part of the semantics of the utterance [22]. We can use the social, pragmatic features of utterances over action to define a game-theoretic semantics for these utterances.

Firstly, a few words on the notion of semantics are in order. There are differences in the meaning of the term *semantics* and in the reasons for, and use of, semantics in the different domains of linguistics, formal logic, programming language theory, and agent communications. We have presented these different notions and purposes in greater detail in [28, Section 3]. Propositions purport to describe some feature of the real-world, and thus may carry truth values. For agent communications involving propositions it is therefore appropriate to view the notion of semantics as something close to standard usage in linguistics: a semantics for well-formed statements about propositions in a dialog is a mapping between the statements and objects in the real world. However, statements over action are usually not intending or purporting to describe some existing reality, and so do not carry truth values. Thus, a different notion of semantics is required for these statements. Following [21], we define the semantics of utterances over action as the external commitments-to-execute-actions referred to by the statements. Valid utterances in properly-undertaken dialogs can be then be viewed as creating, manipulating, assigning, re-assigning and annulling such commitments.

As explained in [28], there are several different ways such semantic mappings could be defined. A game-theoretic semantics is a semantics for statements in some logical language that associates a conceptual game to each well-formed statement of the language. The game is usually imagined to be played by two imaginary players, often named *Protagonist* and *Antagonist*. The statement of the formal language is deemed to be *true* precisely when one of the parties, usually Protagonist, has a strategy to ensure success in the game associated to the statement. By *strategy* is meant a decision-rule telling Protagonist what game moves to play in the game, for each possible prior move of Antagonist, and for each history of moves in the game to that point. Game theoretic semantics were developed by Jaako Hintikka for statements in first-order logic, creating what he called *Independence-Friendly (IF) Logic* [17]. Game semantics have been articulated for propositional and predicate logics [23], linear logic [1], and for probability statements [8], among others. So-called Dutch-book arguments in probability theory (due to Frank Ramsey and Bruno de Finetti) may also be viewed as a game semantics for subjective probability statements, since these arguments involve infinite (and therefore imaginary) gambles between a decision-maker and an imagined book-maker.

Game semantics have also been used to study the properties of formal argumentation systems and dialogue protocols, such as their computational complexity [10], or the extent of truth-convergence under an inquiry dialogue protocol [24], and to identify acceptable sets of arguments in argument frameworks [6, 20]. One could even view the English common-law legal system in game-theoretic terms, as a student of Trevor Bench-Capon, John Henderson, showed in his 2006 PhD thesis [16]. Conceptual games have also found application in mathematical model theory and in theoretical computer science, e.g., [19].

We now present the semantics of the statements defined in Section 2 in terms of two multi-agent dialog games, as follows. For each utterance with the syntactic form:

$$actionloc(\alpha, S, \mathcal{H}, A, U, R)$$

we first associate two specific dialog games, as follows:

Uptake Dialog Game, denoted $UD(\alpha, S, U)$, is a dialog game between agents S and U, played with the rules given in Table 2, and

Revocation Dialog Game, denoted $RD(\alpha, S, U, R)$, is a dialog game between agents S, U and R, played with the rules given in Table 3.

Table 2. Uptake Dialog Game: Outline Rules

Uptake Dialog Game: $UD(\alpha, S, U)$
Dialog Preconditions: A prior utterance of $actionloc(\alpha, S, \mathcal{H}, A, U, R)$.
Dialog Participants: Agents S and U.
Valid locutions: Question, Justify, Accept, Reject, End-dialog
Combination rules: Only agent U may utter Accept or Reject. An agent may only utter Justify following a prior utterance of Question by another agent.
Commitment rules: When and only when U utters Accept, a commitment on agent A to execute action α is created.
Termination rules: The dialog ends upon utterance by U of Accept or Reject, or the utterance of End-dialog by any agent.   The dialog is said to terminate-with-uptake upon utterance by agent U of Accept.

Tables 2 and 3 present outline rules for these two dialogs, respectively. The dialog rules are given here in accordance with the formal specification structure for agent dialog games first articulated in [25]. This structure defines the valid locutions, any rules for utterance and combination of these locutions, any rules for the creation and manipulation of commitments potentially incurred through the utterance of specified locutions, and any rules for termination of the dialogs. For reasons of space, we only present these rules in outline form here. The locutions *Question* and *Justify* have the obvious intended meanings, which are as defined for the Fatio Protocol [26].

We now define the semantics of action statements as follows. The utterance of the statement,

$$actionloc(\alpha, S, \mathcal{H}, A, U, R)$$

creates a commitment on agent A to execute action α precisely when the associated Uptake Dialog Game $UD(\alpha, S, U)$ terminates-with-uptake. This commitment on agent A to execute action α remains in force unless and until the action α is executed by agent A or the associated Revocation Dialog Game, $RD(\alpha, S, U, R)$, ends in termination-with-revocation.

Table 3. **Revoke Dialog Game: Outline Rules**

Revoke Dialog Game: $RD(\alpha, S, U, R)$

Dialog Preconditions:
1. A prior utterance of $actionloc(\alpha, S, \mathcal{H}, A, U, R)$
2. A prior instance of the associated Uptake Dialog Game $UD(\alpha, S, U)$ which terminated-with-uptake
and
3. The commitment on agent A to execute action α remains in force.

Dialog Participants: Agents S, U and R.

Valid locutions: Propose-revoke, Question, Justify, Revoke, End-dialog

Combination rules: Only R may utter Revoke.
An agent may only utter Justify following a prior utterance of Question by another agent.

Commitment rules: When and only when R utters Revoke, the commitment on agent A to execute action α is voided.

Termination rules:
The dialog ends upon utterance by R of Revoke, or the utterance of End-dialog by any agent.

The dialog is said to terminate-with-revocation upon utterance by agent R of Revoke.

The definition here of the semantics of utterances over action in terms of specified agent dialog games means that we have provided explicit procedures for creating and revoking commitments to act, shown by the outline rules of Tables 2 and 3. These procedures are defined in terms only of publicly-observable behaviours, not in terms of any decision or computational processes internal to the agents involved, which means the processes are semantically verifiable

[40], and are in accordance with the first of Hitchcock's *Principles of Rational Mutual Enquiry* [18].[4] The explicit definition of the processes also aids the software engineering of these utterances into agent communications protocols, as shown, for example, [9, 32].

3 Related Work

To the best of our knowledge, there is no prior work directly related to the work of this paper. As mentioned, some of our ideas are inspired by the philosophy of language of Thomas Reid [36] and the philosophy of legal language of Adolf Reinach [35], although neither considers retraction or revocation. Elsewhere in speech act theory, Jürgen Habermas explored the different nature of challenges or rebuttals required by different types of utterances, including statements about actions, although he seems not to have considered either uptake or revocation [14]. Much recent work in computational argumentation has explored argumentation schemes and their associated critical questions (CQs), often proposing formal dialog games to allow participants to argue over the default conclusion of the scheme using the critical questions, for example, [2, 31]. Such approaches may also be viewed as providing a game-theoretic semantics for the scheme and CQs, with the default conclusion of the scheme being adopted precisely when the player designated as Protagonist wins the associated dialog game.

Our approach differs from other work in agent communications on commitments. The social semantics of Singh and Colombetti and their respective colleagues [7, 38] treats utterances in agent dialogs as devices for manipulating the social relationships between the speakers. Our work, focused only statements about actions, is at a lower level of abstraction than social semantics. We assume that a dialog commences with two or more participants joining together with the shared intention of deciding what action or actions to take in some circumstance. There may already be prior social relationships between the participants, which could thereby allow, for example, commands to be uttered legally by one agent to another. However, once a dialog about action commences, we desire to understand how commitments to execute actions (or not to) are created and manipulated by the participants in the dialog. Our focus is therefore on the short-term effects of utterances inside a dialog on commitments, not their longer-term effects on the social relationships between the participants.

---

[4]Namely: **Externalization:** The rules should be formulated in terms of verifiable linguistic behavior.

One could ask why the semantic differences of speech acts identified in Section 1 could not be captured by the notion of agent roles, as in a framework such as that of [41]. The reason is that the role of uptaker or revoker of an utterance is not usually fixed throughout an interaction; it potentially depends on: the type of the utterance (promise, command, etc); the identities of the agent making the utterance, the agent receiving it, and the agent tasked with the action; and possibly also on the history of the dialog to that point. All of these may change through the course of a dialog, particularly if there are embedded dialogs or other complex combinations of dialogs, e.g., [25, 34]; thus, agent roles will usually be too rigid a framework for tracking these abilities to uptake or revoke utterances.

4 Conclusions

In this paper we have presented a formal syntax for utterances over action which allows for different allocations of the responsibilities for doing, for accepting (uptaking), and for revoking action commitments. We then provided a game-theoretic semantics for these utterances, in terms of formal dialog games each involving subsets of the participants specified in the original utterance. The benefits of this approach are several. Firstly, the proposed syntax makes explicit exactly who has responsibility for doing, for accepting, and for revoking an action commitment. Secondly, the syntax allows for every possible allocation of these responsibilities across three different agents, i.e, for all 27 possible combinations. The syntax therefore generalizes from those special cases of utterances over action that human language users have distinguished over the years, namely, promises, commands, requests, prayers, etc. Thirdly, the game-theoretic semantics we have defined gives explicit procedures for agents to accept (or not) a proposed action intention (and thus a procedure for creating a commitment on the part of the intended executor of the action to undertake the action), and for agents to revoke or annul an existing action commitment. These explicit procedures are defined in terms of formal agent dialog games which may readily be implemented in agent communication systems.

In this work we have thus far only considered atomic actions, each undertaken by a single actor. Two avenues of potential future work therefore are to consider utterances involving combinations of actions and to consider actions requiring two or more agents to be executed. Recent research by Rolando Medellin Gasque, for example, has explored dialogs over plans involving multiple actions and actors, work which demonstrates the subtlety of the issues involved when more than one action is considered [30, 31]. Conditional actions, those whose execution depend in some way upon the execution of other actions, and the resulting combinations of action commitments, is another area of potential future work. In [25], we showed that the combination of commitments arising from agent communications is also not necessarily straightforward; as with multiple actions and actors, these issues will require careful treatment.

Acknowledgments

This paper extends and generalizes the ideas presented by the authors at the *Symposium on Logic and Games in MultiAgent Systems (LoGaMAS)*, held in Liverpool, UK, on 16–17 December 2002, under the title of *"Towards a game semantics for logics of practical reasoning."* We are grateful for comments received from the audience on that occasion, particularly Marc Pauly.

Some Personal Recollections

PM: I first met Trevor Bench-Capon in November 1999, just before moving to University of Liverpool to complete my PhD. I had previously seen references to his work, but had not read any of it. In February 2002, I was appointed to a faculty position at Liverpool. A few months later, I was approached by Katie Greenwood (now Atkinson) about doing a PhD. Katie then applied for a Departmental scholarship to do a PhD in the area of agent negotiation under my supervision, and her application was successful. Subsequent to the award of the scholarship, but before she started, Trevor approached me to ask if he could "sit in" on our supervisory meetings. I did not know what that meant, and asked him. He said that he wanted to learn more about the topics of agent interaction and negotiation and thought that witnessing our discussions would help him do this. Still unsure what this involved, I hesitated. He responded by saying that he would just sit quietly in the corner, and not ever utter a word in our meetings. At the time, I did not know Trevor very well, and so I accepted this promise, and allowed him to join us as a silent witness. Fortunately, he did not keep his promise very long. The immensely interesting discussions between the three of us led directly to our joint development of the fruitful model for making and arguing about proposals over action [2], work which built on prior work of both Trevor and myself, as well as others, on qualitative models of practical reasoning involving consequences.[5]

---

[5]For example, [5, 13, 29]. In 1992, Peter McBurney and David Shuker developed a framework for planning and writing large-scale applications for national telecommunications licences which we called the *IPOC Model*. This framework organized materials around the various processes to be undertaken in implementing and launching a public telecommunications network, with each required process described in terms of its required Inputs, the tasks involved in the

In October 2003, Julian Padget of the University of Bath gave an invited research seminar to the Department of Computer Science at the University of Liverpool. In his talk, Julian explained that something he was saying would be obvious to a computer scientist. Realizing that perhaps not everyone in the audience was from the Department, he then added, *"But, of course, not everyone here is necessarily a computer scientist."* Trevor brought laughter to the room with his witty reply, *"Yes — I am only contingently a computer scientist."*

SP: The two stories that I tell most often about Trevor are the following. The first took place in a pub (no surprise for anyone who knows Trevor) (or, come to that, anyone who knows me). My recollection is that the pub was The Cambridge, close to the University of Liverpool campus, but I may be wrong. In any case, Trevor was standing near the bar, pint in one hand, lit cigarette in the other (this was probably in 2001, back when he was a heavy smoker). It was shortly before Easter, and, hoping to find something to tease him about, I asked Trevor what he had given up for Lent. His reply was that, as always, he had given up smoking and drinking. My reply, naturally, was to ask how that squared with him both drinking and smoking, to which he responded "The point of Lent is to contrast human frailty with divine perfection. Failing to give something up is the point". To which there was no answer, except to buy him another drink.

The second took place in Washington DC, at a workshop on argumentation that Trevor, Henry Prakken and I organised as part of a AAAI Fall Symposium Series. These meetings always include a plenary session in which each symposium is presented to an audience made up of attendees from all the events. Often the talks are rather dry, and AAAI usually encourages presenters to try to make them a little lively. In the case of our symposium, Guillermo Simari had agreed to give the talk, and just as he was giving a detailed technical description of an argument, Trevor, who was sitting in the audience shouted "That isn't an argument". Into the stunned silence I replied "Yes it is", and we alternated "No it isn't", "Yes, it is"[6] until the audience realised that this was planned and not some spontaneous heckling.

Bibliography

[1]   Abramsky, S. (1997). Semantics of interaction: an introduction to game semantics. In A. M. Pitts and P. Dybjer, editors, *Semantics and Logics of Computation*, pages 1–31. Cambridge

---

Process itself, its Outputs when successfully executed, and the anticipated Consequences of its execution. One could view a telecommunications licence application as just a very large and sophisticated proposal for action.

[6]Part of the script from the Monty Python "Argument Sketch" [33].

University Press, Cambridge, UK.

[2] Atkinson, K., Bench-Capon, T., and McBurney, P. (2005). A dialogue-game protocol for multi-agent argument over proposals for action. *Journal of Autonomous Agents and Multi-Agent Systems*, **11**(2), 153–171.

[3] Atkinson, K., Girle, R., McBurney, P., and Parsons, S. (2008). Command dialogues. In I. Rahwan and P. Moraitis, editors, *Argumentation in Multi-Agent Systems. Proceedings of the Fifth International Workshop on Argumentation in Multi-Agent Systems (ArgMAS 2008)*, Lecture Notes in Artificial Intelligence 5384, pages 93–106. Springer, Berlin, Germany.

[4] Austin, J. L. (1962). *How To Do Things with Words*. Oxford University Press, Oxford, UK. (Originally delivered as the William James Lectures at Harvard University in 1955.).

[5] Bench-Capon, T. J. M. (2003). Persuasion in practical argument using value-based argumentation frameworks. *Journal of Logic and Computation*, **13**(3), 429–448.

[6] Cayrol, C., Doutre, S., and Mengin, J. (2003). On decision problems related to the preferred semantics for argumentation frameworks. *Journal of Logic and Computation*, **13**(3), 377–403.

[7] Colombetti, M. and Verdicchio, M. (2002). An analysis of agent speech acts as institutional actions. In C. Castelfranchi and W. L. Johnson, editors, *Proceedings of the First International Joint Conference on Autonomous Agents and Multi-Agent Systems (AAMAS 2002), Bologna, Italy*, pages 1157–1164, New York City, NY, USA. ACM Press.

[8] Dawid, A. P. and Vovk, V. G. (1999). Prequential probability: principles and properties. *Bernoulli*, **5**, 125–162.

[9] Doutre, S., McBurney, P., Wooldridge, M., and Barden, W. (2005). Information-seeking agent dialogs with permissions and arguments. Technical Report ULCS-05-010, Department of Computer Science, University of Liverpool, Liverpool, UK.

[10] Dunne, P. E. and Bench-Capon, T. J. M. (2003). Two party immediate response disputes: Properties and efficiency. *Artificial Intelligence*, **149**(2), 221–250.

[11] Engel, J. A., Slattery, C., Ebeling, M., Pogany, E., and Squitieri, A. R. (2003). *The Missile Plains: Frontline of America's Cold War*. US National Parks Service, Minuteman Missile NHS, SD, USA.

[12] FIPA (2002). Communicative Act Library Specification. Standard SC00037J, Foundation for Intelligent Physical Agents.

[13] Fox, J. and Parsons, S. (1998). Arguing about beliefs and actions. In A. Hunter and S. Parsons, editors, *Applications of Uncertainty Formalisms*, volume 1455 of *Lecture Notes in Artificial Intelligence*, pages 266–302. Springer, Berlin, Germany.

[14] Habermas, J. (1984). *The Theory of Communicative Action: Volume 1: Reason and the Rationalization of Society*. Heinemann, London, UK. (Translation by T. McCarthy of: *Theorie des Kommunikativen Handelns, Band I, Handlungsrationalitat und gesellschaftliche Rationalisierung*. Suhrkamp, Frankfurt, Germany. 1981.).

[15] Haldeman, J. (2009). *The Forever War*. Thomas Dunne Books.

[16] Henderson, J. (2006). *A Description of Common Law as a Moving Classification System*. Ph. D., Department of Computer Science, University of Liverpool, Liverpool, UK.

[17] Hintikka, J. and Sandu, G. (1997). Game-theoretical semantics. In J. van Benthem and A. Meulen, editors, *Handbook of Logic and Language*, pages 361–410. Elsevier, Amsterdam, The Netherlands.

[18] Hitchcock, D. (1991). Some principles of rational mutual inquiry. In F. van Eemeren, R. Grootendorst, J. A. Blair, and C. A. Willard, editors, *Proceedings of the Second International Conference on Argumentation*, pages 236–243, Amsterdam, The Netherlands. SICSAT: International Society for the Study of Argumentation.

[19] Hodges, W. (1985). *Building Models by Games*. Cambridge University Press, Cambridge, UK.

[20] Jakobovits, H. and Vermeir, D. (1999). Dialectic semantics for argumentation frameworks. In *Proceedings of the Seventh International Conference on Artificial Intelligence and Law (ICAIL-99)*, pages 63–72, New York, NY, USA. ACM Press.

[21] Johnson, M. W., McBurney, P., and Parsons, S. (2005). A mathematical model of dialog. *Electronic Notes in Theoretical Computer Science*, **141**(5), 33–48.

[22] Levinson, S. C. (1983). *Pragmatics*. Cambridge Textbooks in Linguistics. Cambridge University Press, Cambridge, UK.

[23] Lorenzen, P. and Lorenz, K. (1978). *Dialogische Logik*. Wissenschaftliche Buchgesellschaft, Darmstadt, Germany.

[24] McBurney, P. and Parsons, S. (2001). Representing epistemic uncertainty by means of dialectical argumentation. *Annals of Mathematics and Artificial Intelligence*, **32**(1–4), 125–169.

[25] McBurney, P. and Parsons, S. (2002). Games that agents play: A formal framework for dialogues between autonomous agents. *Journal of Logic, Language and Information*, **11**(3), 315–334.

[26] McBurney, P. and Parsons, S. (2005). Locutions for argumentation in agent interaction protocols. In R. M. van Eijk, M.-P. Huget, and F. Dignum, editors, *Developments in Agent Communication*, Lecture Notes in Artificial Intelligence 3396, pages 209–225. Springer, Berlin, Germany.

[27] McBurney, P. and Parsons, S. (2007). Retraction and revocation in agent deliberation dialogs. *Argumentation*, **21**(3), 269–289.

[28] McBurney, P. and Parsons, S. (2009). Dialogue games for agent argumentation. In I. Rahwan and G. Simari, editors, *Argumentation in Artificial Intelligence*, chapter 13, pages 261–280. Springer, Berlin, Germany.

[29] McBurney, P., Parsons, S., Fox, J., and Glasspool, D. (1999). Consequence logics for cancer risk counselling systems: a specification framework. Technical report, Department of Electronic Engineering, Queen Mary & Westfield College, University of London, London, U.K.

[30] Medellin-Gasque, R., Atkinson, K., McBurney, P., and Bench-Capon, T. (2012). Arguments over co-operative plans. In S. Modgil, N. Oren, and F. Toni, editors, *Theory and Applications of Formal Argumentation*, Lecture Notes in Artificial Intelligence 7131, pages 50–66, Berlin, Germany. Springer.

[31] Medellin-Gasque, R., Atkinson, K., Bench-Capon, T., and McBurney, P. (2013). Strategies for question selection in argumentation about plans. *Argument and Computation. In press.*

[32] Moschoyiannis, S., Bryant, D., Krause, P., and McBurney, P. (2009). Verifiable protocol design for agent argumentation dialogues. In O. Kaynak and E. Damiani, editors, *Proceeedings of the Third International IEEE Conference on Digital Ecosystems and Technologies (IEEE DEST 2009)*, Istanbul, Turkey. IEEE.

[33] Python, M. (1972). http://www.youtube.com/watch?v=kQFKtI6gn9Y.

[34] Reed, C. (1998). Dialogue frames in agent communications. In Y. Demazeau, editor, *Proceedings of the Third International Conference on Multi-Agent Systems (ICMAS-98)*, pages 246–253. IEEE Press.

[35] Reinach, A. (1913). Die apriorischen Grundlagen des bürgerlichen Rechtes. *Jahrbuch für Philosophie und phänomenologische Forschung*, **1**, 685–847. English translation by John F. Crosby, published in *Aletheia*, III (1983), pp. 1–141.

[36] Schuhmann, K. and Smith, B. (1990). Elements of speech act theory in the philosophy of Thomas Reid. *History of Philosophy Quarterly*, **7**, 47–66.

[37] Searle, J. (1969). *Speech Acts: An Essay in the Philosophy of Language*. Cambridge University Press, Cambridge, UK.

[38] Singh, M. P. (1999). An ontology for commitments in multiagent systems: toward a unification of normative concepts. *Artificial Intelligence and Law*, **7**, 97–113.

[39] Trollope, A. (1865). *Can You Forgive Her?* Chapman & Hall.

[40] Wooldridge, M. J. (2000). Semantic issues in the verification of agent communication languages. *Journal of Autonomous Agents and Multi-Agent Systems*, **3**(1), 9–31.

[41] Wooldridge, M. J., Jennings, N. R., and Kinny, D. (2000). The Gaia methodology for agent-oriented analysis and design. *Journal of Autonomous Agents and Multi-Agent Systems*, **3**(3), 285–312.

Relating Ways to Instantiate Abstract Argumentation Frameworks

HENRY PRAKKEN*

Abstract

This paper studies the relation between various ways to instantiate Dung's abstract argumentation frameworks. First the ASPIC$^+$ *framework, which explicitly generates abstract argumentation frameworks, is equivalently reformulated in terms of John Pollock's recursive labelling method, which does not explicitly generate such frameworks. The reformulation arguably facilitates more natural explanations of dialectical argument evaluation. Then a variant is examined of a recent proposal by Wyner, Bench-Capon and Dunne to instantiate abstract argumentation frameworks without defining explicit inferential relations between arguments. The proposal is reformulated in a way that is equivalent to* ASPIC$^+$ *under some limiting assumptions. The proof exploits the equivalence between* ASPIC$^+$ *and Pollock's recursive labellings proven in the first part of the paper.*

Introduction

While most current AI research on argumentation takes its point of departure in [8]'s abstract argumentation framework, there is a tension between approaches which do or do not specify inferential relations between arguments. Examples of the former approach are assumption-based argumentation (initiated in [6]), classical argumentation as studied in [10], and the *ASPIC*($^+$) framework of [7, 19, 15] (recently used in [22]). Examples of the latter approach are preference-based argumentation frameworks [1], abstract resolution semantics (initiated in [13]), [4] value-based argumentation frameworks, [2]'s instantiation of these with an argument scheme for practical reasoning, and [23]'s modelling of rule-based argumentation with Dung's frameworks.

---

*Utrecht University, Department of Information and Computing Sciences, and the University of Groningen, Faculty of Law

As can be seen from these references, Trevor Bench-Capon has throughout his career explored all these ways to use Dung's work. In [4] he took the fully abstract approach, in [2, 23] he defined the structure of arguments but did not allow for inferential relations between them, and in [22] he employed a framework that allows for such relations. It therefore seems appropriate for this volume to further investigate the various ways in which Dung's work can be related to accounts of the structure of argumentation.

In a first contribution I will show that systems for structured argumentation do not have to explicitly produce a Dung-style abstract argumentation framework. I will do so by proving an equivalence between $ASPIC^+$ as formulated in [19, 15] (which explicitly produces Dung-style abstract argumentation frameworks) and a reformulation of $ASPIC^+$ in terms of John Pollock's [17] recursive labelling method (which does not follow this approach). This arguably facilitates more natural explanations of the outcome of dialectical argument evaluation. In a second contribution I will investigate [23]'s way to model structured argumentation without defining explicit inferential relations between arguments. It will turn out that this approach can be formulated in a way that is equivalent to $ASPIC^+$ if some limiting assumptions are made. The proof exploits the equivalence between $ASPIC^+$ and Pollock's recursive labellings proven in the first part of this paper. I will then conclude with some observations on the pros and cons of abstract models of argumentation.

1 Basic formalisms

In this section I review [8]'s abstract argumentation frameworks and the $ASPIC^+$ framework. An *abstract argumentation framework* (AF) is a pair $(\mathcal{A}, \mathcal{D})$, where $\mathcal{A}$ is a set of *arguments* and $\mathcal{D} \subseteq \mathcal{A} \times \mathcal{A}$ is a binary relation of *defeat*. A semantics for AFs returns sets of arguments called *extensions*, which are internally conflict-free and defend themselves against attack. One way to characterise the various semantics is with *labellings*.

Definition 1. A *labelling* of an abstract argumentation framework $(\mathcal{A}, \mathcal{D})$ is any assignment of either the label *in* or *out* (but not both) to zero or more arguments from $\mathcal{A}$ such that:

1. an argument is *in* iff all arguments defeating it are *out*.

2. an argument is *out* iff it is defeated by an argument that is *in*.

Then *stable semantics* labels all arguments, while *grounded semantics* minimises and *preferred semantics* maximises the set of arguments that are labelled *in* and *complete semantics* allows any labelling. Relative to a semantics, an argument is *justified* on the basis of an *AF* if it is labelled *in* in all labellings, it is *overruled* if it is labelled *out* in all labellings, and it is *defensible* if it is neither justified nor overruled.

The *ASPIC*$^+$ framework [19] gives structure to Dung's arguments and defeat relation. It defines arguments as inference trees formed by applying strict or defeasible inference rules to premises formulated in some logical language. Informally, if an inference rule's antecedents are accepted, then if the rule is strict, its consequent must be accepted *no matter what*, while if the rule is defeasible, its consequent must be accepted *if there are no good reasons not to accept it*. Arguments can be attacked on their (non-axiom) premises and on their applications of defeasible inference rules. Some attacks succeed as *defeats*, which is partly determined by preferences. The acceptability status of arguments is then defined by applying any of [8] semantics for abstract argumentation frameworks to the resulting set of arguments with its defeat relation.

ASPIC$^+$ is not a system but a framework for specifying systems. It defines the notion of an abstract *argumentation system* as a structure consisting of a logical language $\mathcal{L}$ closed under negation[1], a set $\mathcal{R}$ consisting of two subsets $\mathcal{R}_s$ and $\mathcal{R}_d$ of strict and defeasible inference rules, and a naming convention n in $\mathcal{L}$ for defeasible rules in order to talk about the applicability of defeasible rules in $\mathcal{L}$. Thus, informally, $n(r)$ is a wff in $\mathcal{L}$ which says that rule $r \in \mathcal{R}$ is applicable. *ASPIC*$^+$ as a framework does not make any assumptions on how the elements of an argumentation system are defined. In *ASPIC*$^+$ argumentation systems are applied to knowledge bases to generate arguments and counterarguments. Combining these with an argument ordering results in argumentation theories, which generate Dung-style *AF*s.

Definition 2. [**Argumentation systems**] An *argumentation system* is a triple $AS = (\mathcal{L}, \mathcal{R}, n)$ where:

- $\mathcal{L}$ is a logical language closed under negation ($\neg$).

- $\mathcal{R} = \mathcal{R}_s \cup \mathcal{R}_d$ is a set of strict ($\mathcal{R}_s$) and defeasible ($\mathcal{R}_d$) inference rules of the form $\varphi_1, \ldots, \varphi_n \to \varphi$ and $\varphi_1, \ldots, \varphi_n \Rightarrow \varphi$ respectively (where φ_i, φ are meta-variables ranging over wff in $\mathcal{L}$), and $\mathcal{R}_s \cap \mathcal{R}_d = \emptyset$.

- $n : \mathcal{R}_d \longrightarrow \mathcal{L}$ is a naming convention for defeasible rules.

We write $\psi = -\varphi$ just in case $\psi = \neg\varphi$ or $\varphi = \neg\psi$.

---

[1]In most papers on *ASPIC*$^+$ negation can be non-symmetric, an idea taken from [6]. In this paper we present the special case with symmetric negation.

Definition 3. [**Knowledge bases**] A *knowledge base* in an $AS = (\mathcal{L}, \mathcal{R}, n)$ is a set $\mathcal{K} \subseteq \mathcal{L}$ consisting of two disjoint subsets $\mathcal{K}_n$ (the *axioms*) and $\mathcal{K}_p$ (the *ordinary premises*).

Intuitively, the axioms are certain knowledge and thus cannot be attacked, whereas the ordinary premises are uncertain and thus can be attacked.

Arguments can be constructed step-by-step from knowledge bases by chaining inference rules into trees. In what follows, for a given argument the function `Prem` returns all its premises, `Conc` returns its conclusion and `Sub` returns all its sub-arguments.

Definition 4. [**Arguments**] An *argument* A on the basis of a knowledge base KB in an argumentation system $(\mathcal{L}, \mathcal{R}, n)$ is:

1. φ if $\varphi \in \mathcal{K}$ with: $\text{Prem}(A) = \{\varphi\}$; $\text{Conc}(A) = \varphi$; $\text{Sub}(A) = \{\varphi\}$; $\text{TopRule}(A) = $ undefined.

2. $A_1, \ldots A_n \to/\Rightarrow \psi$ if $A_1, \ldots, A_n$ are arguments such that there exists a strict/defeasible rule $\text{Conc}(A_1), \ldots, \text{Conc}(A_n) \to/\Rightarrow \psi$ in $\mathcal{R}_s/\mathcal{R}_d$. $\text{Prem}(A) = \text{Prem}(A_1) \cup \ldots \cup \text{Prem}(A_n)$, $\text{Conc}(A) = \psi$, $\text{Sub}(A) = \text{Sub}(A_1) \cup \ldots \cup \text{Sub}(A_n) \cup \{A\}$; $\text{TopRule}(A) = \text{Conc}(A_1), \ldots, \text{Conc}(A_n) \to/\Rightarrow \psi$.

Arguments can be attacked in three ways: on their premises (undermining attack), on their conclusion (rebutting attack) or on an inference step (undercutting attack). The latter two are only possible on applications of defeasible inference rules.

Definition 5. [**Attack**] A *attacks* B iff A *undercuts*, *rebuts* or *undermines* B, where:

• A *undercuts* argument B (on B') iff $\text{Conc}(A) = -n(r)$ and $B' \in \text{Sub}(B)$ such that B''s top rule r is defeasible.

• A *rebuts* argument B (on B') iff $\text{Conc}(A) = -\varphi$ for some $B' \in \text{Sub}(B)$ of the form $B''_1, \ldots, B''_n \Rightarrow \varphi$.

• Argument A *undermines* B (on B') iff $\text{Conc}(A) = -\varphi$ for some $B' = \varphi, \varphi \notin \mathcal{K}_n$.

Undercutting attacks succeed as *defeats* independently of preferences over arguments, since they express exceptions to defeasible inference rules. Rebutting and undermining attacks succeed only if the attacked argument is not stronger than the attacking argument.

Definition 6. [**Defeat**] A *defeats* B iff: A undercuts B, or; A rebuts/undermines B on B' and $A \nprec B'$.

Note that the definitions of attack and defeat explicitly take the subargument relations between arguments into account. In fact, it was recently shown in [20] and [14] that instantiations of Dung's framework that do not do so are severely limited in applicability and run the risk of producing counterintuitive consequences.

Definition 7. Let AT be an *argumentation theory* (AS, KB). A *structured argumentation framework (SAF)* defined by AT, is a triple $\langle \mathcal{A}, \mathcal{C}, \preceq \rangle$ where $\mathcal{A}$ is the set of all finite arguments constructed from KB in AS, $\preceq$ is an ordering on $\mathcal{A}$, and $(X, Y) \in \mathcal{C}$ iff X attacks Y.

Abstract argumentation frameworks are then generated as follows:

Definition 8. [**Argumentation frameworks**] An *abstract argumentation framework (AF) corresponding to a* SAF $= \langle \mathcal{A}, \mathcal{C}, \preceq \rangle$ is a pair $(\mathcal{A}, D)$ such that D is the defeat relation on $\mathcal{A}$ determined by SAF.

Now one way to define the justification status of an argument is as follows (other definitions are possible but for present purposes they do not matter):

Definition 9. A wff $\varphi \in \mathcal{L}$ is *justified* if φ is the conclusion of a justified argument, *defensible* if φ is not justified but the conclusion of a defensible argument, and *overruled* if φ is defeated by a justified argument.

2 Labellings vs. recursive labellings

My view on [8]'s work has always been that it has to be used as the final component of a full-fledged argumentation logic, to define a nonmonotonic consequence notion for the logic. First the structure of arguments must be defined, which will in general be recursive to reflect the step-by-step nature of argumentation. Then a defeat relation must be defined, which will in general have to distinguish between direct and indirect defeat, because of the recursive structure of arguments. Then the resulting set of arguments and the defeat relation defined over it are taken to be a Dung AF. Adopting a semantics for the AF then yields the consequence notion for the logic.

While theoretically this works fine, a practical drawback is that in the thus induced Dung AF the distinction between direct and indirect defeat is left implicit, since in a Dung AF the subargument relation between arguments cannot be shown. For presentation purposes this is somewhat unnatural. Consider the following example of a civil legal case, adapted from [21]. Assume that in a medical malpractice case, a doctor is liable for compensation if the patient was injured because of the doctor's negligence, and that if a patient is injured in a non-risky operation, this is negligence. We also have that an appendicitis operation generally is a non-risky operation but that operations on patients with bad blood circulation are generally risky. Assume finally, that a given patient was injured in an appendicitis operation and that two medical tests gave contradicting results on whether the patient had bad blood circulation. This all can be represented with the following facts and defeasible rules ($\mathcal{R}_d$ consists of r_1-r_6 while $\mathcal{K}$ consists of f_1-f_4; note that for convenience we here use the *ASPIC*$^+$ rules in domain-specific ways).

r_1:	*injury, negligence* $\Rightarrow$ *compensation*	f_1:	*injury*
r_2:	*injury,* $\neg$ *risky operation* $\Rightarrow$ *negligence*	f_2:	*appendicitis*
r_3:	*appendicitis* $\Rightarrow \neg$ *riskyOperation*	f_3:	*medicalTest1*
r_4:	*badCirculation* $\Rightarrow$ *riskyOperation*	f_4:	*medicalTest2*
r_5:	*medicalTest1* $\Rightarrow$ *badCirculation*		
r_6:	*medicalTest2* $\Rightarrow \neg$ *badCirculation*		

We then have the following arguments:

A_1:	*injury*		B_1:	*medicalTests1*
A_2:	*appendicitis*		B_2:	$B_1 \Rightarrow$ *badCirculation*
A_3:	$A_2 \Rightarrow \neg$ *riskyOperation*		B_3:	$B_2 \Rightarrow$ *riskyOperation*
A_4:	$A_1, A_3 \Rightarrow$ *negligence*			
A_5:	$A_1, A_4 \Rightarrow$ *compensation*		C_1:	*medicalTests2*
			C_2:	$C_1 \Rightarrow \neg$ *badCirculation*

Let us first concentrate on the attack relations between the arguments. At first sight it would seem that we have three arguments $A = A_1$-A_5, $B = B_1$-B_3 and $C = C_1$-C_2, such that both A and B and B and C mutually attack each other as in Figure 1. However, upon closer investigation things are more complicated.

Figure 1. Abstract attack graph (simplistic)

First, we have not three but ten arguments. Second, we have not four but seven attack relations: A_3 and B_3 directly rebut each other and as a consequence B_3 indirectly rebuts both A_4 and A_5, namely on A_3. Likewise, B_2 and C_2 directly rebut each other and as a consequence C_2 indirectly rebuts B_3, namely on B_2. So the full abstract attack graph induced by the *ASPIC*$^+$ attack relations is as in Figure 2. In this graph the information is lost that some attack arrows duplicate other attack arrows. For example, the arrows from B_3 to A_4 and A_5 duplicate the arrow from B_3 to A_3.

Therefore, this graph does not adequately show a decision maker which conflicts have to be resolved. When faced with this graph, a decision maker might think that s/he has to determine of seven attack relations whether they result

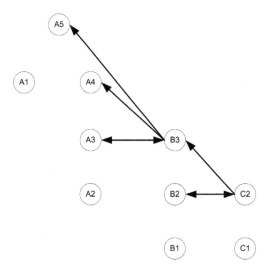

Figure 2. Abstract attack graph (correct)

in defeat, but in fact s/he has to determine this for only four attack relations, namely, those between A_3 and B_2 and between B_2 and C_2. (This in fact illustrates the problems with Preference-based abstract *AFs* [1] and abstract resolution semantics [3], since these approaches cannot recognise that some defeat relations duplicate other defeat relations.) If the attacks are resolved according to Definition 6 then the indirectly defeat relations are correctly computed on the basis of the direct defeat relations, resulting in an abstract argumentation framework with the intuitive outcome. For example, suppose that $A_3 \prec B_3$ and $B_2 \prec C_2$. Then we obtain Figure 3 (which shows the unique labelling in all semantics, in which the arguments that are *in* are coloured gray). However, even though this outcome is intuitive, the process of obtaining it from the abstract attack graph is not well explained by these graphics.

Moreover, the result of the abstract *AF* has to be transported back with Definition 9 to the *SAF* that induced it, which tells us that B_2 and B_3 are *out* in all labellings while all other arguments are *in* in all labellings. Graphically this can be displayed as in Figure 4. Now this graph suggests a more intuitive way to explain how the status of A_5 can be evaluated: A_5 is *in* since it has no direct defeaters and both of its direct subarguments A_1 and A_4 are *in*. In turn, A_1 is in since it is an undefeated fact while A_4 is *in* since it has no direct defeaters and both of its direct subarguments A_1 and A_3 are *in*. In turn, A_3 is *in* since, firstly, its direct defeater B_3 is *out* and, secondly, its direct subargument A_2 is *in*since it is an undefeated fact. Finally, B_3 is *out* since it has a direct defeater that is *in*

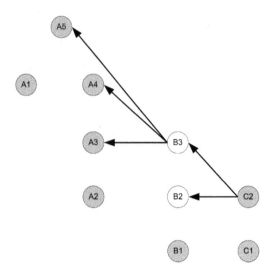

Figure 3. Abstract argumentation framework

namely, C_2, which is is preferred over B_3 and which direct subargument C_3 is *in* since it is an undefeated fact.

Such an explanation arguably shows more clearly why an argument has a certain status, since it looks at both the defeat relations and the inferential support relations between the arguments. In fact, such an explanation directly follows Pollock's [17] recursive definition of 'defeat status assignments' (two other systems with similar recursive definitions are Defeasible Logic [16] and Carneades [9]). I will therefore in the next section adapt this definition to *AS-PIC*$^+$ and then prove equivalence with Definition 1 of labellings for *ASPIC*$^+$.

3   Recursive labellings

To adapt Pollock's [17] recursive definition of 'defeat status assignments' to *ASPIC*$^+$, first the definitions of attack and defeat must be adapted; as in [17] they now only capture direct attack and defeat while their indirect counterparts will now be considered by the recursive labelling definition.

Definition 10. [p-Attack] *A p-attacks B iff A p-undercuts, p-rebuts or p-undermines B, where:*

• *A p-undercuts* argument B iff $\text{Conc}(A) = -n(r)$ and B has a defeasible top rule r.

• *A p-rebuts* argument B iff $\text{Conc}(A) = -\text{Conc}(B)$ and B has a defeasible top rule.

• Argument *A p-undermines* B iff $\text{Conc}(A) = -\varphi$ and $B = \varphi$, $\varphi \notin \mathcal{K}_n$.

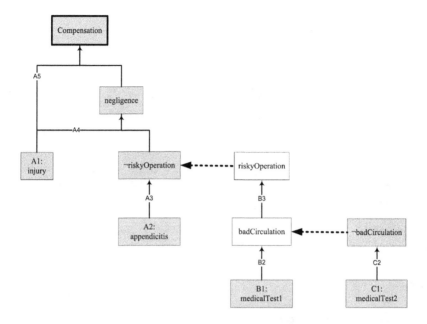

Figure 4. ASPIC+ framework

In our example we have that A_3 and B_3 p-attack each other but B_2 does not p-attack A_4 or A_5. Likewise, B_2 and C_2 p-attack each other but C_2 does not p-attack B_3.

Definition 11. [**p-Defeat**] *A p-defeats B iff:A* p-undercuts B, or; A p-rebuts/p-undermines B and $A \not\prec B$.

It is easy to verify that:

Proposition 1. *A* defeats B iff A p-defeats B or a proper subargument of B.

Proof:

- *A* undermines B iff:
  $\text{Conc}(A) = -\varphi$ and $B = \varphi$, $\varphi \notin \mathcal{K}_n$, or A undermines some subargument B' of B such that B' is a premise of B; iff:
  A p-defeats B or a proper subargument of B.

- *A* rebuts B iff:
  $\text{Conc}(A) = -\text{Conc}(B)$ and B has a defeasible top rule or for some subargument B' of B it holds that $\text{Conc}(A) = -\text{Conc}(B')$ and B' has a defeasible top rule; iff:
  A p-rebuts B or a proper subargument of B.

- A undercuts B iff:

  $\text{Conc}(A) = -n(r)$ and B has a defeasible top rule r or for some subargument B' of B it holds that $\text{Conc}(A) = -n(r)$ and B' has a defeasible top rule r; iff:

  A p-undercuts B or a proper subargument of B.

Then the proposition easily follows. $\square$

Definition 12. A *p-structured argumentation framework (pSAF)* defined by an argumentation theory $AT = (AS, KB)$ is a triple $\langle \mathcal{A}, \mathcal{C}^p, \preceq \rangle$ where $\mathcal{A}$ is the set of all arguments constructed from KB in AS, $\preceq$ is an ordering on $\mathcal{A}$, and $(X, Y) \in \mathcal{C}^p$ iff X p-attacks Y.

Definition 13. [p-Argumentation frameworks] A *p-abstract argumentation framework (pAF) corresponding to a pSAF* = $\langle \mathcal{A}, \mathcal{C}^p, \preceq \rangle$ is a pair $(\mathcal{A}, D)$ such that D is the p-defeat relation on $\mathcal{A}$ determined by *pSAF*.

Definition 14. [p-labellings.]

1. (In, Out) is a *p-labelling* of a *pAF* iff $In \cap Out = \emptyset$ and for all $A \in \mathcal{A}_{pAF}$ it holds that:

   (a) A is labelled *in* iff:

      i. All arguments that p-defeat A are labelled *out*; and
      ii. If A is of the form $B_1, \ldots, B_n \to / \Rightarrow \varphi$ then all of $B_1, \ldots, B_n$ are labelled *in*; and

   (b) A is labelled *out* iff:

      i. A is p-defeated by an argument that is labelled *in*; or
      ii. A is of the form $B_1, \ldots, B_n \to / \Rightarrow \varphi$ and some of $B_1, \ldots, B_n$ are labelled *out*.

   The notions of complete, stable, preferred and grounded labellings are defined as above.

Theorem 2. (In, Out) *is a p-labelling of pAF corresponding to pSAF* = $\langle \mathcal{A}, \mathcal{C}^p, \preceq \rangle$ *iff* (In, Out) *is a labelling of AF corresponding to SAF* = $\langle \mathcal{A}, \mathcal{C}, \preceq \rangle$.

Proof:

From left to right, assume first that A is *in*. We first prove by induction on the structure of A that all subarguments of A are *in*. For $A \in \mathcal{K}$ this holds trivially. If A is of the form $B_1, \ldots, B_n \to / \Rightarrow \varphi$ then if A is *in*, by definition of p-labellings also all of $B_1, \ldots, B_n$ are *in*. By the induction hypothesis all subarguments of all of $B_1, \ldots, B_n$ are also *in*, but then all subarguments of A

are *in*. Now since A is *in*, we have that all B that p-defeat A are *out* and all subarguments of A are *in*. Then all B that p-defeat A are *out* and all B that p-defeat a subargument of A are *out*, but then all B that defeat A are *out*. So constraint (1) on labellings is satisfied.

Assume next that A is *out*. We prove by induction that A is defeated by some argument that is *in*, in which case constraint (2) on labellings is satisfied. For $A \in \mathcal{K}$ this holds trivially, while if A is of the form $B_1, \ldots, B_n \to / \Rightarrow \varphi$ then either some B that p-defeats A is *in* or some B_i is *out*. In the first case, B also defeats A. In the second case, by the induction hypothesis B_i is defeated by an argument that is *in*. But then A is defeated by the same argument.

From right to left, assume first that A is *in*. Then all B that defeat A are *out*. But then all B that p-defeat A or a proper subargument of A are *out*. Next we prove by induction that all proper subarguments of A are *in*. This is trivial if $A \in \mathcal{K}$. Suppose next A is of the form $B_1, \ldots, B_n \to / \Rightarrow \varphi$. Then by the induction hypothesis for all of $B_1, \ldots, B_n$, all their proper subarguments, including the immediate ones, are in. Moreover, by assumption all p-defeaters of any such B_i are *out*. But then all B_i are *in*. Then constraint (1) on p-labellings is satisfied.

Assume next that A is *out*. Then A is defeated by an argument that is *in*. But then either A or a proper subargument A' of A is p-defeated by an argument B that is *in*. In the first case, constraint (2) of p-labellings is satisfied. In the second case A is of the form $B_1, \ldots, B_n \to / \Rightarrow \varphi$. Note that A' is *out* and that A' is a subargument of some B_i. But then B defeats B_i, so since B is *in* we have that B_i is *out*. So constraint (2) on p-labellings is satisfied. $\square$

Since the sets that are labelled, respectively, p-labelled are the same, it immediately follows that the equivalence also holds for the notions of stable, preferred and grounded labellings.

This result is very similar to Hadassa Jakobovits' results in [11, 12] that Pollock's [17] 'labellings' for his inference graphs are equivalent to preferred semantics and that his 'partial labellings' are equivalent to her 'rooted complete labellings'. The main difference is that Pollock's inference graphs are not the same as *ASPIC*$^+$ SAFs (although equivalence should be easy to prove).

With these equivalences established, there is no need any more to translate an *ASPIC*$^+$ argumentation theory into a Dung-style abstract argumentation framework. Instead, the labellings of arguments and the corresponding status of their conclusions can be shown inductively, which, as explained at the end of Section 2, is arguably more natural.

4   Argument structure in purely abstract frameworks

In the second part of the paper I want investigate an idea originally proposed by [23]. Their idea is that arguments in a Dung AF are instantiated as a rule and that the step-by-step nature of arguments is induced by allowing such rules to be attacked by special arguments challenging one of their antecedents, and to in turn allow these arguments to be attacked by a rule with as consequent the challenged antecedent. I will formalise this idea in the definition of a wbd-argumentation theory (*wbd-AF*), in which, given an $ASPIC^+$ argumentation theory, arguments are either rules or items from the knowledge base or *why* φ moves for any φ that is an antecedent of some rule. My aim then is to translate such a *wbd-AF* into an $ASPIC^+$-induced *pAF* and then to investigate correspondences between the labellings of a *wbd-AF* and the p-labellings of the corresponding *pAF* as defined above. If any correspondence is found, then the results of the previous section make it carry over to the Dungean semantics of $ASPIC^+$-induced *AFs*.

It will turn out that correspondences can be found but only under some limiting assumptions. The point is that in the new approach the success of an attack as defeat should completely depend on the last of the arguments, that is, on their top rules. This at least requires that arguments are compared with a last-link argument ordering. Moreover, it excludes the use of non-axiom premises and even the use of strict rules. To see the latter, consider the following example, in which a defeasible rule is attacked by a strict rule:

$$p \Rightarrow_{r1} q$$
$$r \rightarrow \neg q$$

In $ASPIC^+$ with last-link comparison, whether a rebuttal with a strict top rule succeeds depends on how the antecedents of the strict rule (in this case r) are derived. For example, if we have

$$s \Rightarrow_{r2} r$$
$$r_1 < r_2$$

Then the attack with the strict rule succeeds but if we have

$$t \Rightarrow_{r3} r$$
$$r_r < r_1$$

then the attack with the strict rule does not succeed. So whether the attack with the strict rule succeeds depends on how a *why* r attack on the strict rule is counterattacked. So to make [23]'s approach work in general the argument ordering of the wbd-style arguments must be made dependent on the ways the antecedents of the rules can be derived but this defeats the idea of the approach

Table 1. wbd arguments and attacks

Arguments	Attacks
φ $(\varphi \in \mathcal{K})$	
$\varphi_1, \ldots, \varphi_n \Rightarrow_r \varphi$	*why* φ_i $(\varphi_i \in \{\varphi_1, \ldots, \varphi_n\})$ $-\varphi$ $(\varphi \in \mathcal{K})$ $-n(r)$ $(\varphi \in \mathcal{K})$ $\varphi_1, \ldots, \varphi_n \Rightarrow_{r'} -\varphi$
why φ	$\varphi_1, \ldots, \varphi_n \Rightarrow_{r'} -n(r)$ $\varphi_1, \ldots, \varphi_n \Rightarrow_r \varphi$ φ $(\varphi \in \mathcal{K})$

(this is why the nodes in [17]'s defeat graphs are not just well-formed formulas but 'lines of argument' encoding the way a formula is derived; thus if a formula can be derived in more than one way, the graph contains more than one node with the same formula). In fact, this is a problem for any model that defines the evaluation of arguments in a top-down manner without fully constructing the argument before evaluating it, such as also my own dialogue framework in [18]. In that paper I made an assumption that 'backwards extending' an argument in reply to *why* moves cannot make an argument weaker, but then I did not realise how strong that assumption is.

For these reasons I will from now on assume that the set of strict rules is empty and that all premises are axioms. Then with the last link ordering the preference relation between two rule arguments solely depends on their last rules. Note also that in *ASPIC*$^+$ rebutting an argument with an item from $\mathcal{K}_n$ always succeeds, since strict-and-firm arguments (that is, arguments with only strict rules and only axiom premises) are always preferred over all other arguments.

As for the attack relations in the wbd approach, defeasible rules are attacked by any undercutting rule, by any defeasible rule with contradictory consequent, by any item from the knowledge base that contradicts its consequent, and by a *why* φ move for any antecedent φ of the rule. Items from the knowledge base have no attackers while *why* φ moves are attacked by any rule with consequent φ. Table 1 lists all these well-formed arguments and attacks (it assumes all mentioned rules to be in $\mathcal{R}_d$; for convenience, their informal name is sometimes subscripted to the arrow). The defeat relation now equals the attack relation except that an attack of a defeasible rule with a contradictory consequent only succeeds if the attacker is not inferior to its target, that is, only if $r' \not< r$.

This induces a *wbd-AF*, that is, a set of arguments in the just-defined sense with a binary relation of defeat. Formally all this amounts to the following:

Definition 15. Let AS be any argumentation system with no strict rules, KB a knowledge base with no ordinary premises, A^g the set of all arguments given KB and AS as defined in Table 1, C^g the attack relation on A^g as defined in Table 1 and $\leq$ an ordering on R_d. Then the *wbd argumentation framework* corresponding to $(AS, KB, \leq)$ is a pair *wbd-AF* $= (A^g, D^g)$ where D^g is the defeat relation on A^g defined by C^g and $\leq$ as follows: A defeats B iff A attacks B and, in case the attack is as in the fifth line of Table 1, $r' \not< r$.

A *pSAF corresponding to* $(AS, KB, \leq)$ is a triple $(A, C, \preceq)$ where $\preceq$ is the last-link ordering on A induced by $\leq$ as defined in [15]. A *pAF corresponding to* $(AS, KB, \leq)$ is the *pAF* corresponding to *pSAF* as defined in Definition 13.

A *wbd-AF* is *completed* if it (1) contains every possible attack and (2) has no unanswered *why* attacks and (3) K and R_d are defined such that no attack cycles through *why* moves are possible (that is, circular arguments are excluded).

Labellings of completed *wbd-AFs* are now defined in the usual way of Definition 1.

In fact, I am only interested in *wbd-AFs* that are 'grounded' in the knowledge base. Therefore, from now on I will implicitly assume that all *wbd-AFs* are completed. Then a given *wbd-AF* is converted to a *pAF* as follows:

Definition 16. For any *wbd-AF* $G = (A^g, D^g)$ the corresponding *pAF* $G^p = (A^p, D^p)$ is inductively defined as follows.

1. $A \in A^p$ iff:

    (a) $A \in A^g$ and $A \in K$; or

    (b) A is of the form $B_1, \ldots, B_n \Rightarrow \varphi$ and $\mathrm{Conc}(B_1), \ldots, \mathrm{Conc}(B_n) \Rightarrow \varphi \in A^g$ and all of $B_1, \ldots, B_n$ are in A^p.

2. $(A, B) \in D^p$ iff $A, B \in A^p$ and B has a top rule r and (i) $A \in K$ or (ii) A has a top rule $\mathrm{Conc}(A_1), \ldots, \mathrm{Conc}(A_n) \Rightarrow_r' \varphi$ and $(r', r) \in D^g$.

Figure 5 visualises the *wbd-AF* corresponding to the example of Section 2. It assumes that $r_5 < r_6$ and $r_3 < r_4$, corresponding to the last-link argument ordering $A_3 \prec B_3$ and $B_2 \prec C_2$ of our medical negligence example[2]

Proposition 3. For any *wbd-AF* $G = (A^g, D^g)$ corresponding to $(KB, AS, \leq)$ with corresponding *pAF* $G^p = (A^p, D^p)$, and any *pSAF* $= (A, D)$:

---

[2]Defeasible rules are written with $\rightarrow$ instead of $\Rightarrow$ since my drawing program has no double arrow.

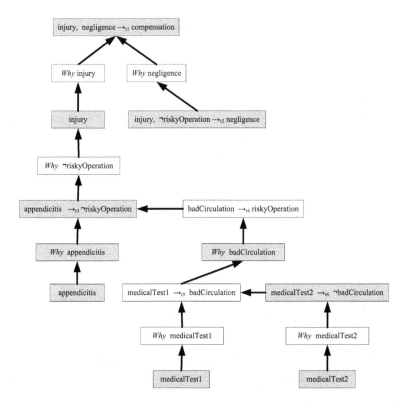

Figure 5. wbd argumentation framework

1. A is an argument in $\mathcal{A}^p$ iff A is an argument in $\mathcal{A}$.

2. $(A, B) \in \mathcal{D}^p$ iff $(A, B) \in \mathcal{D}$.

Proof:
Proof of (1): From left to right follows from the fact that all arguments in $\mathcal{A}^p$ only use elements from $\mathcal{R}_d$ and $\mathcal{K}$ and the structural similarity between Definition 16(1,2) and Definition 4. From right to left is proven with induction on the structure of arguments. For elements of $\mathcal{K}$ this follows immediately from the fact that G is completed. Consider next any argument on the basis of AT of the form $A_1, \ldots, A_n \Rightarrow \varphi$. Then by the induction hypothesis all of $A_1, \ldots, A_n$ are in $\mathcal{A}^p$. Moreover, by construction of $\mathcal{A}^p$ we have that for all such A_i, either $A_i \in \mathcal{K}$ so $A_i \in \mathcal{A}^g$ or A_i is of the form $\mathtt{Conc}(B_1), \ldots, \mathtt{Conc}(B_n) \Rightarrow_{ri} \varphi$ so $r_i \in \mathcal{A}^g$. But then any *why* $\mathtt{Conc}(A_i)$ attack on A can be counterattacked by A_i or r_i, so since G is completed, $A \in \mathcal{A}^g$. But then $A \in \mathcal{A}^p$ by clause (2) of Definition 16.
Proof of (2):

From left to right: If $(A, B) \in \mathcal{D}^p$ then B has a defeasible top rule r. If $A \in \mathcal{K}$ or A has conclusion $-n(r)$ then A p-defeats B regardless of the rule priorities. If A has a defeasible top rule r' then $r' \not< r$ since $(r', r) \in \mathcal{D}^g$. But then A successfully p-rebuts B, so A p-defeats B.

From right to left, note first that by (1) both A and B are in $\mathcal{A}^p$ and then by definition of $\mathcal{A}^p$, A and B are either themselves in $\mathcal{A}^g$ as elements of $\mathcal{K}$ or their top rules are in $\mathcal{A}^g$. Then because of the restrictive assumptions on AT in Definition 15 it holds that A p-defeats B iff B has a defeasible top rule r and either (1) $A \in \mathcal{K}$, in which case $(A, B) \in \mathcal{D}^p$ since $(A, r) \in \mathcal{D}^g$ by row (3) of Table 1, or (2) A has a defeasible top rule r' with (2a) consequent $-n(r)$, in which case $(A, B) \in \mathcal{D}^p$ since $(r', r) \in \mathcal{D}^g$ by row (4) of Table 1, or with (2b) consequent $-\varphi$ (where φ is the consequent of r), in which case $(A, B) \in \mathcal{D}^p$ since $(r', r) \in \mathcal{D}^g$ by row (5) of Table 1 and $r' \not< r$. □

It can be shown that in a *wbd-AF* all arguments in the corresponding *pAF* are 'hidden'. Such hidden arguments are first defined as follows, after which it will be shown that together they correspond to the arguments of the corresponding *pAF*.

Definition 17. For each non-why argument A in G a directed acyclic graph $T = (N, L)$ is inductively defined as follows:

1. $(N_0, L_0) = (\{A\}, \emptyset)$

2.

   (a) $N_{i+1} = N_i \cup \{A^*\}$ if A^* is some argument in G that attacks some why-attacker B of some argument $A^i \in N_i$ such that no attacker of B is in N_i, otherwise $N_{i+n} = N_i$;

   (b) $L_{i+1} = L_i \cup \{(A^*, A^i) \mid A^i \in N_i$ and $\mathrm{Conc}(A^*) \in \mathrm{Ant}(A^i)\}$ if some A^* as defined under (a) exists, otherwise $L_{i+1} = L_i$.

T^A denotes for any non-why argument $A \in G$ the set of all such graphs T for A, while T^G denotes the set of all A^T for any non-why argument A in G.

Definition 18. Let G be a *wbd-AF* with corresponding *pAF* G^p. For any $A^T \in T^G$, the corresponding argument A^p is defined as follows:

1. If $A^T \in \mathcal{K}$ then $A^p = A^T$;

2. If the root of A^T is in $\mathcal{R}^d$ then A^p is of the form $A_1, \ldots, A_n \Rightarrow \mathrm{Conc}(T)$, where $A_1, \ldots, A_n$ correspond to the subtrees $A^{T1}, \ldots, A^{Tn}$ of A^T starting with A's children.

Definitions 17 and 18 are illustrated by the structural similarity of Figures 4 and 5. The idea is that in Figure 5 all *why* moves are removed and the thus disconnected rules and facts are connected by support links.

Proposition 4. For any *wbd-AF* G with corresponding *pAF* G^p:

1. for any $A^T \in T^G$ its corresponding argument A^p is in G^p;

2. for any argument A in G^p there exists a unique $T \in T^G$ such that A corresponds to T.

Proof:
Proof of (1): For elements in $\mathcal{K}$ this is obvious. Next, the induction hypothesis is that for any $A^T \in T^G$ all trees $B^{T1}, \ldots, B^{Tn}$ for all children $B_1, \ldots, B_n$ of A in T correspond to an argument in G^p. By construction of A^T we have that G contains a rule $\mathrm{Conc}(B_1), \ldots, \mathrm{Conc}(B_n) \Rightarrow \mathrm{Conc}(A)$ so by construction of G^p it holds that $B_1, \ldots, B_n \Rightarrow \mathrm{Conc}(A)$ is an argument in G^p; moreover, this argument corresponds to A^T.
Proof of (2): Suppose $A \in G^p$. If $A \in \mathcal{K}$ then $(A, \emptyset) \in T^G$. Assume next A is of the form $B_1, \ldots, B_n \Rightarrow B$ and all B_i correspond to some unique $T_i \in T^G$. By construction of G^p we have that $\mathrm{Conc}(B_1), \ldots, \mathrm{Conc}(B_n) \Rightarrow \mathrm{Conc}(A) \in G$. Then since G is completed, $(N, L) \in T^G$ where $N = T_1, \ldots, T_n \cup \{A\}$ and $L = L_1, \ldots, L_n \cup \{(B_1, A), \ldots, (B_n, A)\}$. Finally, by construction, (N, L) is unique in this sense. □

Corollary 5. Any $A \in G$ that is not a *why* argument is either in G^p or a top rule of some argument in G^p. And any rule or premise of an argument G^p is an argument in G.

Proof:
The second holds by construction of G^p, while the first follows since any A^T corresponds to an argument in G^p as specified in Proposition 4(1). □

Lemma 6. For any labelling L of a *wbd-AF* G, any $A \in G$ is labelled *in* in L iff all defeaters of A are *out* in L and for some $T \in T^A$, all children of A in T are *in* in L.

Proof:
From right to left is immediate, as is the first part from left to right. For the remainder, note that among all defeaters of A that are *out* in L are all its *why* attackers. Then each such attacker has an attacker from $\mathcal{K}$ or $\mathcal{R}_d$ that is *in*. But then by construction of T^A every set consisting of one such attacker for every *why* attacker of A is for some $T \in T^A$ the set of all children of A in T. □

Lemma 7. For any *wbd-AF* G with corresponding *pAF* G^p and all A^T and B^T in G^T it holds that B defeats A iff B^p defeats A^p for any A^p and B^p in G^p corresponding to A^T and B^T.

   Proof: obvious.

Now the following correspondences can be proven between labellings of G and G^p.

Theorem 8. *Let G be a completed wbd-AF corresponding to $(AS, KB, \leq)$ with corresponding pAF G^p and let pAF' correspond to $(AS, KB, \leq)$. Then for any $\varphi \in \mathcal{L}$ it holds that φ is defensible (justified) on the basis of G iff φ is defensible (justified) on the basis of G^p iff φ is defensible (justified) on the basis of pAF'.*

   Proof:
This is proven by proving the following observations:

   1. Any non-why argument $A \in G$ is *in* in some labelling (all labellings) of G iff for some $T \in A^T$ the argument corresponding to T is *in* in some p-labelling (all p-labellings) of G^p.

   2. Any argument $A \in G^p$ is *in* in some p-labelling (all p-labellings) of G^p iff A^T is *in* in some labelling (all labellings) of G, where A^T is the root of some $T \in T^G$ such that A corresponds to T.

   3. (1) and (2) also hold if G^p is replaced by pAF'.

Then (1) and (2) follow from the structural similarity between any A^T and its corresponding argument in G^p and Proposition 4, Corollary 5 and Lemmas 6 and 7. The idea from left to right is that any labelling of G corresponds via T^G with a p-labelling of G^p, since the set of all arguments in G^p corresponding to any element of T^G is precisely the set of all arguments in G^p. For the same reason, from right to left any p-labelling of G^p corresponds via T^G to a labelling of G.
Finally, (3) follows from (1), (2) and Proposition 3. $\square$

This result is illustrated by the correspondence between the (unique) labelling of Figure 5 and the (also unique) p-labelling of Figure 4. A further illustration is given by the following example:

$p \Rightarrow_{r1} q$

$r \Rightarrow_{r2} p$

$s \Rightarrow_{r3} p$

$\Rightarrow_{r4} s$

$\Rightarrow_{r5} \neg s$

$\mathcal{K} = \{r\}$

$r_4 < r_5$

This induces the *wbd-AF* of Figure 6 on the left, with its corresponding *pAF* on the right. This *wbd-AF* has a unique labelling in all semantics, in which

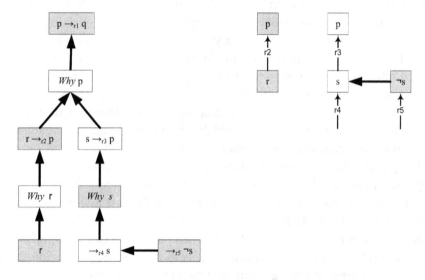

Figure 6. *wbd-AF* with corresponding *pAF*

$p \Rightarrow_{r1} q$ is *in*, but the corresponding G^p contains two alternative arguments with top rule r_1, one of which is *in* but the other is *out* in the (unique) p-labelling of G^p. This example thus shows that in general labellings of a *wbd-AF* do not have the same meaning as (p)-labellings of *SAFs* or *pSAFS*. In a wbd-labelling, that a rule is *in* means that there is *some* acceptable way of deriving its antecedents. By contrast, in a p-labelling, that an argument is *in* means that this argument with a *specifically indicated* way of deriving the antecedents of its top rule is acceptable.

Finally, I briefly compare the approach of this section with [23]. There are some minor differences: [23] make some specific assumptions on the logical object language, which they assume to just consist of propositional literals, that is, atoms and their negations; furthermore, they replace a *why* attack on a rule antecedent by an attack with the contradictory literal. A more important difference is that [23] do not assume a knowledge base but allow atomic arguments for any literal; moreover, such literals can not only be (asymmetrically) attacked by a rule for the original literal but also (symmetrically) by the original literal. As a consequence, the focus in [23] is not on deriving arguments from a knowledge base, which makes a detailed comparison with the present approach not straightforward.

5   Conclusion

This paper has investigated three ways to instantiate [8]'s abstract argumentation framework. The investigations have provided some reasons to believe that when the aim is to model realistic argumentation, too much focus on abstract argumentation frameworks may be harmful. First some presentational drawbacks were identified of systems for structured argumentation with inferential relations between arguments that explicitly model argument evaluation in terms of abstract argumentation frameworks. It was shown that these systems can be reformulated in a way that incorporates Dung's semantics in a stepwise evaluation of arguments, which arguably facilitates more natural explanations of dialectical argumentation evaluation. Then a method for modelling the evaluation of arguments with structure was examined in which the inferential relations between arguments are not taken into account. It turned out that this method only works well under some limiting assumptions, which do not need to be made in a model like $ASPIC^+$ that explicitly models inferential relations between arguments. Thus this paper adds to a growing body of evidence (cf. [20, 14] that adequate models of realistic argumentation should take both the structure of arguments and their inferential relations into account.

6   Afterword – some personal notes on Trevor Bench-Capon and his work

I first met Trevor Bench-Capon at JURIX 1990 in Leiden, The Netherlands, but it was not until the late 1990s that we became closer, starting with a visit by me in april that year to Liverpool, and continued during the famous Bonskeid meeting on argumentation in the Scottish hills in the summer of 2000, where we used to play an outdoors game of chess after every lunch and dinner (chess may be the only field at which I can (only slightly) top Trevor's level. Even with table tennis I suffered some terrible defeats). During my stay in Liverpool in 1999 I gave a talk in which, among other things, I summarised Dung's famous work on abstract argumentation frameworks. If I remember correctly, then neither Trevor nor his close colleague Paul Dunne knew Dung's work at the time. I still remember that especially Paul asked me many questions about

Dung's work during and after my talk, and later it turned out that my visit to Liverpool had sparked a long series of AI journal publications by the two them (I am glad to see that Paul acknowledges my modest historical role in his contribution to this volume).

Over the years Trevor and I found ourselves interacting more and more during conferences and later during the ASPIC project, always to my great pleasure, because of Trevor's intelligence, his knowledge of just about everything, his wisdom and his unbeatable sense of humour. One of the great joys of discussing research with Trevor is that he often shows you another way of looking at things. However, if this way is not quite yours, then such discussions do not always spark immediate collaboration. This may be one of the reasons why we started collaborating relatively late, namely in 2006, during a new visit of me to Liverpool, now for one month.

One of the points at which we did not always fully agree was how the structure of arguments should be accounted for in the context of Dung's abstract frameworks. Although we both agreed and still agree that Dung's work is a great formal tool for the study of argumentation, I have always thought that it should be combined with accounts of the structure of arguments and their inferential relations. In recent years I have become increasingly concerned about the dominance of purely abstract research on argumentation in our field, and in some recent papers I have (partly with Sanjay Modgil) identified some pittfalls of fully abstract approaches [20, 14]. I always found it slightly unfortunate that one of Trevor's best ideas ever (the inclusion of values in models of argumentation) was first formalised at the fully abstract level. Indeed, our first joint publication [5] was an attempt to re-model Trevor's idea (as meanwhile elaborated with Katie Atkinson) in terms of an account of structured argumentation (in fact a preliminary version of the $ASPIC^+$ framework). The work on this paper was a real joy for me (I still have great memories of our exciting lunch-time conversations at Costa's), but I had the impression that Trevor was at that time not yet fully convinced that the $ASPIC^+$-like technical machinery we used is useful. In fact, during one of our lunch meetings he showed me on a napkin how the structure of arguments can be accounted for purely within Dung's abstract frameworks. At that time I found his idea quite exotic, but later I came to realise that it made perfect sense. Section 4 of this paper has been an attempt to acknowledge this by relating Trevor's idea to $ASPIC^+$.

Whatever the merits are of fully abstract approaches to argumentation, the main idea of Trevor's [4], namely that practical argumentation needs to take societal values into account, has been extremely influential in recent years, and rightly so. Moreover, Trevor now also acknowledges the benefits of combining abstract with structured fameworks for argumentation, witness, for example, our recent joint work with Adam Wyner and Katie Atkinson on formalising argument schemes for legal case-based reasoning in ASPIC+ [22]. I hope I am not too unmodest if I claim that this (besides bringing Dung's gospel to Merseyside) is one small point at which I have been able to influence Trevor's work. If so, then this is just a small and insufficient return for the many great insights that he gave me and the many enjoyable moments I could have with him. I truly hope that there will be many more of such moments to come.

Bibliography

[1] L. Amgoud and C. Cayrol. Inferring from inconsistency in preference-based argumentation frameworks. *International Journal of Automated Reasoning*, 29:125–169, 2002.

[2] K.M. Atkinson and T.J.M. Bench-Capon. Practical reasoning as presumptive argumentation using action based alternating transition systems. *Artificial Intelligence*, 171:855–874, 2007.

[3] P. Baroni and M. Giacomin. Resolution-based argumentation semantics. In Ph. Besnard, S. Doutre, and A. Hunter, editors, *Computational Models of Argument. Proceedings of COMMA 2008*, pages 25–36, Amsterdam etc, 2008. IOS Press.

[4] T.J.M. Bench-Capon. Persuasion in practical argument using value-based argumentation frameworks. *Journal of Logic and Computation*, 13:429–448, 2003.

[5] T.J.M. Bench-Capon and H. Prakken. Justifying actions by accruing arguments. In P.E. Dunne and T.B.C. Bench-Capon, editors, *Computational Models of Argument. Proceedings of COMMA 2006*, pages 247–258. IOS Press, Amsterdam etc, 2006.

[6] A. Bondarenko, P.M. Dung, R.A. Kowalski, and F. Toni. An abstract, argumentation-theoretic approach to default reasoning. *Artificial Intelligence*, 93:63–101, 1997.

[7] M. Caminada and L. Amgoud. On the evaluation of argumentation formalisms. *Artificial Intelligence*, 171:286–310, 2007.

[8] P.M. Dung. On the acceptability of arguments and its fundamental role in nonmonotonic reasoning, logic programming, and n–person games. *Artificial Intelligence*, 77:321–357, 1995.

[9] T.F. Gordon, H. Prakken, and D.N. Walton. The Carneades model of argument and burden of proof. *Artificial Intelligence*, 171:875–896, 2007.

[10] N. Gorogiannis and A. Hunter. Instantiating abstract argumentation with classical-logic arguments: postulates and properties. *Artificial Intelligence*, 175:1479–1497, 2011.

[11] H. Jakobovits. *On the Theory of Argumentation Frameworks*. Doctoral dissertation Free University Brussels, 2000.

[12] H. Jakobovits and D. Vermeir. Robust semantics for argumentation frameworks. *Journal of Logic and Computation*, 9:215–261, 1999.

[13] S. Modgil. Hierarchical argumentation. In *Proceedings of the 10th European Conference on Logics in Artificial Intelligence (JELIA)*, pages 319–332, 2006.

[14] S. Modgil and H. Prakken. Resolutions in structured argumentation. In B. Verheij, S. Woltran, and S. Szeider, editors, *Computational Models of Argument. Proceedings of COMMA 2012*, pages 310–321. IOS Press, Amsterdam etc, 2012.

[15] S. Modgil and H. Prakken. A general account of argumentation with preferences. *Artificial Intelligence*, 195:361–397, 2013.

[16] D. Nute. Defeasible logic. In D. Gabbay, C.J. Hogger, and J.A. Robinson, editors, *Handbook of Logic in Artificial Intelligence and Logic Programming*, pages 253–395. Clarendon Press, Oxford, 1994.

[17] J.L. Pollock. *Cognitive Carpentry. A Blueprint for How to Build a Person*. MIT Press, Cambridge, MA, 1995.

[18] H. Prakken. Coherence and flexibility in dialogue games for argumentation. *Journal of Logic and Computation*, 15:1009–1040, 2005.

[19] H. Prakken. An abstract framework for argumentation with structured arguments. *Argument and Computation*, 1:93–124, 2010.

[20] H. Prakken. Some reflections on two current trends in formal argumentation. In *Logic Programs, Norms and Action. Essays in Honour of Marek J. Sergot on the Occasion of his 60th Birthday*, pages 249–272. Springer, Berlin/Heidelberg, 2012.

[21] H. Prakken and G. Sartor. On modelling burdens and standards of proof in structured argumentation. In K.D. Atkinson, editor, *Legal Knowledge and Information Systems. JURIX 2011: The Twenty-fourth Annual Conference*, pages 83–92. IOS Press, Amsterdam etc., 2011.

[22] H. Prakken, A.Z. Wyner, T.J.M. Bench-Capon, and K.D. Atkinson. A formalisation of argumentation schemes for legal case-based reasoning in ASPIC+. *Journal of Logic and Computation*, 2013. In press.

[23] A.Z. Wyner, T.J.M. Bench-Capon, and P.E. Dunne. Instantiating knowledge bases in abstract argumentation frameworks. In *Proceedings of the AAAI Fall 2009 Symposium on The Uses of Computational Argumentation*, pages 76–83. AAAI Press, 2009. Technical Report SS-09-06.

From UUM and CEG to CBR and ICAIL: a Journey in AI and Law

EDWINA RISSLAND*

Abstract

In this note I describe the context that set the stage for my work in case-based reasoning and AI & Law. It covers roughly the decade preceding the first ICAIL in 1987. It is not meant to be a general history of these fields[1] but more a recap of my own personal journey on the road from models for understanding understanding mathematics ("UUM") to example-based reasoning ("EBR") and constrained example generation ("CEG") to case-based reasoning ("CBR") and AI & Law.

1 Understanding Understanding Mathematics: The beginnings, but in mathematics

Having been trained classically as a mathematician, I had always been intrigued by what it takes to *really* understand an area of mathematics that forms a cohesive and roughly circumscribable body of knowledge – a "mini theory" – like continuous functions in real analysis or eigenvalues in linear algebra. To know how the knowledge is interconnected. To know what pieces of information depend – logically, conceptually, pedagogically – on what other pieces. To be able to visualize the mathematical landscape with its peaks and valleys and to know which items of knowledge are like base camps and bridges whose primary purpose is to enable one to scale the summits that are the climaxes of a theory, the *raison* for working one's way through all the preliminaries. To have an arsenal of known examples and counter-examples – and know how to make new ones – to use to cut off dead ends, refine exploration, or suggest entirely new routes to try. There is a lot here, but could it be bundled into a cohesive representation that could help us understand what is involved in the process of understanding mathematics – that is, *understanding understanding*

---

*University of Massachusetts at Amherst, Department of Computer Science
[1]For AI and Law, see [32, 7].

mathematics or UUM – as well as create a framework for building interactive environments for both professional and neophyte mathematicians. This was the subject of my 1977 dissertation at MIT: *Epistemology, Representation, Understanding and Interactive Exploration of Mathematical Theories.*

In this framework I felt that examples and counter-examples should play a central role. I had often found many counter-examples to be exceedingly clever and beautifully crafted to serve reasoning goals like refuting a claim or showing the limits of a concept, and that examples in general seemed just the thing to help one better understand a concept or theorem. But where do they come from? How does one generate them? What role do they play in mathematical knowledge and understanding?

Clearly, examples of all kinds are an essential part of mathematical expertise despite the focus of so many formalists, like those in the Bourbaki group, on the logico-deductive aspects with its 'holy trinity' of definition, theorem and proof. Examples in Bourbaki are mere afterthoughts. Such a purely logic-based view seems to miss large chunks of mathematical knowledge: concrete examples, informal kernels of wisdom, paradigmatic prototypes, generic diagrams, etc. Some of this can be found in compendia of examples and counter-examples in fields like analysis and topology and some in books on problem solving like those by Polya [12] but it is largely underrepresented. To me, the idea that mathematics flows inexorably from definition to claim to proof – a fiction presented in courses like high school plane geometry – seemed simplistic, as much of a caricature of the real process as a Disney portrayal of Beethoven writing a symphony in one fell swoop without cross-outs or backtracking. Neither math nor music follows such a script.

The first goal in my doctoral work was to develop a representation for mathematical knowledge – an epistemology – that not only included extra-logical knowledge like examples[2] but also made them first class objects. Furthermore, the aim was that this framework should capture the rich fabric of interconnections among deductively oriented knowledge (e.g., definitions, theorems) and other types of knowledge including examples, rules of thumb, etc. The second goal was to use this framework to support design of an interactive system that allowed agile exploration and retrieval of mathematical knowledge in a freewheeling hypertext style.[3]

---

[2]For the rest of this note, I will use *examples* to include counter-examples as well as more positive instances

[3]I had learned about Hypertext through Andy van Dam during my undergraduate years at Brown. I took his CS class (AM101-102), then the only CS course offered. It covered everything: from tree search to data structures to numerical methods to compilers and formal languages. It was the only CS course I ever took for credit. I then became an undergraduate as-

The representational framework I developed became Part I of my Ph.D. thesis at MIT [13]. Part II was the specification of an highly interactive on-line environment called GROKKER – in essence, a mathematician's workbench – aimed especially at self-contained mini theories (e.g., matrices and their eigenvalues) and encyclopedic treatises (e.g., Dunford and Schwartz's *Linear Operators*). Part III was the design of an environment to run on top of GROKKER called GROKKER Learning Advisor (GLA) to help neophytes learn the "meta" skills involved in *how to grok* – that is, understand – mathematics. As I wrote in my introduction:

> Heinlein's verb *to grok*, meaning to thoroughly understand, suggests the essence of what is an optimal model of learning: exploration and manipulation of a knowledge base on many levels, from many angles, with facility and spontaneity. To *understand*, or *grok*, a theory one must be able to *travel* freely through it, *experiment* with its items, *survey* its overall mathematical topography, and *interrogate* its encyclopedic data base. One examines relevant examples, perturbs contexts and hypotheses, interactively fiddles with numerical and graphical demonstrations, shifts level of concern from nitty-gritty detail to broad overview, peruses the theory's overall connective structure, and varies the pedagogical exposition. All these techniques are necessary to discover the essence of what makes the theory as a whole or an individual item tick and to grasp the limitations of its truth. The GROKKER SYSTEM is designed to facilitate these processes.

GROKKER and GLA were designed to facilitate queries like:

What is an easy to understand example that illustrates this definition?
For what other concepts or theorems is this example a standard example?
Give an example to show that the converse of this theorem is false.
Give an example to show that this pre-condition is necessary.
What other theorems flow from this result?
What concepts should be known (defined) before tackling this theorem?
Why should I bother to study this result?

In essence, my doctoral enterprise was to develop a "field guide to the structure and understanding of mathematical theories, or in a sense, a field guide for writing field guides."

---

sistant ("schlepp") for Andy. His lab was developing the first hypertext system (called FRESS); his friend Ted Nelson visited from time to time. I immediately "grokked the fullness" of the hypertext way of life, like the freedom to jump and "pmuj" (jump back) through text. I had wished my math texts could be done in such a format.

The representational framework had three classes of frame-style objects, each type embedded into its own directed graph or "space" with its own linkages. Each space also had connections to the other two.

Concepts-space: definitions, mega-principles, and counter-principles connected by *pedagogical ordering* where A → B means concept A precedes concept B definitionally or pedagogically.

Results-space: lemmas, propositions, theorems, etc. connected by *logical support* where A → B means result B depends deductively on result A.

Examples-space: concrete instances, counter-examples, stereotypical model examples, etc. connected by *constructional derivation* where A → B means example A is used in a construction of example B.

Because the links were directed, one could ask about predecessor or successor items. Because the spaces were interconnected, one could ask about items from other spaces – called *dual* items – that were connected to a particular item. For instance, the EXAMPLES-DUAL of a concept or result item contained those items from Examples-space that had something to do with the item: a simple illustration, a motivating example, a limiting counter-example, a prototypical example, etc. If two results or concepts had the same Examples-Dual, they were extensionally identical (as far as the system knew at that time) and thus highly similar or closely related. If two items had identical dual sets (e.g., the duals of two result items contained the same concepts and examples), they were essentially the same and could be said to be *dual equivalent*. One could use the dual idea to move through the spaces. For instance, one could ask to see the concepts referenced by the results that referenced a particular example: $C(R(example))$. Or the examples linked to results that were linked a particular example: $E(R(example))$. One could also use the inherent directionality in the spaces to retrieve pre- and post-duals. For instance, the pre-examples-dual of an item, $(<E)(x)$, would be those examples that come before (point to) the item x, such as introductory start-up examples; the pre-concepts-dual in $(<C)(R(example))$ would be those concepts coming before results that reference an example.

My framework also included: (1) a taxonomy for each of the three spaces; (2) a Michelin-style "worth rating" of 0 to 4 stars where a 3-star item was a very important item worth a "detour," a 4-star item, a "journey" in itself, that is, worth learning its ingredient knowledge so that it can be fully understood, and 1-and 2-star items, not so much; and (3) tags to mark pedagogical trails (PTRAILS) through the spaces, like those used in the exposition of a particular teacher or textbook, and tags to keep track of user explorations.

The epistemological classes for examples included:

start-up examples – perspicuous, simple cases needing minimal prior
knowledge, good for getting started;
reference examples – cases that one refers to over and over again, no
matter one's level of expertise;
model examples – generic paradigmatic cases or prototypes;
counter examples – limiting or falsifying cases;
anomalous examples – exceptional, pathological, or unexplained
(weird) cases.

In addition to definitions, the taxonomy for concepts included classes of useful
kernels of wisdom:

mega principles – positive rules of thumb, maxims, summarizations
in a nutshell;
counter principles – negative or cautionary guidance.

An example of a mega-principle (MP) is *Try extreme cases.* MPs are like the
heuristics found in Polya's books (e.g., *How To Solve It*). Others like *Continuous functions are smooth* capture an idea in a nutshell; while not necessarily technically true, they are useful nonetheless. An example of a counter-principle (CP) is *Watch out for the case of N=0.* CPs are akin to "dangerous
curves" in Bourbaki's treatises.

My taxonomy was neither exclusive nor exhaustive. For instance, an example could be classified as both a reference example and a counter-example if
it were used in these two different ways. It certainly was also not stationary
since the taxonomic classes of an item could change. For instance, a start-up
example could become a standard reference.

In summary, the representation and epistemology were quite rich. They
were illustrated in three standard areas from the undergraduate mathematics
curriculum (calculus, linear algebra, real analysis).[4] The project made several
valuable contributions to 'meta-mathematics', AI, and cognitive science. In
particular, it gave first class status to examples and facilitated exploring linkages among them and other more traditional aspects of mathematical knowledge. It supported design of a highly interactive mathematician's workbench
(GROKKER) and a system (GLA) to help neophytes learn how to understand
a body of mathematics. It spelled out skills and information needed for understanding mathematics and understanding the understanding process [15]. Its
major shortcoming was that it was far too static: no new theorems were proved,
no new concepts defined, and no new examples constructed. It suffered from
the classic knowledge acquisition bottleneck: someone (me) needed to input

---

[4]Later, my students and I would use them in areas of high school math [19].

the knowledge into the framework. Upon finishing my doctoral project, I felt "it was now appropriate to investigate the evolutionary aspects of mathematical knowledge" [14].

Looking back at this effort with our current understanding, there are two more aspects worth noting. First, another shortcoming: the "indexing" of items was static in the sense that items were accessible only through already memorialized links. The idea of dynamic indexing computed on the fly based on the problem at hand – a hallmark of CBR – was yet to come, for instance, in HYPO and its progeny, and the dynamic memory systems of Schank's group at Yale. Second, another strength: as came to be standard later in CBR systems, an example (problem case) could cause retrieval of other examples (cases). In my framework this could occur through in-space and dual links:

> (1) via links in the Examples-space graph: predecessor, successor, predecessor of a predecessor, etc.
> (2) via dual links: either singly like using the examples-dual of a concept or result item, E(x), or in composite applications like E(R(example)), (<E)(C(example)), etc.

GROKKER was the first framework to explicitly link example objects to each other (in the Examples-space) and also with items like definitions, principles, and theorems in the other spaces.[5] Although the linkages were hard coded, the actual set of retrieved items was dynamically computed. That is, even though all the examples associated with a result or concept were already linked in the knowledge base, the set of examples retrieved through the duals were gathered on demand. This allowed for different sets of examples to be retrieved for different applications of the dual idea as well as for different states of the knowledge base (or the user). The intertwining of examples with other types of knowledge, with various modes of reasoning like the "proofs and refutation" dialectic of Lakatos [9], and with concepts and concept formation would remain a long-standing interest of mine [20].

Even though I saw how my work could stand in a synergistic relationship with work in theorem proving, I decided to leave the dynamics of Results-space to others like Woody Bledsoe at the University of Texas, who led an effort in automatic (non-resolution) theorem proving. Instead, I wanted to fo-

---

[5]Lenat's 1977 AM did connect examples with concepts and results in the sense that there was a slot for examples in their frame representations. AM could also produce simple examples (typically integers). However, examples were not first class objects: they were not themselves represented or linked to other examples. One could not ask questions like *What other concepts use this example?*

cus on making the example-based aspects more dynamic. As I said in the conclusions of my thesis,

> how one example is built from others is a very important topic for further research ... It would be extremely worthwhile to scrutinize how in the course of proving or disproving a statement, we embellish examples to reinforce or deny our hunches.

By the end of 1977, while a postdoc at MIT, I would become well immersed in my efforts to study *Example-Based Reasoning* (EBR), particularly, *Example Generation*.

2 EBR and CEG: Precursors to CBR

To gather ideas about EBR, I made some forays into cognitive science style studies in which I taped, transcribed, and analyzed example generation protocols. Given that the examples to be generated were to satisfy prescribed constraints, I called the process *Constrained Example Generation or CEG*.[6] I had already collected some CEG protocols from students in a freshman seminar I taught at MIT in the fall of 1976. I now set up additional "loud thinking" sessions with more colleagues and students, like those at UMass once I joined the faculty there in 1979. At this point, I was still focused on mathematics.

Two examples of the type of CEG problems I posed are [16, 17]:

> (1) *Give an example of a quadrilateral that has exactly three equal sides.*
> (2) *Give an example of a non-negative, continuous function defined on the entire real line, with the value 1000 at $x = 1$, and with area under its curve less than 1/1000.*

Protocols exhibited two styles of CEG: (1) *retrieval-plus-modification*, and (2) *construction from scratch*. Retrieval appeared to be from a subject's memory of existing examples – an *Examples Knowledge Base* or *EKB* – and the modifications were various procedures performed on the examples. Once a new example was created to solve a problem, it could be used in subsequent CEG problems, and thus could be said to have been added to a subject's EKB.

For instance, for the quadrilateral problem, one subject took a square and modified it into a trapezoid by "stretching" one side into a longer base; another took an equilateral triangle and "opened it up" to form a quadrilateral. These

---

[6]Given that the examples were often to be used in a larger reasoning context like limiting or refuting a claim, CEG was a name that could also stand for counter-example generation or counter *exempli gratia* (e.g.).

are examples of the retrieval-plus-modify strategy where often a well-known reference example (square, equilateral triangle) is modified with various procedures (stretch, open up) to produce an example that satisfies the desiderata. Note that the square is from the 'right' class of objects (quadrilaterals) whereas the triangle satisfies the other constraint (exactly three equal sides). Some subjects constructed quadrilaterals from scratch with a "cascading" process of drawing in succession three lines of equal length (not at right angles) and then connecting the endpoint of the third with the starting point of the first. Constructions could be 'buggy' like drawing four sides with appropriate lengths and then connecting the first and last (giving a 5-sided figure).

These two types of CEG behaviors were also observed for impossible CEG problems, like producing a quadrilateral with exactly three equal sides and exactly three equal angles. This is not possible; there is a conflict between the angle and length constraints. Nonetheless on this problem, subjects who followed a retrieval-plus-modify strategy often started with a well-known figure like a square or equilateral triangle. Those following the cascading construction paid careful attention to angles and lengths of sides.

For the "1000–1/1000" problem, protocols showed similar strategies like retrieval-plus-modification. For instance, one subject took a function like a normal distribution, "moved it to the right" to center it over x=1, made it "skinny" by squeezing in the sides, and "stretched it" so that its apex was the point (1, 1000). This subject then said that demonstrating that this function actually has area under its curve less than 1/1000 would a "bother", and noted, "my candidate function is smoother than it need be, ...so, let me relax it to a hat function" (a skinny triangle) because "I know how to find the area of triangles" and to insure the 1/1000 constraint, make it be zero to both the left and right of the triangle. Another subject took the function that is constant 0 and modified it to be 1000 at x=1 (thus introducing a discontinuity), and then fixed up the discontinuity by "smoothing" out the function by making it piecewise linear (another hat function). Both of these protocols started from well-known examples – the normal distribution and the zero function – and modified them. Interestingly, both made them symmetric about and having a max of 1000 at x=1. Neither of these "constraints" was required; rather, they seemed to be implicit defaults or predilections of the subjects.

In other protocols in the function domain, subjects used construction strategies like "curly brackets" to put together functions to satisfy the constraints. For instance, as a solution to the problem "Give a function on the unit interval that goes from the point (0,0) to the point (1,1)," one subject offered

$f(x) = 0$ for $x \leq \frac{1}{2}$

$f(x) = 1$ for $x > \frac{1}{2}$

Of course, many subjects just gave the identity function, $f(x)=x$, an *über* standard reference. When asked in subsequent problem for a function that went from (0,0) to (1,1) and was not one-to-one, the first subject contentedly said, "See the above." This was a nice re-use of a prior solution.

3 From EBR to CBR. From Math to Law.

As interesting as CEG in mathematics was, I found that most colleagues in my AI/Cognitive Science communities were really a bit mathephobic. They certainly didn't want to hear about areas of mathematics, like eigenvalues and continuous functions, that had the richness necessary for the sort of reasoning and representation issues I wanted to study.

Thus I started looking for other domains. I believed that the process of generating bespoke examples was ubiquitous. Mathematicians weren't the only ones to engage in CEG. For instance, linguists generate so-called "star sentences" in studies of syntax and these can be quite artful and nicely intertwined with the development of a grammar. In computer science, from my own experience I knew I often followed a retrieval-plus-modification strategy in constructing programs and data: if I could get away with tweaking old code or test cases to generate needed new ones, I'd do it. (But I would revert to a construction-from-scratch approach if the program got too kludgy or I ran into too many conflicting modifications and fixes.)

In 1979-80 during my first year on the faculty at UMass, I began a project to build a CEG system and an environment to experiment with CEG architectures.[7] Based on protocol data and ideas from my models of mathematical knowledge, we built a CEG shell that included: (1) an Examples Knowledge Base (EKB) with linkages and a taxonomy of example types; (2) a Retriever module; (3) a Modification module that used a library of domain-specific modifications; (4) a Judgment module to evaluate attributes of an example; (5) a Construction module that did only instantiation of model examples or procedural formulations of concepts, and (6) an Executive module to coordinate the modules and set retrieval, modification, and overall problem-solving policies[16, 17, 29]. For instance, the retrieval policy could dictate that examples most recently added to the EKB were to be considered first or that reference examples were to be considered before other types. Modifications

---

[7]The CEG team included my students Raj Wall and Sally Waisbrot and my colleague Elliot Soloway. CEG was instantiated in a variety of mini-topics: from lines and slopes in high school algebra to learning racquetball. Because Elliot and I shared an interest in teaching LISP programming, we also experimented with CEG for generating instructional LISP examples.

were selected using a GPS (difference operator table) approach and modification policies (e.g., try most successful modifications first). They were applied in conjunction with an agenda mechanism and an alias EKB; this essentially amounted to heuristic search in Examples-space. Except for construction through instantiation of a prototype, we shied away from construction (from scratch); it was really too hard to tackle at that time (and perhaps ever). There were also overall policies to handle situations like thrashing in which a new modification obliterates satisfaction of a previously satisfied constraint ('goal clobbers brother goal').

My then colleague Elliot Soloway[8] and I created a version of CEG to generate specified instructional examples in LISP. For instance, to illustrate the idea of "depth" of an atom, our system could produce a list to satisfy the requirements of being of length 3 and having depth of its first atom equal to 2. The system started with a standard reference example like (A B C) and then pushed the first element deeper: ((A) B C). Or it could produce a list that satisfies the requirements that it be made of 0's and 1's, be longer than 2, and have at least one element deeper than 1. This instantiation of CEG used modification procedures like "make deeper", "make longer," etc. The basic idea was to *satisfy as many of the constraint as possible through retrieval* and then *"rectify a candidate example along each of the unsatisfied dimensions."* This really engendered a sort of hill climbing with respect to constraints satisfied [28].

Even in this exceedingly simple domain, we bumped into many hard questions such as how to order working on the constraints not satisfied, how to select modification procedures, and how to manage constraint (goal) interaction.[9] For instance to give an example of a list of length 5 with an embedded sublist of length 2, the system could start with (A B C), add two elements to create the list (A B C 1 2), and then further modify this list by using the "make-a-group" procedure to arrive at (A B C (1 2)), but this list would now have violated the length constraint, which of course could be fixed by adding another element. The point is that constraint interaction can be tricky, and it is possible, just as in the quadrilateral mini-world, to encounter difficulties in trying to satisfy constraints. We concluded that "a purely GPS approach is not sufficient to handle the complexity of constraint interaction" [28].[10]

---

[8]Elliot and I overlapped for two academic years. In 1981, he left for Yale. He is now at the University of Michigan.

[9]Such problems also arose in later "problem-solving" CBR projects. Hammond's CHEF tried to address many of them.

[10]CEG predated work on constraint satisfaction problem solving (CSP). It would be interesting to see how CSP techniques might now be used in the service of CEG.

CEG led to my serendipitous first contact in 1980 with the AI & Law community – or rather pre-community since no formal gatherings would happen for seven more years – when I presented a paper [16] on CEG and "retrieval-plus-modification" (in mathematics and elementary LISP) in the same session as Thorne McCarty presented a paper on TAXMAN II and "prototype-plus-deformations" (in corporate tax law) at the Third National Conference of the Canadian Society for Computational Studies of Intelligence, held in Victoria, BC, in May 1980.[11] There was an astonishing resonance between our interests. We were in fact presenting what were to become some of our most central research interests – more like passions – that endure to the present.

Also, at about this time, others in AI, particularly those in Schank's group at Yale, were becoming increasingly interested in "cases" and "case memory". I met many of the Yale group at the Second Cognitive Science Conference held at Yale in June 1980[12] where I delivered a talk "Remarks on Example Generation." This conference was rich in presentation of new ideas. It included talks by Schank and Norman on MOPs (Memory Organization Packets), Gentner on structure mapping, and Kolodner on retrieval from memory. In retrospect, one might even call it a landmark gathering. What would become the CBR community was beginning to emerge with two of its founding tributaries of example-based reasoning (mine) and dynamic memory (Schank's) already present in 1980.

In 1980, I was still using the terms *examples* and *example-based reasoning*. Shortly thereafter, when I became engaged in the legal domain, I started using the terms *cases* and *case-based reasoning* but would restrict them to the legal domain, and use example language for other ones. However, the Yale group liked to talk about *cases* (even though there was not one legal domain in their portfolio). They were a juggernaut, and so instead of fighting over nomenclature, I eventually switched to talking of cases and CBR instead of examples and EBR.

With regard to CBR, the CEG system can lay claim to being one of the very first CBR systems. Since it re-used old cases to solve new problems with modification – later called "adaptation" – CEG was really of the "problem-solving" genus of CBR systems. While Hammond's case-based planner CHEF [8] is usually held up as the first of this type of CBR system, a good case

---

[11] We both also presented papers at IJCAI-81 (also held in BC, but in Vancouver): I on CEG in a session on Learning and he on Prototypes and Deformations in a session on Knowledge Representation.

[12] Actually, our first meeting was in 1977 when I gave a colloquium at Yale where I talked about my thesis work, which did include example-based aspects, and (probably) not much about example generation.

could be made for CEG's landmark status as well. In any case, CEG was the only true problem-solving (adaptation) style CBR system that my group ever built; all the others were "interpretive" CBR systems or hybrid CBR systems employing interpretive CBR (e.g., CABARET, BankXX, SPIRE) in which a new (problem) case is interpreted in light of past, relevant cases, as is done in appellate law.[13]

Two aspects of CEG are worth noting. First, we found the idea of modification with respect to a property to be very useful indeed. CEG's modifications to make an example 'have more' of a particular property – like smoothness of a function or depth of an atom in a list – used one of the essential ingredients of what came to be known as (HYPO-style) *dimensions*: a sense of direction for making a case have more/less or be stronger/weaker with respect to a particular property through manipulation of one or more key features (later called *focal slots*). Other aspects of dimensions, like their use as a retrieval mechanism, or as a way to focus on particular aspects of case, or a way to compare cases or assess similarity (e.g., in claim lattices) were yet to come. CEG modifications used a procedural representation unlike those in HYPO that had their own explicit frame-based representations, which included procedural aspects. Nevertheless, CEG contained important pre-cursors to some key aspects of HYPO and CBR in general.

Second, I had always believed that examples – and thus CEG – were intimately tied to other reasoning goals like refutation or evidence gathering and had long been a fan of Lakatos, Polya, Kuhn, and others who had written eloquently about this. Thus, at some point the larger context of *where* the constraints come from needed to be addressed. This is the problem of *constraint generation*. The intertwining of reasoning with examples (cases) and non-example entities (like rules) was a theme that would be a focus in later projects like my group's CABARET and those of others like Karl Branting and John Zeleznikow [27, 6, 10, 33, 7].

4   The Transition to Hypotheticals, CBR, and AI & Law

In appellate law, there seemed to me to be an intriguing taxonomy of cases being used: cases of 'first impression', 'landmark' cases, etc. It reminded me of my taxonomy for examples. My interest was fueled by reading a book written by Vern Countryman, a bankruptcy expert at Harvard Law School, on the Douglas opinions that I had received as a present. Subsequently, I met with him over an informal lunch, which included Oliver Selfridge, in spring 1981. I

---

[13] HYPO created hypos using modification and thus included aspects of adaptation-type CBR. The line is often not so clear.

remember saying how I thought Supreme Court cases might be an interesting place to study examples. His reply was: read Llewellyn and start with contract law.

Thus the following academic year (1981-82), I began weekly treks to Harvard to sit in as a backbencher in the 1L Contracts course taught by Gerry Frug.[14] It was more interesting and more fun than I ever could have imagined. Even the first day provided a terrific datum of EBR/CEG when Frug began the class by saying to one of the students: "Mr. Cramer, I promise to give you ten thousand dollars." Immediately the class was launched into the world of consideration, reliance, etc. and a sequence of hypotheticals that built upon the seed case of *Dougherty v. Salt* to address the master question in contracts of "what promises should the law enforce" [18, 21]. The Mr Cramer hypo was a spectacular start-up example.

Armed with data from my observations from Harvard Law School and preliminary explorations in other areas like programming and linguistics with colleagues at UMass, I submitted a proposal to study EBR and example generation in mathematics, law, linguistics, and computer science to the US National Science Foundation. I was encouraged by a supportive program director at NSF and was awarded a generous grant.[15] As it turned out, the other domains, while interesting, couldn't hold a candle to law. Not only did I find that the law an exceedingly rich domain for this research, but also I believed in its importance and its beauty. I was hooked. This research vein on EBR in law concerning hypotheticals seemed limitless. It set the stage for my work on hypos and interpretive CBR.

In mathematics, there is no distinction between "real" and "hypothetical" examples; all examples are as real or make-believe as any other. However, in law, there is a difference. One cannot manufacture real (litigated) cases, but one can certainly create hypotheticals. Hypos are an essential tool in law school Socratic dialogues and in appellate oral argument. They probe and push the responder to consider the limitations and ramifications of a point of view. They help address the "gaps, conflicts and ambiguities" inherent in law. They act sometimes as counter-examples do in mathematics, sometimes as standard references, sometimes as easy start-ups, sometimes as helpful illus-

---

[14]In Frug's class, I also met up with one of my former MIT students who had taken my freshman seminar and participated in the original CEG protocols. I remember that he immediately saw the connection with hypos and what I was up to.

[15]The NSF grant gave me great freedom to pursue this line of research. It was this experience with NSF and my cognizant Program Director (PD) Henry Hamburger that planted the idea that someday I would like to "repay" NSF for its generous support by doing service in Washington. Twenty years later, I did so: I served as a PD in IIS/CISE for two rotations (2003-07, 2010-12).

trations, sometimes as cautionary worst cases. They play different roles in advocacy, adjudication, and advice giving, but in all contexts hypos can serve an important role. But where do they come from? How can one generate them to serve other goals like refutation or illustration? What is the knowledge underlying the process?

Classroom observations and analysis of oral argument transcripts showed that hypos were often generated in sequences that emphasized a particular aspect. Sometimes, the sequences manipulated the generality of the parties involved, like changing the parties' names (e.g., to A and B) or their attractiveness as plaintiff or defendant (e.g., poor, old, famous, kindly). Some modifications were perfectly general and could be used in any area. Others were much more doctrine-specific like changing the perceived value ("consideration") involved in a promissory exchange. For instance, this is the beginning of a sequence of hypos from my 1L contracts course with Frug [18]:

> Hypo1: Aunt Tillie says, "Charlie, you are such a nice boy; I promise to give you $10,000."
>
> Hypo2: Charlie says, "Dear Aunt Tillie, I can't take something for nothing, let me give you my third grade painting."
>
> Hypo3: Same as Hypo2 except Charlie promises to mow Tillie's lawn.
>
> Hypo4: Same as Hypo2, except Charlie's last name is Picasso.

These hypos are built on the seed case of *Dougherty v. Salt*, an assigned case for class, as well as Mr. Cramer's hypo. The sequence moves cases along the *dimension* of the value of the items involved.

It seemed clear to me that the CEG approach could prove useful in generating hypos. Some central issues to investigate would be:

> What cases are to be used as the "seed" or starting cases for a hypo or sequence of them?
>
> What sort of modifications can be used?
>
> In sequences of hypos, what sort of movement is there along dimensions?
>
> How are desiderata for the hypos chosen based on goals of argument or Socratic dialogue?[16]

To delve deeper into these questions in the law, I spent the academic year 1982-83 at Harvard Law School as a Fellow of Law and Computer Science. Although I concentrated on completing the 1L curriculum (torts, property, civil procedure, etc.), which I had begun in 1981-82 with contracts, I also took some upper level courses like Constitutional Law. The year provided me with a

---

[16]In later work, David Skalak and I laid out some of the various strategies, like slippery slope or strawman arguments, and the type of cases and hypos needed to implement them [34].

windfall of data about hypos, cases, argument, and legal reasoning in general, and served as data for several papers during the early 1980s.

5 HYPO and its progeny

In 1982, Kevin Ashley became a graduate student at UMass and we began a long and productive collaboration. We began by focusing full bore on the problem of generating hypotheticals using the core CEG approach of modification along known, legally important aspects, which we then began to explicitly call *dimensions*. This grew into the subject of Ashley's MS thesis in 1984. A 1984 AAAI paper entitled *Explaining and Arguing with Examples* reported on this work, as well as work of another of my MS students Eduardo Valcarce on using custom-tailored examples in on-line help systems for VAX/VMS commands[17] and a LOGO-like programming language.

For the hypos, we focused on the problem of making a case stronger or weaker in favor of the plaintiff or defendant through modification of known cases and hypos stored in an Examples Knowledge Base.[18] We used trade secrets law as our domain. In the AAAI-84 paper, we introduced the terminology of *dimensional analysis* and *dimensions* "along which a hypo can be modified in ways that have legal significance for one or the other party" and indicated how they are used for case retrieval. We listed some specific dimensions that we found in the legal literature about trade secrets, including "unfair competitive advantage" and "telltale signs of misappropriation."

To illustrate our approach, we showed how "dimension- and example-directed modification" could be used to create telling hypos based on known cases from the EKB. For instance we showed how one could manipulate the amounts of time and money involved in bringing a product to market to create new hypos addressing the dimension of competitive advantage. This 1984 paper was the one in which HYPO made its debut. Although we actually used the name HYPO but once in this paper, it was the watershed paper that launched the era of HYPO-style programs and interpretive CBR.

By the conclusion of 1984-85, the HYPO Project had become a major focus in my lab. Work on intelligent user interfaces ("IUIs"), on-line help, CEG in mathematics, computer science and other fields took a back seat. I was now firmly committed to the legal domain. For me, law was more than just a

---

[17]VAX/VMS was a product of the now extinct Digital Equipment Corporation (DEC). We applied CEG to produce examples customized to a user and the user's context for presentation in explanation templates ("TEXPLATES") containing chunks of canned text and places to insert customized examples. Valcarce and I demo'd the system for DEC in February 1985.

[18]We were still using the terminology of examples: Examples Knowledge Base, Example-Based Reasoning, etc.

domain of application in which to study issues of representation and reasoning, it became the driver for my research. Deep synergies exist between the fields of AI and law, and each has much to teach and learn from the other [23]. By the mid-1980s I was wholly engaged by the goal of using AI techniques to explicate and model various aspects of legal reasoning, like using hypotheticals in oral argument. While I certainly continued to pursue projects that used EBR/CBR ideas in other areas, it was the law that really intrigued me.

For the 1985-86 academic year, I spent my first sabbatical from UMass further immersed in the law. I spent the fall semester at Harvard Law School as a Lecturer on Law and the spring semester at Stanford Law School (and also at Stanford's Knowledge Systems Lab) as a Visiting Scholar. At Harvard, I taught a seminar *Artificial Intelligence and Legal Reasoning* for 2Ls, 3Ls, and LL.M. students. This began more than a dozen years at Harvard Law School as a Lecturer on Law where I taught this upper level seminar and a practicum in building expert systems. I also continued to sit in on courses (e.g., Federal tax, bankruptcy) as a way to gather interesting data and delve further into law.

By 1987, the HYPO project had become quite mature. As a model of legal argument, it had grown to encompass much more then generation of legal hypotheticals. In May 1987, at the first ICAIL, Kevin and I presented a pair of papers [24, 3] that described a well-developed HYPO to the first official meeting of the AI and Law community.[19] In February 1988, Kevin was awarded his Ph.D. His dissertation *Modelling Legal Argument: Reasoning with Cases and Hypotheticals* spelled out in full the now familiar key features of HYPO: dimensional analysis, most on-point cases ("mopc's"), claim lattices, 3-ply arguments, etc. My grant from NSF and a grant from ONR supported this work. In 1990, it was published as the second book in the MIT Press series on AI and Law [2], of which Thorne McCarty and I were editors. That spring at the March 1988 IEEE International Conference on Artificial Intelligence Applications (CAIA), we published a paper that succinctly presented the main ideas of HYPO; it was awarded top prize as a paper authored/co-authored by a graduate student [4].

By the summer of 1988, HYPO as Kevin's Ph.D. project was complete and he left for a yearlong appointment as a Visiting Scientist at IBM's T.J. Watson Research Center in Yorktown Heights. In September 1989, he joined the faculty at the University of Pittsburgh in both the Law School and the Program in Intelligent Systems.

---

[19]This inaugural conference was held at Northeastern University in Boston and hosted by Carole Hafner and Don Berman, who would partner a series of landmark papers over the course of several subsequent ICAILs.

At Pitt, Kevin continued work with HYPO-style systems that tackled various law and AI problems like teaching law students *how* to argue, most notably in the CATO project of Vincent Aleven's 1997 Ph.D. CATO was a landmark in intelligent tutoring systems. It also made significant contributions to CBR, especially with its notion of *factor hierarchies* [1]. The SIROCCO system of Bruce McLaren's 1999 thesis brought principles and rules into the case-based mix to bear on problems in ethics [11]. These second-generation HYPO-style systems from Ashley's group used *factors* instead of dimensions. Factors were a significant departure from dimensions in my group's systems since a factor, if applicable in a case, is presumed a priori to be beneficial to the position of a particular side [5, 25].

Meanwhile, my group continued to build HYPO-style systems (with dimensions, not factors). In the fall of 1986, David Skalak had become a graduate student at UMass and joined my group. Around this time, we began a project to build "E-HYPO", an environment intended to provide a skeleton for building case-based systems modeled on HYPO, analogously to how EMYCIN was used for building rule-based systems modeled on MYCIN. We built a scaled down version of HYPO using it.

Using ideas from our homegrown E-HYPO environment, we began work in fall 1988 on a completely new project – CABARET – to explore problems in statutory interpretation, particularly, how to interleave reasoning with cases and reasoning with rules,[20] and also how to integrate machine learning into CBR. David Skalak played a lead role in all this work. CABARET used an agenda-based architecture driven by the needs of argument in statutory law to coordinate HYPO-style CBR and classic rule-based reasoning (RBR) [27]. CABARET monitored its CBR and RBR modules, and based on observations and reasoning goals, it used control rules to post new tasks on the agenda. CABARET thus pursued best-first heuristic search among tasks of statutory interpretation. We began with two domains: "passing/speeding" concerning motor vehicles and the "home office deduction" from US tax law. The latter became our primary focus. It was an area rich with open-textured predicates, rules to interpret requirements, and a plethora of cases about tax controversies. We first reported on this work at ICAIL 1989 held in Vancouver. At this conference, I also gave a paper using dimensions to analyze hypotheticals from U.S. Supreme Court oral arguments [22].

CABARET's control rules included general ones like *If RBR fails, try CBR*. A similar heuristic to switch modes on failure (e.g., when the rules run out

---

[20]CABARET had several types of rules in its rule-base: legal (statutory) rules, rules of thumb for determining satisfaction of a predicate, definitional rules for predicates, etc.

or fail) had been used by Gardner [35] in her groundbreaking research, which used rules and cases to analyze "issue spotter" type questions found on law school and bar exams in order to determine which facts raise interesting or important legal issuers and to make the jurisprudential distinction between hard and easy questions of law. In addition to standard RBR, CABARET could use rule-based near misses, that is, situations in which all but one of a rule's prerequisites are satisfied.[21] For instance, there were "broadening" heuristics like *If there is a rule-based near miss and one wants the rule to succeed, try satisfying the missed predicate with use of cases*, or *finding cases to show that the missed predicate is really not necessary*. In essence, the control rules implemented a three-tiered model of argument with cases and rules: high-level *argument strategies* (e.g., broadening, discrediting), tactical *argument moves* (e.g., distinguishing, analogizing), and basic *argument primitives* (e.g., dimensional methods) [34].

My group continued to use HYPO-style CBR in several research projects that involved argument, search, and information retrieval. For instance, BankXX, first reported on at ICAIL 1993, explored the use of heuristic search to serve the needs of information gathering for argument [31]. It used evaluation functions that took into consideration types of information – best supporting cases, best contrary cases, applicable legal theories, prototype stories, etc. – needed to make a good argument. It used innovative groupings of information into various spaces, such as those for legal theories and for prototypical legal scenarios and stories.

SPIRE, first reported on at ICAIL 1995, showed how HYPO-style case-based analysis could drive classical information retrieval through automatic query generation using text from the cases in the top tiers of a claim lattice [26]. It showed how a modest case base could not only spur effective retrieval but also remediate the *staleness problem* for case bases: that is, once a case base (or any knowledge base) is constructed, eventually there will be items of great relevance that will not be included because they occurred afterwards. For instance, SPIRE found maximally on-point cases concerning the home office deduction (e.g., *Dudley* and *Soliman* cases) that had not been included in the original case base (constructed many years earlier for the CABARET project). In fact, *Soliman* had not yet been litigated when the original case base was constructed. SPIRE actually found all three versions of the *Soliman* case as it made its way up the appellate ladder from the Tax Court, to Federal

---

[21]HYPO also defined a near miss, but for dimensions: when all prerequisites except those associated with the focal slot are satisfied. This led to mechanisms in HYPO like the *extended* claim lattice.

appeals court, and finally to the U. S. Supreme Court. (*Soliman* is the only home office deduction case decided by the U. S. Supreme Court – at least at that time – and is thus of supreme importance.) By being able to retrieve highly on-point "after-occurring" cases – that is, those that occurred *after* the case base was constructed – SPIRE demonstrated a method for addressing the staleness problem, even with a small, older "in house" case base. SPIRE also demonstrated the clear advantage of "thinking" (doing case-based analysis) before "acting" (doing information retrieval).

One robust and enduring conclusion from all these projects was the clear efficacy of using dimensions, *mopc*'s, and claim lattices. This continues to be borne out again and again, for instance in recent work on "gray cygnets" presented at ICAIL 2011 [30].

6 Intersecting journeys through a rich landscape

The first ICAIL was held in 1987. Thus, I have now reached the endpoint of my personal travelogue through the decade preceding it. As I said at the outset, it was not meant to be a complete history but a personal one. ICAIL 1987 marked the beginning of the AI and Law community, as we now know it. A few years later (1992), our research journal *Artificial Intelligence and Law* was established. From this point on, there was a cohesive community with a steadily growing body of accomplishments [7].

While I started my journey with a focus on examples and cases and then branched out to paths exploring rules and hybrid systems, our honoree Trevor was making a journey that could be said to travel in the opposite direction: from rules to cases. For instance, Trevor's two papers at ICAIL 1987 reported on applying rule-based systems (in PROLOG) to the problem of formulating legislation in the United Kingdom, particularly in the area of supplementary government benefits in welfare law. Even though this focus continued for many ICAIL cycles, Trevor eventually also turned to considering case-based reasoning.

Trevor's stream of work with Giovanni Sartor and Henry Prakken aimed to give a sound formalization for many aspects of case-based argument, for instance, in a paper at ICAIL 2001. His research has made several other points of contact with CBR, argument, heuristic search, etc. At ICAIL 2005 in Bologna, Trevor co-authored a paper with Alison Chorley on the use of heuristic search in the service of argument and another with Katie Atkinson on principles of social values and desires underlying case-based argument.

On a few occasions, Trevor and I have traveled together on the same road for case-oriented quests, for instance, to revisit the ideas of factors and dimensions in HYPO- and CATO-style CBR [5]. In this 2001 paper, we explored these ideas in a set of classic "wild animal" cases concerning the doctrine of "possession" from American property law: *Pierson v. Post* involving hunted foxes, *Keeble v. Hickeringill* involving wild ducks, and *Young v. Hitchens* involving purloined fish, etc. These joint pursuits have been jolly as well as scholarly excursions.

No doubt these have not been the last of such magnificent joint outings. So, in conclusion I convey all my best wishes to Trevor for his future journeys and hope they will include some spirited hunts through the land of cases. *Tally ho!*

Bibliography

[1] V. Aleven. Using background knowledge in case-based legal reasoning: a computational model and an intelligent learning environment. *Artificial Intelligence*, 150(1-2):183–237, 2003.

[2] K.D. Ashley. *Modeling Legal Argument: Reasoning with Cases and Hypotheticals*. MIT Press, Cambridge, MA, 1990.

[3] K.D. Ashley and E.L. Rissland. But, see, accord: Generating blue book citations in HYPO. In *Proceedings of the First International Conference on Artificial Intelligence and Law*, pages 67–74, New York, 1987. ACM Press.

[4] K.D. Ashley and E.L. Rissland. A case-based approach to modeling legal expertise. *IEEE Expert*, 3(3):70–77, 1988.

[5] T.J.M. Bench-Capon and E. L. Rissland. Back to the future: dimensions revisited. In B. Verheij et al., editor, *Legal Knowledge and Information Systems. JURIX 2001: The Fourteenth Annual Conference*, pages 41–52, Amsterdam etc, 2001. IOS Press.

[6] L.K. Branting. Building explanations from rules and structured cases. *International Journal of Man-Machine Studies*, 34(6):797–837, 1991.

[7] T.J.M. Bench-Capon et al. A history of AI and law in 50 papers: 25 years of the international conference on AI and law. *Artificial Intelligence and Law*, 20(3):215–319, 2012.

[8] K.J. Hammond. Planning and goal interaction: The use of past solutions in present situations. In *Proceedings of the Third National Conference on Artificial Intelligence (AAAI-83)*, pages 148–151, 1983.

[9] I. Lakatos. *Proofs and Refutations*. Cambridge University Press, Cambridge, 1976.

[10] C. Marling, E. L. Rissland, and A. Aamodt. Integrations with case-based reasoning. *The Knowledge Engineering Review*, 20(3):241–246, 2005.

[11] B.M. McLaren. Extensionally defining principles and cases in ethics: An AI model. *Artificial Intelligence*, 150(1-2):145–181, 2003.

[12] G. Polya. *How to Solve it*. Princeton University Press, Princeton, New Jersey, second edition, 1957.

[13] E.L. Rissland (Michener). *Epistemology, Representation, Understanding and Interactive Exploration of Mathematical Theories.* PhD thesis, Department of Mathematics, MIT, Cambridge, MA, 1977.

[14] E.L. Rissland. The structure of mathematical knowledge. Technical Report 472, MIT Artificial Intelligence Laboratory, Cambridge, MA, 1978.

[15] E.L. Rissland (Michener). Understanding understanding mathematics. *Cognitive Science,* 2(4):361–383, 1978.

[16] E.L. Rissland. Example generation. In *Proceedings of the Third National Conference of the Canadian Society for Computational Studies of Intelligence,* pages 280–288, Victoria, BC, 1980.

[17] E.L. Rissland. Constrained example generation. COINS Technical Report 81-24, Department of Computer and Information Science, University of Massachusetts/Amherst, Amherst, MA, 1981.

[18] E.L. Rissland. Examples in the legal domain: Hypotheticals in contract law. In *Proceedings of the Fourth Annual Cognitive Science Conference,* pages 96–99, Univ. of Michigan, Ann Arbor, 1982.

[19] E.L. Rissland. The structure of knowledge in complex domains. In S.F. Chipman, J.W. Segal, and R. Glaser, editors, *Thinking and Learning Skills: Research and Open Questions,* pages 107–126. Lawrence Erlbaum Associates, Inc., Hillsdale, NJ, 1984a.

[20] E.L. Rissland. The ubiquitous dialectic. In *Proceedings of the Sixth European Conference on Artificial Intelligence (ECAI-84),* pages 367–372, 1984b.

[21] E.L. Rissland. Learning how to argue: Using hypotheticals. In J.L. Kolodner and C. Reisbeck, editors, *Experience, Memory, and Reasoning,* pages 115–126. Lawrence Erlbaum Associates, Inc., Hillsdale, NJ, 1986.

[22] E.L. Rissland. Dimension-based analysis of hypotheticals from Supreme Court oral arguments. In *Proceedings of the Second International Conference on Artificial Intelligence and Law,* pages 111–120, New York, 1989. ACM Press.

[23] E.L. Rissland. Artificial intelligence and law: Stepping stones to a model of legal reasoning. *Yale Law Journal,* 99(8):1957–1982, 1990.

[24] E.L. Rissland and K.D. Ashley. A case-based system for trade secrets law. In *Proceedings of the First International Conference on Artificial Intelligence and Law,* pages 60–66, New York, 1987. ACM Press.

[25] E.L. Rissland and K.D. Ashley. A note on dimensions and factors. *Artificial Intelligence and Law,* 10(1-3):65–77, 2002.

[26] E.L. Rissland and J.J. Daniels. The synergistic application of CBR to IR. *Artificial Intelligence Review,* 10(1-3):441–475, 1996. Special Issue on the use of AI in Information Retrieval.

[27] E.L. Rissland and D.B. Skalak. CABARET: statutory interpretation in a hybrid architecture. *International Journal of Man-Machine Studies,* 34:839–887, 1991.

[28] E.L. Rissland and E.M. Soloway. Overview of an example generation system. In *Proceedings of the First National Conference on Artificial Intelligence (AAAI-80),* pages 256–258,

1980.

[29] E.L. Rissland and E.M. Soloway. Constrained example generation: A testbed for studying issues in learning. In *Proceedings of the Seventh International Joint Conference on Artificial Intelligence (IJCAI-81)*, pages 162–164, 1981.

[30] E.L. Rissland and X. Xu. Catching gray cygnets: An initial exploration. In *Proceedings of the Thirteenth International Conference on Artificial Intelligence and Law*, pages 151–160, New York, 2011. ACM Press.

[31] E.L. Rissland, D.B. Skalak, and M.T. Friedman. BankXX: Supporting legal arguments through heuristic retrieval. *Artificial Intelligence and Law*, 4(1):1–71, 1996.

[32] E.L. Rissland, K.D. Ashley, and R.P. Loui. AI and law: A fruitful synergy. *Artificial Intelligence*, 150(1-2):1–17, 2003.

[33] E.L. Rissland, K.D. Ashley, and L.K. Branting. Case-based reasoning and law. *The Knowledge Engineering Review*, 20(3):293–298, 2005.

[34] D.B. Skalak and E.L. Rissland. Arguments and cases. an inevitable intertwining. *Artificial Intelligence and Law*, 1(1):3–44, 1992.

[35] A. vdL. Gardner. *An Artificial Intelligence Approach to Legal Reasoning*. MIT Press, Cambridge, MA, 1987.

Reasoning with Values: Quantitative Assessments Without Numbers

GIOVANNI SARTOR[*]

Abstract

AI & law research has so far mainly addressed values through argumentation schemes and case based reasoning. The present paper is meant to address a complementary feature of value-based reasoning, namely, the extent to which it may include quantitative reasoning, according to arithmetical constraints. Relying on some work on cognitive and evolutionary psychology it is argued that processing non-symbolic approximate continuous magnitudes is a fundamental cognitive capacity, which seems to be deployed also when we are reasoning with values. A model is developed for determining the impact of a choice on different values, assessing the utilities so produced and merging these utilities into an overall evaluation, which may be used in comparisons. Finally, it is shown how quantitative proportionality assessments may be constrained by the requirement of consistency with precedents.

Introduction

Recent research within AI & law has focused on legal reasoning with values, following the work of Berman and Hafner [6]. In particular, Trevor Bench-Capon has played a leading role in this line of research. In a number of contributions he has provided diverse innovative analyses of how values may be used to address conflicts of argument, how they may be connected to factors and rules, how they provide a fundamental ingredients in constructing legal theories and identifying inference schemes for value-driven or teleological reasoning [4, 7, 3, 2, 5]. Recent research within AI & law has focused on legal reasoning with values, following the work of Berman and Hafner [6]. In particular, Trevor Bench-Capon has played a leading role in this line of research.

---

[*]University of Bologna, Faculty of Law, and European University Institute of Florence, Law Department

In a number of contributions he has provided diverse innovative analyses of how values may be used to address conflicts of argument, how they may be connected to factors and rules, how they provide a fundamental ingredients in constructing legal theories and identifying inference schemes for value-driven or teleological reasoning [4, 7, 3, 2, 5].

AI & law research has so far mainly addressed values through logic, argumentation schemes and case based reasoning (see, for instance, Ashley [1]). The present paper is meant to address a complementary feature of value-based reasoning, namely, the extent to which this kind of reasoning may include quantitative reasoning, according to arithmetical constraints. There is in fact a parallel aspect in reasoning with values, namely an assessment of the merit of alternative actions, an assessment that is performed by processing magnitudes concerning the impact of such actions on the realisation of values, the proportional utilities so delivered, and the weights of the values. Even though this processing does not use symbolically expressed numbers, it still deals with quantities (by adding them, subtracting, multiplying, etc.), and should comply with the basic laws of arithmetic. Relying on some work on cognitive and evolutionary psychology it is observed that processing non-symbolic approximate continuous magnitudes is a fundamental cognitive capacity, which seems to be deployed also when we are reasoning with values. This capacity needs to be integrated with logic and argumentation to provide a comprehensive account of value-based reasoning.

On the basis of this assumption, a conceptual framework is developed for reasoning with values. Then ways to determine the impacts of a choice on values are considered, and ways to determine the associated utilities and merge utilities into a single measure of the merit of that choice. Some issues pertaining to the comparison of alternative choices are also addressed.

Finally it is considered how value-based assessments may be constrained by the requirement of consistency with assessments of the same kind.

1 Quantitative reasoning without (symbolically expressed) numbers

When we are to assess whether a decision α has failed to duly realise some values, we need to compare the extent to which the relevant values are realised by α and the extent to which they would be realised if a different choice β were made instead of α (where β may consist in not interfering with the status quo, or in changing it in a different way). Moreover, as we shall see, we need to take into account the differential merit or utility that is provided by the implementation of different choices.

This raises the issue of how we are going to determine the impact of a choice on all values at stake and aggregate such impacts into a determination of the overall benefit or loss that is provided by that choice, as compared with different possible choices. I shall not consider here the further (or preliminary) issues of what should be considered as a value, with what importance, which involves patterns of reasoning (and anthropological, ethical, legal, and political issues) which go beyond the scope of this paper.

If we could obtain appropriate numbers,[1] it seems that some mathematics should provide the answer on the merit of a choice. For this purpose we should need numbers expressing the different impacts of our choices (in all possible scenarios) on the realisation of the values at stake and functions connecting such impacts to the overall gains or losses they produce, with regard to all values. However, in most legal cases we do not seem to have sensible ways for assigning such numbers and constructing the corresponding functions. Nor have we an exhaustive set of preferences between all possible combinations of the different realisations of values, which may be represented as a utility function, in accordance with the so-called representation theorems used in economics.[2] This makes quantitative methods used in decision theory and cost-benefit analysis not directly applicable to many legal contexts, and in particular, to constitutional decisions involving impacts on different values.[3]

It seems that one explanation of the fact that we are able to make reasonable choices on the basis of their impacts on different values, even though we cannot sensibly not express this impacts through numbers, is that people (in particular, legislators and judges) possess some (more or less inborn) capacity to reason quantitatively which is non-numerical. This assumption is not meant to exclude that other ways of reasoning may also be significant for this purpose, such as the capacity of making analogies out of cases, or of building arguments. We rather integrate these different skills in complex value assessment.

---

[1] I use the term "number" to refer only to the cases where a quantity is expressed with the symbols (the numerals) or a particular number system. When a quantity is represented (e.g. graphically, or mentally) without the use of such symbols, I use the term "magnitude".

[2] According to the so-called Morgenstern-Von Neumann representation theorem, if we have a set of preferences among alternatives, and these preferences are complete, transitive, independent and continuous, then we can build a utility function assigning a numerical utility to each alternative, in such a way that any alternative (strictly) preferred to another would have a higher utility than the latter.

[3] This does not exclude that the methods of decision theory and cost-benefit analysis can be usefully deployed in many cases; for a technical account of multi-criteria decision-making, see Keeney and Raiffa [11].

To model our intuitive quantitative assessments, we have two possible alternative approaches. The first approach consists in assuming that this non-numerical capacity for quantitative reasoning is limited to ordinal comparison between quantities: without numbers we are able to assess that a certain object is more or less than another (with regard to dimensions such as length, volume, weight, speed, etc.), but we cannot say how much the one is more than the other. The second approach, which I find more plausible, consists in assuming that this capacity also covers cardinal measures: even without numbers we are able to assess (though in a very approximate way) the size of an object or the extent of its difference from another. To express such non-numerical cardinal evaluations we often refine our ordinal assessment with adverbs (we say, that this object is a little, fairly, a lot larger, or smaller, or quicker, etc., than that object). We can sometimes map such evaluations into numbers, even without referring to a general unit of measure and without engaging in explicit numerical computations (we may just say that an entity is about a half, two times, three times larger, or smaller, or quicker, etc., than another). For instance not only can we compare two lines and establish which one is longer, but we can say that one line is twice longer that the other, or that a line is the sum of the two lines of different sizes, without the need of making numerical calculations.

In fact, animals are to not only able to order objects according to their size, but they can perform tasks that involve processing magnitudes: they compute distances by summing up the extent of successive displacements, they make visits to caches according to the difference between the time when the food was stored and its expected rotting time, they remain in different locations according to ratios between time spent and rewards obtained, etc. From this evidence the hypothesis can be made that a developed mathematical competence is quite widespread in the animal kingdom:

> Research with vertebrates, some of which have not shared a common ancestor with man since before the rise of the dinosaurs, implies that they represent both countable and uncountable quantity by means of mental magnitudes . . . The system of arithmetical reasoning with these mental magnitudes is closed under the basic operations of arithmetic, that is, mental magnitudes may be mentally added, subtracted, multiplied, and divided without restriction [10, p. 259].

Similarly, experiments with humans show that we can do computations with quantities without associating numerical symbols to such quantities; see [9].

Thus it seems that there exists an inborn ability to represent and mathematically process mental magnitudes, which is deployed without translating these magnitudes into the linguistic symbols (the numerals) of a number system. Contrary to a famous statement by the mathematician Leopold Kronecker ("God made the integers; all else is the work of man") it seems that God (or natural evolution) endowed us with the primitive ability to store and process continuous (though approximated, or noisy) mental magnitudes,[4] quantities that are only mappable into real numbers, since they include also negative magnitudes, fractions, and even irrational magnitudes, such a certain square roots. On the top of this ability, humans have the additional possibility of using symbols for expressing such quantities and making them more precise. Our mind, however, continues to map numerical values into analogical magnitudes, and we resort to the latter when making quick, unreflected judgments.

According to John Pollock [13, Ch. 3] this capacity for intuitive cardinal assessment of quantities, which he calls "analogical quantitative cognition", applies not only to lengths, weights or volumes, but also to our likes and dislikes, and to the realisation of our values.

I shall accept the assumption that humans have a basic (and largely inborn, though improvable by training and experience) intuitive capacity for non-symbolic quantitative reasoning, a capacity that includes not only assessing and comparing magnitudes, but also performing on such magnitudes approximate mathematical operations: sums, subtractions, proportions, multiplications and divisions (and even approximate differentiation and integration). I shall argue that exactly this capacity is involved in assessing impacts on values according to proportionality. We can deploy it in choices concerning our private life (choosing a car or a computer by balancing design, performance, and cost; choosing an restaurant by considering quality of food, service and price, choosing a course of studies balancing interest and work-opportunities, etc.) but also when public choices have to be taken or assessed. For engaging in this kind of intuitive, or "analogical" quantitative reasoning, we do not need to translate quantities into numbers through measurement (which is an

---

[4]Thus, apparently, these findings of contemporary cognitive science seem to validate Leibniz's principle of continuity (often expressed by the Latin saying *natura non facit saltus*), at least with regard to the mental processing of quantitative information: "I also take it for granted that every created being is subject to change [...] and even that this change is continuous in each." (G. W. Leibniz. Monadology. 1720, Section 10, translation by N. Rescher. G.W. Leibniz's Monadology: An Edition for Students. Pittsburgh: University of Pittsburgh Press, 1991). There are various methods for dealing with approximate quantities, but here I cannot even attempt at discussing them, and moreover the general account here provided is meant to be neutral in this regard as much as possible. For a review of methods for reasoning for uncertainty, see for instance, Parsons [12].

ability that only humans possess, and in many domains only after adequate schooling): usually we just rely on our intuitive appreciation of the quantities involved and of their relations. When more precision is needed and numerical quantification makes sense, we may move to symbolically expressed numbers, and test and refine our intuitions. The nature of this mathematical capacity entails that mathematical relationships do not hold only among symbolically expressed numbers: they also constrain the process of our intuitive-analogical quantitative reasoning. Thus such relationships can be used as a standard of rationality for that reasoning, and for facilitating the transition to numerical quantification, when possible and convenient. Finally, note that the assumption that we can reason with approximate quantities does not entail that we can precisely assess such quantities, nor that we can always determine with certainty whether one object's magnitude is bigger than another's. For instance, we may sometimes (though not in most cases) remain uncertain when comparing the lengths of two twisted lines, or the volumes of two solid objects. Similarly we may sometimes (though not in most cases) remain in doubt concerning the impacts of our choices on our values, and the comparative merits of such choices.

In the following section, I shall examine teleological reasoning in law as an instance of non-numerical quantitative reasoning and I shall derive some implications of this idea.

2   Basic concepts

I shall specify certain notions that are needed in order to proceed in the analysis. First of all I assume that we can quantify the level of the realisation of a value in a particular situation (where a situation is an actual or possible set of circumstances, including social and institutional arrangements).

Definition 1.   (Realisation-quantity of a value) The realisation-quantity of a value v in a particular situation is the extent up to which v is realised in case that situation obtains. Let us write $\mathtt{Real}_v(s)$ to denote the realisation-quantity of value v in situation s. We correspondingly denote as $\mathtt{Real}_v(s_c)$, or simply $\mathtt{Real}_v$, the level of realisation of v in the current situation s_c (the present state of affairs). Thus $\mathtt{Real}_v = q$ means that in the current situation the value v is realised in quantity q.

We can express our assessment of the realisation-quantity of a value in non-numerical term (e.g., we may say that privacy is protected to a sufficient extent in Country x, while its protection is low in Country y, that a large freedom of speech is enjoyed by the citizen of Country w, etc.) or in numerical term, when appropriate numerical indicators are available (as for GDP per head, employment rate, etc.). For some values (transparency, democracy, economic freedom, equality, non-discrimination, etc.) proxies are available according to various measurements, such as those that are used for ranking countries according to their levels of welfare or of protection of human rights. However, even when no such proxies are available (or when they are not known to us) we still engage in quantitative assessments, even while being aware that such assessments are inevitable noisy, approximate and revisable.

Such assessments may be different according to different conceptions of the values at issue, but, I would argue, different people usually show quite some consistency in making them. For instance, I think that very few people would disagree that a 50% increase in the revenue per head (with the same distribution) would provide a much higher welfare, that storing personal data for a longer time or making them accessible to a larger set of people would involve a limitation to privacy, that extending the time for detention without judicial authorisation would additionally restrain individual liberty.

We may wonder, however, whether it is really possible to compare situations where values are realised in different ways. Assume for instance that we have to compare a situation where privacy is well protected against governmental interference but much less protected against commercial interference, and a situation where privacy is well-protected again commercial interference, and much less protected against governmental interference. This is a real issue, but I think that it does not affect the theoretical model here provided. In case there really is a competition between two different aspects of value (we can increase privacy towards governmental bodies only by reducing privacy toward private bodies, or, more plausibly, given a fixed amount of resources available for the welfare of dependant people, we can increase the welfare of old people only by decreasing welfare for children), it is better to see the two aspects as distinct values, to be comparatively assessed taking their conflict into account.

Besides assuming that we can quantify the extent of the realisation of a value, we may assume that there is also a quantity consisting in the benefit or utility that is delivered by the fact that a value is realised up to a certain extent in a certain situation.

Definition 2. (Utility-quantity concerning a value) The utility-quantity concerning a value v, in a certain situation, is the amount of utility provided by the realisation of v in that situation. We write $\mathrm{Ut}_v s$ to denote the utility which is obtained with regard to value v, in situation s, where the value is realised up to the quantity $\mathrm{Real}_v s$. Thus, $\mathrm{Ut}_v s = q$ means that such utility is quantity q.

Note that here I use utility as a "neutral" term denoting the amount of goodness (or badness, when the utility is negative) that is provided by a choice, without making any assumption on the nature or distribution of such good-ness. Thus the "utility" of a choice includes the assessment all of its aspects and consequences that interfere with relevant values, increasing or decreasing their realisation.[5]

In the following I shall consider how to move from the realisation a value to the utility that is provided by that realisation. Obviously, people's assessment of the utility of the realisation of a value may be quite variable, and in particu-lar, more variable than their assessment of the realisation-quantity of a value. However, some relations between such assessments may be considered to be invariant.

First of all, since values are by definition good things, we can assume that the utility provided by the realisation of a value, increases as the realisation-quantity of that value increases. Thus we assume that relation between the realisation of a value and the corresponding utility is a monotonic function, and indeed a strictly increasing one. We take this as a defeasible assumption, which expresses what is usually the case, and does not exclude that in certain cases over-realisation of a value can be counterproductive.

Assumption 1. (Increasing utility from values) A higher realisation of a value provides a higher utility. In other words, when the realisation-quantity of value v increases, also its utility-quantity increases: if the realisation-quantity of v in a situation s_2 is higher that the realisation-quantity of v in s_1, than also the utility-quantity of v in situation s_2 is higher than its utility-quantity in s_1. In other words, if $\text{Real}_v(s_1) < \text{Real}_v(s_2)$ then $\text{Ut}_v(s_1) < \text{Ut}_v(s_2)$.

Thus the utility resulting from the realisation of a value v will increase pro-gressively, when v's realisation-quantity increases. For instance, a higher level of a value such as health, or environmental quality, or privacy, or freedom of speech, etc., gives more utility than a lower level of the same value, all the rest (the realisation-quantity of the other values) remaining equal. Moreover, as we shall see in the following the extent of this increase progressively dimin-

---

[5]In particular, I do not assume a utilitarian approach, according to which utility is to be viewed as happiness or preference satisfaction. On the contrary, here "utility" refers to the sum of all impacts on all (legally relevant) communal and individual values, since I assume that such impacts are independent. In principle, such utility might also be specified in such a way that the distribution of individual opportunities is subject to some fairness requirements. Then, such opportunities, as they follow from the realisation of the relevant values, according to their importance, would need to be allocated according to a scheme that is fair enough, in the sense that it balances the requirement of distributive fairness against the importance of increasing the total realization of the concerned values. Here however, I shall not examine whether including fairness requirement in the model here proposed would require a relaxation of some of its assumption, such as the assumption of the independence of the utilities obtained by realising different values.

ishes as the realisation-quantity of the value gets higher (there is a diminishing marginal utility), but the relationship above still holds.

On the basis of the notions introduced, we can address impacts of actions (choices) on the realisation of values. We use Greek letters $\alpha, \beta, \ldots$ as variables ranging over actions. We assume that actions have outcomes, namely, they make a change in the status quo, with one exception: the null action *nil* consists in letting things as they are (letting the status quo), or better, letting things evolve without our intervention.

To simplify things let us assume that each action has only just outcome, i.e., we assume a deterministic framework (otherwise we have to expand the current framework with probabilities): the unique outcome of an action α is the situation that would result from performing α in the current situation.

We are now able to specify the impact of an action α to a value v, namely, the change the action α can make to the realisation of v. This is the difference between the extent up to which v would be realised by α and the extent up to which it would be realised by not doing anything, i.e., by the null action *nil*.

Definition 3. (Realisation Impact) The realisation impact of an action α on a value v is the difference between the realisation-quantities of v resulting from α and from *nil*. Let us denote the outcome of action α, namely, the situation resulting from its performance in the current situation, as $\text{out}(\alpha)$ and the realisation impact (the differential realisation) of an action α on a value v as $\Delta\text{Real}_v(\alpha)$. Then $\Delta\text{Real}_v(\alpha) = \text{Real}_v\text{out}(\alpha) - \text{Real}_v\text{out}(nil)$.

For instance if α is a law prohibiting the use of a polluting substance which is currently in use in industrial processes, the realisation impact of α on health is the increased level of health that results from not having any longer the pollution caused by that substance, while α's realisation impact on productivity, is the decreased level of productivity which results from not using the substance in production processes.

The notion of realisation impact allows us to define what it means to promote or demote a value: promoting means increasing (having a positive impact on) the value's level of realisation and demoting means decreasing (having a negative impact on) it, as compared to *nil*.

Definition 4. (Promotion and demotion of a value) An action α promotes a value v if its realisation impact on v is positive ($\Delta\text{Real}_v(\alpha) > 0$); it demotes v if its realisation impact on v is negative ($\Delta\text{Real}_v(\alpha) < 0$).

Thus a legislative choice which prohibits the use of a polluting substance may promote health and demote productivity; a legislative measure that makes internet provider liability for violations of data-protection by their subscribers, may promote data protection and demote freedom of speech, etc.

We can also characterise the utility of an action with regard to a value, as the differential utility-impact provided by that action with regard to that value: this is a measure of the difference in utility provided by the fact that the value is realised to a higher or lower extent.

Definition 5. (Utility-impact of an action on a value) The utility-impact of an action α on a value v is the difference between the utility-quantity by v resulting from α and from nil.

Thus in the above case of the prohibition α of the use of a polluting substance, we can say that since α, as compared with the status quo, promotes the value of health, while demoting the value of productivity, it increases the utility by concerning health, and decreases the utility by concerning productivity.

Corollary 2. (Realisation- and utility-impact of nil) The above definitions entail that the realisation impact of nil on any value is 0, and so is nil's utility impact. Let us denote the utility impact of an action α on a value v as $\Delta\mathtt{Ut}_v(\alpha)$. Then $\Delta\mathtt{Ut}_v(\alpha) = \mathtt{Ut}_v\mathtt{out}(\alpha) - \mathtt{Ut}_v\mathtt{out}(nil)$.

3   Impacts on single values

The notions we have described enable us to compare the impact of different choices on different values. First of all we need to introduce a way to express that a choice α is superior to β with regard to its aggregate impact on a set of values.

Definition 6. (Superiority with regard to a set of values) We say that choice α is superior to choice β with regard to a set of values $\{v_1, \ldots, v_n\}$ and write $\alpha \succ_{\{v_1,\ldots,v_n\}} \beta$, if α's utility-impact on this set is higher than β's utility-impact on the same set. In other words $\alpha \succ_{\{v_1,\ldots,v_n\}} \beta$ if and only if $\Delta\mathtt{Ut}_{\{v_1,\ldots,v_n\}}\alpha > \Delta\mathtt{Ut}_{\{v_1,\ldots,v_n\}}\beta$.

Note that since the utility-impact of nil is null (0), then a choice α is superior to nil with regard to a set of value, wherever the choice has a positive utility-impact on that set.

Thus, for instance, in the environmental domain a measure α that prohibits the use of polluting substance, promoting health and demoting of productivity, is superior to nil, in case its utility-impact with regard to the combination of health and productivity is positive. In such a case we would write: $\alpha \succ_{\{health, productivity\}} nil$.

We will come back later on how to establish superior utility with regard to a set of values. Let us first address impacts on a single value. When we are considering just one value, we can say that whenever the realisation-impact on that value is positive, then the utility-impact on it is positive, given Assumption 1 (higher realisation of a value provides a higher utility by that value). But a higher utility by a value entails superiority with regard to that value. In other words, since (a) $\Delta \text{Real}_v \alpha > \Delta \text{Real}_v \beta$ entails $\Delta \text{Ut}_v \alpha > \Delta \text{Ut}_v \beta$ and (b) the latter entails $\alpha \succ_v \beta$, we can conclude (c) that $\Delta \text{Real}_v \alpha > \Delta \text{Real}_v \beta$ entails $\alpha \succ_v \beta$. This leads us to the following corollary.

Corollary 3. (Superiority (with regard to a value), according to contribution) Whenever α's realisation-impact on value v is higher than β's, then α is superior to β with regard to v ($\alpha \succ_v \beta$): $\Delta \text{Real}_v \alpha > \Delta \text{Real}_v \beta$ entails $\alpha \succ_v \beta$.

Note that this corollary also applies to the comparison of a choice α with *nil*. Since *nil* provides 0 differential contribution to the realisation of any value (the differential contribution of a choice being its difference with regard to the contribution of *nil*), any choice giving a positive marginal contribution would be better than *nil*, and any choice giving a negative marginal contribution would be worse than it.

For instance since a law allowing wiretapping only on the basis of a judicial warrant (α) has a positive impact on privacy and a negative impact on crime prevention, in comparison to the current regulation (the status quo, i.e., *nil*), which allows also police authorities to wiretap any communication in their criminal investigations (*nil*), we can say that $\alpha \succ_{privacy} nil$, while $nil \succ_{crime\_prevention} \alpha$.

4 Pareto superiority

We can extend the comparison to choices having an impact on multiple values. For this purpose, we shall make a simplifying assumption, namely, the assumption that the utilities we derive from the realisation of different values are independent, i.e., that the utility-impact with regard to set of values is just the sum of the utility-impacts we obtain from the separate realisation of each of them. This assumption may be questionable: for instance it may be argued that we enjoy more a given quantity of freedom of speech, or access culture, when we are not starving, or when we have political liberties as well (so that it makes more sense for us to discuss political matters). However, for the sake of simplicity, it is convenient to make the independence assumption.[6]

Assumption 4. (Independence of the utilities from different values) Given a choice α having an impact on values $v_1, \ldots, v_n$, the utility-impact of α with regard to the set of those values is the sum $i_1 + \ldots + i_n$ of the utility-impacts $i_1, \ldots, i_n$ of α with regard to each of such values. In other words $\Delta \mathsf{Ut}_{\{v_1,\ldots,v_n\}}\alpha = \Delta \mathsf{Ut}_{v_1}\alpha + \ldots + \Delta \mathsf{Ut}_{v_n}\alpha$.

For instance, consider a law exempting host providers from liability for the privacy violations committed by their users, as compared to a situation where providers are considered to be liable for such a violation. The total utility provided by such a law results from the sum of the utility-impacts it provides on the different values involved, its positive utility-impact on freedom of expression, freedom of information and economic efficiency, and its negative utility-impact on privacy.

The easy case is when α, as compared to β, provides a higher realisation of some values, and does not provide a lower realisation of any other value. In this case we say that α is Pareto-superior to β.

Definition 7. (Pareto superiority) We say that choice α is Pareto superior to β if there exists a value v_1 such that the realisation impact of α on v_1 is higher than β's and for no value v_2 the realisation impact of β on v_2 is higher than α's. In other words α is Pareto-superior to β with regard to $\{v_1, \ldots, v_n\}$ if (a) there exists a $v_i \in \{v_1, \ldots, v_n\}$ such that $\Delta \mathsf{Real}_{v_i}\alpha > \Delta \mathsf{Real}_{v_i}\beta$ and (b) there exists no $v_j \in \{v_1, \ldots, v_n\}$ such that $\Delta \mathsf{Real}_{v_j}\beta > \Delta \mathsf{Real}_{v_j}\alpha$. In this case we also say that β is Pareto-inferior to α.

Given that a sum $x_1 + \ldots + x_n$ is bigger than a sum $y_1 + \ldots + y_n$ whenever some x_i is bigger than y_i and no y_j is bigger than x_j, the following corollary follows from the definition of Pareto superiority, the assumption that a higher realisation of a value provides a higher utility, and the assumption of the independence of the utilities from values.

Corollary 5. (Pareto superiority entails overall superiority.) If α is Pareto superior to β with regard to a set of values then α is superior tout court to β with regard to the same set: If α is Pareto-superior to β with regard to $\{v_1, \ldots, v_n\}$ then $\alpha \succ_{\{v_1,\ldots,v_n\}} \beta$.

Consider for instance that a legislator is discussing whether to raise the length of copyright from the status 70 years (the status quo) to 90 years after the death of the author, and assume that the two lengths are equivalent with

---

[6]On how to handle cases when this assumption does not hold, see Pollock [13].

regard to the incentive to produce new works, but the shorter term contributes more to the value of knowledge. In such a case we can say that the shorter term is Pareto superior, and thus superior tout court to the longer one.

A legislator's choice which, likes this one, is Pareto inferior to *nil* (to the status quo) is particularly condemnable: it makes things worse in some regards, while providing no advantage in any other regards. Such choices may however take place, as a consequence of mistakes in appreciating the social impacts of a new regulation, or as a consequence of the fact that the legislators are pursuing private interests rather than public values.

Note that the cognitive capacities that are needed for assessing Pareto superiority are limited: we just need to be able to assess whether the differential impact on the realisation of single values is positive or negative. We do not need to establish the magnitude or such impacts, nor the magnitude of the utility they deliver.

5 Comparative evaluations without Pareto superiority

In many cases however, legislative choices are not Pareto inferior to the status quo: they promote some value, and demote some other values. For instance, a regulation increasing privacy protection may likely decrease freedom of speech, or a regulation increasing environmental protection may decrease productivity or economic freedom.

To evaluate choices having such impacts, we need to find a way of adding up gains and losses, providing a single outcome, on the basis of which to evaluate each choice as a whole. This means that the utilities provided by impacts on distinct values must somehow be comparable, and subject to elementary arithmetical operations (sum, subtraction, comparison).

Let us assume, as above, that we have an approximate way for assessing the current realisation-quantity of a value v (such as privacy, freedom of speech, welfare, environmental quality, transparency, political freedom, etc.), which may or not be expressed in numerical way, and a way of assessing the impact of a particular action α on the realisation of v. Given this information, we want to establish what it the utility-impact of α by v, namely, we want to assess the utility-impact of the fact that v's realisation has been increased of decreased to a certain extent. And we want to express this utility-assessment in an absolute cardinal quantity, namely, a quantity that is homogenous to the quantities through which we express the utility-impacts of this choice on other values at stake, so that these quantities can be added to make up the overall assessment of the utility generated or destroyed by this choice. We want find a way of accomplishing this task that not only makes sense (it is likely to provide a sensible outcome), but is also psychologically plausible, given the above considerations about intuitive quantitative reasoning.

To establish in this way the utility-impact (gain or loss) concerning each value, it may be useful to perform two steps. First of all we want to assess an impact on the realisation of the value, in a way that is independent of any particular unit of measure. We intuitively make some assessment when saying that a certain choice would provide a (very) big or a (very) small gain or loss with regard to a certain value.

Two different frames of reference seem to be usable for such a judgment. On the one hand we could quantify increases or decreases as proportions of what the full realisation of that value (achievable within what are taken as the boundaries of the given framework) would be. On the other hand we could quantifying the same increases or decreases as proportions of what is the current realisation level of that value. I think that we use both frames, when using number, but also when deploying analogical magnitudes. Thus we may say that the GDP per head in a poor county has increased a little in absolute terms (viewing the increase as a fraction of what is the GDP per head in the richest countries), but that it has increased a lot relatively its previous level. Similarly, we may say that a liberalisation measure in an authoritarian regime provides a little increase in freedom of the press in absolute terms, but a huge increase relatively to the previous level.

I would argue that in practical situation an intermediate position can be taken. We assess the level of realisation of a value as a proportion of what might seem the maximum realisation that is concretely available under the existing conditions, within the constraints that we see as unsurpassable (the maximum realisation resulting from actions we view as practicable). As a common-sense example, consider a person who is considering what career to undertake, and is considering what kind of revenue and work satisfaction he or she may obtain from different professions. The range of revenue-quantities and satisfaction-quantities the person is considering would probably end at the top of the levels of revenue and satisfaction that person considers to be reasonably achievable.

The same takes place also with regard to public choices, whose impact on the relevant values are to be considered within this feasibility horizon: changes in the GDP would be assessed with reference to the maximal achievable GDP, and similarly changes in privacy or freedom of speech.

Thus, an action α's proportional impact on the realisation level of value v could be defines as the proportion between the increase or decrease in the realisation of v brought about by α and the maximum amount of such realisation that is viewed as realisable by the agent.

Definition 8. (Proportional impact on the realisation of a value) The proportional impact of an action α on the realisation of a value v is the proportion between α's realisation impact on v and the reasonably achievable maximum level of v, denoted as $\texttt{MaxReal}_v\alpha$: $\Delta\texttt{PropReal}_v\alpha = \frac{\Delta\texttt{Real}_v\alpha}{\texttt{MaxReal}_v\alpha}$.

Similarly, we need to define the proportional contribution an action to the utility deriving from the realisation of a value, as a proportion of the utility that can be obtained by the maximal feasible realisation of that value.

Definition 9. (Proportional impact on the utility by a value) The proportional impact of an action α on the utility provided by the realisation of value v is the proportion between α's utility-impact on v and the utility provided by the maximal, reasonably achievable, realisation of v, denoted as $\texttt{MaxUt}_v\alpha$: $\Delta\texttt{PropUt}_v\alpha = \frac{\Delta\texttt{Ut}_v\alpha}{\texttt{MaxUt}_v\alpha}$.

The next step is to determine what is the change in the proportional utility that corresponds to a change in proportional realisation. The relation between the two changes is not constant, since the realisation of a value has decreasing marginal utility: this means that the same change in the realisation of a value will provide less (more) utility the higher (the lower) the position of the realisation interval at issue.

Assumption 6. (Decreasing marginal utility of the realisation of a value) A change in the realisation-quantity of value v, from quantity q_i to quantity q_j (the difference between q_i and q_j being constant) provides a smaller utility-difference the higher is the position of interval $[q_i, q_j]$.[7]

Thus, for instance, a proportional loss in the realisation of revenue (or of privacy) of 1/10 determines a higher loss if it is the passage from 5/10 to 4/10 than if it is the passage from 9/10 to 8/10.

Corollary 7. (From decreasing marginal utility) The hypothesis of the decreasing marginal utility has the following implications:

- The utility loss resulting from a diminution in the realisation of a value is higher than the utility gain which is provided by an equal increase in the realisation of the same value.

- A greater decrease in the realisation of a value causes a proportionally greater decrease in the utility generated by the value; a greater increase

---

[7]In mathematical terms, we would say that the function connecting a value to its utility, is such that its second derivative is negative. This too, however, has to be taken as what happens in most of the cases, namely, as a defeasible assumption.

in the realisation of a value causes a proportionally smaller increase in the utility by that value.

After establishing the proportional contribution of a choice to the utility provided by a value (note that the approximate magnitudes would be located in a range from 0 to 1, being proportions of the maximum achievable utility) we need to find a way of having homogeneous quantities for the utilities provided by the realisation of different values. For this purpose we need to assign weighs to values.

Definition 10. (Weight of a value) The weight of a value v, denoted as w_v, is a quantity expressing the importance of value v relatively to the other values.

Obviously, more important values, such as personal freedom, or freedom of speech will have a higher weight, while less important values, such as privacy or transparency will have a lower weight. The idea of assigning weights to values may seem to introduce arbitrariness in balancing, due to the difficulty of comparing different values. However, our experience tells us that we often engage in such comparisons, and we can come to determinations (approximate quantities) that are sufficient to support our choices, and even to come to shared conclusions. In fact, Sen [15, p. 297] observes that fact that there are "reasonable variations (or inescapable ambiguities) in the choice of relative weights" does not exclude that a shared assessment, with a sufficient precision, can be made under many circumstances. In particular, agreement on the fact that the weights at issue fall within certain ranges is often sufficient.

We are now in a condition to provide a quantitative characterisation of the absolute utility of an action with regard to a value.

Definition 11. (Absolute utility-impact on a value) The absolute utility-impact of action α on value v is the proportional impact of α on the utility concerning v multiplied by the weight of v: $\Delta \mathtt{Ut}_v \alpha = \Delta \mathtt{PropUt}_v \alpha * w_v$.

This allows us to give content to the idea that the utility of a choice is the sum of its impacts on all relevant values at stake. The elements to be summed up consist in the absolute utility-impacts concerning each value, which are obtained by multiplying the proportional utility-impact on that value, for the weight of the value.

Definition 12. (Utility of an action) The utility of action α with regard to a set of values $\{v_1, \ldots, v_n\}$, is the sum $i_1 + \ldots + i_n$ of the absolute utility-impacts of α on each of such values: $\Delta \mathtt{Ut}_{\{v_1,\ldots,v_n\}} \alpha = \Delta \mathtt{Ut}_{v_1} \alpha + \ldots + \Delta \mathtt{Ut}_{v_n} \alpha$.

By separating positive and negative elements, in the set of the utility-impacts of α we get the notion of outweighing: the positive impacts of α outweigh its negative impacts, if their sum is higher than the sum of the negative elements.

Definition 13. (Positive impact, negative impact and outweighing) The positive impact of action α on value-set $\{v_1, \ldots, v_n\}$ is the sum of its impacts on the values whose realisation it increases; α's negative impact on $\{v_1, \ldots, v_n\}$ is the sum of its impacts on the values whose realisation it decreases. The positive impact can be expressed as: $\Delta\text{PosUt}_{\{v_1,\ldots,v_n\}}\alpha = \Sigma_{\Delta\text{Ut}_{vi}>0}\Delta\text{Ut}_{v_i}$. The negative impact is correspondingly: $\Delta\text{NegUt}_{\{v_1,\ldots,v_n\}}\alpha = \Sigma_{\Delta\text{Ut}_{vi}<0}|\Delta\text{Ut}_{v_i}|$.

We use positive quantities for negative impacts (given that the absolute value $|-x|$ of a negative number $-x$ is the positive number x), since we want to express the negative impact through a positive quantity, which can be compared with the quantity of the positive impact.

Corollary 8. (From the notion of outweighing) The following statements are equivalent:

- α's utility is larger (smaller) than 0, i.e., $\Delta\text{Ut}_{\{v_1,\ldots,v_n\}}\alpha \geq 0$;

- α's positive (negative) utility-impact on values in $\{v_1, \ldots, v_n\}$ is larger than α's negative (positive) utility-impact on values in $\{v_1, \ldots, v_n\}$: $\Delta\text{PosUt}_{\{v_1,\ldots,v_n\}}\alpha > \Delta\text{NegUt}_{\{v_1,\ldots,v_n\}}\alpha$;

- α's positive (negative) utility-impact on values in $\{v_1, \ldots, v_n\}$ outweighs α's negative (positive) utility-impact on values in $\{v_1, \ldots, v_n\}$;

- the proportion between α's positive (negative) utility-impact on values in $\{v_1, \ldots, v_n\}$ and α's negative (positive) utility-impact on values in $\{v_1, \ldots, v_n\}$ is bigger than 1: $\frac{\Delta\text{PosUt}_{\{v_1,\ldots,v_n\}}\alpha}{\Delta\text{NegUt}_{\{v_1,\ldots,v_n\}}\alpha} > 1$.

The last item of Corollary 8, in its negative form provides a generalisation of the so-called weight formula proposed by Robert Alexy. In fact Alexy formula, which provides the proportion between negative and positive impacts, has the form: $W_{[v_i,v_j]}\alpha = \frac{I_{v_i,\alpha}*W_{v_i}}{I_{v_j,\alpha}*W_{v_j}}$. In our terms $W_{[v_i,v_j]}\alpha$, which Alexy calls the concrete weight of the (demoted) value v_i as opposed to the (promoted) value v_j, in case α, corresponds to the proportion between the negative impact of α on v_i and its positive impact on v_j (which are obtained by multiplying the importance of the impact on the value for its weight), namely, to $\frac{|\Delta\text{Ut}_{v_i}\alpha|}{\Delta\text{Ut}_{v_j}\alpha}$, which amounts to $\frac{|\Delta\text{PropUt}_{v_i}\alpha|*w_{v_i}}{\Delta\text{PropUt}_{v_j}\alpha*w_{v_j}}$. According to Alexy a choice is wrong when the proportion between its negative impacts and its positive impacts is higher then 1, ie., when $\frac{\Delta \text{NegUt}_{\{v_1,...,v_n\}}\alpha}{\Delta \text{PosUt}_{\{v_1,...,v_n\}}\alpha} > 1$.

Finally, we can define the utility of an action α relatively to an alternative action β.

Definition 14. (Utility of an action relatively to another action) The utility of action α relatively to action β, with regard to a set of values $\{v_1, \ldots, v_n\}$ is the difference between the absolute utility of α and β with regard to those values: $\Delta \text{Ut}_{\{v_1,...,v_n\}}(\alpha, \beta) = \Delta \text{Ut}_{\{v_1,...,v_n\}}\alpha - \Delta \text{Ut}_{\{v_1,...,v_n\}}\beta$.

This entails that superiority can also be specified on the basis of relative utility.

Corollary 9. Action α is superior to action β when the utility of α relatively to β is positive: $\alpha \succ_{\{v_1,...,v_n\}} \beta$ if and only if $\Delta \text{Ut}_{\{v_1,...,v_n\}}(\alpha, \beta) > 0$.

Another interesting corollary is that it may happen that given a set of actions, the action that is superior to all actions in the set is not superior to all of them with regard to any single value.

Corollary 10. Superiority does not necessarily require maximality with regard to a single value, when at least three choices are compared with regard to at least two values. More precisely, given an option option set $\{o_1, o_2, \ldots, o_m\}$ and a value set $\{v_1, \ldots, v_n\}$ it is possible that there is an option $o^* \in \{o_1, o_2, \ldots , o_m\}$ such that $o^* \succ_{\{v_1,...,v_n\}} o_i$ for every $o_i \neq o^*$ but there is no $v_j \in \{v_1, \ldots, v_n\}$ such that for every o_i it holds that $o^* \succ_{v_i} o_i$.

For instance, given three possible choices α, β, γ, it may be the case that γ is superior to both α and β with regard to value set $\{v_1, v_2\}$ while being inferior to α with regard to v_1 and to β with regard to v_2. This happens when $0 < \Delta \text{Ut}_{v_1}(\alpha, \gamma) < \Delta \text{Ut}_{v_2}(\gamma, \alpha)$ and $0 < \Delta \text{Ut}_{v_2}(\beta, \gamma) < \Delta \text{Ut}_{v_2}(\gamma, \beta)$.

This is the case when γ represents an adeguate compromise between the values that are best promoted by α and β. Consider for instance how with regard to the conflict between privacy and security, the best choice may be one that does not maximise neither of the two values, providing a compromise between them. For instance, the intermediate choice of keeping DNA data from suspects only for a short time, with appropriate warranties, may be preferable, all things considered, to both the most privacy favourable option (not storing the data at all) and the most security favourable option (keeping the data indefinitely).

6 Consistency in balancing

The idea that quantitative reasoning with non-numerical magnitudes has a valuable function in the application of the law can be challenged by pointing to the arbitrariness of the inputs of such a reasoning: even though balancing is constrained by arithmetic, it operates on magnitudes that are idiosyncratic contents of the minds of individual decision-makers (or reviewers). How can there be convergence in the outcomes of such reasoning, and how can any social control over such outcomes be effective if any outcome would be possible by changing subjective input quantities?

I think, however, that the following hypothesis can be made. We learn the magnitudes to be associated to our values (the proportional utilities of their realisation and their weights) by processing the inputs we get from our inborn attitudes, education, and personal experience, possibly though inductive/abductive patterns of reasoning which deliver both adjustments and explanations of our intuitive assessments (inference to the best explanation). Moreover we can consider what reasons support or attack the quantitative assessment we are inclined to make, and thus subject them to critical review, though monological or dialogical argumentation.

When we are assumed to adopt a single and shared point of view (the legal point of view), our assessments are additionally constrained by the need that they fit with the past expressions — value norms contained in constitutions and legislative documents, other explicit statements on the absolute and comparative importance of impacts and values, decisions of individual cases involving impacts on such values, legislative rules addressing value conflicts — of the point of view we are adopting.

I cannot here provide an analysis of how we can determine the measure of fit of a new assessment with a certain past history of teleological reasoning, which may involve also incompatible decisions, giving conflicting clues.[8]

Let us first mention two basic cases, where reasoning *a fortiori* on the basis of previous assessments gives clear indications. Assume that α, involving a demotion of value v_d and the promotion of value v_p, was assessed as being proportionate (v_d and v_p being the only values at stake). Now consider a new decision β involving a smaller (in absolute number) demotion of v_d and an equal or greater promotion of v_p (again, v_d and v_p being the only values at stake): clearly, β must be considered proportionate as well. This follows from the inequalities $|\Delta\mathtt{PropUt}_{v_d}\alpha| > |\Delta\mathtt{PropUt}_{v_d}\beta|$ and $\Delta\mathtt{PropUt}_{v_p}\alpha \leq$

---

[8]On the idea of fit, see Dworkin [8, Ch. 7]. On the connection between value-based reasoning and the interpretation of rules or the determination of their priorities see in particular Bench-Capon and Sartor [4, pp. 97--142] and Prakken [14, pp. 49--57].

$\Delta\texttt{PropUt}_{v_p}\beta$. In fact, such inequalities entail that $\Delta\texttt{Ut}_{v_p}\alpha - |\Delta\texttt{Ut}_{v_d}\alpha| < \Delta\texttt{Ut}_{v_d}\beta - |\Delta\texttt{Ut}_{v_p}\beta|$, i.e., that $\Delta\texttt{Ut}_{\{v_d,v_p\}}\alpha < \Delta\texttt{Ut}_{\{v_d,v_p\}}\beta$. Since we know that α's utility $\Delta\texttt{Ut}_{\{v_d,v_p\}}\alpha$ is superior to 0 (α is proportionate) and that β's utility $\Delta\texttt{Ut}_{\{v_d,v_p\}}\beta$ is superior to α's, it follows that also β's utility is superior to 0, namely, that β is proportionate.

Assume on the contrary that α, involving a demotion of value v_d and the promotion of value v_p was assessed as non-proportionate. Consider a decision β involving a greater demotion of v_p and a smaller or equal promotion of v_d: clearly, β must be considered disproportionate as well. This follows from the inequalities $|\Delta\texttt{PropUt}_{v_d}\alpha| < |\Delta\texttt{PropUt}_{v_d}\beta|$ and $\Delta\texttt{PropUt}_{v_p}\alpha \geq \Delta\texttt{PropUt}_{v_p}\beta$. Such inequalities entail that $\Delta\texttt{Ut}_{v_p}\alpha - |\Delta\texttt{Ut}_{v_d}\alpha| < \Delta\texttt{Ut}_{v_d}\beta - |\Delta\texttt{Ut}_{v_p}\beta|$, i.e., that $\Delta\texttt{Ut}_{\{v_d,v_p\}}\alpha > \Delta\texttt{Ut}_{\{v_d,v_p\}}\beta$. Since we know that α's utility is inferior to 0 (α is disproportionate), and that β's utility is inferior to α's, it follows that also β's utility is inferior to 0, namely, that β is disproportionate.

These ideas can be further generalised, as this simple example will shows. Assume that I have to assess whether a choice α that demotes value v_1 and promotes v_2 (for instance, a choice to store DNA samples of all citizens for 20 years, which demotes their privacy and promotes their security) provides an acceptable balance, i.e., whether $\Delta\texttt{PropUt}_{\{v_1,v_2\}}\alpha \geq 0$. Assume that in the past a choice β which involved storing DNA samples of all citizens accused of a crime for a 10 years was considered to be unacceptable, since its negative impact on privacy outweighed the gain in security. Assume also that it is agreed that by increasing the conservation time (by adopting β rather than α), the damage to privacy is proportionally increased to a larger extent than the gain in security: $\dfrac{\Delta\texttt{PropUt}_{v_1}\beta}{\Delta\texttt{PropUt}_{v_1}\alpha} > \dfrac{\Delta\texttt{PropUt}_{v_2}\beta}{\Delta\texttt{PropUt}_{v_2}\alpha}$.[9] Given such premises, any assessment according to which the new law would provide a positive balance (by subtracting losses and adding gains) would be inconsistent with the previous decision. In fact it is easy to observe that $\Delta\texttt{Ut}_{\{v_1,v_2\}}\alpha = \Delta\texttt{Ut}_{v_1}\alpha + \Delta\texttt{Ut}_{v_2}\alpha = \Delta\texttt{PropUt}_{v_1}\alpha * w_{v_1} + \Delta\texttt{PropUt}_{v_2}\alpha * w_{v_2}$. Thus whatever quantities w_{v_1} and w_{v_2} we attribute to the weight of v_1 and v_2, it must be the case that in this sum the negative number $\Delta\texttt{PropUt}_{v_1}\alpha * w_{v_1}$ has an absolute value which is larger than the absolute value of the positive number $\Delta\texttt{PropUt}_{v_2}\alpha * w_{v_2}$ (since this is needed to explain the precedent): $|\Delta\texttt{PropUt}_{v_1}\alpha * w_{v_1}| > \Delta\texttt{PropUt}_{v_2}\alpha * w_{v_2}$. Then by multiplying the first number for $\dfrac{\Delta\texttt{PropUt}_{v_1}\beta}{\Delta\texttt{PropUt}_{v_1}\alpha}$ and simplifying we get $\Delta\texttt{PropUt}_{v_1}\beta * w_{v_1}$, and similarly by multiplying the second number for $\dfrac{\Delta\texttt{PropUt}_{v_2}\beta}{\Delta\texttt{PropUt}_{v_2}\alpha}$ and simplifying we get $\Delta\texttt{PropUt}_{v_2}\beta * w_{v_2}$. Thus we must con-

---

[9]An economist would say that v_1 is more elastic than v_2 with regard to the conservation time.

clude that the also these results must be, in absolute value, such as the first one is bigger than the second: $|\Delta \text{PropUt}_{v_1} \beta * w_{v_1}| > \Delta \text{PropUt}_{v_2} \beta * w_{v_2}$. This follows indeed from the fact that for all numbers a_1, a_2, b_1, b_2 if $a_1 > b_1$ and $a_2 > b_2$ then also $a_1 * a_2 > b_1 * b_2$. Therefore also the second sum must give a negative result: $\Delta \text{PropUt}_{v_1} \beta * w_{v_1} + \Delta \text{PropUt}_{v_2} \beta * w_{v_2} < 0$.

More generally, any assignments of weights to v_1 and v_2 that would satisfactorily explain the disproportionality of the 10 years term, would also determine the disproportionality a longer term. Thus, the need to explain the disproportionality of the 10 year storage term would impose an assignment of weights entailing the disproportionality, for instance, 20 years term.

7 Conclusions

I have argued that teleological reasoning includes the assessment of impacts upon relevant values, which may be viewed as a kind of approximate quantitative reasoning, even when we are unable to assign symbolic numerals to the concerned magnitudes. We engage in this reasoning both when making common-sense private choices, and when participating in public decision-making. Non-numerical quantitative reasoning involves certain rationality conditions, and first of all it should normally respect the usual arithmetical relationships, which indicate general constraints on the processing of quantitative information. Thus arithmetical relationships can also be viewed as default standards of rationality to be applied by legal reasoners (legislators, interpreters and judges) when engaging in proportionality assessments.

These quantitative assessments result from the intuitive appreciations of the importance of the values at issue and of the intensity of impacts on their realisation, but can be supported or attacked through arguments, addressing all relevant aspects at stake (the identification of values, the assessment of priorities, the determination of impacts, etc.) and can be related to precedent cases. Thus arguments and cases can provide both inputs and constraints to the intuitive quantitative assessments I have considered. How this may happen will be the matter for future work, which hopefully will enable me to develop this preliminary sketch, validate it and integrate it with existing research.

Bibliography

[1] Kevin D. Ashley. Ontological requirements for analogical, teleological, and hypothetical legal reasoning. In *Proceedings of the 12th International Conference on Artificial Intelligence and Law (ICAIL'09)*, pages 1–10. ACM, 2009.

[2] Trevor J. M. Bench-Capon. Relating values in a series of supreme court decisions. In Katie Atkinson, editor, *Legal Knowledge and Information Systems. JURIX 2011: The Twenty-Fourth Annual Conference*, pages 13–22. IOS press, Amsterdam, 2011.

[3] Trevor J. M. Bench-Capon and Henry Prakken. Using argument schemes for hypothetical reasoning in law. *Artificial Intelligence and Law*, 18:153–74, 2010.

[4] Trevor J. M. Bench-Capon and Giovanni Sartor. A model of legal reasoning with cases incorporating theories and values. *Artificial Intelligence*, 150:97–142, 2003.

[5] Trevor J. M. Bench-Capon, Henry Prakken, and R. Visser. Argument schemes for two-phase democratic deliberation. In *Proceedings of the 13th International Conference on Artificial Intelligence and Law (ICAIL'11)*, pages 21–30. ACM Press, New York, 2011.

[6] Donald H. Berman and Carole D. Hafner. Representing teleological structure in case-based reasoning: The missing link. In *Proceedings of the Fourth International Conference on Artificial Intelligence and Law (ICAIL'93)*, pages 50–9. ACM Press, New York, 1993.

[7] Alison Chorley and Trevor J. M. Bench-Capon. An empirical investigation of reasoning with legal cases through theory construction and application. *Artificial intelligence and Law*, 13:323–371, 2005.

[8] Ronald M. Dworkin. *Law's Empire*. Kermode, London, 1986.

[9] C. R. Gallistel and Rochel Gelman. Mathematical cognition. In *The Cambridge Handbook of Thinking and Reasoning*. Cambridge University Press, Cambridge, 2005.

[10] C. R. Gallistel, Rochel Gelman, and Sara Cordes. The cultural and evolutionary history of the real numbers. In Stephen C. Levinson and Pierre Jaisson, editors, *Evolution and culture*, pages 247–74. MIT, Cambridge, Mass., 2006.

[11] Ralph Keeney and Howard Raiffa. *Decisions with Multiple Objectives: Preferences and Trade Offs*. Cambridge University Press, Cambridge, Mass., 1993.

[12] Simon Parsons. *Qualitative Methods for Reasoning Under Uncertainty*. MIT Press, Cambridge, Mass, 2001.

[13] John L. Pollock. *Thinking about Acting: Logical Foundations for Rational Decision Making*. Oxford University Press, Oxford, 2006.

[14] Henry Prakken. An exercise in formalising teleological case-based reasoning (extended abstract). In J Breukers, R. Leenes, and R. Winkels, editors, *Legal Knowledge and Information Systems. JURIX 2000: The Thirteenth Annual Conference*, pages 49–57. IOS Press, Amsterdam, 2000.

[15] Amartya Sen. *The Idea of Justice*. Belknap, 2009.

FuzziCalc: The Fuzzy Logic Spreadsheet

MAREK SERGOT[*]

Abstract

This short note reports on joint work with Trevor Bench-Capon on Fuzzi-Calc, an advanced, revolutionary, innovative fuzzy inference system whose social and commercial potential remains untapped. I summarise the design, theoretical foundations, and implementation, and sketch three illustrative applications. Some conclusions are drawn.

Introduction

In 1985 Trevor Bench-Capon and I wrote an article on possible approaches to the formal treatment of open texture in law [3]. The first part of the paper was an introduction to the concept of open texture and connections to the related concept of vagueness. (Professor Bench-Capon was responsible for most of that section.) The rest of the paper discussed three possible approaches. The first was approximation: the observation that for many practical purposes, especially in the everyday administration of law, a vague or open-textured concept could be and in practice often is substituted by an approximating crisp concept. (Professor Bench-Capon was responsible for most of that section.) The second approach was fuzzy logic. We speculated that sooner or later someone would suggest the application of fuzzy logic, either in Zadeh's original formulation [6] or in some modified form, to the treatment not only of vagueness but of open-texture in law. We wanted to pre-empt that suggestion and record several fundamental objections to it. (Professor Bench-Capon was responsible for most of that section.) The third approach, and the one we picked out as the most promising and deserving of further study, was a sketch of how open texture could be addressed through argumentation. (Professor Bench-Capon was responsible for most of the ideas in that section.)

Besides his fundamental contributions to the theory of argumentation and its applications, Trevor Bench-Capon has gone on to pursue the lines of research

---

[*]Imperial College London, Department of Computing

we had identified in the concluding part of our paper: to demonstrate how example-driven, case-based reasoning approaches to legal precedent can be reconciled and reconstructed in terms of argumentation, see e.g. [5] *inter alia*, and to look at the evaluation of arguments and questions of what it is that makes an argument persuasive.

My original idea for this *Festschrift* contribution was to follow up some of the ideas in his seminal paper [4] on value-based argumentation and in particular the very convincing examples used there to illustrate its application to the treatment of moral dilemmas. Subsequent developments in joint work with Katie Atkinson [1, 2] produced a methodology for constructing value-based argumentation frameworks for practical reasoning. I thought I might look at how these methods address some of the classic problems in moral and ethical reasoning, or produce an implementation to automate the methodology, or both. However, that turned out to be a much larger undertaking than I had allowed for. The implementation in particular turns up a number of points of detail and further questions that deserve careful discussion and a much longer and detailed exposition than would be appropriate for this volume. I will save it for another occasion.

Still, I could not let this celebration pass without making some contribution. I have picked out another, less well known piece of joint work, the design and development of a prototype system that came to be known as FuzziCalc (The Fuzzy Logic Spreasheet). That work could not be published previously because of commercial embargoes and other constraints. It grew out of our discussions on the possible applications of fuzzy logic to aspects of law, and built on earlier ideas Trevor Bench-Capon had sketched out to me on the representation of vague concepts in rule-based expert systems. FuzziCalc was subsequently developed to industrial strength by Charlotte Anne Software[1]. The industrial versions will not be covered in this short note.

1 Design and implementation

The design and operation of FuzziCalc is perhaps easiest to explain by reference to a specific concrete example. The application we used to drive the development was a system designed to provide qualified advice about suggested careers based on a person's performance in school examinations.

Input to the system were the numerical marks obtained by the subject in school examinations. In the implementation, these appeared in a column of cells on the left hand side of the screen. We experimented with other arrangements, for instance, diagonal from top-right to bottom-left of the screen, but

---

[1]Company motto: *lucrum per obfuscandum.*

ergonomic studies identified the columnar arrangement as the most natural and appealing. Output from the system were the suggested careers for that person, qualified by truth value. These appeared in a column of cells on the right hand side of the screen, ordered by truth value, highest to lowest. A modification to an examination mark in an input data cell generated an immediate revision of the list of suggested careers, as in a conventional spreadsheet, except of course that in FuzziCalc's more sophisticated manifestation, all computations are qualified to indicate the truth of computed values.

In fuzzy logic as introduced in [6], the truth value assigned to a proposition such as 'the subject is suited to a career in journalism' is not restricted to the two values *true* and *false* but can be any value in the real interval between 0 and 1, with 0 corresponding to *false* and 1 to *true*. Thus, for example, if it is 0.693 true that Peter is suited to a career in journalism and 0.618 true that Jim is suited to a career in journalism, then not only is Peter more suited to a career in journalism than Jim, but we have a precise measure of how much truer the first statement is than the second. The value of having such precision at our disposal will not be lost on the reader. It is important to stress that fuzzy truth values are *not* to be confused with probabilities or likelihood measures of any kind. We are not concerned with the *probability* that Peter is suited to a career in journalism (for what could *that* possibly mean?) but the degree to which it is true that he is so suited, which is of course quite clear.

Knowledge about the characteristics and requirements of various career paths was encoded in the form of biconditional rules such as the following:

```
journalism ↔
    (English:good ∨ English:very-good) ∧
    Science:weak ∧
    Mathematics:weak ∧
    (History:good ∨ Geography:good)
```

The rule is for illustration only. The actual rules employed were more elaborate than that shown here. Also not shown is the concrete syntax provided in FuzziCalc to make the formulation of rules more concise. An intermediate concept such as Science:weak could be defined in similar fashion, for example (in simplified form, for the sake of illustration):

```
Science:weak ↔
    (Chemistry:weak ∧ Physics:weak)
```

Now, armed with truth values for the various factors appearing in the antecedents of rules (English:good, Mathematics:weak, and so on), it is a straightforward matter to calculate the truth value of the consequents of a rule (in the example, `journalism`) and of any intermediate concepts. In Zadeh's original formulation, the truth value of the conjunction $P \wedge Q$ is the minimum of the truth values of P and Q and the truth value of the disjunction $P \vee Q$ is the maximum of the truth values of P and Q. Many other variations have since been proposed; I will comment briefly below.

It remains to specify how the truth value of a factor such as `English:good` can be determined from the marks obtained in school examinations. This is done by means of a *truth profile*. A truth profile for a factor F is a mapping from (in the example, examination marks) to the real interval $[0, 1]$. Certain restrictions have to be imposed to ensure that truth profiles are sufficiently well behaved but these are technical details that need not detain us.

Example: examination marks of 30, 40, 50, 60, 70, 80 for English might map to truth values for `English:good` of (for illustration) 0.1, 0.2, 0.35, 0.9, 0.75, 0.6, respectively, to truth values for `English:very-good` of (say) 0, 0, 0.1, 0.2, 0.8, 0.95, to truth values for `English:weak` of (say) 1, 0.85, 0.3, 0.05, 0, 0, respectively, and so on.

Truth profiles Clearly, determining the truth profile for a given factor is no trivial matter. We experimented with many different shapes: Gaussians, sinusoidal curves of various kinds, more or less angular wave forms, and many others.

Correct choice of truth profile was determined through a rigorous process of structured disciplined debate, supported by extensive scholarship, and diagrams drawn using different coloured pens. The use of different coloured pens is important. It increases confidence and helps to ensure accuracy. It would obviously be a nonsense if we were to compute the truth value of `English:very-good` as 0.709 (say) when the actual truth value was only 0.686. It is essential to get these details right.

Much of our investigations throughout the development phases centred on establishing the correct shape for truth. Towards the end of that period, we came across a scholarly work in which the author argued by reference to historical sources[2] that truth is in fact *spherical* (in the material sense). Further exploration led to the development of a more advanced FuzziCalc engine employing ellipsoidal truth values instead of simple real numbers and a revolutionary three-dimensional spreadsheet as interface[3]. The details cannot be presented here for reasons I am not at liberty to disclose, or even refer to.

---

[2]Parmenides (c. 500 B.C.) though the reference is almost certainly spurious.

[3]Alternatively: a two-dimensional spreadsheet with three columns.

Technical problem 1 A technical problem that emerged early in the first prototype was that in many cases the system was unable to compute any output for a given set of input data. Worse, this also had the unsettling effect that the modification of an examination mark on the left hand side of the screen could often result in the complete disappearance from the screen of career possibilities on the right. The problem can be traced to the fact that there are many persons whose abilities, as measured by examination performance in school subjects, make them unsuited to any particular career. The knowledge base we had constructed merely reflected that fact. The problem remained unsolved until a flash of inspiration by Professor Bench-Capon illuminated the way forward. His insight was to observe that in practice persons unsuited to any particular career were ideally suited to a career in the Civil Service[4]. This remarkable insight led to the incorporation of a default conclusion (in the application, 'Civil Service') with truth value 1 to be triggered in the absence of any other computed value. The required modifications to the implementation of the engine and its theoretical underpinnings are immediate. I omit the details since they are easily reconstructed.

Technical problem 2 Efficiency of an inference engine is often an obstacle to its effective deployment. The problem in FuzziCalc was that the inference engine was *too fast*, which undermined the user's credibility that anything of significance was being computed. We were faced with two seemingly irreconcilable requirements: users need to be persuaded that an inference engine is labouring over its computations on the one hand, but demand an instant response to changes in input data values on the other. The problem was eventually solved by developing a compilation technique that transformed the Fuzzi-Calc knowledge base into an efficient internal form when loaded by the user (or in modern terminology, when the 'app was opened'). The required transformation is so trivial however that we merely performed a series of heavy but completely pointless numerical calculations in order to give the illusion that something significant was happening. At that point the FuzziCalc engine was ready to accept user input (it had been 'unleashed' in the technical jargon).

Evaluation This was a fully functional proof-of-concept prototype. (In contrast to the references one sometimes sees in the literature to 'non-functional' prototypes, by which is meant usually 'non-functioning'.) No claims were made for the accuracy of the knowledge base. We took no responsibility for

---

[4]This was true in the United Kingdom in the 1980s. We did not investigate whether it is a universal phenomenon. In modern times 'University administration' is probably the most widely applicable analogue.

regrets and disappointments resulting from making life choices on the basis of FuzziCalc computations.

2 Two applications

FuzziCalc was applied to a range of important and substantial applications, of which I will sketch briefly just two.

2.1 Destination Advice for Travellers (*DAFT*)

DAFT was a system which offered advice to travellers seeking the perfect holiday, based on earlier preliminary work by Trevor Bench-Capon. The knowledge base specified in FuzziCalc rules the features and characteristics of popular holiday destinations: good beaches, sunshine, historical sites, culture, night life, facilities for children, cheap wine, availability of authentic English cuisine, and so on. Input to the system, on the left hand side of the screen, was a list of all such factors together with a slider for each which the user moved to record his or her own subjective assessment of the importance of that factor, in a scale from -10 (absence essential) to 10 (presence essential) with 0 indicating indifference. Output, on the right hand side of the screen, was an ordered list of suggested holiday destinations, qualified by truth value, naturally. Details of the knowledge base are proprietary and cannot be revealed. Truth profiles for each of the subjective factors were constructed following the methodology described above.

Evaluation: empirical, qualitative. *DAFT* was demonstrated at a series of international workshops and conferences, either as part of the industrial exhibition or informally during lunch and coffee breaks. Delegates were invited to try out the system for themselves, FuzziCalc's immediately intuitive interface making further detailed instruction unnecessary. User responses were carefully recorded. They divided roughly into two equal parts: those who responded 'Do you know, I have always wanted to go there!' and those who replied 'That is amazing. I went there once. It was the best holiday I ever had!'

Comment: This unanimously enthusiastic response was most gratifying, yet it also raised an important research question. Everyone knows that Morocco, say, enjoys sunshine and that Rome has a rich collection of historical sites but besides commonplace information of that sort, the rules in the *DAFT* knowledge base were compiled *without knowing anything about the destinations covered* and *nothing* about the features we claimed they possessed. It is remarkable that the system was nevertheless able to generate detailed advice that, without exception, was perceived as valuable and accurate by its users. The explanation of how this could happen remains to be investigated.

2.2 Case law and precedent (*CLAP* and *CLAP-dash*)

The *CLAP* system and its subsequent refinement *CLAP-dash* were built to evaluate the potential applications of FuzziCalc to the construction of case law databases and the search for matching precedents. The *CLAP* knowledge base consisted of FuzziCalc rules whose consequent was a reference to a previously decided legal case and whose antecedent listed the factors deemed to have been influential in deciding the case, qualified by fuzzy terms such as *important*, *very-important*, *minor*, *negligible*, and so on. User input, as in *DAFT*, was the list of all potential influencing factors with sliders for recording the estimated degree of relevance of that factor to the new case to be analysed. Output from the system was an ordered list of previous cases, with a precise measure of how true it is that their decision applies to the circumstances of the new case.

For *CLAP*, accurate determination of the correct truth profiles turned out to be extremely problematic, which no amount of rigorous debate or coloured pens could resolve. Sometimes a smooth sinusoidal curve worked well; in other application domains a sharp saw-toothed shape for truth was clearly right. The extended version *CLAP-dash* provided therefore a wide range of truth profiles, giving the user the option of choosing between them *at run-time*. A strong argument was also put forward that for application to legal precedent, Zadeh's original truth tables had dubious theoretical basis, and that other variations modelled legal reasoning more accurately. The user was also given the option of choosing at run-time between different fuzzy logic calculi.

Evaluation: anecdotal. The *CLAP-dash* was demonstrated at an important international conference to an audience of lawyers and legal practitioners. The response was unanimously enthusiastic: 'Why, this is exactly the tool we have been waiting for!' was typical. In order to make the evaluation more systematic, each member of the audience was asked to rate the system. There were two choices: 'excellent' and 'superb'. Rankings divided roughly equally. (One assessor added a hand-written comment asking whether 'excellent' was better than 'superb' or 'superb' was better than 'excellent'. His or her ranking was discarded.)

For all its technical sophistication, the *CLAP-dash* experiment must be judged a failure. The knowledge base of cases had been deliberately constructed to demonstrate that the output depended critically on choice of truth profile and choice of fuzzy logic. Thus, if the shape of truth profile was changed from, say, sinusoidal to saw-tooth, a completely different set of legal precedents came into view in the right hand column. Disconcertingly, this did not dampen in any way the enthusiasm of the evaluation group. We call this 'the *DAFT* phenomenon'.

3   Conclusion

This account is of dubious historical and technical accuracy, though it is probably no worse in this respect than many of the published papers in the literature on applications of logic to representation problems in computer science. The truth of that last remark I would estimate at 0.887, or possibly a little higher.

FuzziCalc is an inference system whose foundations are built on shifting sand and whose conclusions ought therefore to be taken *cum grano salis*—a satisfyingly littoral metaphor on which to close an article dedicated to a person born in a naval establishment who has chosen to spend nearly all of his professional life in one of the world's great industrial ports.

This note reports on joint work with Trevor Bench-Capon. I am however solely responsible for any mistakes or misunderstandings, deliberate or otherwise. Technical details of FuzziCalc are by kind permission of Charlotte Anne Software.

Bibliography

[1]   K. Atkinson and T. Bench-Capon. Addressing moral problems through practical reasoning. In Lou Goble and Ch. Meyer, John-Jules, editors, *Deontic Logic and Artificial Normative Systems*, volume 4048 of *Lecture Notes in Computer Science*, pages 8–23. Springer, 2006.

[2]   K. Atkinson and T. Bench-Capon. Practical reasoning as presumptive argumentation using action based alternating transition systems. *Artificial Intelligence*, 171(10):855–874, 2007.

[3]   T. J. M. Bench-Capon and M. J. Sergot. Towards a rule-based representation of open texture in law. In Charles Walter, editor, *Computing Power and Legal Language*, pages 39–60. Greenwood/Quorum Press, Westport, 1988.

[4]   T.J.M. Bench-Capon. Persuasion in practical argument using value-based argumentation frameworks. *Journal of Logic and Computation*, 13(3):429–448, 2003.

[5]   Trevor Bench-Capon and Giovanni Sartor. A model of legal reasoning with cases incorporating theories and values. *Artificial Intelligence*, 150(1):97–143, 2003.

[6]   L. Zadeh. Fuzzy logic and approximate reasoning. *Synthese*, 30:407–428, 1975.

Arguments about Values

BART VERHEIJ*

Abstract

Arguments are more or less persuasive depending on the values their outcomes promote and demote. This idea, closely related to Perelman's ideas work on argumentation, has been formally modeled by Bench-Capon in his well-known Value-Based Argumentation Frameworks, based on Dung's abstract argumentation. In this paper, the question is addressed how arguments about which values are promoted and demoted can be modeled. A proposal is made to model Value-Based Argumentation Frameworks in DefLog, a language that extends Dung's abstract argumentation, while keeping central definitions such as preferred and stable extensions. Since DefLog allows the modeling of support of support, attack of support, support of attack, and attack of attack, it becomes possible to model arguments about whether a value is promoted or demoted in case an argument is accepted.

Introduction

Trevor Bench-Capon is a respected and prolific author with a broad range of interests. Many will recognize the experience that a topic one just becomes excited about, turns out to have been addressed by someone before, sometimes already a long time ago. In the areas of *Artificial Intelligence and Law* and *Argument and Computation* chances are high that this someone is Trevor. I propose to dub this the *Bench-Capon effect*, in analogy with its philosophical counterpart, the Aristotle effect, that the major questions of philosophy have also been addressed by Aristotle.

For me personally a recent example of the Bench-Capon effect - there are more - is the investigation of argumentation in connection with quantitative techniques.[1] I was aware of Trevor's emphasis on the fact that there are not

---

*University of Groningen, Institute of Artificial Intelligence and Cognitive Engineering
[1]See [23], and also the recently started NWO-funded project on forensic Bayesian networks 'Designing and Understanding Forensic Bayesian Networks with Arguments and Scenarios'; www.ai.rug.nl/~verheij/nwofs/.

only all-or-nothing factors in case-based argumentation, but also gradual dimensions going from one extreme via intermediate values to another extreme (e.g., [4, 6]). In the context of a case about the possible voidance of an employee's dismissal, an example factor is whether the employee has forged a diploma or not, and an example of a dimension is the degree of damage caused by the employee (cf. examples used by [18]). In the mentioned work, the emphasis is on a discrete spectrum of qualitative degrees. For instance, Bench-Capon and Sartor [6] follow the well-known work by Berman and Hafner [7], when they discuss a series of cases concerning the hunting of wild animals, about the legal issue whether the loss of game should be compensated or not. In the proposal by Bench-Capon and Sartor, the dimension of control can take on values *no-contact, seen, started, wounded, mortally-wounded, captured*, each value of the dimension expressing a gradually higher level of control of the hunted animal. There is also a hint of quantitative approaches, when remarks are made on the extension of the qualitative version of gradual dimensions to a quantitative version. Preliminary experiments related to Thagard's theory of explanatory coherence [19, 9] are reported in [5].

All this I knew. My surprise came when I discovered Trevor's paper 'Neural networks and open texture' [1],[2], in which an attempt is made to learn the rationale underlying legal cases, given only a set of decided cases. By the use of neural network technology, this work has a profoundly numeric, quantitative flavor, while retaining the connection to qualitative reasoning. The chosen domain concerns a welfare benefit to be paid to senior citizens visiting their hospitalized spouse, for which a set of decided cases was constructed artificially. The variables are chosen so as to provide a representative set of possibilities: The variable 'sex' is for instance represented as a Boolean, while the combined capital resources of the spouses are modeled using a numeric variable with a threshold. The paper draws partly positive and partly negative conclusions: Bench-Capon writes (p. 292): 'Neural networks are capable of producing a high degree of success in classifying cases in domains where the factors involved in the classification are unknown.' But he also finds that the patterns in a given set of decisions do not determine the rules that led to the decisions. (See also my discussion of this paper in [3], Section 5.6.)

Trevor's work is highly cited, and his most cited work is on value-based argumentation [2].[3] In this work, it is argued that disagreements cannot always be solved conclusively, and that hence the role of persuasion and of the

---

[2]Trevor himself played a pivotal role in this discovery: it was on a long list of possible papers to be discussed in [3].

[3]Google Scholar's author profile for Trevor J.M. Bench Capon (accessed July 9, 2013) records 6877 citations, 3278 of which since 2008, an h-index of 41, and 425 citations for [2].

values promoted by arguments should be emphasized. Here Trevor follows Perelman. In [2], argument attack succeeds depending on the preferences of the values promoted. As a model, Bench-Capon proposes an extension of Dung's abstract argumentation frameworks [11], called value-based argumentation frameworks.

In value-based argumentation frameworks, it is statically modeled which arguments promote or demote which values. As a result, there is no reasoning *about* which values are promoted or demoted. That is the question addressed in the present paper: How can arguments about which values are promoted and demoted be modeled?

An example can be found in the Dutch debate about the gradual elimination of home mortgage interest deduction. That political debate can only be understood when considering arguments about which values are promoted or demoted, and which of these are preferred. For instance, for a laissez-faire oriented liberal, the current system of interest deduction would be seen as demoting the value of a free house market, thereby artificially inflating house prices. However, the Dutch political party that one would expect to be closest to laissez-faire liberalism (the VVD, currently providing the prime minister), has always fiercely opposed the gradual elimination of the interest deduction system. A key reason for the VVD seems to be that the system tends to especially benefit high-income citizens, and hence has as a side effect that it softens the high tax rates for higher incomes. So a VVD liberal will argue that the interest deduction system promotes the value of keeping taxes low for higher incomes.

In the following, Trevor's proposal about value-based argumentation is discussed (Section 2). Then the DefLog theory of structured arguments is presented (Section 3), followed by a proposal for modeling Trevor's value-based argumentation in DefLog (Section 4). Using a characteristic property of DefLog, namely that it models arguments about attack and support, a discussion of the modeling of arguments about values follows (Section 5).

1 Value-based argumentation

In AI & Law, Berman and Hafner [7] may have been the first to emphasize the need for the computational modeling of the role of the values and goals underlying legal decisions. Bench-Capon [2] builds on their work, but also pays tribute to the ground-breaking rhetorician and dialectician Perelman, who wrote (with Olbrechts-Tyteca):

> If men oppose each other concerning a decision to be taken, it is not because they commit some error of logic or calculation. They discuss apropos the applicable rule, the ends to be considered, the meaning to be given to values, the interpretation and characterisation of facts. ([12], as quoted in [2])

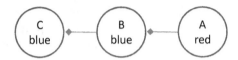

Figure 1. A value-based argumentation framework with two values (adapted from [2], p. 437)

Hence, it is not to be expected that actual arguments about a decision to be taken can be conclusively settled. Bench-Capon focuses on a decision by a judge on a case where two sides argue for their position, and writes that the 'arguments [of both sides] may all be sound. But their arguments will not have equal value for the judge charged with deciding the case: the case will be decided by the judge preferring one argument over the other.' As a result, mathematical proof is not an appropriate model of the kind of arguments used when taking decisions, as acceptance of such arguments depends on the values of the audience addressed.

Bench-Capon [2] presents a formal account of what is needed for the modeling of the role of values in argumentation. In the account, he uses Dung's abstract argumentation frameworks [11] as a starting point. Mathematically, Dung's abstract argumentation frameworks are directed graphs, where the nodes represent arguments, and the directed edges argument attack. Bench-Capon's central notion is that of a value-based argumentation framework (Definition 5.1). Formally, a value-based argumentation framework, or VAF for short, is an abstract argumentation framework in which each argument has an associated (abstract) value. The intended meaning of the value associated with an argument is that the value is promoted by accepting the argument. For instance, when parliament discusses a policy about raising taxes, the argument may focus on the values of social equality and of enterprise. Accepting a tax raise will demote the value of enterprise and promote the value of social equality. Bench-Capon also defines audience-specific argumentation frameworks (Definition 5.2). In an audience-specific argumentation framework, the values have an associated preference relation, that express the preferences of some audience. For instance, the Labour Party may prefer the value of social equality, and the Conservative Party that of enterprise.

In Bench-Capon's model, an argument A *defeats* an argument B *for an audience a* if A attacks B and the value associated with B is not preferred to the value associated with A for audience a. An attack succeeds for instance when the arguments promote the same value, or when there is no preference between the values. Bench-Capon continues to define variations of Dung's notions of argument acceptability, admissibility and preferred extension, relative to audience attack.

Bench-Capon uses a VAF with two values *red* and *blue* as an example (Figure 1). In the underlying abstract argumentation framework, there are three arguments A, B and C. A attacks B and B attacks C. The argumentation framework has a unique preferred extension (which is also grounded and stable), in which A and C are accepted and B rejected. In the framework, accepting the argument A promotes the value *red* and accepting the argument B or C promotes *blue*. Hence, for an audience preferring *red* to *blue*, defeat for the audience coincides with the underlying attack relation. In the corresponding unique preferred extension, A and C are accepted and B rejected, modeling that an audience preferring *red* accepts A and C, and rejects B. However, for an audience preferring *blue*, A does not defeat B. So for such an audience, A can exist side by side B, while B defeats C. This models that, for an audience preferring the value *blue*, A and B are accepted and C is rejected.

Bench-Capon illustrates value-based argumentation by considering the case of a diabetic who almost collapses into a coma by lack of insulin, and therefore enters the house of another diabetic, and uses her insulin. Bench-Capon models the roles of the value of protection against property right infringement and of saving one's life.

2 Structured arguments: the DefLog approach

Dung's abstract argumentation frameworks [11] have had an immense impact on the formal study of argumentation, as evidenced by its exceptionally high number of citations.[4] The paper focused on argument attack and its properties, uncovering the mathematical intricacy of the concept. Also a new puzzle arose, namely how argument attack is related to argument support. Dung himself contributed especially to one approach for the combination of attack and support, namely assumption-based argumentation [10]. A related influential approach is the ASPIC+-framework [15], which can be regarded as a modernized version of the model developed in close collaboration by Prakken and Sartor [16, 17], after incorporating the experiences in the European ASPIC project.

The formal argumentation model that combines support and attack used in this paper is DefLog [21]. We discuss a number of characteristic properties.

1. DefLog models both support and attack between arguments.

---

[4]Google Scholar records 1915 citations (July 9, 2013).

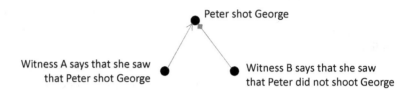

Figure 2. Support and attack

This first property is illustrated in Figure 2. The claim that Peter shot George is supported on the grounds of the testimony by witness A who says she saw that Peter shot George. The claim is also attacked by a testimony since witness B says she saw that Peter did not shoot George. DefLog uses a logical language with two connectives: a conditional for the representation of support combined with a negation operator for the representation of attack.

Modeling the arguments in Figure 2 requires two DefLog sentences:

$$a \rightarrow p; b \rightarrow \times p. \tag{1.1}$$

Here a expresses the claim about the testimony by A, b the claim about the testimony by B, and p the claim that Peter shot George. The conditional $a \rightarrow p$ expresses that given A's testimony, it is supported that Peter shot George. The sentence $b \rightarrow \times p$ expresses that given B's testimony, it is attacked that Peter shot George. It depends on whether a and b are assumed what can be said about the justification of p. When only a is assumed as a premise, there is only an argument for p, making p justified. When only b is assumed as a premise, there is only an argument against p, and p is not justified. When both a and b are assumed as premises, there is one argument for p and one argument against p. As no information is available that solves the conflict between the testimonies, it is undetermined whether Peter shot George. In the DefLog formalization, this corresponds to the fact that the theory consisting of the four sentences $a \rightarrow p$, $b \rightarrow \times p$, a, and b does not have a stable extension in which p has a value.

  2. DefLog models arguments about the issue whether an argument supports or attacks another argument.

The second property is illustrated in Figure 3, where arguments are provided about whether a witness testimony that Peter shot George supports the claim

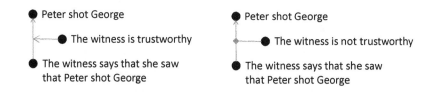

Figure 3. Arguments about support

that Peter shot George. On the left-hand side, it is argued that the testimony indeed supports the claim since the witness is trustworthy. In contrast, on the right-hand side, it is attacked that the testimony supports the claim since the witness is not trustworthy. The right-hand side argument is an example of what since Pollock [13, 14] is called undercutting attack.

Modeling the arguments on the left-hand side in DefLog requires a nested conditional:

$$t \rightarrow (w \rightarrow p). \tag{1.2}$$

Here w expresses the witness testimony about the claim p that Peter shot George, and t the trustworthiness of the testimony. The nested conditional expresses that, given the trustworthiness of the witness, it is supported that, given the testimony, the claim is supported. Assuming t as a premise, it is justified that $w \rightarrow p$, i.e., that, given the testimony, the claim is supported. Assuming also w as a premise, the claim p that Peter shot George is justified.

Modeling the undercutter on the right-hand side, requires this nested conditional:

$$n \rightarrow \times(w \rightarrow p). \tag{1.3}$$

Here n expresses that the witness is not trustworthy. The nested conditional expresses that if the witness is not trustworthy it is attacked that, given the testimony, the claim is supported. The examples in Figure 3 can be adapted for arguments about attack, e.g., by considering a witness who says that she saw Peter *not* shoot George.

Figure 4 gives an overview of the four ways of arguing about support and attack in DefLog: support of support, attack of support, support of attack, and attack of attack.

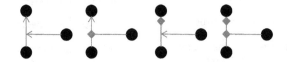

Figure 4. The four ways of arguing about support and attack in DefLog

3. In DefLog, the arguments supporting and attacking claims are expressed by sentences.

The third property has already been illustrated in the examples above. Every node in the graphs corresponds to a sentence. Also the arrows in the diagrams correspond to sentences, then with a conditional structure. The point is made since, following Dung [11], one influential way of modeling argumentation considers the argument nodes as structured arguments, in particular as (defeasible) Modus Ponens-based derivations. The attack relation is then considered to be between such derivations. Such a formalization separates an argument support layer from an argument attack layer in the model, which are then later reconnected when considering argumentative warrant (e.g., [15]). Instead, in DefLog's sentence-based approach, claims about support and attack are treated on a par. Layers that more strongly separate support and attack are not needed. In DefLog, sentences express prima facie assumptions that are assigned a justification status in light of the other available information: justified, defeated, or undetermined (cf. labeling approaches to argumentation with labels 'in', 'out' and 'undecided').

4. DefLog extends the expressiveness of Dung's abstract argumentation frameworks, generalizing its preferred and stable semantics.

Dung's preferred semantics is based on the notion of admissibility, following the idea that an argument is only acceptable when it can be defended against attacks by other arguments. DefLog's semantics is based on the related notion of dialectical justification, which uses a slightly stronger constraint, namely that an argument is only dialectically justified when it can be defended against all conflicts. Since attacks by other arguments are examples of conflicts, dialectical justification requires, in general, a stronger defense. Dialectical justification implies admissibility, but not in general vice versa. Verheij [21] shows that the two notions coincide when restricting to the expressiveness of Dung's

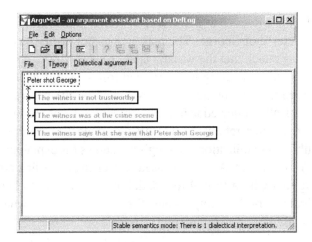

Figure 5. An argument against support in ArguMed

abstract argumentation. To show this, a selection of DefLog's more general theories is made that directly correspond to Dung's abstract argumentation frameworks: these are called Dung theories, defined as DefLog theories that only contain elementary sentences and sentences of the form $\alpha \rightarrow \times\beta$, where α and β are elementary. Dung theories have a straightforward translation to a Dung-style abstract argumentation framework, and vice versa: an elementary sentence corresponds to an argument, and a sentence $\alpha \rightarrow \times\beta$ to the attack of the argument β by the argument α. Since for Dung theories admissibility and dialectical justification coincide (Proposition 6.1), it follows that the DefLog analogs of preferred and stable extensions correspond exactly to Dung's preferred and stable extensions. It is also explained that when the richer DefLog language is used, admissibility is not a sufficiently strong notion of defense, when one wants to characterize the number of extensions (Theorem 4.3): then the stronger notion of dialectical justification is needed.

5. DefLog has been implemented in the argumentation software ArguMed. ArguMed diagrams and evaluates arguments, and has been assessed in user experiments.

The DefLog language and its formalization have been developed in parallel with a series of implemented argument assistance tools [20, 22]. Figure 5 shows an example of an argument against support in ArguMed (cf. the under-cutting argument at the right-hand side of Figure 3). As shown, in ArguMed based on DefLog, reasons for and against conclusions can be composite, i.e., consist of several conjuncts. In Figure 5, the reason for the claim that Peter shot

George is that the witness was at the crime scene *and* that the witness says that she saw that Peter shot George. The reason does not justify its conclusion, by the undercutting attack that the witness is not trustworthy.

ArguMed based on DefLog was designed following the experiences in different prototype implementations, and evaluated on the basis of user experiences systematically collected using test protocols. ArguMed implements DefLog's dialectical interpretations, and DefLog's dialectical interpretations are a formally faithful generalization of Dung's semantics (as explained under Property 4 above). As a result, ArguMed based on DefLog is the first argumentation diagramming tool with a formal foundation corresponding to Dung's semantics. Specifically, ArguMed implements the stable semantics when only Dung sentences are used.

3   Value-based arguments in DefLog

The first step towards our proposal to model arguments about values is to show how value-based arguments can be modeled in DefLog. We start with a discussion of Bench-Capon's example [2] of a value-based argumentation framework (VAF) with two values (cf. the example in Figure 1). We propose a translation of a VAF to DefLog using three steps:

1. *Given a VAF, translate the underlying abstract argumentation framework to the corresponding Dung sentences in DefLog.*

   This step models the attack relation between arguments, when the values are ignored. For the example in Figure 1 these sentences are:

$$A \to \times B; B \to \times C. \tag{1.4}$$

2. *For each value V promoted by an argument X, add the conditional that expresses the support of V by X.*

   This step models which values are promoted by accepting which arguments. For the example we get:

$$A \to red; B \to blue; C \to blue. \tag{1.5}$$

3. *For every pair of arguments X and Y, and pair of values V and W, such that X attacks Y, X promotes V, Y promotes W, and W is preferred to V, add an attack of an attack, namely that the preference attacks that X attacks Y.*

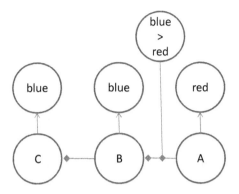

Figure 6. The example of Figure 1; translation to DefLog

This step models that an attack between arguments depends on the value preferences. For the example we get:

$$(blue > red) \rightarrow \times (A \rightarrow \times B). \tag{1.6}$$

We make use of a connective $>$ for expressing preferences, that is not a part of DefLog proper. This is unproblematic now that preference statements do not influence the DefLog semantics other than by their use in nested conditionals that result from this translation step. As a result, a sentence $blue > red$ behaves like an elementary proposition, that however by its structure is connected to the sentences $blue$ and red.

This translation of the VAF of Figure 1 is depicted in Figure 6. If we now assume the three arguments A, B, and C, but not the value preference, DefLog evaluates A and C as justified, and B as defeated (by the attack by A). Both values red and $blue$ are justified, expressing that they are promoted: red since A is justified, and $blue$ since C is justified. When we do assume the value preference, DefLog evaluates A and B as justified, as they no longer attack each other, and C as defeated (by the attack by B). Again both values are justified/promoted, but $blue$ is now promoted by B. The results in this DefLog translation correspond to what happens in Bench-Capon's VAF model.

In Figure 7, it is shown how different value preferences, modeling different audiences can be modeled. The two different value preferences indicated exclude each other, representing that they are different choices of an audience. In

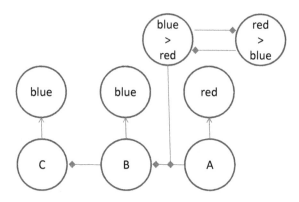

Figure 7. The example of Figure 1; two preference orderings, representing two audiences

the added preferential choice $red > blue$, the attack between A and B remains unaffected, and we have that A and C are justified, and B is defeated.

The translations discussed show informally how the apparatus of DefLog can be used to model Bench-Capon's value-based argumentation frameworks. A next step would be to evaluate the proposal by developing and proving a precise formal correspondence. Since the translation is so close to Bench-Capon's definitions, and both DefLog and VAFs are close to Dung's abstract argumentation frameworks, formal correspondence results can likely be developed.

4   Arguments about values

The next step of this essay is about the modeling of arguments about values: What if arguments are produced about which values are promoted and which demoted? What if there can be several values promoted or demoted? By the proposal for the modeling of value-based arguments in terms of DefLog's support and attack, as presented in Section 4, the full power of DefLog's nested support and attack model is now available: support of support, support of attack, attack of support, and attack of attack (Figure 4).

In the introduction (Section 1), we discussed the Dutch policy concerning home mortgage interest deduction. It can be argued that such a policy demotes the value of a free house market (V1), and promotes the value of keeping (net) taxes low for higher incomes (V2). A laissez-faire liberal could argue that home mortgage interest deduction demotes the first value, and a VVD-liberal that it promotes the second value. The VVD-liberal can argue against interest

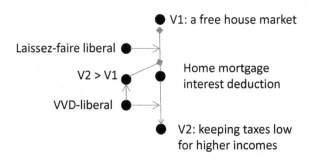

Figure 8. Arguing about values in DefLog

deduction demoting the value of a free market by a preference of the value of low taxes for higher incomes to the value of a free house market (though perhaps not too explicitly, because of the risk that the VVD is then more regarded as a party favoring the interests of those who don't need support). A model of the corresponding arguments about values in DefLog is shown in Figure 8.

Note that since DefLog models both support and attack, both the promotion and the demotion of a value can be modeled directly: promotion by support, and demotion by attack. The arguments about demotion and promotion of the two types of liberals have been indicated. Also the role of the preference of the VVD liberal is shown; here as an argument against the demotion of the value of a free house market. Their role in determining which policy would be preferred can be modeled as in Section 4. Note also that here the same policy has two associated values, and not just a single value, as in [2].

A side remark: for reasons of national politics, in particular the Dutch necessity of coalition formation, the preferences of VVD-liberals have recently changed slightly, and allowed for a mild reform of the home mortgage interest deduction system.

5 Conclusion: a tribute to Trevor Bench-Capon

I started this text with the explication of an analogy between Aristotle and Bench-Capon. This led me to read the Wikipedia page on the one I know least about.[5] One does not have to read far to find that the analogy is much stronger than just that between the Aristotle and Bench-Capon effects, play-

---

[5]en.wikipedia.org/wiki/Aristotle; version February 27, 2013.

fully coined in the introduction. Other matching factors include: productivity; elegant writing; emphasis on dialogue and argument, both in method and in subject matter; emphasis on personal and social values; promoting one's values by living them; the existence of hidden writing gems; being an example to follow and learn from, cf. Aristotle's medieval Muslim nickname المعلم الأول — the First Teacher. The matching factors have a strong correlation to the values that constitute a good life, both in general and in the academy. I am happy that the strength of the value-based analogy makes the following conclusive truth persuasive. Paraphrasing Cicero on Aristotle:[6]

Flumen orationis aureum fundens Bench-Capon

As the best dialecticians, such as Aristotle, Perelman and Bench-Capon know, but formalists sometimes forget: good form must always follow good content. The beautiful color of Bench-Capon's words is not just in their form, but matches the power of what they express.

Bibliography

[1] T. Bench-Capon. Neural networks and open texture. In *Proceedings of the Fourth International Conference on Artificial Intelligence and Law*, pages 292–297. ACM Press, New York (New York), 1993.

[2] T. Bench-Capon. Persuasion in practical argument using value-based argumentation frameworks. *Journal of Logic and Computation*, 13(3):429–448, 2003.

[3] T. Bench-Capon, M. Araszkiewicz, K. Ashley, K. Atkinson, F. Bex, F. Borges, D. Bourcier, D. Bourgine, J. Conrad, E. Francesconi, T. Gordon, G. Governatori, J. Leidner, D. Lewis, R. Loui, L. McCarty, H. Prakken, F. Schilder, E. Schweighofer, P. Thompson, A. Tyrrell, B. Verheij, D. Walton, and A. Wyner. A history of AI and law in 50 papers: 25 years of the international conference on AI and law. *Artificial Intelligence and Law*, 20(3):215–319, 2012.

[4] T. Bench-Capon and E. Rissland. Back to the future: Dimensions revisited. In *Legal Knowledge and Information Systems. Proceedings of JURIX 2001*, pages 41–52. IOS Press, Amsterdam, 2001.

[5] T. Bench-Capon and G. Sartor. A quantitative approach to theory coherence. In *Legal Knowledge and Information Systems. Proceedings of JURIX 2001*, pages 53–62. IOS Press, Amsterdam, 2001.

[6] T. Bench-Capon and G. Sartor. A model of legal reasoning with cases incorporating theories and values. *Artificial Intelligence*, 150(1):97–143, 2003.

[7] D. Berman and C. Hafner. Representing teleological structure in case based reasoning: The missing link. In *Proceedings of the Fourth International Conference on Artificial Intelligence and Law*, pages 50–59. ACM Press, New York (New York), 1993.

---

[6] 'Flumen orationis aureum fundens Aristoteles', in Cicero's Academica. One translation is: Aristotle with his golden river of words (cf. [8], 127).

[8] J. Blakesley. *A Life of Aristotle, Including a Critical Discussion of Some Questions of Literary History Connected with His Works.* J. and J.J. Deighton, Cambridge, 1839.

[9] J. Blakesley. *Coherence in Thought and Action.* The MIT Press, Cambridge (Massachusetts), 2001.

[10] A. Bondarenko, P. Dung, R. Kowalski, and F. Toni. An abstract, argumentation-theoretic approach to default reasoning. *Artificial Intelligence*, 93:63–101, 1997.

[11] P. Dung. On the acceptability of arguments and its fundamental role in nonmonotonic reasoning, logic programming and n-person games. *Artificial Intelligence*, 77:321–357, 1995.

[12] C. Perelman and L. Olbrechts-Tyteca. *The New Rhetoric: A Treatise on Argumentation [English translation of La nouvelle rhÈtorique: TraitÈ de líargumentation].* University of Notre Dame Press, Notre Dame (Indiana), 1958/1969.

[13] J. Pollock. Defeasible reasoning. *Cognitive Science*, 11(4):481–518, 1987.

[14] J. Pollock. *Cognitive Carpentry: A Blueprint for How to Build a Person.* The MIT Press, Cambridge (Massachusetts), 1995.

[15] H. Prakken. An abstract framework for argumentation with structured arguments. *Argument and Computation*, 1(2):93–124, 2010.

[16] H. Prakken and G. Sartor. A dialectical model of assessing conflicting arguments in legal reasoning. *Artificial Intelligence and Law*, 4:331–368, 2007.

[17] H. Prakken and G. Sartor. Modelling reasoning with precedents in a formal dialogue game. *Artificial Intelligence and Law*, 6:231–287, 2007.

[18] B. Roth. *Case-Based Reasoning in the Law. A Formal Theory of Reasoning by Case Comparison. Dissertation.* Universiteit Maastricht, Maastricht, 2003.

[19] P. Thagard. *Conceptual Revolutions.* Princeton University Press, Princeton (New Jersey), 1992.

[20] B. Verheij. Artificial argument assistants for defeasible argumentation. *Artificial Intelligence*, 150(1–2):291–324, 2003.

[21] B. Verheij. DefLog: on the logical interpretation of prima facie justified assumptions. *Journal of Logic and Computation*, 13(3):319–346, 2003.

[22] B. Verheij. *Virtual Arguments. On the Design of Argument Assistants for Lawyers and Other Arguers.* T.M.C. Asser Press, The Hague, 2005.

[23] B. Verheij. Jumping to conclusions. a logico-probabilistic foundation for defeasible rule-based arguments. In L. Fariñas del Cerro, A. Herzig, and J. Mengin, editors, *13th European Conference on Logics in Artificial Intelligence, JELIA 2012. Toulouse, France, September 2012. Proceedings (LNAI 7519)*, pages 411–423. Springer, Berlin, 2012.

Value-Based Practical Reasoning

DOUGLAS WALTON*

Introduction

Surely one of the most important contributions of Trevor Bench-Capon to computer science, and especially to artificial intelligence and law, and for that matter to argumentation theory and cognitive science generally, is the model of value-based practical reasoning he has given us. He introduced value-based argumentation frameworks (VAF's) in [8] [7] [9], and then applied this framework to practical reasoning, yielding the argumentation scheme for value-based practical reasoning, in a series of papers with his colleagues Katie Atkinson and Peter McBurney. The first one appears to be [14]. Greenwood was the unmarried name of Katie Atkinson. Before 2003 there had been several books and numerous articles written on the subject of practical reasoning, and of course the notion originally derived from Aristotle.

The literature in philosophy was almost exclusively concentrated on what could be called instrumental practical reasoning, a notion that did not take values explicitly into account, even though some philosophers recognized the importance of values in practical reasoning. But the only argumentation model of practical reasoning previously put forward [23] concentrated exclusively on instrumental practical reasoning, the assumption being that the values-laden variant contained so many complexities of its own that getting a basic notion practical reasoning without considering the role of values in it was the best place to start. Previous to 2002, there was simply no idea of how a value-based model of practical reasoning could be added on to the existing argumentation model. Much less was there any idea of how such a notion of value-based practical reasoning could be formally modeled or implemented computationally. So what Trevor and his colleagues have given us is a tool of no small importance for many fields. The significance of the potential applications and philosophical implications of it should not be taken lightly.

Having a value-based version of the argumentation scheme for practical reasoning will no doubt prove to be extremely useful, not only in the field of artifi-

*University of Windsor, Centre for Research in Reasoning, Argumentation and Rhetoric

cial intelligence and law, but in many applications of argumentation theory and methods, including law itself. But there are many questions that arise concerning the relationship between the new value-based version of practical reasoning and the old simpler model of practical reasoning that does not take values into account. Also, there are more critical questions matching the value-based version of the scheme, and therefore questions are raised generally about how both kinds of critical questions should be used in evaluating practical reasoning, and how they fit together. Another basic question is how the value-based version and the older and simpler version of the argumentation scheme for practical reasoning fit together. Is one a special instance of the other? Is the value-based version the more general scheme so that the other scheme fits into it as a special instance? Or is the other scheme the more general one, so that the value-based scheme is an extension of the more basic scheme?

There have long been questions about the argumentation scheme and critical questions for practical reasoning that can prove troublesome to those trying to apply this scheme to argumentation in natural language discourse. Some users of this scheme have found it difficult to distinguish in particular cases between instances of practical reasoning and instances of argument from negative consequences. Argument from negative consequences is a particularly common type of argument, perhaps even the most common type of argument in political discourse, as recent studies at University of Windsor [17] have suggested. But asking about side effects of a projected course of action that could be used to fulfill a goal in practical reasoning is in fact one of the critical questions matching the basic scheme for practical reasoning. Is argument from negative consequences a distinctive type of counterattacking argument in its own right, or is it better seen as a critical question matching the scheme for practical reasoning? Or can it fulfill both these roles?

Another question raised is that since there appear to be around sixteen critical questions matching the value-based scheme for practical reasoning, could there be some way to make this list of schemes more manageable? For example, perhaps critical questions could be classified into subcategories in a tree structure so that it would be easier for a user to keep them in mind. At any rate, these are the questions that will be explored in this paper. Finally, good answers are hard to come by quickly in this new and vital area of investigation in argumentation, but still, it is worth moving ahead by trying to provide answers to them since practical reasoning is so important as a foundational mode of reasoning in argumentation studies.

1 Simple Practical Reasoning and its Extensions

The simplest and most basic kind of practical inference that is readily famil-iar to all of us can be represented in the following scheme according to the account of it given in [24] (p. 300-301). The first-person pronoun 'I' repre-sents an agent. More correctly, it could be called a rational agent of the kind described by Wooldridge [29], an entity that has goals, some (though possi-bly incomplete) knowledge of its circumstances, and the capability of acting to alter those circumstances and to perceive (some of) the consequences of so acting.

Goal Premise: I have a goal, G.
Means Premise: Carrying out this action A is a means to realize G.
Conclusion: I ought (practically speaking) to carry out this action A.

This simplest form of practical reasoning can be represented by the decision-making structure in visualized in figure 1.

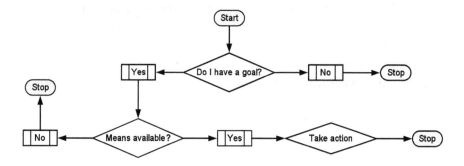

Figure 1. Simple Practical Reasoning

This form of practical inference is much too simple to represent realistic cases of the use of practical reasoning. An agent may have many goals, they may conflict, a chain of actions may be required, and there may be many ways to carry out a goal. Because practical reasoning is generally a defeasible form of argumentation, the basic evaluation procedure recommended in [24] (p. 301) is to begin by asking one or more of a set of basic critical questions. Six of the most basic critical questions are listed below.

CQ1: Are there alternative actions available other than action A?
CQ2: Is G a possible (realistic) goal?
CQ3: Are there other goals that might conflict with G?

CQ4: Are there negative consequences of bringing about *A* that should be considered?

CQ5: Is *A* the best or most acceptable of the alternatives?

CQ6: Are intervening actions required to get from *A* to *G*?

To get some idea of how these critical questions work, let's start with a relatively simple example from [23] (p. 89-90). Bob wants to balance his budget. He observes that the heating bill for his house has a large item in his budget. Let's suppose Bob already possesses a wood stove, a chainsaw and a trailer to carry wood. He is now in a position to take action, except he must have some source of wood to cut. Let's suppose he has a permit to cut wood in a woodland area designated by the government. So now, in order to carry out his goal, he hitches up his trailer to his car, and puts the chainsaw in the car. Next, he has to drive to the woodland area, which involves a lengthy collection of intervening actions, stopping at stop lights, putting his foot on the accelerator or the brake, and so forth. When it gets to the woodland area, he has to find some suitable trees, select one to start with, and then get his equipment unloaded and ready to start cutting a tree. He then has to go through a sequence of actions that would be familiar to him if he is very experienced with cutting trees with his chain saw.

If Bob's chain saw is new, or a rental unit that he is not familiar with, he might need to the instructions given for starting his chain saw [23] (p. 89).

1. Switch on the ignition (push the stop switch to the left so that the 1 is visible).

2. Pull out the choke control.

3. Push down the throttle safety catch.

4. Open the throttle fully.

5. Push the starting throttle ratchet backwards. Now all controls are in starting position and the chain saw is ready to be started.

6. Put your right foot on the plate beneath the rear handle.

7. Grasp the front handle with your left hand and press the saw against the ground.

8. Grasp the starter handle with your right hand and pull out the starting cord slowly until the starter pawls engage.

9. Give the starting cord a short sharp tug.

When analyzing what appears to be a simple teleological action like getting someone for the fireplace, studying even what appears to be an obvious case that can be summed up as one action typically leads to the need to break it down into a sequence of actions that might be quite lengthy. We often don't think about these intervening actions because they are routine. We do them habitually without thinking about them. But in studying any realistic case, it can be seen that they involve some sequences of actions that are comparable to computer programs.

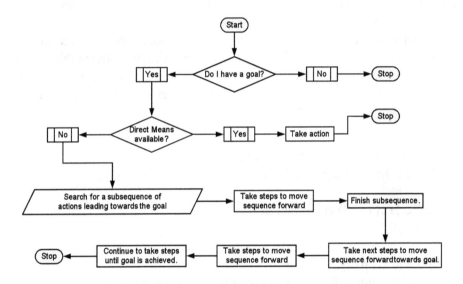

Figure 2. Practical Reasoning with Intervening Actions

There is a first step, and intervening sequence of steps, and finally a last step that represents the outcome. In such cases, the model of simple practical reasoning shown in figure 1 will not work. We have to make the model more complex by taking the need for intervening subsequences of actions into account. A rough attempt at a more adequate model is shown in figure 2.

But now what about the other critical questions? We need an even more complex model that not only takes subsequences of chained actions into account, but also accounts for the realistic possibilities at there may be a choice of several different actions each of which by itself represents a means to achieving the goal. In order to factor in these other critical questions, the model of practical reasoning as a sequence of steps in the thinking of a rational agent as it goes through thinking required to move towards its goal starts to get much more complex. Complex sequences of practical reasoning of these kinds have already been widely studied in the field of AI planning. But here our aim is only to get a model of the schema for practical reasoning along with a set of matching critical questions.

2   The BDI and Commitment Models

The dominant approach is the belief-desire-intention (BDI) model, which uses 'intention' (or other variants like 'want' or 'desire') in place of the term 'goal' in the first premise. In this model the cognitive architecture of an agent is made up of a set of beliefs as well as a set of desires or intentions. In particular, an agent is said to have beliefs about its circumstances such that carrying out some particular action or set of action in those circumstances could be a means to realizing its intention. Clarke [12] (p. 17) posited a simple model of this sort in which E is a want or intention, M is a means (an action) that might potentially lead to the satisfaction of this want, and C is a set of circumstances of the agent's choice situation.

> I want E
> My doing M is a means to attaining E if C obtains
> Hence I should (ought to) do M

Clarke [12] (p. 3) cited the following example as fitting his version of the scheme.

> I want to keep dry.
> Taking this umbrella is a means of keeping dry if it rains [because it will rain].
> Hence I should take this umbrella.

This version expressing the major premise as a want fits the BDI (belief-desire intention) model.

The BDI model has been widely adopted in cognitive science and computing, especially in work on artificial intelligence [10]; [11]; [6]; [20]; [29]; [19]). On this model of how a cognitive agent reasons, the agent possesses a set of beliefs that are continually being updated by sensory input coming in from its environment as it moves forward taking actions, and a set of desires (wants) that form its intentions. On the BDI model, a distinction can be made between goals and intentions. There seems to be little firm agreement on how to draw this distinction precisely, but one way is that an agent's intentions can be defined as a subset of its goals - persistent goals that are stable over time and are not easily given up as the agent continues to act.

The BDI accounts which represent the dominant model of practical reasoning in philosophy appear to be directed to modeling the behavior of a person who is trying to decide what to do based on information about the circumstances that might be changing as the situation evolves. Hence the model is based on the notion of an agent taking action based on its beliefs and intentions, desires and wants. It is possible to take a different approach to practical reasoning, however, where the object is to model the reasoning of a robot that is built to act autonomously in accord with goals that have been programmed into it by continually moving through a set of circumstances recorded in its memory and perceived by its sensors as it navigates through the circumstances.

Such a rational agent would need to have several important characteristics. First obviously it needs to have goals and the capability to carry out actions that might realize those goals, or in some instances might steer away from the realization of those goals. It must have some knowledge contained in its memory representing information about its circumstances and about the external world generally. As it steers its way through the circumstances it must have the capability for feedback, requiring the capability to observe the consequences of its actions and the capability to steer them towards its goals. It must have the capability to mesh abstract goals with particular actions, and hence it needs to have some resources for dealing with abstraction. It must have the capability to look forward into the future by constructing hypotheses about possible future consequences of its actions. It must have the capability to comparatively examine different possible alternative courses of action to determine which course might better steer towards fulfillment of its goals, or might lead to entrance of fulfillment of its goals. It must have a memory that has the capability of keeping track of its actions so that it can organize them, and so it can tell which actions have had certain consequences in the past.

These are the basic characteristics it must have, but at a higher level it might have four other characteristics, if it is to be an especially intelligent agent. One is plasticity meaning the characteristic to act in a flexible way moving forward and adapting to information new circumstances. A second one is the characteristic of persistence, referring to trying an alternative course of action if one action being considered turns out to be impossible or not useful towards reaching a goal. A third one is planning capability, built on the agent's capability of constructing hypotheses about possible future consequences of its actions and its capability of estimating the most likely consequences of its actions in normal situations of the kind is familiar with, or has had some experience with.

A fourth one is criticism, referring to the ability to see defects in its own action plans, including inconsistencies and practical difficulties.

An agent of this sort can be programmed with goals in the form of propositions that can be more concrete or more abstract. For example if my goal is health, that goal is quite abstract. It may be nontrivial to operationalize it in a specific case where I have to make a decision about my health on the basis of what I know or don't know. Or my goal might be to lose weight. This is a more specific goal, but still quite general. It might be much more specific. For example my goal may be to lose ten pounds within the next six months. A goal in this sense of the word can be represented as a proposition that is inserted into the memory of the agent to represent the commitment that the agent has adopted. For example, if an agent says it is his goal to lose ten pounds with the next six months, or that he intends to do so, or uses some comparable expression of the sort, it can be inferred that he has taken on a commitment to do whatever he can to lose ten pounds within the next six months. Presumably, in the case of a nonhuman agent like a robot, it has a goal because it has been programmed to act in such a way as to try to bring about some proposition and its commitment store if it has the resources to do so, and if the possibility of doing so becomes possible in the circumstances that it confronts.

A goal in this sense does not have to be an intention, a want or desire of the agent. It is often described that way, but such a description is somewhat misleading, or even anthropomorphic. A goal can be understood as a state of the world that an agent is aiming at. This world state can be represented in the agent's knowledge base (or in its commitment set, in an argumentation model) as one or more propositions. To call this (or these) propositions a goal for some agent is simply to say that the agent is committed to bringing about this world state, or to arrange for its bringing about, and acts accordingly. Typically, an agent will maintain this objective for an extended period of time, which is to say that the agent is committed to the achievement of the world state.

We tend to think of a rational agent of this sort as a solitary decision maker who looks at both sides of a choice and examines the pros and cons of each course of action it contemplates undertaking. But in a multiagent context, such a decision maker would engage in group deliberations in cases where the group shares common goals, to some degree, common knowledge of a set of circumstances in which a choice that affects all of them has to be made, and can put forward and criticize proposals for action [3]. The basic structure of a single agent, or the way a group of agents collaborates in deliberation to make a decision on action, is basically the same in that in both instances the argumentation and the outcome of the decision-making procedure is based on practical reasoning.

The problem with using the concept of intention as the primitive constant in the major premise of the scheme for practical reasoning is the difficulty of knowing what the intention of an agent really is in a given case. We can all easily recognize that it is extremely difficult very often in everyday life to try and figure out what the intention of another agent really is. Indeed, one might add that it may involve considerable speculative guesswork to try to figure out even what one's own intention is in some situation where one is making a decision to act, or has made such a decision. Both intentions and beliefs, the other key primitive notion in the BDI model, are private psychological notions internal to an agent, while commitments are statements externally and verbally accepted by an agent in a communicative context. The BDI model is clearly necessary and important in cognitive science in the fields of psychology and law, because the notions of motive and intention are fundamentally important in these fields. However, precisely because of the richness of these notions, and the difficulty of determining them in particular cases, it introduces of complexity in using them in the simplest form of the argumentation scheme for practical reasoning.

An alternative approach is to take goals as statements that the agent has expressed or formulated in a public way, based on what he has said and committed himself to, either through as speech or actions. On this approach, a goal is simply a proposition stated or accepted by an agent. On the commitment model of argumentation, there is a dialogue structure in which each contributes speech acts and each party has a commitment set containing the propositions it has accepted, judging by its speech acts in the previous dialogue [27]. In such a formal dialogue model, as each move is made, propositions are inserted into or retracted from an agent's commitment store according to protocols (rules governing the moves) [15] [16]. The commitment model represents a weaker logic-based approach, as opposed to the richer psychological approach of the BDI model. The two models are certainly related to each other, and one approach to investigating both of them is to begin with the commitment model, which is simpler and more open to logical analysis, and them move from there to the investigation of the BDI model. On the commitment model, practical reasoning is modeled in a dialogue format which utilizes the device of a set of critical questions matching an argumentation scheme in order to evaluate the application of the scheme to a case.

3   Argument from Consequences

Suppose that Bob has now gotten his chain saw started, and has selected the first tree he wants to cut down. He steps towards the tree, but then realizes that if he makes the cut from the front, the way he originally planned, there is a very good chance that the tree will fall back towards him and cause him serious injury. Therefore, using practical reasoning, he moves around to a different angle and makes the cut in such a way that the tree will fall away from him. Here Bob has used argument from negative consequences as follows.

> If I cut the tree from the front, it will have consequences for me.
> These consequences are highly negative.
> Therefore I will not cut the tree from the front.

Because of these negative consequences, Bob searches around for an alternative course of action that might lead to his goal of cutting down a tree without the negative consequences of injuring him. He sees that if he cuts the tree from a different angle, it will fall away from him, and so the cutting of the tree will not have these negative consequences. So he chooses the alternative course of action. This conclusion assumes however that the alternative course of action does not also have some negative consequences, especially ones that might be even worse than the original set of negative consequences.

To model this kind of reasoning, we have to construct a decision-making flowchart that takes negative consequences of a proposed course of action into account. This model needs to be capable of considering the question of whether the negative consequences are bad enough that they outweigh the goal. In other words, the negative consequences have to be weighed against the goal. This process of weighing the negative value of the consequences against the positive value of the goal might suggest that values are now involved. In other words, it suggests that we are now already doing value-based practical reasoning and not just simple instrumental practical reasoning of the kind that does not involve values. This observation exposes a general problem. Could it be that because the side effects critical question entails classifying consequences as good or bad, values are inextricably bound up with even the simpler forms of practical reasoning. This in turn suggests that perhaps there is no such thing as simple instrumental practical reasoning, because all practical reasoning involves values. Here we have a central problem, assuming we want to draw a distinction between two kinds of practical reasoning, instrumental practical reasoning versus value-based practical reasoning.

Practical reasoning is commonly used in advertising, for example in health product ads [25]. Typical examples cite positive consequences of taking the medication, but will also offer a long list of side effects. For example an ad for the pain reliever medication Cymbalta (*Newsweek*, December 31, 2012, 12-14) tells us that Cymbalta can help to significantly reduce chronic low back pain. This good consequence can be seen as representing the goal of someone who takes this medication. However, the ad also states a long list of side effects included under the heading of important safety information. This list includes itching, upper belly pain, headache, weakness or feeling unsteady, confusion, problems in concentrating, high fever, confusion, stiff muscles, muscle twitching, racing heart rate, abnormal bleeding, serious possibly life-threatening skin reactions, abnormal mood (mania), racing thoughts, talking more or faster than usual, reckless behaviour, and seizures or convulsions. It may be presumed that all of these side effects may be taken to be bad consequences. They may be taken to be reasons to at least consider not taking the drug, or to stop taking it if the side effects are so bad as to be intolerable.

Each side effect in the list may be taken as an instance of the side effects critical question. But should any of these side effects actually be experienced by the person taking the drug, the critical question is transformed into an argument from negative consequences. Now it is an argument against continuing to take the drug. However, the person will have to weigh the negative consequences against the positive benefits of the drug in helping with back pain. It is a question of balancing how bad the back pain is against how bad the side effects are.

4 Value-based Practical Reasoning

Atkinson, Bench-Capon and McBurney, [5] (p. 166) - and before that in [14] - formulated their model of value-based practical reasoning said to be an extension of Walton's instrumental practical reasoning scheme as follows.

In the circumstances R
we should perform action A
to achieve new circumstances S
which will realize some goal G
which will promote some value V

The first version of this scheme that I found was in [14] (p. 22). Matching this scheme Atkinson, Bench-Capon and McBurney [5] (p. 165-167) cited ten critical questions, labeled as follows.

CQ1a: Are there alternative ways of realizing the same consequences?
CQ1b: Are there alternative ways of realizing the same goal?
CQ1c: Are there alternative ways of promoting the same value?
CQ3a: Would doing action A promote some other value?
CQ3b: Does doing action A preclude some other action which would promote
some other value?
CQ4a: Does doing action A have a side effect which demotes the value V?
CQ4b: Does doing action A have a side effect which demotes some other
value?
CQ5: Are the circumstances such that doing action A will bring about
goal G?
CQ6: Does goal G promote value V?
CQ7: Is goal G possible?

In this list, all the critical questions concern values, except for CQ1a, CQ1b, CQ5 and CQ7.

In addition to this main list of ten critical questions, Atkinson, Bench-Capon and McBurney [5] stated that some of these critical questions need to address eight other issues. First they state (p. 166-167) that that an answer to CQ5 needs to address four issues:

(a) Whether the believed circumstances R are possible.
(b) Whether the believed circumstances R are true.
(c) Assuming both of these, whether the action A has the stated consequences S.
(d) Assuming all of these, whether the action A will bring about the desired goal G.

Second, they state (p. 167) CQ6 needs to address two issues:

(a) Whether goal G does realize the value intended; and
(b) Whether the value proposed is indeed a legitimate value.

Third, they state (p. 167) that CQ7 needs to address two additional issues:

(a) Whether the situation S believed by agent a to result from doing action A is a possible state of affairs.
(b) Whether the particular aspects of situation S represented by G are possible.

These issues can be reformulated as questions, and indeed they do seem to represent additional critical questions that can be subsumes under the original seven. This extended reformulation would give us a grand total of eighteen critical questions. Only the issues in the second group concern values. The comments of Atkinson, Bench-Capon and McBurney suggest that subsets of the eight issues identified above can be fitted under the concerns of specific critical questions. In light of these matters, it is interesting to compare the later list of sixteen critical questions offered where it is said that Walton's original four critical questions associated with his (instrumental) scheme have been extended to address the elements in the value-based scheme, producing an expanded list with eighteen critical questions. In this new list of critical question [2] (p. 141), has been reduced to the following sixteen.

CQ1: Are the believed circumstances true?
CQ2: Assuming the circumstances, does the action have the stated consequences?
CQ3: Assuming the circumstances and that the action has the stated consequences, will the action bring about the desired goal?
CQ4: Does the goal realise the value stated?
CQ5: Are there alternative ways of realising the same consequences?
CQ6: Are there alternative ways of realising the same goal?
CQ7: Are there alternative ways of promoting the same value?
CQ8: Does doing the action have a side effect which demotes the value?
CQ9: Does doing the action have a side effect which demotes some other value?
CQ10: Does doing the action promote some other value?
CQ11: Does doing the action preclude some other action which would promote some other value?
CQ12: Are the circumstances as described possible?
CQ13: Is the action possible?
CQ14: Are the consequences as described possible?
CQ15: Can the desired goal be realised?
CQ16: Is the value indeed a legitimate value?

The two that appear to be missing from the original list are these ones: (1) Are the circumstances such that doing action *A* will bring about goal *G*? (2) Are the particular aspects of situation *S* represented by *G* possible?

Citing [3], the technical report [4] (p. 3) tells us that there are sixteen critical questions matching the scheme for value-based practical reasoning. The latter source is especially interesting for our purposes in that it proposes [4] (p. 3) that the list of critical questions can be subdivided into three distinct categories relating to the nature of the attack: "issues relating to the belief as to what is the case; issues relating to desires as to what should be the case; and issues relating to representation concerning the language being used and the logic being deployed in the argument".

However, another way of classifying the sixteen critical questions that seems to me easier to identify and apply is set out below, classifying them into seven categories.

1. Belief about circumstances: CQ1, CQ12

2. Consequences: CQ2, CQ3, CQ8, CQ9, CQ14

3. The action being considered (not just its consequences): CQ 10, CQ11, CQ13

4. Goal: CQ4, CQ15,

5. Alternatives: CQ5, CQ6, CQ7

6. CQ16 is only about values.

7. All are about values except CQ1, CQ2, CQ3, CQ5, CQ6, CQ12, CQ13, CQ14.

What would be helpful is to divide the critical questions into categories so that we could have made critical questions and then sub-questions under these main critical questions. That way we could have a tree structure of critical questions where the user starts with the basic critical questions and then probes into the given argument in a more detailed way by asking further sub questions. Of course the sub questions can also have some questions, and so the problem of the completeness of practical reasoning as a defeasible form of argumentation is posed. Basically, the answer to this question is that practical reasoning is inherently defeasible when employed under conditions of changing circumstances and incomplete information about all the circumstances. The closure problem can only be solved by viewing practical reasoning is a form of argumentation set into a dialogue structure with an opening and a closing stage. This is not an impossible project to carry out because Atkinson, Bench-Capon and McBurney view practical reasoning this way as a form of argument that needs to be set into a framework of dialogue.

So what I have proposed above as a way of classifying the critical questions, based on the comments of Atkinson Bench-Capon and McBurney, might serve as a beginning point for such a classification project. However, the problem I have is to make sense of some of the critical questions in the list of sixteen. For example consider critical questions CQ3, which asks whether the action will bring about the desired goal? What does this question made? Does it mean that the action that is being considered will be sufficient all by itself to carry out the goal? Or does it mean that the action, taken along with a lot of other sub-actions along the way in a sequence of the kind described above in the chain saw example, will bring about the desired goal? Or does it mean that the action, although it may not be sufficient by itself, is a necessary condition for bringing about the desired goal that can be sufficient in the circumstances, perhaps taken along with some other actions that are also required?

5   Critical Questions and Premises

In a book published fifteen years ago [23] I set out an argumentation scheme for a form of goal-directed, knowledge-based reasoning that concludes in an action, called practical reasoning. In this analysis, two argumentation schemes for practical reasoning were postulated: a necessary condition scheme and a sufficient condition scheme. Here is the necessary condition scheme [23] (p. 48).

(*N1*) My goal is to bring about A (*Goal Premise*).
(*N2*) I reasonably consider on the given information that bringing about at least one of $[B_0, B_1,...,B_n]$ is necessary to bring about A (*Alternatives Premise*).
(*N3*) I have selected one member B_i as an acceptable, or as the most acceptable necessary condition for A (*Selection Premise*).
(*N4*) Nothing unchangeable prevents me from bringing about B_i as far as I know (*Practicality Premise*).
(*N5*) Bringing about A is more acceptable to me than not bringing about B_i (*Side Effects Premise*).
Therefore, it is required that I bring about B_i (*Conclusion*).

The sufficient condition scheme is the same [23], except that in its premises (N2) and (N3), the expression 'sufficient condition' must be substituted for 'necessary condition'. This way of framing the scheme is interesting because it takes the approach of incorporating the critical questions into the scheme itself by treating them as premises (in some cases additional premises).

In a table Atkinson, Bench-Capon and McBurney [5] (p. 174) reconfigure the critical questions for their scheme for value-based practical reasoning as set of sixteen attacks representing what they call "the nature of conflict for critical questions" The reader can also see by scanning over the list of these attacks given below how each attack is said to be associated with a specific critical question. The label of the critical question is given to the right of each attack.

1. Disagree with the description of the current situation CQ5b

2. Disagree with the consequences of the proposed action CQ5c

3. Disagree that the desired features are part of the consequences CQ5d

4. Disagree that these features promote the desired value CQ6a

5. Believe that the consequences can be realized by some alternative action CQ1a

6. Believe that the desired features can be realized through some alternative action CQ1b

7. Believe that the desired value can be realized in an alternative way CQ1c

8. Believe that the action has undesirable side effects which demote the desired value CQ4a

9. Believe that the action has undesirable side effects which demote some other desired value CQ4b

10. Agree that the action should be performed, but for different reasons CQ3a

11. Believe that the action will preclude some more desirable action CQ3b

12. Believe that the action is impossible CQ2

13. Believe that the circumstances as described are not possible CQ5a

14. Believe that the consequences as described are not possible CQ7a

15. Believe that the desired features cannot be realized CQ7b

16. Disagree that the desired value is worth promoting CQ6b

The association of the prior list of critical questions with a list of what are taken to be typical types of argument attacks on practical reasoning is interesting from the point of view of argumentation theory for a number of reasons. First, it raises the question of whether each of the critical questions could be reconfigured as a positive assertion or statement of some sort that expresses the content of the critical question. This issue of whether the questions can be re-formulated as statements has been discussed in the literature on argumentation [26]. Second, it presents quite an expanded list of critical questions matching scheme for practical reasoning, one might almost say a proliferation of critical questions. Third, it suggests the possibility that some of the critical questions matching the scheme for practical reasoning could be classified under others, suggesting a way of organizing the critical questions in some way that might prove useful to users of the scheme.

This approach has now been systematically worked out in the Carneades Argumentation System, which manages critical questions matching a scheme by treating them as premises of the scheme and classifying them as assumption or exceptions [13]. The ordinary premises are the ones explicitly stated in the argumentation scheme are classified as assumptions. But here are also assumptions in the form of additional premises that are assumed to hold, just like the ordinary premises, but if questioned automatically fail to hold unless the proponent of the argument gives some evidence to support the premise. Exceptions are also additional premises, but they are assumed not to hold as exceptions unless evidence to back them up is given by the critical questioner. They do not defeat the argument unless the questioner gives backup evidence to support the question.

The following entry for 'argument from practical reasoning', citing [1] as the source, can be found in the catalogue of schemes in the Carneades Argumentation System (http://carneades.github.com/).

Argument from Practical Reasoning

id: practical-reasoning
strict: false
direction: pro
conclusion: Action A should be performed.
premises:

- $S1$ is the case in the current circumstances.

- Performing A in $S1$ would bring about $S2$.

- G would be realized in $S2$.

- Achieving the goal G would promote the value V.

assumptions:

- V is a legitimate value.

- *G* is a worthy goal.

- Action *A* is possible.

exceptions:

- There exists an action that would bring about *S1* more effectively than *A*.

- There exists an action that would realize the goal *G* more effectively than *A*.

- There exists an action that would promote the value *V* more effectively than *A*.

- Performing *A* in *S1* would have side-effects which demote *V* or some other value.

What are called 'premises' in the list above are the so-called ordinary premises of the scheme for argument from practical reasoning.

Now the question is raised how the critical questions proposed in [1] can be classified as assumptions or exceptions in order to deal with the problem of burden of proof posed by them. Some recommendations on this and related questions of how to configure the scheme for practical reasoning and its set of matching critical questions are given in the conclusions section.

6   Conclusions and Questions for Further Work

One problem with the current version of this scheme is that it may not take into account the kind of situation where there are conflicting goals for the agent. Consider the military planning example from [23] (p. 64). In this case, a soldier wants to locate the enemy position, but in order for them to do that it is necessary for him to stand on a hill and make visual observations. However, if he does this he may reveal the location of his unit the enemy. So he has two goals. One is to locate the enemy position, while the other is not to reveal the location of this unit the enemy. The problem is that these two goals are in conflict.

Of course the purpose of value-based practical reasoning is precisely to resolve such goal conflicts by means of an ordering of values using value priorities. But even before a practical reasoning agent gets to this step, it may be important for it to recognize a conflict between two of its goals as a basis for proceeding further. Therefore, it was argued in [23] but one of the critical questions matching this scheme for practical reasoning should be the question of whether there is a conflict of goals that can be identified. At very least, the critical question should ask whether there are other goals that the agent should take into consideration, in addition to the goal G that is the primary goal being considered in the argumentation scheme. The recommendation is to add the premise 'there is another goal G' that is incompatible with G as an additional exception to the current list.

But also there is another critical question to be considered. This is the question of whether the goal G is possible, one of the questions that was taken into account in the version of the value-based scheme put forward in [1]. The recommendation suggested is that the premise 'G is possible' should be added under the list of exceptions.

Finally, there is a third additional critical question that ought to be taken into account. This is the question concerning intervening actions. As shown by the chain saw example, typically working towards a goal involves carrying out not just one action but a sequence of actions where each one is required (often a particular order) to be performed in order to move toward the goal. Thus is to ask whether there are intervening actions required to move from the action A to the goal G.

To deal with these issues, the following amended version of the Carneades scheme is put forward as the appropriate scheme for value-based reasoning practical reasoning with its matching set of critical questions is proposed.

Argument from Value-based Practical Reasoning

id: practical-reasoning
strict: false
direction: pro
conclusion: Action *A* should be performed.
premises:

- *S1* is the case in the current circumstances.

- Performing *A* in *S1* would bring about *S2*.

- *G* would be realized in *S2*.

- Achieving the goal *G* would promote the value *V*.

assumptions:

- *V* is a legitimate value.

- *G* is possible.

- *G* is a worthy goal.

- Action *A* is possible.

exceptions:

- There exists an action that would bring about *S1* more effectively than *A*.

- There exists an action that would realize the goal *G* more effectively than *A*.

- There are intervening actions required to move from the action *A* to the goal *G*.

- There exists an action that would promote the value *V* more effectively than *A*.

- Performing *A* in *S1* would have side-effects which demote *V* or some other value.

- There is another goal *G/* that is incompatible with *G*

However, in addition a scheme for Instrumental Practical Reasoning that contains no mention of values is put forward for consideration.

Argument from Instrumental Practical Reasoning

id: practical-reasoning
strict: false
direction: pro
conclusion: Action *A* should be performed.
premises:

- *S1* is the case in the current circumstances.

- Performing *A* in *S1* would bring about *S2*.

- *G* would be realized in *S2*.

assumptions:

- *G* is possible.

- Action *A* is possible.

exceptions:

- There exists an action that would bring about *S1* more effectively than *A*.

- There exists an action that would realize the goal *G* more effectively than *A*.

- There are intervening actions required to move from the action *A* to the goal *G*.

- There exists an action that would promote the value *V* more effectively than *A*.

- Performing *A* in *S1* would have side-effects that need to be taken into account.

- There is another goal *G*/ that is incompatible with *G*

The scheme for value-based practical reasoning, on this approach, is an extension of the scheme for instrumental practical reasoning. This is a useful way of designing a theory of practical reasoning as a form of argument that can be applied to real cases of argumentation because the simpler purely instrumental version of the scheme can be applied when values are not at issue.

There is one complication however. The side effects critical question is usually expressed as asking whether there are negative side consequences of the action A. The example of the side effect of the Cymbalta medication discussed in section 3 is the classic kind of case so often encountered. The question is whether the potential negative consequences of the medication are "negative" (bad) because they have a negative value for the agent. If so, then the side effects critical question cannot be purely instrumental in nature. It has to be a value-based consideration. If so, then all practical reasoning has to be value-based practical reasoning. How to separate out these schemes and distinguish between them in a useful manner also involved some related schemes.

Argument from negative consequences cites the consequences of a proposed course of action as a reason against taking that action. The following scheme is from [22] (p. 75).

Premise: If *A* is brought about, negative consequences will plausibly occur.
Conclusion: *A* should not be brought about.

Of course there is also a matching scheme for argument from positive consequences.

Premise: If *A* is brought about, positive consequences will plausibly occur.
Conclusion: *A* should be brought about.

According to [22] (p. 76-77), there are three critical questions match either scheme.

CQ1. How strong is the probability or plausibility that these cited consequences will (may, might, must) occur?
CQ2. What evidence, if any, supported the claim that these consequences will (may, might, must) occur if A is brought about?
CQ3. Are there consequences of the opposite value that ought to be taken into account?

Both schemes appear to be species of value-based argumentation. But are they really? Bench-Capon takes as values abstract notions like 'health', 'security', 'patriotism', and so forth that support goals. But in arguments from positive and negative consequences, the term 'values' appears to be used in a different way, closer to what Stevenson [21] called positive and negative values [18].

It also needs to be taken into account that there are schemes for arguments from positive and negative values [28] (p. 321). In these schemes, a judgment of positive value is taken as a reason supporting commitment to a goal, while a judgment of negative value is taken as a reason going against commitment to a goal. So these schemes have to be factored in.

So future work on classification of argumentation schemes needs to much more carefully study how this cluster of schemes fits together so that some of them can be classified as subspecies of others. Until this work of scheme classification achieves fits these schemes together into a unified system, the conclusions drawn here have to be tentative.

Bibliography

[1] K. Atkinson and T. J. M. Bench-Capon. Practical reasoning as presumptive argumentation using action based alternating transition systems. *Artificial Intelligence*, 171(10–15):855–874, 2007.

[2] K. Atkinson and T. J. M. Bench-Capon. Addressing moral problems through practical reasoning. *Journal of Applied Logic*, 6(2):135–151, 2008.

[3] K. Atkinson, T. J. M. Bench-Capon, and P. McBurney. Parmenides: Facilitating democratic debate. In R. Traunmüller, editor, *EGOV*, volume 3183 of *Lecture Notes in Computer Science*, pages 313–316. Springer, 2004.

[4] K. Atkinson, T. J. M. Bench-Capon, and P. McBurney. Agent decision making using argumentation about actions. Technical Report ULCS-5-006, University of Liverpool, 2005.

[5] K. Atkinson, T. J. M. Bench-Capon, and P. McBurney. Computational representation of practical argument. *Synthese*, 152(2):157–206, 2006.

[6] R. Audi. *Practical Reasoning*. London: Routledge, 1989.

[7] T. Bench-Capon. Agreeing to differ: Modelling persuasive dialogue between parties without a consensus about values. *Informal Logic*, 22(3):231–245, 2002.

[8] T. J. M. Bench-Capon. The missing link revisited: The role of teleology in representing legal argument. *Artificial Intelligence and Law*, 10(1-3):79–94, 2002.

[9] T. J. M. Bench-Capon. Persuasion in practical argument using value-based argumentation frameworks. *Journal of Logic and Computation*, 13(3):429–448, 2003.

[10] M. E. Bratman. *Intention, Plans, and Practical Reason*. Harvard University Press, Cambridge, MA, 1987.

[11] M. E. Bratman, D. J. Israel, and M. E. Pollack. Plans and resource-bounded practical reasoning. *Computational Intelligence*, 4:349–355, 1988.

[12] D. S. Clarke. *Practical Inferences*. London: Routledge, 1985.

[13] T. F. Gordon, H. Prakken, and D. Walton. The Carneades model of argument and burden of proof. *Artificial Intelligence*, 171(10-15):875–896, 2007.

[14] K. Greenwood, T. J. M. Bench-Capon, and P. McBurney. Towards a computational account of persuasion in law. In *Proceedings of the Ninth International Conference on AI and Law (ICAIL 2003)*, pages 22–31, 2003.

[15] C. L. Hamblin. *Fallacies*. London: Methuen, 1970.

[16] C. L. Hamblin. Mathematical models of dialogue. *Theoria*, 37:130–155, 1971.

[17] H. Hansen and D. Walton. Argument kinds and argument roles in the ontario provincial election. *Journal of Argumentation in Context*, 2013.

[18] F. Macagno and D. Walton. *Emotive Language in Argumentation*. Cambridge: Cambridge University Press, 2013.

[19] F. Paglieri and C. Castelfranchi. Arguments as belief structures. In D. Hitchcock and D. Farr, editors, *The Uses of Argument: Proceedings of a Conference at McMaster University*, pages 356–367. Ontario Society for the Study of Argumentation, 2005.

[20] J. L. Pollock. *Cognitive Carpentry*. The MIT Press: Cambridge, MA, 1995.

[21] C. Stevenson. *Ethics and Language*. New Haven: Yale University Press, 1944.

[22] D. Walton. *Argumentation Schemes for Presumptive Reasoning*. Mahwah, New Jersey: L. Erlbaum Associates, 1990.

[23] D. Walton. *Practical Reasoning: Goal-Driven, Knowledge-Based, Action-Guiding Argumentation*. Savage, Maryland: Rowman and Littlefield, 1990.

[24] D. Walton. *Fundamentals of Critical Argumentation*. Cambridge: Cambridge University Press, 2006.

[25] D. Walton. The structure of argumentation in health product messages. *Argument and Computation*, 1(3):179–198, 2010.

[26] D. Walton and D. Godden. The nature and status of critical questions in argumentation schemes. In D. Hitchcock and D. Farr, editors, *The Uses of Argument: Proceedings of a Conference at McMaster University*, pages 476–484. Ontario Society for the Study of Argumentation, 2005.

[27] D. Walton and E. Krabbe. *Commitment in Dialogue*. Albany: SUNY Press, 1995.

[28] D. Walton, C. Reed, and F. Macagno. *Argumentation Schemes*. Cambridge: Cambridge University Press, 2008.

[29] M. Wooldridge. *An Introduction to MultiAgent Systems*. Chichester: Wiley, 2002.